J W Sargent

620 425

Slavery.

F

John W. Sargent
Newburyport
Mass

SELECTIONS

FROM THE

WRITINGS AND SPEECHES

OF

WILLIAM LLOYD GARRISON.

WITH AN APPENDIX.

> ' O, my brethren! I have told
> Most BITTER TRUTH, but without bitterness.
> Nor deem my zeal or factious or mis-timed;
> For never can true courage dwell with them,
> Who, playing tricks with Conscience, dare not look
> At their own vices.' — COLERIDGE.

BOSTON:

R. F. WALLCUT, 21 CORNHILL.

1852.

J. B. YERRINTON AND SON,
PRINTERS,
21 CORNHILL.

Contents.

iv CONTENTS.

Preface.

HAVING been the first publicly to unfurl the banner of IMMEDIATE and UNCONDITIONAL EMANCIPATION in this country, and to expose the true character, tendency and design of the AMERICAN COLONIZATION SOCIETY, as the handmaid of SLAVERY, it is not surprising that, for a period of more than twenty years, (occupied unceasingly and uncompromisingly in advocating the cause of a people 'meted out and trodden under foot,') WILLIAM LLOYD GARRISON has been subjected to every kind of popular odium, misrepresentation, and abuse. Nor is it singular, that, in view of the religious sanctions which have been thrown around the horrible slave system, North and South, (and, therefore, the necessity imposed upon him to arraign and expose the American church and clergy as stained with blood and deeply polluted,) he has been every where stigmatized as a heretic and an 'infidel,' by the same class and in the spirit which cried out against Jesus, that he was 'not of God, because he did not keep the Sabbath day,' and accused him of having a devil. The mode of attacking the true Reformer is essentially the same in every age : he is ever at first pronounced guilty of heresy and sedition, though no one is more loyal or more orthodox than

1*

himself—orthodox in his regard for the truth, and loyal
in his support of a righteous government. It is the infatuation of those, who are terrified and inflamed at his appearance, to imagine, that if they can succeed in destroying
his reputation, or, more certainly still, his life, the cause
which he espouses will sink with him out of sight, and
out of the world, for ever. Hence their eagerness for
his crucifixion—justifying themselves by the plea, 'We
have a law, and by that law he ought to die'—'It is better
that one man should die, than that the whole nation should
perish.'

> 'The man is thought a knave or fool,
>   Or bigot plotting crime,
> Who, for the advancement of his kind,
>   Is wiser than his time.
> For him the hemlock shall distil ; .
>   For him the axe be bared ;
> For him the gibbet shall be built ;
>   For him the stake prepared ;
> Him shall the scorn and wrath of men
>   Pursue with deadly aim ;
> And malice, envy, spite and lies,
>   Shall desecrate his name ;
> But Truth shall conquer at the last,
>   For round and round we run,
> And ever the right comes uppermost,
>   And ever is justice done.'

Of the thousands who have joined in the absurd outcries
against Mr. GARRISON, it may be safely presumed that
many of them, being entirely devoid of candor, have yet

to read the first sentence he has ever written, on any subject; while many others have had no opportunity to obtain his sentiments, embodied in a convenient form, who, nevertheless, honestly suppose that what they have heard so constantly reiterated against him must be true. For the sake of the latter class, in particular, as well as to subserve the cause of Reform in general, it has been deemed advisable to make the following SELECTIONS FROM THE WRITINGS OF MR. GARRISON; containing, as they do, his severest denunciations, his strongest impeachments, and his most radical sentiments touching the various reformatory enterprises in which his feelings are so deeply enlisted. It is a volume both for his friends and his enemies; for the latter, to reveal to them the folly and injustice of their treatment of one whose spirit breathes only of 'peace on earth and good will towards men,' whatever their clime and complexion; and for the former, to strengthen and animate them in their coöperative labors for the advancement of that glorious period, when Liberty shall be proclaimed throughout all the land, to all the inhabitants thereof.

We purposely abstain from making any comments of our own on the career of Mr. GARRISON, by whom praise is subordinated to principle, to whom censure gives no uneasiness, and whose characteristic language (uttered in the midst of fiery trials) has uniformly been—'Is the inquiry made, how do I bear up under my adversities? I answer—like the oak—like the Alps—unshaken, storm-proof. Opposition, and abuse, and slander, and prejudice,

and judicial tyranny, are like oil to the flame of my zeal.
I am not discouraged, but more confident than ever. Am I
to be frightened by dungeons and chains? I will not hold
my peace. The cause is worthy of the loftiest ambition
and the noblest genius. To it I am wedded, as long as I
shall have a pen to wield, or a voice to speak. Poverty
may assail me with her hungry whelps; Persecution may
light its fires; Slander may spit out her venom; and
Judicial Power attempt to intimidate; all will be in vain.
Wherever oppression, fraud and violence exist, I am for
exposing to merited infamy the robber and the tyrant;
wherever there is a virtuous struggle for liberty, there
is my heart.' Whether this language was uttered in the
spirit of self-inflation or bombast, or whether it emanated
from a sincere and earnest mind, let the rise and progress
of the Anti-Slavery enterprise, since it was uttered, determine.

If Mr. GARRISON has had the most formidable opposition
to contend with, and received an unequalled amount of
abuse, he has also been greatly cheered and strengthened
by the generous appreciation and warm commendations of
the friends of impartial freedom, on both sides of the
Atlantic; such, for example, as are embodied in the following poetical effusions, elicited by a kindred sympathy for
the enslaved on the part of their authors. They are here-
with appended, not merely on account of their personal testimonies, but also because of their intrinsic excellence, both
as to style and sentiment.

THE DAY OF SMALL THINGS.

BY JAMES RUSSELL LOWELL.

'Sometime afterward, it was reported to me by the city officers, that they had ferreted out the paper and its editor. His office was an obscure hole; his only visible auxiliary a negro boy; and his supporters a few very insignificant persons, of all colors.' — LETTER OF HON. H. G. OTIS.

IN a small chamber, friendless and unseen,
    Toiled o'er his types one poor, unlearned young man;
The place was dark, unfurnitured and mean,
    Yet there the freedom of a race began.

Help came but slowly; surely, no man yet
    Put lever to the heavy world with less;
What need of help ? — He knew how types were set,
    He had a dauntless spirit and a press.

Such earnest natures are the fiery pith,
    The compact nucleus round which systems grow;
Mass after mass becomes inspired therewith,
    And whirls impregnate with the central glow.

O Truth! O Freedom! how are ye still born
    In the rude stable, in the manger nursed!
What humble hands unbar those gates of morn,
    Through which the splendors of the new day burst!

What! shall one monk, scarce known beyond his cell,
    Front Rome's far-reaching bolts, and scorn her frown ?
Brave LUTHER answered, Yes! — that thunder's swell
    Rocked Europe, and discharmed the triple crown.

' Whatever can be known of earth, we know,'
    Sneered Europe's wise men, in their snail-shells curled;
No! said one man in Genoa; and that No
    Out of the dark created this New World.

Who is it will not dare himself to trust ?
    Who is it hath not strength to stand alone ?
Who is it thwarts and bilks the inward must ?
    He and his works like sand from earth are blown.

Men of a thousand shifts and wiles, look here!
  See one straight-forward conscience put in pawn
To win a world! See the obedient sphere,
  By bravery's simple gravitation drawn!

Shall we not heed the lesson taught of old,
  And by the Present's lips repeated still,
In our own single manhood to be bold,
  Fortressed in conscience and impregnable will?

We stride the river daily at its spring,
  Nor in our childish thoughtlessness foresee
What myriad vassal streams shall tribute bring,
  How like an equal it shall greet the sea.

O small beginnings, ye are great and strong,
  Based on a faithful heart and weariless brain;
Ye build the future fair, ye conquer wrong,
  Ye earn the crown, and wear it not in vain!

TO WILLIAM LLOYD GARRISON.

BY JOHN GREENLEAF WHITTIER.

CHAMPION of those who groan beneath
  Oppression's iron hand,
In view of penury, hate and death,
  I see thee fearless stand;
Still bearing up thy lofty brow,
  In the steadfast strength of truth,
In manhood sealing well the vow
  And promise of thy youth.

Go on!—for thou hast chosen well;
  On in the strength of God!
Long as one human heart shall swell
  Beneath the tyrant's rod.

Speak in a slumbering nation's ear,
    As thou hast ever spoken,
Until the dead in sin shall hear—
    The fetter's link be broken!

I love thee with a brother's love—
    I feel my pulses thrill,
To mark thy spirit soar above
    The cloud of human ill;
My heart hath leaped to answer thine,
    And echo back thy words,
As leaps the warrior's at the shine
    And flash of kindred swords!

They tell me thou art rash and vain—
    A searcher after fame;
That thou art striving but to gain
    A long enduring name;
That thou hast nerved the Afric's hand,
    And steeled the Afric's heart,
To shake aloft his vengeful brand,
    And rend his chain apart.

Have I not known thee well, and read
    Thy mighty purpose long,
And watched the trials which have made
    Thy human spirit strong?
And shall the slanderer's demon breath
    Avail with one like me,
To dim the sunshine of my faith,
    And earnest trust in thee?

Go on!—the dagger's point may glare
    Amid thy pathway's gloom—
The fate which sternly threatens there,
    Is glorious martyrdom!
Then, onward, with a martyr's zeal—
    Press on to thy reward—
The hour when man shall only kneel
    Before his Father—GOD!

TO·WILLIAM LLOYD GARRISON.

BY THOMAS W. HIGGINSON.

'T is not that deeds like thine need my poor praise,
  When, though commending not each word of strife,
  I yet would thank thee for thy manly life,
Thou rugged LUTHER of these latter days!
O! when will men look through thine ardent phrase
  To the true depth of that devoted heart,
  Where selfish hope or fear had never part
To swerve thee, with the crowd, from Truth's plain ways!
When that day comes, thy brothers, wiser grown,
  Shall reverence struggling man's true friend in thee,
Thy life of stern devotion shall atone
  For some few words that seemed too rough to be,
And they shall grave upon thy funeral stone,
  'THIS MAN SPOKE TRUTH, AND HELPED US TO GROW FREE!'

Cambridge, Massachusetts.

TO WILLIAM LLOYD GARRISON.

BY ALONZO LEWIS.

THY God has cast thee in a noble mould,
  And poured thy fabric full of living soul,
  That fills, informs, and animates the whole,
As if we saw a visioned form unrolled!
And thou go'st forward with Ithuriel's spear,
  To combat with the evils of the world;
  And thy keen falchion-shafts on high are hurled,
To fill Oppression with a deadly fear,
  And drive him from his hold in Freedom's land,
  Where he has marshalled forth a mail-clad band,
Armed with the scourge of torture. Like a knight
  Who battled for the Cross in days of old,
  With Truth thy shield, go forward, and be bold,
And may God aid thee in the glorious fight!

SELECTIONS

FROM THE WRITINGS OF

WILLIAM LLOYD GARRISON.

Exposure of the American Colonization Society.

IN attacking the system of slavery, I clearly foresaw all that has happened to me. I knew, at the commencement, that my motives would be impeached, my warnings ridiculed, my person persecuted, my sanity doubted, my life jeoparded: but the clank of the prisoner's chains broke upon my ear — it entered deeply into my soul — I looked up to Heaven for strength to sustain me in the perilous work of emancipation — and my resolution was taken.

In opposing the American Colonization Society, I have also counted the cost, and as clearly foreseen the formidable opposition which will be arrayed against me. Many of the clergy are enlisted in its support: their influence is powerful. Men of wealth and elevated station are among its contributors: wealth and station are almost omnipotent. The press has been seduced into its support: the press is a potent engine. Moreover, the Society is artfully based upon and defended by popular prejudice; it takes advantage

2

of wicked and preposterous opinions, and hence its success. These things grieve, they cannot deter me. 'Truth is mighty, and will prevail.' It is able to make falsehood blush, tear from hypocrisy its 'mask, annihilate prejudice, overthrow persecution, and break every fetter.

I am constrained to declare, with the utmost sincerity, that I look upon the Colonization scheme as inadequate in its design, injurious in its operation, and contrary to sound principle ; and the more scrupulously I examine its pretensions, the stronger is my conviction of its sinfulness. Nay, were Jehovah to speak in an audible voice from his holy habitation, I am persuaded that his language would be, ' Who hath required this at your hands ? '

It consoles me to believe that no man, who knows me personally or by reputation, will suspect the honesty of my skepticism. If I were politic, and intent only on my own preferment or pecuniary interest, I should swim with the strong tide of public sentiment, instead of breasting its powerful influence. The hazard is too great, the labor too burdensome, the remuneration too uncertain, the contest too unequal, to induce a selfish adventurer to assail a combination so formidable. Disinterested opposition and sincere conviction, however, are not conclusive proofs of individual rectitude; for a man may very honestly do mischief, and not be aware of his error. Indeed, it is in this light I view many of the friends of African colonization. I concede to them benevolence of purpose and expansiveness of heart; but, in my opinion, they are laboring under the same delusion as that which swayed Saul of Tarsus — persecuting the blacks even unto a strange country, and verily believing that they are doing God service. I blame them, nevertheless, for taking this mighty scheme upon trust; for not perceiving and rejecting the monstrous doctrines avowed by the master spirits in this crusade ; and for feeling so indifferent to the moral, political and social advancement of the free people of color in this, their only legitimate home.

In the progress of this discussion, I shall have occasion to use very plain, and sometimes very severe language. This would be an unpleasant task, did not duty imperiously demand its application. To give offence I am loath, but more to hide or modify the truth. I shall deal with the Society in its collective form—as one body—and not with individuals. While I shall be necessitated to marshal individual opinions in review, I protest, *ab origine*, against the supposition, that indiscriminate censure is intended, or that every friend of the Society cherishes similar views. He to whom my reprehension does not apply, will not receive it. It is obviously impossible, in attacking a numerous and multiform combination, to exhibit private dissimilarities, or in every instance to discriminate between the various shades of opinion. It is sufficient that exceptions are made. My warfare is against the AMERICAN COLONIZATION SOCIETY. If I shall identify its general, preponderating, and clearly developed traits, it must stand or fall as they shall prove benevolent or selfish.

I bring to this momentous investigation an unbiased mind, a lively sense of accountability to God, and devout aspirations for divine guidance.

It is only about two years since I was induced to examine the claims of the Colonization Society upon the patronage and confidence of the nation. I went to this examination with a mind biased by preconceived opinions favorable to the Society, and rather for the purpose of defending it against opposition than of bringing it into disrepute. Every thing, apart from its principles, was calculated to secure my friendship. Nothing but its revolting features could have induced me to turn loathingly away from its embrace. I had some little reputation to sustain; many of my friends were colonizationists; I saw that eminent statesmen and honorable men were enlisted in the enterprise; the great body of the clergy gave their unqualified support to it; every Fourth of July, the charities of the nation were secured in its behalf; wherever I turned my eye in the free States, I saw nothing but unanimity; wherever my ear caught a sound, I heard nothing but excessive panegyric. No individual had ventured to blow the trumpet of alarm, or exert his energies to counteract the influence of the scheme. If an assailant had occasionally appeared, he had either fired a random shot and retreated, or found in the inefficiency of the Society the only cause for hostility. It was at this crisis, and with such an array of motives before me to bias my judgment, that I resolved to make a close and candid examination of the subject.

I went, first of all, to the fountain head—to the African Repository and the Reports of the Society. I was not long in discovering sentiments which seemed to me as abhorrent to humanity as contrary to reason. I perused page after page, first with perplexity, then with astonishment, and finally with indignation. I found little else than sinful palliations, fatal concessions, vain expectations, exaggerated statements, unfriendly representations, glaring contradictions, naked terrors, deceptive assurances, unrelenting prejudices, and unchristian denunciations. I collected together the publications of auxiliary societies, in order to discern some redeeming traits; but I found them marred and disfigured with the same disgusting details. I courted the acquaintance of eminent colonizationists, that I might learn how far their private sentiments agreed with those which were so offensive in print; and I found no dissimilarity between them. I listened to discourses from the pulpit in favor of the Society; and the same moral obliquities were seen in minister and people.

These discoveries affected my mind so deeply that I could not rest. I endeavored to explain away the meaning of plain and obvious language; I made liberal concessions for good motives and unsuspicious confidence; I resorted to many expedients to vindicate the disinterested benevolence of the Society; but I could not rest. The sun in its mid-day splendor was not more clear and palpable to my vision, than the anti-christian and anti-republican character of this association. It was evident to me that the great mass of its supporters at the North did not realize its dangerous tendency. They were told that it was designed to effect the ultimate emancipation of the slaves—to improve the condition of the free people of color—to abolish the foreign slave trade—to reclaim and evangelize benighted Africa—and various other marvels. Anxious to do something for the colored population—they knew not what—and having no other plan presented to their view, they eagerly embraced a scheme which was so big with promise, and which required of them nothing but a small contribution annually. Perceiving the fatality of this delusion, I was urged by an irresistible impulse to attempt its removal. I could not turn a deaf ear to the cries of the slaves, nor throw off the obligations which my Creator had fastened upon me. Yet, in view of the inequalities of the contest, of the obstacles which towered like mountains in my path, and of my own littleness, I trembled, and exclaimed in the language of Jeremiah,—'Ah, Lord God! behold I cannot speak: for I am a child.' But I was immediately strengthened by these interrogations: 'Is any thing too hard for the Lord?' Is Error, though unwittingly supported by a host of good men, stronger than Truth? Are Right and Wrong convertible terms, dependant upon popular opinion? Oh, no! Then I will go forward in the strength of the Lord of hosts—in the name of Truth—and under the banner of Right. As it is not by might nor by

2*

power, but by the Spirit of God, that great moral changes
are effected, I am encouraged to fight valiantly in this good
cause, believing that I shall 'come off conqueror'—yet not
I, but Truth and Justice. It is in such a contest that one
shall chase a thousand, and two put ten thousand to flight.
'The Lord disappointeth the devices of the crafty, so that
their hands cannot perform their enterprise. He taketh the
wise in their own craftiness; and the counsel of the froward
is carried headlong.' 'Because the foolishness of God is
wiser than men; and the weakness of God is stronger than
men.'

Probably I may be interrogated by individuals,—'Why do
you object to a colony in Africa? Are you not willing people should choose their own places of residence? And if
the blacks are willing to remove, why throw obstacles in
their path, or deprecate their withdrawal? All go voluntarily: of what, then, do you complain? Is not the colony
at Liberia in a flourishing condition, and expanding beyond
the most sanguine expectations of its founders?'

Pertinent questions deserve pertinent answers. I say,
then, in reply, that I do not object to a colony, *in the abstract*—to use the popular phraseology of the day. In other
words, I am entirely willing men should be as free as the
birds in choosing the time when, the mode how, and the
place to which they shall migrate. The power of locomotion
was given to be used at will: as beings of intelligence and
enterprise,

> 'The world is all before them, where to choose
> Their place of rest, and Providence their guide.'

The emigration from New-England to the far West is constant and large. Almost every city, town or village suffers
annually by the departure of some of its adventurous inhabitants. Companies have been formed to go and possess the
Oregon territory—an enterprise hazardous and unpromising

in the extreme. The old States are distributing their population over the whole continent, with unexampled fruitful-
ness and liberality. But why this restless, roving, unsatisfied
disposition? Is it because those who cherish it are treated
as the offscouring of all flesh, in the place of their birth?
or because they do not possess equal rights and privileges
with other citizens? or because they are the victims of incorrigible hate and prejudice? or because they are told that
they must choose between exilement and perpetual degradation? or because the density of population renders it impossible for them to obtain preferment and competence here?
or because they are estranged by oppression and scorn? or
because they cherish no attachment to their native soil, to
the scenes of their childhood and youth, or to the institutions
of government? or because they consider themselves as
dwellers in a strange land, and feel a burning desire, a feverish longing to return home? No. They lie under no odious
disabilities, whether imposed by public opinion or by legislative power; to them the path of preferment is wide open;
they sustain a solid and honorable reputation; they not only
can rise, but have risen, and may soar still higher, to responsible stations and affluent circumstances; no calamity afflicts,
no burden depresses, no reproach excludes, no despondency
enfeebles them; and they love the spot of their nativity
almost to idolatry. The air of heaven is not freer or more
buoyant than they. Theirs is a spirit of curiosity and adventurous enterprise, impelled by no malignant influences, but
by the spontaneous promptings of the mind. Far different
is the case of our colored population. Their voluntary banishment is compulsory—they are ' forced to turn volunteers '
—as will be shown in other parts of this work.

The following proposition is self-evident: The success
of an enterprise furnishes no proof that it is in accordance
with justice, or that it meets the approbation of God, or that

it ought to be prosecuted to its consummation, or that it is
the fruit of disinterested benevolence.

I do not doubt that the Colony at Liberia, by a prodigal
expenditure of life and money, will ultimately flourish; but
a good result can never hallow or atone for persecution.

The doctrine, that the ' end sanctifies the means,' belongs,
I trust, exclusively to the creed of the Jesuits. If I were
sure that the Society would accomplish the entire regeneration of Africa by its present measures, my detestation of
its principles would not abate one jot, nor would I bestow
upon it the smallest modicum of praise. Never shall the
fruits of the mercy and overruling providence of God,—ever
bringing good out of evil, and light out of darkness,—be
ascribed to the prejudice or tyranny of man.

It is certain that many a poor native African has been led
to embrace the gospel, in consequence of his transportation
to our shores, who else had lived and died a heathen. Is the
slave trade therefore a blessing? Suppose one of those
wretches, who are engaged in this nefarious commerce, were
brought before the Supreme Court, and on being convicted,
should be asked by the Judge, whether he had aught to say
why sentence of death should not be pronounced upon him.
And suppose the culprit should espy some of his sable victims in court, whom he knew had made a profession of faith,
and he should boldly reply—' May it please your Honor, I
abducted these people away from their homes, it is true ;
but they were poor, miserable, benighted idolators, and must
have inevitably remained as such unto the hour of their
death, if I had not brought them to this land of Christianity
and Bibles, where they have been taught a knowledge of the
true God, and are now rejoicing in hope of a glorious immortality. I therefore offer as a conclusive reason why sentence
should not be pronounced, *that I have rescued souls from
perdition.*' Would the villain be acquitted, and, instead of

a halter, receive the panegyric of the Court for his conduct?

Let not, then, any imaginary or real prosperity of the settlement at Liberia lead any individual to applaud the Colonization Society, reckless whether it be actuated by mistaken philanthropy, or perverted generosity, or selfish policy, or unchristian prejudice.

I should oppose this Society, even were its doctrines harmless. It imperatively and effectually seals the lips of a vast number of influential and pious men, who, for fear of giving offence to those slaveholders with whom they associate, and thereby leading to a dissolution of the compact, dare not expose the flagrant enormities of the system of slavery, nor denounce the crime of holding human beings in bondage. They dare not lead to the onset against the forces of tyranny; and if *they* shrink from the conflict, how shall the victory be won? I do not mean to aver, that, in their sermons, or addresses, or private conversations, they never allude to the subject of slavery; for they do so frequently, or at least every Fourth of July. But my complaint is, that they content themselves with representing slavery as an evil,—a misfortune,—a calamity which has been entailed upon us by former generations,—*and not as an individual* CRIME, embracing in its folds robbery, cruelty, oppression and piracy. They do not identify the criminals; they make no direct, pungent, earnest appeal to the consciences of menstealers; by consenting to walk arm-in-arm with them, they virtually agree to abstain from all offensive remarks, and to aim entirely at the expulsion of the free people of color; their lugubrious exclamations, and solemn animadversions, and reproachful reflections, are altogether indefinite; they ' go about, and about, and all the way round to nothing;' they generalize, they shoot into the air, they do not disturb the repose nor wound the complacency of the sinner; ' they

have put no difference between the holy and profane, neither
have they shewed difference between the unclean and the
clean.' Thus has free inquiry been suppressed, and a universal fear created, and the tongue of the boldest silenced,
and the sleep of death fastened upon the nation. ' Truth
has fallen in the streets, and equity cannot enter.' The
plague is raging with unwonted fatality; but no *cordon
sanitaire* is established—no adequate remedy sought. The
tide of moral death is constantly rising and widening; but
no efforts are made to stay its desolating career. The fire
of God's indignation is kindling against us, and thick darkness covers the heavens, and the hour of retribution is at
hand; but we are obstinate in our transgression, we refuse
to repent, we impiously throw the burden of our guilt upon
our predecessors, we affect resignation to our unfortunate
lot, we descant upon the mysterious dispensations of Providence, and we deem ourselves objects of God's compassion
rather than of his displeasure!

Were the American Colonization Society bending its energies directly to the immediate abolition of slavery; seeking
to enlighten and consolidate public opinion, on this momentous subject; faithfully exposing the awful guilt of the owners of slaves; manfully contending for the bestowal of equal
rights upon our free colored population in this their native
land; assiduously endeavoring to uproot the prejudices of
society; and holding no fellowship with oppressors; my
opposition to it would cease. It might continue, without
censure, to bestow its charities upon such as spontaneously
desire to remove to Africa, whether animated by religious
considerations, or the hope of bettering their temporal condition. But, alas! its governing spirit and purpose are of
an opposite character.

The popularity of the Society is not attributable to its
merits, but exclusively to its congeniality with those unchris-

tian prejudices which have so long been cherished against a sable complexion. It is agreeable to slaveholders, because it is striving to remove a class of persons who they fear may stir up their slaves to rebellion. All who avow undying hostility to the people of color are in favor of it; all who shrink from acknowledging them as brethren and friends, or who make them a distinct and inferior caste, or who deny the possibility of elevating them in the scale of improvement here, most heartily embrace it.

To Africa this country owes a debt larger than she is able to liquidate. Most intensely do I desire to see that ill-fated continent transformed into the abode of civilization, of the arts and sciences, of true religion, of liberty, and of all that adds to the dignity, the renown, and the temporal and eternal happiness of man. Shame and confusion of face belong to the Church, that she has so long disregarded the claims of Africa upon her sympathies, prayers, and lib- erality — claims as much superior as its wrongs to those of any other portion of the globe. It is indeed most strange, that, like the Priest and the Levite, she should have ' passed by on the other side,' and left the victim of thieves to bleed and sicken and die. As the Africans were the only people doomed to perpetual servitude, and to be the prey of kid- nappers, she should long since have directed almost her undivided efforts to civilize and convert them,— not by estab- lishing colonies of ignorant and selfish foreigners among them, who will seize every opportunity to overreach or oppress, as interest or ambition shall instigate, — but by send- ing intelligent, pious missionaries; men fearing God and eschewing evil — living evidences of the excellence of Chris- tianity — having but one object, not the possession of wealth, or the obtainment of power, or the gratification of selfish- ness, but the salvation of the soul. Had she made this attempt, as she was bound to have made it by every principle of justice, and every feeling of humanity, a century ago, Africa would have been, at the present day, ' redeemed, regenerated, and disenthralled, and the slavery of her children brought to an end. No pirates would now haunt her coast, to desolate her villages with fire and sword, in order to supply a Christian people with hewers of wood and drawers of water. How much has been needlessly lost to the world by this criminal neglect!

,The conception of evangelizing a heathenish country by sending to it an illiterate, degraded and irreligious population, belongs exclusively to the advocates of African colonization. For absurdity and inaptitude, it stands, and must for ever stand, without a parallel. Of all the offspring of prejudice and oppression, it is the most shapeless and unnatural.

No man of refined sensibility can contemplate the fate of the aborigines of this country, without shuddering at the consequences of colonization; and if *they* melted away at the presence of the Pilgrims and their descendants, like frost before the meridian blaze of the sun, — if *they* fell to the earth like the leaves of the forest before the autumnal blast, by the settlement of men reputedly humane, wise and pious, in their vicinage, — what can be our hopes for the preservation of the Africans, associated with a population degraded by slavery, and, to a lamentable extent, destitute of religious and secular knowledge? The argument, that the difference of complexion between our forefathers and the aborigines (which is not a distinctive feature between the settlers at Liberia and the natives) was the real cause of this deadly enmity, is more specious than solid. Conduct, not color, secures friendship or excites antipathy, as it happens to be just or unjust. The venerated William Penn and his pacific followers furnish a case in point.

I avow it — the natural tendency of the colony at Liberia excites the most melancholy apprehensions in my mind. Its

birth was conceived in blood, and its footsteps will be marked with blood down to old age—the blood of the poor natives
—unless a special interposition of Divine Providence prevent such a calamity. The emigrants will be eager in the
acquisition of wealth, ease and power; and, having superior
skill and discernment in trade, they will outwit and defraud
the natives as often as occasion permits. This knavish
treatment once detected,—as it surely will be, for even an
uncivilized people may soon learn that they have been cheat-
ed,—will provoke retaliation, and stir up the worst passions
of the human breast. Bloody conflicts will ensue, in which
the colonists will be victorious. This success will serve to
increase the enmity of the natives, and to perpetuate the
murderous struggle; until, by their subjugation, the colonists
obtain undisputed possession of the land.

Heaven grant that these fears may prove to be only the
offspring of a distracted mind! May the colonists be so just
in their intercourse with the Africans, as never to tarnish
their own integrity; so pacific, as to disarm violence and
perpetuate good will; so benevolent, as to excite gratitude
and diffuse joy wherever their names shall be known; and
so holy, as to exalt the Christian religion in the eyes of an
idolatrous nation! But he must be grossly ignorant of
human nature, or strangely infatuated, who believes that
they will always, or commonly, present such an example.

Examine this scheme. More than one-sixth portion of
the American people—confessedly the most vicious and dangerous portion—are to be transported to the shores of Africa,
by means which are hereafter to be considered, and at an
expense which we shall not stop now to calculate, for the
purpose of civilizing and evangelizing Africa, and of improving their own condition! Here, then, are two ignorant and
depraved nations to be regenerated instead of one—two
huge and heterogeneous masses of moral contagion min-

3

gled together benevolently for the preservation of each!
One of these is so deplorably stupid, or so unfathomably deep
in degradation, (such is the argument,) that, although surrounded by ten millions of people living under the full blaze
of gospel light, who have every desirable facility to elevate
and save it, it never can rise until it be removed at least
four thousand miles from their vicinage!—and yet it is first
to be evangelized in a barbarous land, by a feeble, inadequate process, before it can be qualified to evangelize the
other nation! In other words, men who are intellectually
and morally blind are violently removed from light effulgent
into thick darkness, in order that they may obtain light themselves and diffuse light among others! Ignorance is sent
to instruct ignorance, ungodliness to exhort ungodliness, vice
to stop the progress of vice, and depravity to reform depravity! All that is abhorrent to our moral sense, or dangerous
to our quietude, or villanous in human nature, we benevolently disgorge upon Africa, for her temporal and eternal
welfare! We propose to build upon her shores, for her
glory and defence, colonies framed of materials which we
discard as worthless for our own use, and which possess no
fitness or durability! Admirable consistency! surprising
wisdom! unexampled benevolence! As rationally might
we think of exhausting the ocean by multiplying the number of its tributaries, or extinguishing a fire by piling fuel
upon it.

Lastly. Any scheme of proselytism, which requires for
its protection the erection of forts and the use of murderous
weapons, is opposed to the genius of Christianity, and radically wrong. If the gospel cannot be propagated but by the
aid of the sword,—if its success is to depend upon the military science and prowess of its apostles,—it were better to
leave the pagan world in darkness. Yet the first specimen
of benevolence and piety, which the colonists gave to the

natives, was the building of a fort, and supplying it with arms and ammunition! This was an earnest manifestation of that ' peace on earth, good will to man,' which these expatriated missionaries were sent to inculcate! . How eminently calculated to inspire the confidence, excite the gratitude, and accelerate the conversion of the Africans! Their ' dread of the great guns of the Islanders,' (to adopt the language of Mr. Ashmun,) must from the beginning have made a deep and salutary impression upon their minds; and when, not long afterward, ' every shot ' from these guns ' *spent its force in a solid mass of living human flesh* '—their own flesh—they must have experienced an entire regeneration! Bullets and cannon balls argue with resistless effect, and as easily convert a barbarous as a civilized people. One sanguinary conflict was sufficient to spread the glad tidings of salvation among a thousand tribes, almost with the rapidity of light!

But—says an objector—these reflections come too late. The colony is planted, whatever may be its influence. What do you recommend? Its immediate abandonment to want and ruin? Shall we not bestow upon it our charities, and commend it to the protection of Heaven?

I answer. Let the colony continue to receive the aid, and elicit the prayers of the good and benevolent. Still let it remain within the pale of Christian sympathy. Blot it not out of existence. But let it henceforth develop itself naturally. Crowd not its population. Let transportation cease. Seek no longer to exile millions of our colored countrymen. For, assuredly, if the Colonization Society succeed in its efforts to remove thousands of their number annually, it cannot inflict a heavier curse upon Africa, or more speedily accomplish the entire subversion of the colony.

But—the objector asks—how shall we evangelize Africa? In the same manner as we have evangelized the Sandwich and Society Islands, and portions of Burmah, Hindostan, and other lands. By sending missionaries of the Cross indeed, who shall neither build forts nor trust in weapons of war; who shall be actuated by a holy zeal and genuine love; who shall be qualified to instruct, admonish, enlighten, and convert; who shall not by their examples impugn the precepts, nor subject to suspicion the excellence of the Word of Life; who shall not be covered with pollution and shame as with a garment, nor add to the ignorance, sin and corruption of paganism; and who shall abhor dishonesty, violence and treachery. Such men have been found to volunteer their services for the redemption of a lost world; and such men may now be found to embark in the same glorious enterprise. A hundred evangelists like these, dispersed along the shores and in the interior of Africa, would destroy more idols, make more progress in civilizing the natives, suppress more wars, unite in amity more hostile tribes, and convert more souls to Christ, in ten years, than a colony of twenty thousand ignorant, uncultivated, selfish emigrants in a century. Such a mission would be consonant with reason and common sense; nor could it fail to receive the approbation of God. How simple and comprehensive was the command of the Saviour to his disciples! Not—' Drive out from among yourselves those whom you despise, or against whom you cherish a strong antipathy; those who need to be instructed and converted themselves; those who are the dregs of society, made vicious and helpless by oppression and public opinion; those who are beyond the reach of the gospel in a Christian land; those whose complexions are not precisely like yours; drive out these to evangelize the nations which are in heathenish darkness'! But—' Go ye into all the world, and preach the gospel to every creature.'

But—says the objector—the climate of Africa is fatal to white men.

So is the climate of India. But our missionaries have not counted their lives dear unto themselves. As fast as one is cut down, another stands ready to supply his place.

But the objection is fallacious. If white missionaries cannot, black ones can survive in Africa. What, then, is our duty? Obviously to educate colored young men of genius, enterprise and piety, expressly to carry the 'glad tidings of great joy' to her shores. Enough, I venture to affirm, stand ready to be sent, if they can be first qualified for their mission. If our free colored population were brought into our schools, and raised from their present low estate, I am confident that an army of Christian volunteers would go out from their ranks, by a divine impulse, to redeem their African brethren from the bondage of idolatry and the dominion of spiritual death.

If I must become a colonizationist, I insist upon being consistent: there must be no disagreement between my creed and practice. I must be able to give a reason why all our tall citizens should not conspire to remove their more diminutive brethren, and all the corpulent to remove the lean and lank, and all the strong to remove the weak, and all the educated to remove the ignorant, and all the rich to remove the poor, as readily as for the removal of those whose skin is 'not colored like my own;' for Nature has sinned as culpably in diversifying the size as the complexion of her progeny, and Fortune in the distribution of her gifts has been equally fickle. I cannot perceive that I am more excusable in desiring the banishment of my neighbor, because his skin is darker than mine, than I should be in desiring his banishment, because he is a smaller or feebler man than myself. Surely it would be sinful for a black man to repine and murmur, to impeach the wisdom and goodness of God, because he was made with a sable complexion; and dare I be guilty of such an impeachment, by persecuting him on account of

3*

his color? I dare not: I would as soon deny the existence of my Creator as quarrel with the workmanship of his hands. I rejoice that he has made one star to differ from another star in glory; that he has not given to the sun the softness and tranquillity of the moon, nor to the moon the intensity and magnificence of the sun; that he presents to the eye every conceivable shape, and aspect, and color, in the gorgeous and multifarious productions of nature; and I do not rejoice the less, but admire and exalt him the more, that, notwithstanding he has made of one blood the whole family of man, he has made the whole family of man to differ in personal appearance, complexion and habits.

Of this I am sure: no man, who is truly willing to admit the people of color to an equality with himself, can see any insuperable difficulty in effecting their elevation. When, therefore, I hear an individual—especially a professor of religion—contending that they can never enjoy equal rights in this country, I cannot help suspecting the genuineness of his own republicanism or piety, or thinking that the beam is in his own eye. My Bible assures me that the day is coming when even the ' wolf shall dwell with the lamb, and the leopard shall lie down with the kid, and the wolf and the young lion and the fatling together;' and if this be possible, I see no cause why those of the same species—God's rational creatures—fellow-countrymen, in truth, cannot dwell in harmony together.

How atrociously hypocritical, how consummately despicable, how incorrigibly tyrannical, must this whole nation appear in the eyes of the people of Europe!—professing to be the friends of the colored race, actuated by the purest motives of benevolence toward them, desirous of making atonement for past wrongs, challenging the admiration of the world for their patriotism, philanthropy and piety—and yet (hear, O heaven! and be astonished, O earth!) shamelessly proclaiming, with a voice louder than thunder, with an aspect malignant as sin, that while their colored countrymen remain among them, they must be deprived of the invaluable privileges of freemen, treated as inferior beings, separated by the brand of indelible ignominy, trampled beneath their feet, and debased to a level with brute beasts! Yea, that they may as soon change their complexion as rise from their degradation! that no device of philanthropy can benefit them here! that they constitute a class, out of which no individual can be elevated, and below which none can be depressed! that no talents however great, no piety however pure and devoted, no patriotism however ardent, no industry however great, no wealth however abundant, can raise them to a footing of equality with the whites! that, 'let them toil from youth to old age in the honorable pursuit of wisdom— let them store their minds with the most valuable researches of science and literature—and let them add to a highly gifted and cultivated intellect, a piety pure, undefiled, and unspotted from the world, it is all nothing—they would not be received into the very lowest walks of society; admiration of such uncommon beings would mingle with disgust!' Yea, that 'there is a broad and impassable line of demarcation between every man who has one drop of African blood in his veins, and every other class in the community'! Yea, that 'the habits, the feelings, all the prejudices of society— prejudices which neither refinement, nor argument, nor education, nor RELIGION itself, can subdue—mark the people of color, whether bond or free, as the subjects of a degradation inevitable and incurable'! Yea, that 'Christianity cannot do for them here, what it will do for them in Africa'! Yea, that 'this is not the fault of the colored man, NOR OF THE WHITE MAN, nor of Christianity; but AN ORDINATION OF PROVIDENCE, *and no more to be changed than the* LAWS OF NATURE'!!

Again I ask, are we pagans, are we savages, are we devils?
Search the records of heathenism, and sentiments more hostile to the spirit of the gospel, or of a more black and blasphemous complexion than these, cannot be found. I believe
that they are libels upon the character of my countrymen,
which time will wipe off. I call upon the spirits of the just
made perfect in heaven, upon all who have experienced the
love of God in their souls here below, upon the Christian
converts in India and the islands of the sea, to sustain me in
the assertion, that there is power enough in the religion of
Jesus Christ to melt down the most stubborn prejudices, to
overthrow the highest walls of partition, to break the strongest caste, to improve and elevate the most degraded, to unite
in fellowship the most hostile, and to equalize and bless all
its recipients. Make me sure that there is not, and I will
give it up, now and for ever. 'In Christ Jesus, all are one:
there is neither Jew nor Greek, there is neither bond nor
free, there is neither male nor female.'

These sentiments were not uttered by infidels, nor by
the low and vile, but in many instances by professors of
religion and ministers of the gospel; and in almost every
instance, by reputedly the most enlightened, patriotic and
benevolent men in the land! Tell it not abroad! publish it
not in the streets of Calcutta! Even the eminent President
of Union College, (Rev. Dr. Nott,) could so far depart,
unguardedly, I hope, from Christian love and duty, as to utter
language like this in an address in behalf of the Colonization Society :—' With us they (the free people of color) have
been degraded by slavery, and *still further degraded by the
mockery of nominal freedom.*' This charge is not true.
We have not, it is certain, treated our colored brethren
as the law of kindness and the ties of brotherhood demand;
but have we outdone Southern slaveholders in cruelty?
Were it true, to forge new fetters for the limbs of these

degraded beings would be an act of benevolence. But their condition is as much superior to that of the slaves, as happiness is to misery: indeed, it admits of no comparison. Again he says: ' *We have endeavored*, but endeavored in vain, *to restore them either to self-respect, or to the respect of others.*' It is painful to contradict so worthy an individual; but nothing is more certain than that this statement is altogether erroneous. We have derided, we have shunned, we have neglected them, in every possible manner. They have had to rise, not only under the mountainous weight of their own vice and ignorance, but also under the heavy and constant pressure of our contempt and injustice. In despite of us, they have done well. Again: ' *It is not our fault that we have failed ;* it is not theirs.' We *are* wholly and exclusively in fault. What have we done to raise them up from the earth? What have we not done to keep them down? Once more: 'It has resulted from a cause over which neither they, nor we, can ever have control.' In other words, they have been made with skins ' not colored like our own,' and therefore we cannot recognise them as fellow-countrymen, or treat them like rational beings! One sixth of our whole population must, FOR EVER, in this land, remain a wretched, ignorant and degraded race ; and yet nobody is culpable—*none but the Creator*, who has made us incapable of doing unto others as we would have them do unto us! Now, if this be not an impeachment of Infinite Goodness, I cannot define it. The same sentiment is reiterated by a writer in the Southern Religious Telegraph, who says—'The exclusion of the free black from the civil and literary privileges of our country depends on another circumstance than that of character—a circumstance, which, as it was entirely beyond his control, so it is unchangeable, and will for ever operate. This circumstance is—*he is a black man*' *! !* And the Board of Managers of the Parent

Society, in their Fifteenth Annual Report, declare that ' *an ordination of Providence*' prevents the general improvement of the people of color in this land! How is our country dishonored, how are the requirements of the gospel contemned, by this ungodly plea! Having satisfied himself that the Creator is alone blameable for the past and present degradation of the free blacks, Dr. Nott draws the natural and unavoidable inference that ' here, therefore, they must be *for ever debased, for ever useless, for ever a nuisance, for ever a calamity ;*' and then gravely declares, (mark the climax!) ' and yet THEY, AND THEY ONLY, are qualified for colonizing Africa '! ' Why, then,' he asks, ' *in the name of God,*' (the abrupt appeal, in this connection, seems almost profane,) ' should we hesitate to encourage their departure ? '

Nature, we are constantly assured, has raised up impassable barriers between the races. But Southern slaveholders have clearly demonstrated, that an amalgamation with their slaves is not only possible, but a very easy matter, and eminently productive. It neither ends in abortion nor produces monsters. In truth, it is often so difficult in the slave States to distinguish between the fruits of this intercourse and the children of white parents, that witnesses are summoned at court to solve the problem! Talk of the barriers of Nature, when the land swarms with living refutations of the statement! Happy indeed would it be for many a female slave, if such a barrier could exist during the period of her servitude, to protect her from the lust of her master.

In France, England, Spain, and other countries, persons of color maintain as high a rank, and are treated as honorably, as any other class of the inhabitants, in despite of the ' impassable barriers of Nature.' Yet it is proclaimed to the world by the Colonization Society, that the American people can never be as republican in their feelings and practices as

Frenchmen, Spaniards or Englishmen! Nay, that religion itself cannot subdue their malignant prejudices, nor induce them to treat their dark-skinned brethren in accordance with their professions of republicanism! My countrymen! is it so? Are you willing thus to be held up as tyrants and hypocrites for ever? as less magnanimous and just than the populace of Europe? No—no! I cannot give you up as incorrigibly wicked, nor my country as sealed over to destruction. My confidence remains like the oak—like the Alps—unshaken, storm-proof. I am not discouraged; I am not distrustful. I still place an unwavering reliance upon the omnipotence of truth. I still believe that the demands of justice will be satisfied; that the voice of bleeding humanity will melt the most obdurate heart; and that the land will be redeemed and regenerated by an enlightened and energetic public opinion. As long as there remains among us a single copy of the Declaration of Independence, or of the New Testament, I will not despair of the social and political elevation of my black countrymen. Already a rallying-cry is heard from the East and the West, from the North and the South; towns and cities and states are in commotion; volunteers are trooping to the field; the spirit of freedom and the fiend of oppression are in mortal conflict, and all neutrality is at an end. Already the line of division is drawn; on one side are the friends of truth and liberty, with their banner floating high in the air, on which are inscribed, in letters of light, ' IMMEDIATE ABOLITION '—' NO COMPROMISE WITH OPPRESSORS '—' EQUAL RIGHTS '—' NO EXPATRIA-TION '—' DUTY, AND NOT CONSEQUENCES '—' LET JUSTICE BE DONE, THOUGH THE HEAVENS FALL!' On the opposite side stand the supporters and apologists of slavery, in mighty array, with a black flag, on which are seen, in bloody characters, ' AFRICAN COLONIZATION '—' GRADUAL ABOLI-TION '—' RIGHTS OF PROPERTY '—' NO EQUALITY'—' EXPUL-

SION OF THE BLACKS '—' PROTECTION TO TYRANTS !' Who
can doubt the issue of this controversy, or which side has
the approbation of the Lord of hosts?

See how suddenly, by a touch of the Colonization wand,
those who, in one breath, are denounced as ' nuisances,'
can be transformed into enlightened citizens and excellent
Christians — to hide the iniquity of their expulsion !

In the month of June, 1830, I happened to peruse a number of the Southern Religious Telegraph, in which I found
an essay, enforcing the duty of clergymen to take up collec-
tions in aid of the funds of the Colonization Society, on the
then approaching Fourth of July. After an appropriate
introductory paragraph, the writer says:

'But—we have a plea like a peace-offering to man and to God.
We answer poor blind Africa in her complaint—that we have her
children, and that they have served on our plantations. And we
tell her, look at their returning! We took them barbarous, though
measurably free,—untaught—rude—without science—without the
true religion—without philosophy—and strangers to the best civil
governments. And now we return them to her bosom, with the
mechanic arts, with science, with philosophy, with civilization, with
republican feelings, and above all, with the true knowledge of the
true God, and the way of salvation through the Redeemer.'

' The mechanic arts' ! With whom did they serve their
apprenticeship? ' With philosophy' ! In what colleges
were they taught? It is strange that we should be so anxious to get rid of these scientific men of color, these philosophers, these republicans, these Christians, and that we
should shun their company as if they were afflicted with the
hydrophobia, or carried a deadly pestilence in their train!
Certainly, they must have singular notions of the Christian
religion which tolerates—or, rather, which is so perverted as
to tolerate—the oppression of God's rational creatures by its
professors! They must feel a peculiar kind of brotherly

love for those good men, who banded together to remove them to Africa, because they were too proud to associate familiarly with men of a sable complexion! But the writer proceeds :

'We tell her, look at the little colony on her shores. We tell her, look to the consequences that must flow to all her borders from religion, and science, and knowledge, and civilization, and republican government! And then we ask her—*is not one ship load of emigrants returning with these multiplied blessings, worth more to her than a million of her barbarous sons ?'*

So! every ship load of ignorant and helpless emigrants is to more than compensate Africa for every million of her children who have been kidnapped, buried in the ocean and on the land, tortured with savage cruelty, and held in perpetual servitude! Truly, this is a compendious method of balancing accounts. In the sight of God, of Africa, and of the world, we are consequently blameless, and rather praiseworthy, for our past transgressions. It is such sophistry as is contained in the foregoing extract, that kindles my indignation into a blaze. I abhor cant, I abhor hypocrisy; and if some of the advocates of the Colonization Society do not deal largely in both, I am unable to comprehend the meaning of those terms.

Instead of returning to those, whom they have so deeply injured, with repenting and undissembling love; instead of seeking to conciliate and remunerate the victims of their prejudice and oppression; instead of resolving to break the yoke of servitude, and let the oppressed go free; it seems to be the only anxiety and aim of the American people, to outwit the vengeance of Heaven, and strengthen the bulwarks of tyranny, by expelling the free people of color, and effecting such a diminution of the number of slaves as shall give the white population a triumphant and irresistible supe-

4

riority! ' *Check the increase!* ' is their cry——' let us retain
in everlasting bondage as many as we can, safely. To do
justly is not our intention; we only mean to remove the sur-
plus of our present stock; we think we shall be able, by
this prudent device, to oppress and rob with impunity. Our
present wailing is not for our heinous crimes, but only
because our avarice and cruelty have carried us beyond our
ability to protect ourselves: we lament, not because we hold
so large a number in fetters of iron, but because we cannot
safely hold more!'

Ye crafty calculators! ye greedy and relentless tyrants!
ye contemners of justice and mercy! ye pale-faced usurpers! my soul spurns you with unspeakable disgust. Know
ye not that the reward of your hands shall be given you?
' Wo unto them that decree unrighteous decrees, and that
write grievousness which they have prescribed; to turn aside
the needy from judgment, and to take away the right from
the poor, that widows may be their prey, and that they may
rob the fatherless! And what will ye do in the day of vis-
itation, and in the desolation which shall come from far? to
whom will ye flee for help? and where will ye leave your
glory?' ' What mean ye that ye beat my people to pieces,
and grind the face of the poor? saith the Lord God of hosts.'
' Behold, the hire of the laborers which have reaped down
your fields, which is of you kept back by fraud, crieth; and
the cries of them which have reaped are entered into the
ear of the Lord of Sabaoth.' Repent! repent! now, in
sackcloth and ashes. Think not to succeed in your expul-
sive crusade; you cannot hide your motives from the Great
Searcher of hearts; and if a sinful worm of the dust, like
myself, is fired with indignation at your dastardly behavior
and mean conspiracy to evade repentance and punishment,
how must the anger of Him, whose holiness and justice are
infinite, burn against you? Is it not a fearful thing to fall

into the hands of the living God? You may plot by day and by night; you may heap together the treasures of the land, and multiply and enlarge your combinations, to extricate yourselves from peril; but you cannot succeed. Your only alternative is, either to redress the wrongs of the oppressed now, and humble yourselves before God, or prepare for the chastisements of Heaven. I repeat it—REPENT-ANCE or PUNISHMENT must be yours.

The Colonization Society deters a large number of masters from liberating their slaves, and hence directly perpetuates the evils of slavery: it deters them for two reasons—an unwillingness to augment the wretchedness of those who are in servitude, by turning them loose upon the country, and a dread of increasing the number of their enemies. It creates and nourishes the bitterest animosity against the free blacks. It has spread an alarm among all classes of society, in all parts of the country; and acting under this fearful impulse, they begin to persecute, believing self-preservation imperiously calls for this severe treatment. It is constantly thundering in the ears of the slave States—'Your free blacks contaminate your slaves, excite their deadliest hate, and are a source of horrid danger to yourselves! They must be removed, or your destruction is inevitable.' What is their response? Precisely such as might be expected—'We know it; we dread the presence of this class; their influence over our slaves weakens our power, and endangers our safety; they must, they shall be expatriated, or be crushed to the earth if they remain!' It says to the free States—'Your colored population can never be rendered serviceable, intelligent or loyal; they will only, and always, serve to increase your taxes, crowd your poor-houses and penitentiaries, and corrupt and impoverish society!' Again, what is the natural response?—'It is even so; they are offensive to the eye, and a pest in community; theirs is now, and must inevitably be, without a reversal of the laws of nature, the lot of vagabonds; it were useless to attempt their intellectual and moral improvement among ourselves; and therefore be this their alternative — either to emigrate to Liberia, or remain for ever a despicable caste in this country!'

Hence the enactment of those sanguinary laws, which disgrace our statute books; hence, too, the increasing disposition which is every where seen to render the situation of the free blacks intolerable. Never was it so pitiable and distressing — so full of peril and anxiety — so burdened with misery, despondency and scorn; never were the prejudices of society so virulent and implacable against them; never were their prospects so dark, and dreary, and hopeless; never was the hand of power so heavily laid upon their limbs; never were they so restricted in regard to locomotion and the advantages of education, as at the present time. Athwart their sky scarcely darts a single ray of light — above and around them darkness reigns, and an angry tempest is mustering its fearful strength, and 'thunders are uttering their voices.' Treachery is seeking to decoy, and violence to expel them. For all this, and more than this, and more that is to come, the American Colonization Society is responsible. And no better evidence is needed than this: their persecution, traducement and wretchedness increase in exact ratio with the influence, popularity and extension of this Society! The fact is undeniable, and it is conclusive. For it is absurd to suppose, that, as the disposition and ability of an association to alleviate misery increase, so will the degradation and suffering of the objects of its charities.

If the American Colonization Society were indeed actuated by the purest motives and the best feelings toward the objects of its supervision; if it were not based upon injustice,

fraud, persecution and incorrigible prejudice ; still, if its purpose be contrary to the wishes and injurious to the interests
of the free people of color, it ought not to receive the countenance of the public. Even the trees of the forest are
keenly susceptible to every touch of violence, and seem to
deprecate transplantation to a foreign soil. Even birds and
animals pine in exile from their native haunts ; their local
attachments are wonderful ; they migrate only to return
again at the earliest opportunity. Perhaps there is not a
living thing, from the hugest animal down to the minutest
animalcule, whose pleasant associations are not circumscrib-
ed, or that has not some favorite retreats. This universal
preference, this love of home, seems to be the element of
being, — a constitutional attribute given by the all-wise Creator to bind each separate tribe or community within intelligent and well-defined limits : for, in its absence, order would
be banished from the world, collision between the countless orders of creation would be perpetual, and violence
would depopulate the world with more than pestilential
rapidity.

Shall it be said that beings endowed with high intellectual
powers, sustaining the most important relations, created for
social enjoyments, and made but a little lower than the
angels — shall it be said that their local attachments are less
tenacious than those of trees, and birds, and beasts, and
insects ? I know that the blacks are classed by some, who
scarcely give any evidence of their own humanity but their
shape, among the brute creation : but are they below the
brutes ? or are they more insensible to rude assaults than
forest-trees ?

'Men,' says an erratic but powerful writer — 'men are
like trees : they delight in a rude soil — they strike their
roots downward with a perpetual effort, and heave their proud
branches upward in perpetual strife. Are they to be remov-

4*

ed ? — you must tear up the very earth with their roots, and rock, and ore, and impurity, or they perish. They cannot be translated with safety. Something of their home — a little of their native soil, must cling to them forever, or they die.'

This love of home, of neighborhood, of country, is inherent in the human breast. It accompanies the child from its earliest reminiscence up to old age : it is written upon every tangible and permanent object within the habitual cognizance of the eye — upon stone, and tree, and rivulet — upon the green hill, and the verdant plain, and the opulent valley — upon house, and garden, and steeple-spire — upon the soil, whether it be rough or smooth, sandy or hard, barren or luxuriant.

No one will understand me to maintain, that population should never be thinned by foreign emigration ; but only that such an emigration is unnatural. The great mass of a neighborhood or country must necessarily be stable : only fractions are cast off, and float away on the tide of adventure. Individual enterprise or estrangement is one thing : the translation of an entire people to an unknown clime, another. The former may be moved by a single impulse — by a love of novelty, or a desire of gain, or a hope of preferment ; he leaves no perceptible void in society. The latter can never be expatriated but by some extraordinary calamity, or by the application of intolerable restraints. They must first be rendered broken-hearted or loaded with chains — hope must not merely sicken but die — cord after cord must be sundered — ere they will seek another home.

African colonization is directly and irreconcilably opposed to the wishes of our colored population, as a body. Their desires ought to be tenderly regarded. In all my intercourse with them, in various towns and cities, I have never seen one of their number who was friendly to this scheme ; and I have not been backward in canvassing their opinions on this subject. They are as unanimously opposed to a removal to Africa, as the Cherokees from the council-fires and graves of their fathers. It is remarkable, too, that they are as united in their respect and esteem for the republic of Hayti. But this is their country — they are resolute against every migratory plot, and willing to rely on the justice of the nation for an ultimate restoration to all their lost rights and privileges. What is the fact? Through the instrumentality of BENJAMIN LUNDY, the distinguished and veteran champion of emancipation, a great highway has been opened to the Haytien republic, over which our colored population may travel toll free, and at the end of their brief journey be the free occupants of the soil, and meet such a reception as was never yet given to any sojourners in any country, since the departure of Israel out of Egypt. One would think, that, with such inducements and under such circumstances, this broad thoroughfare would present a most animating spectacle ; that the bustle and roar of a journeying multitude would fall upon the ear like the strife of the ocean, or the distant thunder of the retiring storm ; and that the song of the oppressor and the oppressed, a song of deliverance to each, would go up to heaven, till its echoes were seemingly the responses of angels and justified spirits. But it is not so. Only here and there a traveller is seen to enter upon the road—there is no noise of preparation or departure ; but a silence, deeper than the breathlessness of midnight, rests upon our land—not a shout of joy is heard throughout our borders !

Whatever may be the result of this great controversy, I shall have the consolation of believing that no efforts were lacking, on my part, to uproot the prejudices of my countrymen, to persuade them to walk in the path of duty and shun the precipice of expediency, to undo the heavy burdens and let the oppressed go free at once, to warn them of the danger of expelling the people of color from their native land, and to convince them of the necessity of abandoning a dangerous and chimerical, as well as unchristian and anti-republican association. For these efforts I have hitherto suffered reproach and persecution, must expect to suffer, and am willing to suffer to the end.*

The Dangers of the Nation.

Fifty-three years ago, the Fourth of July was a proud day for our country. It clearly and accurately defined the rights of man; it made no vulgar alterations in the established usages of society.; it presented a revelation adapted to the common sense of mankind; it vindicated the omnipotence of public opinion over the machinery of kingly government; it shook, as with the voice of a great earthquake, thrones which were seemingly propped up with Atlantean pillars; it gave an impulse to the heart of the world, which yet thrills to its extremities.

It may be profitable to inquire, whether the piety which founded, and the patriotism which achieved our liberties, remain unimpaired in principle, undiminished in devotion. Possibly our Samson is sleeping in the lap of Delilah, with

---

* Extracted from a pamphlet, published in 1832, entitled 'THOUGHTS ON AFRICAN COLONIZATION: or an Impartial Exhibition of the Doctrines, Principles and Purposes of the American Colonization Society. Together with the Resolutions, Addresses and Remonstrances of the Free People of Color. By WILLIAM LLOYD GARRISON.'

his locks shorn and his strength departed. Possibly his
enemies have put out his eyes, and bound him with fetters
of brass, and compelled him to grind in the prison-house;
and if, in his rage and blindness, he find the pillars of the
fabric, woe to those for whose sport he is led forth!

For many years, the true friends of their country have
witnessed the return of this great jubilee with a terror, that
no consolation could remove, and with a grief, that no flattery could assuage. They have seen, that, instead of being
distinguished for rationality of feeling and purity of purpose,
it has exhibited the perversion of reason and the madness of
intemperance. Patriotism has degenerated into mere animal indulgence; or, rather, into the most offensive personalities. Liberty has gone hand in hand with licentiousness—
her gait unsteady, her face bloated, her robe bedraggled in
the dust. It seems as if men had agreed, by common
consent, that an act, which, on any other day, would impeach
a fair reputation, on this, should help enlarge that reputation.
The love of country has been tested by the exact number
of libations poured forth, the most guns fired, the greatest
number of toasts swallowed, and the loudest professions of
loyalty to the Union, uttered over the wine-cup.

Indeed, so dear is Liberty to many, that they cannot make
too free with her charms: they owe her so much, that they
owe the Most High nothing. It would shock their sensibility,
and tarnish their reputation as patriots, to be caught at a
religious celebration of our national anniversary. The day,
they argue, should be properly appreciated; and, unless a
man gets gloriously inebriated, either at home or in the
streets, at his own or a public table, in digesting his own good
sayings or those of others—unless he declaims roundly in
praise of freedom, and drinks perdition to tyrants—it shows
that he is either a monarchist or a bigot.

But it is not the direct, palpable, and widely extensive mischief to public morals, which alone makes the Fourth of July the worst and most disastrous day in the whole three hundred and sixty-five. There is, if possible, a corruption more deep—an intoxication more fascinating and deadly. It is that torrent of flattery, artfully sweetened and spiced, which is poured out for the thirsty multitude to swallow; it is that thriftless prodigality of praise, that presumptuous defi- ance of danger, that treacherous assurance of security, that impudent assumption of ignorance, that pompous declama- tion of vanity, that lying attestation of falsehood, from the lips of tumid orators, which are poisoning our life-blood.

We are a vain people, and our love of praise is inordinate. We imagine, and are annually taught to believe, that the republic is immortal; that its flight, like a strong angel's, has been perpetually upward, till it has soared above the impu- rities of earth, and beyond the remotest star; and, having attained perfection, is forever out of the reach of circum- stance and change. An earthquake may rock all Europe, and ingulph empires at a stroke; but it cannot raise an inch of republican territory, nor disturb the composure of a plat- ter on our shelves. The ocean may gather up its forces for a second deluge, and overtop the tallest mountains; but our ark will float securely when the world is drowned. The storm may thicken around us; but a smile from the goddess of Liberty will disperse the gloom, and build a rainbow wherever she turns her eye. We shall remain ' till the heav- ens be no more.'

It is this fatal delusion, which so terrifies men of reflection and foresight; which makes the Christian shudder at the prospect before us, and the Patriot weep in despair; which, unless the mercy of God interpose, seals the doom of our country. .

When a people become so infatuated as to deny the exist- ence, and to doubt the possibility of danger; when they

hear the language of reproof with angry emotions, and ridicule the remonstrances of wisdom as the croakings of imbecility; when they imagine every virtue to dwell in mere
liberty, and are content to take the shadow for the substance,
the name for the object, the promise for the possession, there
is no extreme of folly into which they cannot be led, no
vice which they will not patronise, no error which they will
not adopt, no pitfall into which they will not stumble.

At such a crisis, the reason of men becomes more obtuse
than animal instinct. The frugal and industrious ant does
not wait till the cold winds of winter stiffen her legs, before
she stores her provisions; the bird of passage migrates when
autumn expires; the deer needs only to hear the bark of the
hounds, and, without waiting for their approach, he tosses
back his broad antlers, and dashes onward with the speed of
an arrow. But a nation of infatuated freemen take no warning from history; they learn nothing from experience. To
their vision, the signs of the times are always ominous of
good. Like the inhabitants of Jerusalem, they must hear
the avenger thundering at their gates, and see their destiny
prefigured by dreadful omens in the heavens, before they
will acknowledge that the judgments of God are sure. They
must tread on the cinders of a national coflnagration, and
count the number of smoking ruins, before they will believe
in the combustibleness of the republic.

. ' Our fate,' says a distinguished essayist, ' is not foretold
by signs and wonders: the meteors do not indeed glare in
the form of types, and print it legibly in the sky: but our
warning is as distinct, and almost as awful, as if it were
announced in thunder by the concussion of all the elements.' .

I know that this may be viewed as the phantasm of a disordered imagination. I know, too, it is easy to persuade
ourselves that we shall escape those maladies, which have

destroyed other nations. But, how closely soever a republic may resemble the human body in its liability to disease and death, the instance is not on record, where a people expired on account of excessive watchfulness over their own health, or of any premature apprehension of decay; and there is no national epitaph which says, ' they were well, they wished to be better, they took physic, and died.'

I speak not as a partisan or an opponent of any man or measures, when I say, that our politics are rotten to the core. *We* boast of our freedom, who go shackled to the polls, year after year, by tens, and hundreds, and thousands! *We* talk of free agency, who are the veriest machines—the merest automata—in the hands of unprincipled jugglers! *We* prate of integrity, and virtue, and independence, who sell our birthright for office, and who, nine times in ten, do not get Esau's bargain—no, not even a mess of pottage! Is it republicanism to say, that the majority can do no wrong? Then I am not a republican. Is it aristocracy to say, that the people sometimes shamefully abuse their high trust? Then I am an aristocrat. Rely upon it, the republic does not bear a charmed life: our prescriptions, administered through the medium of the ballot-box—the mouth of the political body—may kill or cure, according to the nature of the disease, and our wisdom in applying the remedy. It is possible that a people may bear the title of freemen, who execute the work of slaves. To the dullest observer of the signs of the times, it must be apparent, that we are rapidly approximating to this condition. Never were our boasts of liberty so inflated as at this moment—never were they greater mockeries. We are governed, not by our sober judgments, but by our passions: we are led by our ears, not by our understandings.

Wherein do we differ from the ancient Romans? What shall save us, from their fate?

'It is remarkable,' says a writer, to whom all history was as familiar as his alphabet, 'it is remarkable that Cicero, with all his dignity and good sense, found it a popular seasoning of his harangue, six years *after* Julius Cæsar had established a monarchy, and only six months *before* Octavius totally subverted the commonwealth, to say: "It is not possible for the people of Rome to be slaves, whom the gods have destined to the command of all nations. Other nations may endure slavery, but the proper end and business of the Roman people is liberty."'

But there is another evil, which, if we had to contend against nothing else, should make us quake for the issue. It is a gangrene preying upon our vitals—an earthquake rumbling under our feet—a mine accumulating materials for a national catastrophe. It should make this a day of fasting and prayer, not of boisterous merriment and idle pageantry, —a day of great lamentation, not of congratulatory joy. It should spike every cannon, and haul down every banner. Our garb should be sackcloth—our heads bowed in the dust—our supplications, for the pardon and assistance of Heaven.

Last week, this city was made breathless by a trial of considerable magnitude. The court chamber was inundated for hours, day after day, with a dense and living tide, which swept along like the rush of a mountain torrent. Tiers of human bodies were piled up to the walls, with almost miraculous condensation and ingenuity. It seemed as if men abhorred a vacuum equally with Nature: they would suspend themselves, as it were, by a nail, and stand upon air with the aid of a peg. Although it was a barren, ineloquent subject, and the crowd immense, there was no perceptible want of interest—no evidence of impatience. The cause was important, involving the reputation of a distinguished citizen. There was a struggle for mastery between two giants—a

5

test of strength in tossing mountains of law. The excitement was natural.

I stand up here in a more solemn court, to assist in a far greater cause; not to impeach the character of one man, but of a whole people—not to recover the sum of a hundred thousand dollars, but to obtain the liberation of two millions of wretched, degraded beings, who are pining in hopeless bondage—over whose sufferings scarcely an eye weeps, or a heart melts, or a tongue pleads either to God or man. I regret that a better advocate had not been found, to enchain your attention, and to warm your blood. Whatever fallacy, however, may appear in the argument, there is no flaw in the indictment; what the speaker lacks, the cause will supply.

Sirs, I am not come to tell you that slavery is a curse, debasing in its effect, cruel in its operation, fatal in its continuance. The day and the occasion require no such revelation. I do not claim the discovery as my own, 'that all men are born equal,' and that among their inalienable rights are 'life, liberty, and the pursuit of happiness.' Were I addressing any other than a free and Christian assembly, the enforcement of this truth might be pertinent. Neither do I intend to analyze the horrors of slavery for your inspection, nor to freeze your blood with authentic recitals of savage cruelty. Nor will time allow me to explore even a furlong of that immense wilderness of suffering, which remains unsubdued in our land. I take it for granted that the existence of these evils is acknowledged, if not rightly understood. My object is to define and enforce our duty, as Christians and Philanthropists.

On a subject so exhaustless, it will be impossible, in the moiety of an address, to unfold all the facts which are necessary to its full development. In view of it, my heart wells up like a living fountain, which time cannot exhaust, for it is perpetual. Let this be considered as the preface of a noble work, which your inventive sympathies must elabo-'rate and complete.

I assume, as distinct and defensible propositions,

I. That the slaves of this country, whether we consider their moral, intellectual or social condition, are pre-eminently entitled to the prayers, and sympathies, and charities of the American people; and that their claims for redress are as strong as those of any Americans could be, in a similar condition.

II. That, as the free States — by which I mean non-slave-holding States — are constitutionally involved in the guilt of slavery, by adhering to a national compact that sanctions it; and in the danger, by liability to be called upon for aid in case of insurrection; they have the right to remonstrate against its continuance, and it is their duty to assist in its overthrow.

III. That no justificative plea for the perpetuity of slavery can be found in the condition of its victims; and no barrier against our righteous interference, in the laws which authorize the buying, selling and possessing of slaves, nor in the hazard of a collision with slaveholders.

IV. That education and freedom will elevate our colored population to a rank with the whites — making them useful, intelligent and peaceable citizens.

In the first place, it will be readily admitted, that it is the duty of every nation primarily to administer relief to its own necessities, to cure its own maladies, to instruct its own children, and to watch over its own interests. He is 'worse than an infidel,' who neglects his own household, and squanders his earnings upon strangers; and the policy of that nation is unwise, which seeks to proselyte other portions of the globe at the expense of its safety and happiness. Let me not be misunderstood. My benevolence is neither con-

tracted nor selfish.   I pity that man whose heart is not larger
than a whole continent.   I despise the littleness of that patriotism which blusters only for its own rights, and, stretched
to its utmost dimensions, scarcely covers its native territory;
which adopts as its creed, the right to act independently,
even to the verge of licentiousness, without restraint, and to
tyrannize wherever it can with impunity.   This sort of patriotism is common.   I suspect the reality, and deny the pro-
ductiveness of that piety, which confines its operations to a
particular spot — if that spot be less than the whole earth;
nor scoops out, in every direction, new channels for the
waters of life.   Christian charity, while it ' begins at home,'
goes abroad in search of misery.   It is as copious as the sun
in heaven.   It does not, like the Nile, make a partial inun-
dation, and then withdraw; but it perpetually overflows, and
fertilizes every barren spot.   It is restricted only by the
exact number of God's suffering creatures.   But I mean to
say, that, while we are aiding and instructing foreigners, we
ought not to forget our own degraded countrymen; that
neither duty nor honesty requires us to defraud ourselves, that
we may enrich others.

The condition of the slaves, in a religious point of view,
is deplorable, entitling them to a higher consideration, on our
part, than any other race; higher than the Turks or Chinese,
for they have the privileges of instruction; higher than the
Pagans, for they are not dwellers in a gospel land; higher
than our red men of the forest, for we do not bind them with
gyves, nor treat them as chattels.

And here let me ask, what has Christianity done, by direct
effort, for our slave population?   Comparatively nothing.
She has explored the isles of the ocean for objects of com-
miseration; but, amazing stupidity! she can gaze without
emotion on a multitude of miserable beings at home, large
enough to constitute a nation of freemen, whom tyranny has

heathenized by law. In her public services, they are seldom remembered, and in her private donations they are forgotten. From one end of the country to the other, her charitable societies form golden links of benevolence, and scatter their contributions like rain-drops over a parched heath; but they bring no sustenance to the perishing slave. The blood of souls is upon her garments, yet she heeds not the stain. The clankings of the prisoner's chains strike upon her ear, but they cannot penetrate her heart.

I have said, that the claims of the slaves for redress are as strong as those of any Americans could be, in a similar condition. Does any man deny the position? The proof, then, is found in the fact, that a very large proportion of our colored population were born on our soil, and are therefore entitled to all the privileges of American citizens. This is their country by birth, not by adoption. Their children possess the same inherent and unalienable rights as ours; and it is a crime of the blackest dye to load them with fetters.

Every Fourth of July, our Declaration of Independence is produced, with a sublime indignation, to set forth the tyranny of the mother country, and to challenge the admiration of the world. But what a pitiful detail of grievances does this document present, in comparison with the wrongs which our slaves endure! In the one case, it is hardly the plucking of a hair from the head; in the other, it is the crushing of a live body on the wheel; the stings of the wasp contrasted with the tortures of the inquisition. Before God, I must say, that such a glaring contradiction, as exists between our creed and practice, the annals of six thousand years cannot parallel. In view of it, I am ashamed of my country. I am sick of our unmeaning declamation in praise of liberty and equality; of our hypocritical cant about the unalienable rights of man. I could not, for my right hand, stand

5*

up before a European assembly, and exult that I am an American citizen, and denounce the usurpations of a kingly government as wicked and unjust; or, should I make the attempt, the recollection of my country's barbarity and despotism would blister my lips, and cover my cheeks with burning blushes of shame.

Will this be termed a rhetorical flourish? Will any man coldly accuse me of intemperate zeal? I will borrow, then, a ray of humanity from one of the brightest stars in our American galaxy, whose light will gather new effulgence to the end of time. 'This, sirs, is a cause, that would be dishonored and betrayed, if I contented myself with appealing only to the understanding. It is too cold, and its processes are too slow for the occasion. I desire to thank God, that, since he has given me an intellect so fallible, he has impressed upon me an instinct that is sure. On a question of shame and honor—liberty and oppression—reasoning is sometimes useless, and worse. I feel the decision in my pulse: if it throws no light upon the brain, it kindles a fire at the 'heart.'

Let us suppose that endurance has passed its bounds, and that the slaves, goaded to desperation by the cruelty of their oppressors, have girded on the armor of vengeance. Let us endeavor to imagine the appeal which they would publish to the world, in extenuation of their revolt. The preamble might be taken from our own Declaration of Independence, with a few slight alterations. Then what a detail of wrongs would follow! Speaking at first from the shores of Africa, and changing their situation with the course of events, they would say:

'They, (the American people,) arrogantly styling themselves the champions of freedom, for a long course of years have been guilty of the most cruel and protracted tyranny. They have invaded our territories, depopulated our villages,

and kindled among us the flames of an exterminating war.
They have wedged us into the holds of their ' floating hells,'
with suffocating compactness, and without distinction of age
or sex—allowing us neither to inhale the invigorating air of
heaven, nor to witness the cheering light of the sun, neither
wholesome food nor change of raiment—by which treatment
thousands have expired under the most horrible sufferings.
They have brought us to a free and Christian land, (so called,) and sold us in their market-places like cattle—even in
the proud Capital of their Union, and within sight of their
legislative halls, where Tyranny struts in the semblance of
Liberty.   They have cruelly torn the wife from her husband,
the mother from her daughter, and children from their
parents, and sold them into perpetual exile.   They have
confined us in loathsome cells and secret prisons—driven us
in large droves from State to State, beneath a burning sky,
half naked, and heavily manacled—nay, retaken and sold
many, who had by years of toil obtained their liberation.
They have compelled us ' to till their ground, to carry them,
to fan them when they sleep, and tremble when they wake,'
and rewarded us only with stripes, and hunger, and nakedness.   They have lacerated our bodies with whips, and
brands, and knives, for the most innocent and trifling offen-
ces, and often solely to gratify their malignant propensities ;
nor do they esteem it a crime worthy of death to murder us
at will.   Nor have they deprived us merely of our liberties.
They would destroy our souls, by endeavoring to deprive us
of the means of instruction—of a knowledge of God, and
Jesus Christ, and the Holy Spirit, and a way of salvation :
at the same time, they have taxed the whole country (our own
labor among other things) to instruct and enlighten those
who are at a great remove from them, whom they never fettered nor maimed, whose condition is not so dark or pitiable as our own.   They have ———'

But why need I proceed ?   My powers of description are
inadequate to the task.   A greater than Jefferson would fail.
Only the pen of the recording angel can declare their manifold wrongs and sufferings ; and the revelation will not be
made till the day of judgment.

We say, that the disabilities imposed upon our fathers, by
the mother country, furnished just cause for rebellion ;
that their removal was paramount to every other consideration ; and that the slaughter of our oppressors was a justifiable act ; for we should resist unto blood to save our liberties.
Suppose that to-morrow should bring us tidings that the slaves
at the South had revolted, *en masse*, and were spreading
devastation and death among the white population.   Should
we celebrate their achievements in song, and justify their
terrible excesses ?   And why not, if our creed be right?
Their wrongs are unspeakably grievous, and liberty is the
birthright of every man.

We say, that France was justified in assisting our fathers
to maintain their independence ; and that, as a nation, we
owe her our liveliest gratitude for her timely interference.
Suppose, in case of a revolt, that she, or some other European power, should furnish our slaves with guns and ammunition, and pour her troops into our land.   Would it be
treacherous or cruel ?   Why, according to our revolutionary
credenda?   The argument, tremendous as it is, is against
us !   WELL, IT MAY BE DONE.   At a fit moment, a foreign
foe may stir up a rebellion, and arm every black, and take
the lead in the enterprise.   The attempt would not be difficult ; the result can be easily imagined.

We say, that the imprisonment of an inconsiderable number of our seamen, by Great Britain, authorized the late war ;
and we boast of our promptitude to redress their wrongs.
More than a million of native-born citizens are at this moment
enduring the galling yoke of slavery.   Who cries for jus-

tice? None. ' But they are blacks!' True, and they are also men; and, moreover, they are Americans by birth.

If it be said, (which assertion is false,) that the present race are beyond recovery; then I reply, in the language of a warm-hearted philanthropist, ' Let us make no more slaves. Let us shiver to atoms those galling fetters, under the pressure of which so many hearts have bursted. Let us not shackle the limbs of the future workmanship of God. Let us pour into their minds the fertilizing streams of piety and knowledge; imbue their hearts with gratitude for extending to them this heaven's best boon; and suffer their souls to walk abroad in their majesty.'

It may be objected, that the laws of the slave States form insurmountable barriers to any interference on our part.

Answer. I grant that we have not the right, and I trust not the disposition, to use coercive measures. But do these laws hinder our prayers, or obstruct the flow of our sympathies? Cannot our charities alleviate the condition of the slave, and perhaps break his fetters? Can we not operate upon public sentiment, (the lever that can move the moral world,) by way of remonstrance, advice, or entreaty? Is Christianity so powerful, that she can tame the red men of our forests, and abolish the Burman caste, and overthrow the gods of Paganism, and liberate lands over which the darkness of Superstition has lain for ages; and yet so weak, in her own dwelling-place, that she can make no impression upon her civil code? Can she contend successfully with cannibals, and yet be conquered by her own children?

Suppose that, by a miracle, the slaves should suddenly become white. Would you shut your eyes upon their sufferings, and calmly talk of constitutional limitations? No; your voice would peal in the ears of the taskmasters like deep thunder; you would carry the Constitution by force, if it could not be taken by treaty; patriotic assemblies would

congregate at the corner of every street; the old Cradle of
Liberty would rock to a deeper tone than ever echoed therein
at British aggression; the pulpit would acquire new and
unusual eloquence from our holy religion. The argument,
that these white slaves are degraded, would not then obtain.
You would say, it is enough that they are white, and in
bondage, and they ought immediately to be set free. You
would multiply your schools of instruction, and your temples
of worship, and rely upon them for security.

But the plea is prevalent, that any interference by the free
States, however benevolent or cautious it might be, would
only irritate and inflame the jealousies of the South, and
retard the cause of emancipation.

If any man believes that slavery can be abolished without a struggle with the worst passions of human nature,
quietly, harmoniously, he cherishes a delusion. It can
never be done, unless the age of miracles return. No; we
must expect a collision, full of sharp asperities and bitterness. We shall have to contend with the insolence, and
pride, and selfishness, of many a heartless being. But these
can be easily conquered by meekness, and perseverance,
and prayer.

It is often despondingly said, that the evil of slavery is
beyond our control. Dreadful conclusion, that puts the seal
of death upon our country's existence! If we cannot conquer the monster in his infancy, while his cartilages are tender and his limbs powerless, how shall we escape his wrath
when he goes forth a gigantic cannibal, seeking whom he
may devour? If we cannot safely unloose two millions of
slaves now, how shall we bind upwards of TWENTY MILLIONS
at the close of the present century? But there is no cause
for despair. We have seen how readily, and with what
ease, that horrid gorgon, Intemperance, has been checked in
its ravages. Let us take courage. Moral influence, when

in vigorous exercise, is irresistible. It has an immortal essence. It can no more be trod out of existence by the iron foot of time, or by the ponderous march of iniquity, than matter can be annihilated. It may disappear for a time ; but it lives in some shape or other, in some place or other, and will rise with renovated strength. Let us, then, be up and doing. In the simple and stirring language of the stout-hearted LUNDY, ' all the friends of the cause must go to work, keep to work, hold on, and never give up.'

Years may elapse before the completion of the achievement; generations of blacks may go down to the grave, manacled and lacerated, without a hope for their children ; the philanthropists, who are now pleading in behalf of the oppressed, may not live to witness the dawn which will precede the glorious day of universal emancipation; but the work will go on — laborers in the cause will multiply — new resources will be discovered — the victory will be obtained, worth the desperate struggle of a thousand years. Or, if defeat follow, woe to the safety of this people ! The nation will be shaken as if by a mighty earthquake. A cry of horror, a cry of revenge, will go up to heaven in the darkness of midnight, and re-echo from every cloud. Blood will flow like water — the blood of guilty men, and of innocent women and children. Then will be heard lamentations and weeping, such as will blot out the remembrance of the horrors of St. Domingo. The terrible judgments of an incensed God will complete the catastrophe of republican America.

And since so much is to be done for our country; since so many prejudices are to be dispelled, obstacles vanquished, interests secured, blessings obtained ; since the cause of emancipation must progress heavily, and meet with much unhallowed opposition, why delay the work ? There must be a beginning, and now is a propitious time — perhaps the

last opportunity that will be granted us by a long-suffering
God.   No temporising, lukewarm measures will avail aught.
We must put our shoulder to the wheel, and heave with
our united strength.   Let us not look coldly on, and see
our southern brethren contending single-handed against an
all-powerful foe — faint, weary, borne down to the earth.
We are all alike guilty.   Slavery is strictly a national sin.
New-England money has been expended in buying human
flesh; New-England ships have been freighted with sable
victims; New-England men have assisted in forging the fetters of those who groan in bondage.

  . I call upon the ambassadors of Christ every where to
make known this proclamation: 'Thus saith the Lord God
of the Africans, Let this people go, that they may serve
me.'   I ask them to 'proclaim liberty to the captives, and
the opening of the prison to them that are bound' — to light
up a flame of philanthropy, that shall burn till all Africa be
redeemed from the night of moral death, and the song of
deliverance be heard throughout her borders.

  I call upon the churches of the living God to lead in this
great enterprise.   If the soul be immortal, priceless, save
it from redeemless woe.   Let them combine their energies,
and systematize their plans, for the rescue of suffering
humanity.   Let them pour out their supplications to heaven
in behalf of the slave.   Prayer is omnipotent: its breath can
melt adamantine rocks — its touch can break the stoutest
chains.   Let anti-slavery charity-boxes stand uppermost
among those for missionary, tract and educational purposes.
On this subject, Christians have been asleep; let them shake
off their slumbers, and arm for the holy contest.

  I call upon our New-England women to form charitable
associations to relieve the degraded of their sex.   As yet,
an appeal to their sympathies was never made in vain.
They outstrip us in every benevolent race.   Females are

doing much for the cause at the South; let their example be imitated, and their exertions surpassed, at the North.

I call upon the great body of newspaper editors to keep this subject constantly before their readers; to sound the trumpet of alarm, and to plead eloquently for the rights of man. They must give the tone to public sentiment. One press may ignite twenty; a city may warm a State; a State may impart a generous heat to a whole country.

I call upon the American people to enfranchise a spot, over which they hold complete sovereignty; to cleanse that worse than Augean stable, the District of Columbia, from its foul impurities. I conjure them to select those as Representatives, who are not too ignorant to know, too blind to see, nor too timid to perform their duty.

I will say, finally, that I tremble for the republic while slavery exists therein. If I look up to God for success, no smile of mercy or forgiveness dispels the gloom of futurity; if to our resources, they are daily diminishing; if to all history, our destruction is not only possible, but almost certain. Why should we slumber at this momentous crisis? If our hearts were dead to every throb of humanity; if it were lawful to oppress, where power is ample; still, if we had any regard for our safety and happiness, we should strive to crush the Vampyre which is feeding upon our life-blood. All the selfishness of our nature cries aloud for a better security. Our own vices are too strong for us, and keep us in perpetual alarm; how, in addition to these, shall we be able to contend successfully with millions of armed and desperate men, as we must eventually, if slavery do not cease?*

---

* Extracted from an Address, delivered in Park Street Church, Boston, July 4th, 1829.

6

Commencement of the Liberator.

In the month of August, I issued proposals for publishing 'THE LIBERATOR' in Washington city; but the enterprise, though hailed approvingly in different sections of the country, was palsied by public indifference. Since that time, the removal of the 'Genius of Universal Emancipation' to the Seat of Government has rendered less imperious the establishment of a similar periodical in that quarter.

During my recent tour for the purpose of exciting the minds of the people by a series of discourses on the subject of slavery, every place that I visited gave fresh evidence of the fact, that a greater revolution in public sentiment was to be effected in the free States—and particularly in New England—than at the South. I found contempt more bitter, opposition more active, detraction more relentless, prejudice more stubborn, and apathy more frozen, than among slave owners themselves. Of course, there were individual exceptions to the contrary. This state of things afflicted, but did not dishearten me. I determined, at every hazard, to lift up the standard of emancipation in the eyes of the nation, within sight of Bunker Hill, and in the birth-place of liberty. That standard is now unfurled; and long may it float, unhurt by the spoliations of time or the missiles of a desperate foe; yea, till every chain be broken, and every bondman set free! Let Southern oppressors tremble; let their secret abettors tremble; let their Northern apologists tremble; let all the enemies of the persecuted blacks tremble.

Assenting to the 'self-evident truths' maintained in the American Declaration of Independence, 'that all men are created equal, and endowed by their Creator with certain inalienable rights—among which are life, liberty, and the pursuit of happiness,' I shall strenuously contend for the

immediate enfranchisement of our slave population. In
Park Street Church, on the Fourth of July, 1829, in an
address on slavery, I unreflectingly assented to the popular
but pernicious doctrine of gradual abolition. I seize this
opportunity to make a full and unequivocal recantation, and
thus publicly to ask pardon of my God, of my country, and
of my brethren, the poor slaves, for having uttered a sentiment so full of timidity, injustice and absurdity. A similar
recantation, from my pen, was published in the 'Genius of
Universal Emancipation,' at Baltimore, in September, 1829.
My conscience is now satisfied.

I am aware, that many object to the severity of my language; but is there not cause for severity? I will be as
harsh as truth, and as uncompromising as justice. On this
subject, I do not wish to think, or speak, or write, with moderation. No! no! Tell a man, whose house is on fire, to
give a moderate alarm; tell him to moderately rescue his
wife from the hands of the ravisher; tell the mother to gradually extricate her babe from the fire into which it has fallen;
but urge me not to use moderation in a cause like the present! I am in earnest. I will not equivocate—I will not
excuse—I will not retreat a single inch—AND I WILL BE
HEARD. The apathy of the people is enough to make every
statue leap from its pedestal, and to hasten the resurrection
of the dead.

It is pretended, that I am retarding the cause of emancipation by the coarseness of my invective, and the precipitancy of my measures. The charge is not true. On this
question, my influence, humble as it is, is felt at this moment
to a considerable extent, and shall be felt in coming years—
not perniciously, but beneficially—not as a curse, but as a
blessing; and POSTERITY WILL BEAR TESTIMONY THAT I WAS
RIGHT. I desire to thank God, that he enables me to disregard 'the fear of man which bringeth a snare,' and to speak

his truth in its simplicity and power.   And here I close with this fresh dedication :—

> ' Oppression ! I have seen thee, face to face,
>   And met thy cruel eye and cloudy brow ;
>   But thy soul-withering glance I fear not now—
>   For dread to prouder feelings doth give place,
>   Of deep abhorrence ! Scorning the disgrace
>   Of slavish knees that at thy footstool bow,
>   I also kneel—but with far other vow
>   Do hail thee and thy herd of hirelings base :—
>   I swear, while life-blood warms my throbbing veins,
>   Still to oppose and thwart, with heart and hand,
>   Thy brutalizing sway—till Afric's chains
>   Are burst, and Freedom rules the rescued land,
>   Trampling Oppression and his iron rod :—
>   Such is the vow I take—so help me, God ! '

BOSTON, January 1, 1831.

Universal Emancipation.

> Though distant be the hour, yet come it must —
>   Oh ! hasten it, in mercy, righteous Heaven !
> When Afric's sons, uprising from the dust,
>   Shall stand erect — their galling fetters riven ;
>   When from his throne Oppression shall be driven,
> An exiled monster, powerless through all time ;
>   When freedom — glorious freedom, shall be given
> To every race, complexion, caste, and clime,
> And Nature's sable hue shall cease to be a crime !
>
> Wo if it come with storm, and blood, and fire,
>   When midnight darkness veils the earth and sky !
> Wo to the innocent babe — the guilty sire —
>   Mother and daughter — friends of kindred tie !

Stranger and citizen alike shall die!
Red-handed Slaughter his revenge shall feed,
And Havoc yell his ominous death-cry,
And wild Despair in vain for mercy plead —
While Hell itself shall shrink, and sicken at the deed!

Thou who avengest blood! long-suffering Lord!
My guilty country from destruction save!
Let Justice sheath her sharp and terrible sword,
And Mercy rescue, e'en as from the grave!
Oh! for the sake of those who firmly brave
The lust of Power — the tyranny of Law —
To bring redemption to the fettered slave —
Fearless, though few — Thy presence ne'er withdraw,
But quench the kindling flames of hot, rebellious war!

And ye — sad victims of base Avarice!
Hunted like beasts, and trodden like the earth;
Bought and sold daily, at a paltry price —
The scorn of tyrants, and of fools the mirth —
Your souls debased from their immortal birth —
Bear meekly — as ye 've borne — your cruel woes;
Ease follows pain — light, darkness — plenty, dearth: —
So time shall give you freedom and repose,
And high exalt your heads above your bitter foes!

Not by the sword shall your deliverance be;
Not by the shedding of your masters' blood;
Not by rebellion — or foul treachery,
Upspringing suddenly, like swelling flood:
Revenge and rapine ne'er did bring forth good.
God's time is best! — nor will it long delay:
Even now your barren cause begins to bud,
And glorious shall the fruit be! — Watch and pray,
For, lo! the kindling dawn, that ushers in the day!

6*

Declaration of Sentiments

OF THE AMERICAN ANTI-SLAVERY CONVENTION.

The Convention assembled in the city of Philadelphia, to organize a National Anti-Slavery Society, promptly seize the opportunity to promulgate the following Declaration of Sentiments, as cherished by them in relation to the enslavement of one-sixth portion of the American people.

More than fifty-seven years have elapsed, since a band of patriots convened in this place, to devise measures for the deliverance of this country from a foreign yoke. The corner-stone upon which they founded the Temple of Freedom was broadly this—'that all men are created equal; that they are endowed by their Creator with certain inalienable rights; that among these are life, LIBERTY, and the pursuit of happiness.' At the sound of their trumpet-call, three millions of people rose up as from the sleep of death, and rushed to the strife of blood; deeming it more glorious to die instantly as freemen, than desirable to live one hour as slaves. They were few in number—poor in resources; but the honest conviction that Truth, Justice and Right were on their side, made them invincible.

We have met together for the achievement of an enterprise, without which that of our fathers is incomplete; and which, for its magnitude, solemnity, and probable results upon the destiny of the world, as far transcends theirs as moral truth does physical force.

In purity of motive, in earnestness of zeal, in decision of purpose, in intrepidity of action, in steadfastness of faith, in sincerity of spirit, we would not be inferior to them.

Their principles led them to wage war against their oppressors, and to spill human blood like water, in order to be free.

. Ours forbid the doing of evil that good may come, and lead us to reject, and to entreat the oppressed to reject, the use of all carnal weapons for deliverance from bondage ; relying solely upon those which are spiritual, and mighty through God to the pulling down of strong holds.

Their measures were physical resistance — the marshalling in arms — the hostile array — the mortal encounter. Ours shall be such only as the opposition of moral purity to moral corruption — the destruction of error by the potency of truth — the overthrow of prejudice by the power of love — and the abolition of slavery by the spirit of repentance.

Their grievances, great as they were, were trifling in comparison with the wrongs and sufferings of those for whom we plead. Our fathers were never slaves — never bought and sold like cattle — never shut out from the light of knowledge and religion — never subjected to the lash of brutal taskmasters.

But those, for whose emancipation we are striving — constituting at the present time at least one-sixth part of our countrymen — are recognized by law, and treated by their fellow-beings, as marketable commodities, as goods and chattels, as brute beasts ; are plundered daily of the fruits of their toil without redress ; really enjoy no constitutional nor legal protection from licentious and murderous outrages upon their persons ; and are ruthlessly torn asunder — the tender babe from the arms of its frantic mother — the heart-broken wife from her weeping husband — at the caprice or pleasure of irresponsible tyrants. For the crime of having a dark complexion, they suffer the pangs of hunger, the infliction of stripes, the ignominy of brutal servitude. They are kept in heathenish darkness by laws expressly enacted to make their instruction a criminal offence.

These are the prominent circumstances in the condition of more than two millions of our people, the proof of which may be found in thousands of indisputable facts, and in the laws of the slaveholding States.

Hence we maintain — that, in view of the civil and religious privileges of this nation, the guilt of its oppression is unequalled by any other on the face of the earth; and, therefore, that it is bound to repent instantly, to undo the heavy burdens, and to let the oppressed go free.

We further maintain — that no man has a right to enslave or imbrute his brother — to hold or acknowledge him, for one moment, as a piece of merchandize — to keep back his hire by fraud — or to brutalize his mind, by denying him the means of intellectual, social and moral improvement.

The right to enjoy liberty is inalienable. To invade it is to usurp the prerogative of Jehovah. Every man has a right to his own body — to the products of his own labor — to the protection of law — and to the common advantages of society. It is piracy to buy or steal a native African, and subject him to servitude. Surely, the sin is as great to enslave an American as an African.

Therefore we believe and affirm — that there is no difference, in principle, between the African slave trade and American slavery:

That every American citizen, who detains a human being in involuntary bondage as his property, is, according to Scripture, (Ex. xxi. 16,) a man-stealer:

That the slaves ought instantly to be set free, and brought under the protection of law:

That if they had lived from the time of Pharaoh down to the present period, and had been entailed through successive generations, their right to be free could never have been alienated, but their claims would have constantly risen in solemnity:

That all those laws which are now in force, admitting the right of slavery, are therefore, before God, utterly null and void; being an audacious usurpation of the Divine prerogative, a daring infringement on the law of nature, a base overthrow of the very foundations of the social compact, a complete extinction of all the relations, endearments and obligations of mankind, and a presumptuous transgression of all the holy commandments; and that therefore they ought instantly to be abrogated.

We further believe and affirm — that all persons of color, who possess the qualifications which are demanded of others, ought to be admitted forthwith to the enjoyment of the same privileges, and the exercise of the same prerogatives, as others; and that the paths of preferment, of wealth, and of intelligence, should be opened as widely to them as to persons of a white complexion.

We maintain that no compensation should be given to the planters emancipating their slaves:

Because it would be a surrender of the great fundamental principle, that man cannot hold property in man:

Because slavery is a crime, and therefore is not an article to be sold:

Because the holders of slaves are not the just proprietors of what they claim; freeing the slave is not depriving them of property, but restoring it to its rightful owner; it is not wronging the master, but righting the slave — restoring him to himself:

Because immediate and general emancipation would only destroy nominal, not real property; it would not amputate a limb or break a bone of the slaves, but by infusing motives into their breasts, would make them doubly valuable to the masters as free laborers; and

Because, if compensation is to be given at all, it should be given to the outraged and guiltless slaves, and not to those who have plundered and abused them.

We regard as delusive, cruel and dangerous, any scheme of expatriation which pretends to aid, either directly or indirectly, in the emancipation of the slaves, or to be a substitute for the immediate and total abolition of slavery.

We fully and unanimously recognise the sovereignty of each State, to legislate exclusively on the subject of the slavery which is tolerated within its limits; we concede that Congress, under the present national compact, has no right to interfere with any of the slave States, in relation to this momentous subject:

But we maintain that Congress has a right, and is solemnly bound, to suppress the domestic slave trade between the several States, and to abolish slavery in those portions of our territory which the Constitution has placed under its exclusive jurisdiction.

We also maintain that there are, at the present time, the highest obligations resting upon the people of the free States to remove slavery by moral and political action, as prescribed in the Constitution of the United States. They are now living under a pledge of their tremendous physical force, to fasten the galling fetters of tyranny upon the limbs of millions in the Southern States; they are liable to be called at any moment to suppress a general insurrection of the slaves; they authorize the slave owner to vote for three-fifths of his slaves as property, and thus enable him to perpetuate his oppression; they support a standing army at the South for its protection; and they seize the slave, who has escaped into their territories, and send him back to be tortured by an enraged master or a brutal driver. This relation to slavery is criminal, and full of danger: IT MUST BE BROKEN UP.

These are our views and principles — these our designs and measures. With entire confidence in the overruling justice of God, we plant ourselves upon the Declaration of our Independence and the truths of Divine Revelation, as upon the Everlasting Rock.

We shall organize Anti-Slavery Societies, if possible, in every city, town and village in our land.

We shall send forth agents to lift up the voice of remonstrance, of warning, of entreaty, and of rebuke.

We shall circulate, unsparingly and extensively, anti-slavery tracts and periodicals.

We shall enlist the pulpit and the press in the cause of the suffering and the dumb.

We shall aim at a purification of the churches from all participation in the guilt of slavery.

We shall encourage the labor of freemen rather than that of slaves, by giving a preference to their productions : and

We shall spare no exertions nor means to bring the whole nation to speedy repentance.

Our trust for victory is solely in God. We may be personally defeated, but our principles never! Truth, Justice, Reason, Humanity, must and will gloriously triumph. Already a host is coming up to the help of the Lord against the mighty, and the prospect before us is full of encouragement.

Submitting this Declaration to the candid examination of the people of this country, and of the friends of liberty throughout the world, we hereby affix our signatures to it; pledging ourselves that, under the guidance and by the help of Almighty God, we will do all that in us lies, consistently with this Declaration of our principles, to overthrow the most execrable system of slavery that has ever been witnessed upon earth; to deliver our land from its deadliest curse; to wipe out the foulest stain which rests upon our national escutcheon; and to secure to the colored population of the United States, all the rights and privileges which belong to them as men, and as Americans — come what may to our persons, our interests, or our reputation — whether we live to witness the triumph of Liberty, Justice and Humanity, or perish untimely as martyrs in this great, benevolent, and holy cause.

Done at Philadelphia, December 6th, A. D. 1833.

Declaration of Sentiments

ADOPTED BY THE PEACE CONVENTION, HELD IN BOSTON,
SEPTEMBER 18, 19 AND 20, 1838.

Assembled in Convention, from various sections of the American Union, for the promotion of peace on earth and good will among men, we, the undersigned, regard it as due to ourselves, to the cause which we love, to the country in which we live, and to the world, to publish a Declaration, expressive of the principles we cherish, the purposes we aim to accomplish, and the measures we shall adopt to carry forward the work of peaceful and universal reformation.

We cannot acknowledge allegiance to any human government; neither can we oppose any such government, by a resort to physical force. We recognize but one King and Lawgiver, one Judge and Ruler of mankind. We are bound by the laws of a kingdom which is not of this world; the subjects of which are forbidden to fight; in which Mercy and Truth are met together, and Righteousness and Peace have kissed each other; which has no state lines, no national partitions, no geographical boundaries; in which there is no distinction of rank, or division of caste, or inequality of sex; the officers of which are Peace, its exactors Righteousness, its walls Salvation, and its gates Praise; and which is destined to break in pieces and consume all other kingdoms.

Our country is the world, our countrymen are all mankind. We love the land of our nativity, only as we love all other lands. The interests, rights, and liberties of American citizens are no more dear to us, than are those of the whole human race. Hence, we can allow no appeal to patriotism, to revenge any national insult or injury. The Prince of Peace, under whose stainless banner we rally, came not to destroy, but to save, even the worst of enemies. He has left us an example, that we should follow his steps. 'God commendeth his love towards us, in that while we were yet sinners, Christ died for us.'

We conceive, that if a nation has no right to defend itself against foreign enemies, or to punish its invaders, no individual possesses that right in his own case. The unit cannot be of greater importance than the aggregate. If one man may take life, to obtain or defend his rights, the same license must necessarily be granted to communities, states, and nations. If he may use a dagger or a pistol, they may employ cannon, bomb-shells, land and naval forces. The means of self-preservation must be in proportion to the magnitude of interests at stake, and the number of lives exposed to destruction. But if a rapacious and blood-thirsty soldiery, thronging these shores from abroad, with intent to commit rapine and destroy life, may not be resisted by the people or magistracy, then ought no resistance to be offered to domestic troublers of the public peace, or of private security. No obligation can rest upon Americans to regard foreigners as more sacred in their persons than themselves, or to give them a monopoly of wrong-doing with impunity.

The dogma, that all the governments of the world are approvingly ordained of God, and that the powers that be in the United States, in Russia, in Turkey, are in accordance with His will, is not less absurd than impious. It makes the impartial Author of human freedom and equality, unequal and tyrannical. It cannot be affirmed, that the powers that be, in any nation, are actuated by the spirit, or guided by the example of Christ, in the treatment of enemies: therefore, they cannot be agreeable to the will of God: and, therefore, their overthrow, by a spiritual regeneration of their subjects, is inevitable.

We register our testimony, not only against all wars, whether offensive or defensive, but all preparations for war;

7

against every naval ship, every arsenal, every fortification; against the militia system and a standing army; against all military chieftains and soldiers; against all monuments commemorative of victory over a foreign foe, all trophies won in battle, all celebrations in honor of military or naval exploits; against all appropriations for the defence of a nation by force and arms on the part of any legislative body; against every edict of government, requiring of its subjects military service. Hence, we deem it unlawful to bear arms, or to hold a military office.

As every human government is upheld by physical strength, and its laws are enforced virtually at the point of the bayonet, we cannot hold any office which imposes upon its incumbent the obligation to do right, on pain of imprisonment or death. We therefore voluntarily exclude ourselves from every legislative and judicial body, and repudiate all human politics, worldly honors, and stations of authority. If *we* cannot occupy a seat in the legislature, or on the bench, neither can we elect *others* to act as our substitutes in any such capacity.

It follows, that we cannot sue any man at law, to compel him by force to restore any thing which he may have wrongfully taken from us or others; but, if he has seized our coat, we shall surrender up our cloak, rather than subject him to punishment.

We believe that the penal code of the old covenant, An eye for an eye, and a tooth for a tooth, has been abrogated by Jesus Christ; and that, under the new covenant, the forgiveness, instead of the punishment of enemies, has been enjoined upon all his disciples, in all cases whatsoever. To extort money from enemies, or set them upon a pillory, or cast them into prison, or hang them upon a gallows, is obviously not to forgive, but to take retribution. ' Vengeance is mine—I will repay, saith the Lord.'

The history of mankind is crowded with evidences, proving that physical coercion is not adapted to moral regeneration; that the sinful disposition of man can be subdued only
by love; that evil can be exterminated from the earth only
by goodness; that it is not safe to rely upon an arm of flesh,
upon man, whose breath is in his nostrils, to preserve us from
harm; that there is great security in being gentle, harmless,
long-suffering, and abundant in mercy; that it is only the
meek who shall inherit the earth, for the violent, who resort
to the sword, shall perish with the sword. Hence, as a
measure of sound policy, of safety to property, life, and
liberty, of public quietude and private enjoyment, as well as
on the ground of allegiance to Him who is King of kings,
and Lord of lords, we cordially adopt the non-resistance
principle; being confident that it provides for all possible
consequences, will ensure all things needful to us, is armed
with omnipotent power, and must ultimately triumph over
every assailing force.

We advocate no jacobinical doctrines. The spirit of jacobinism is the spirit of retaliation, violence and murder. It
neither fears God, nor regards man. We would be filled
with the spirit of Christ. If we abide by our principles, it
is impossible for us to be disorderly, or plot treason, or participate in any evil work: we shall submit to every ordinance
of man, for the Lord's sake; obey all the requirements of
government, except such as we deem contrary to the commands of the gospel; and in no wise resist the operation of
law, except by meekly submitting to the penalty of disobedience.

But, while we shall adhere to the doctrines of non-resistance and passive submission to enemies, we purpose, in a
moral and spiritual sense, to speak and act boldly in the
cause of God; to assail iniquity in high places and in low
places; to apply our principles to all existing civil, political,

legal, and ecclesiastical institutions; and to hasten the time, when the kingdoms of this world shall become the king-doms of our Lord and of his Christ, and he shall reign for ever.

It appears to us a self-evident truth, that, whatever the gospel is designed to destroy at any period of the world, being contrary to it, ought now to be abandoned. If, then, the time is predicted, when swords shall be beaten into plough-shares, and spears into pruning-hooks, and men shall not learn the art of war any more, it follows that all who manufacture, sell, or wield those deadly weapons, do thus array themselves against the peaceful dominion of the Son of God on earth.

Having thus briefly, but frankly, stated our principles and purposes, we proceed to specify the measures we propose to adopt, in carrying our object into effect.

We expect to prevail through the foolishness of preach-ing—striving to commend ourselves unto every man's con-science, in the sight of God. From the press, we shall promulgate our sentiments as widely as practicable. We shall endeavor to secure the co-operation of all persons, of whatever name or sect. The triumphant progress of the cause of Temperance and of Abolition in our land, through the instrumentality of benevolent and voluntary associations, encourages us to combine our own means and efforts for the promotion of a still greater cause. Hence we shall employ lecturers, circulate tracts and publications, form societies, and petition our state and national governments in relation to the subject of Universal Peace. It will be our leading ob-ject to devise ways and means for effecting a radical change in the views, feelings and practices of society respecting the sinfulness of war, and the treatment of enemies.

In entering upon the great work before us, we are not unmindful that, in its prosecution, we may be called to test our sincerity, even as in a fiery ordeal. It may subject us to insult, outrage, suffering, yea, even death itself. We anticipate no small amount of misconception, misrepresentation, calumny. Tumults may arise against us. The ungodly and violent, the proud and pharisaical, the ambitious and tyrannical, principalities and powers, and spiritual wickedness in high places, may combine to crush us. So they treated the Messiah, whose example we are humbly striving to imitate. If we suffer with him, we know that we shall reign with him. We shall not be afraid of their terror, neither be troubled. Our confidence is in the Lord Almighty, not in man. Having withdrawn from human protection, what can sustain us but that faith which overcomes the world? We shall not think it strange concerning the fiery trial which is to try us, as though some strange thing had happened unto us; but rejoice, inasmuch as we are partakers of Christ's sufferings. Wherefore, we commit the keeping of our souls to God, in well-doing, as unto a faithful Creator. 'For every one that forsakes houses, or brethren, or sisters, or father, or mother, or wife, or children, or lands, for Christ's sake, shall receive an hundred fold, and shall inherit everlasting life.'

Firmly relying upon the certain and universal triumph of the sentiments contained in this Declaration, however formidable may be the opposition arrayed against them, in solemn testimony of our faith in their divine origin, we hereby affix our signatures to it; commending it to the reason and conscience of mankind, giving ourselves no anxiety as to what may befall us, and resolving, in the strength of the Lord God, calmly and meekly to abide the issue.

7*

Patriotism and Christianity --- Kossuth and Jesus.

Since the disastrous termination of the struggle for liberty and independence on the part of the Italian people, all eyes are fastened upon Hungary, bravely coping with the colossal powers of Austria and Russia, and as yet undismayed and unconquered. Her final triumph, in the present sanguinary conflict, is possible, but not at all probable. In the course of another month, authentic intelligence will doubtless be received, that, like Rome, she no longer contends with her oppressors, but submits to wear the yoke and drag the chain of a degrading servitude.

A great national emergency usually lifts from obscurity to eminence, men of extraordinary genius, talent, courage, self-sacrifice, patriotism, piety. Hungary has at the head of her forces three notable chieftains — Kossuth, Bem, Georgy. Of these, Kossuth appears to be the Washington. His presence electrifies, his appeals inspire his countrymen, with almost magical effect. What he proposes, they ratify — what he desires, they execute — where he leads or points the way, they ' rush to glory or the grave ' — with a promptitude, an obedience, a valor, unsurpassed in the history of nations.

As specimens of the power of his genius and the eloquence of his rhetoric, read the proclamations from his pen to his countrymen. They are of a peculiar type, and singularly imbued with a religious sentiment, without the appearance of eccentricity or cant. ' Our trust is in the God of righteousness ' — ' We can hope in nothing but a just God and our own strength ' — ' God has chosen us to redeem the people from physical bondage by our victory, as Christ has redeemed humanity from spiritual bondage ' — ' God is just ; his power is almighty ; he hallows the battle-field for the weak, and the strength of the mighty and the wicked is broken '—' God of our fathers, and God of the nations! God of the warriors of Arpad! O Father! Father of our fathers! Hallow their dust with Thy grace, that the ashes of my fallen heroic brethren may rest in peace! Leave us not, great God of battles!' Such are the constant declarations and invocations of Kossuth, designed alike to animate the hearts of the Hungarians, and to secure the benediction of Heaven. It is impossible to describe their effect on the popular mind.

Kossuth is, unquestionably, a sublime specimen of what the world calls ' patriotism.' He is a model ' patriot.' To his country, he gives himself unreservedly; to effect its freedom from the Austrian yoke, he has suffered every thing but death, and stands ready to offer up his life at any moment; in its independence will be realized his highest aspirations. The press is every where extolling his virtues, and ranking him among the foremost heroes of the world. Whether he succeed or fail, he has associated his name with that of Tell, of Wallace, of Hamden, of Washington; and his memory will be cherished by succeeding generations.

What then? Is Kossuth worthy of imitation? Is his example such as should be held up for universal acceptance? Is his spirit truly noble, expansive, sublime? Is his piety of a genuine quality, neither tinctured with fanaticism, nor sullied by passion? He calls upon his countrymen to seize the axe, the scythe, the sword, the firebrand, every weapon of death and destruction within their reach, and wield them with exterminating effect against their Austrian and Russian invaders. What then? Is war justifiable? Is there, can there be, such a thing as a justifiable war? Is it true that we may do evil, that good may come—that the end sanctifies the means—that Hungary is reduced to such an extremity, that she is not only innocent, but deserving of praise, in destroying her enemies? What is war? Is it not the opposite of peace, as slavery is of liberty, as sin is of holiness, as Belial is of Christ? And is slavery some-times to be enforced—is sin in cases of emergency to be committed—is Belial occasionally to be preferred to Christ, as circumstances may require? These are grave questions, and the redemption of the world is dependant on the answers that may be given to them.

What is this Hungarian war in its features and effects? Wherein does it differ from any other war, animated by the spirit of hatred and revenge, and prosecuted by a resort to murderous weapons? Is not human blood flowing like water—are not the wounded, dying and dead, multiplying like the withered leaves of autumn at the touch of frost— are not homes made desolate, and firesides voiceless, and fields barren? On the score of forbearance, kindness, mag-nanimity, wherein do the Hungarians exceed their enemies? They neither give nor ask for quarter. Their weapons of defence are the weapons with which they are assailed—the weapons of tyranny in all ages!

'Ah! you overlook the wide difference that exists between the conflicting parties! The object of Hungary is laudable and noble—her freedom and independence! That of Aus-tria is tyrannous and diabolical—the subjection of Hungary to her iron will!'

No, I do not forget, but admit the fact. It is because I remember it, that I groan in spirit to see a good object defended by the same weapons and the same measures as those which are used to uphold a bad object. The better the object, the less need, the less justification there is to behave as they do, who have one that is altogether execra-ble. Eye for eye, tooth for tooth, life for life, is not the way to redeem or bless our race. Sword against sword, cannon against cannon, army against army, is it thus that love and

good-will are diffused through the world, or that right con-
quers wrong ? Why not, then, seek by falsehood to counteract falsehood — by cruelty to terminate cruelty — by sin
to abolish sin ? Can men gather grapes from thorns, or figs
from thistles ?

Hungary has already sustained a frightful loss of life, and
the dead bodies of her people cover her soil. She is enduring all the horrors of a merciless war, and how shall these
be depicted ? And what if she fail in this unequal strife ?
Kossuth tells his countrymen, that, in case of defeat, they
must fall a prey to famine — for their ruthless invaders, as
they stalk murderously onward, leave slaughter, flame, misery and famine in their track, and wherever they appear,
ploughing and sowing are useless. He warns them that, if
they allow themselves to be conquered, they must be prepared to experience all imaginable tribulation. Already,
' the enemy has ravaged everything with fire and sword.
How many cities and villages has not his flaming torch laid
in ashes ! '

This is the Hungarian view of this dreadful conflict. But
the Austrian is scarcely less appalling. The sufferings of
the allied invaders have been indescribably severe, and their
losses at least as great as those whom they are endeavoring
to subjugate. It is our duty to remember the fate of all who
are involved in this war, whether they are on the right or on
the wrong side ; for they are all brothers by creation, members of the same great human family, and under the most
sacred obligations to love and do good to each other. Our
computation must include all the suffering and evil that are
the legitimate consequences of the war, on both sides, or we
shall fail to see it as it is.

The piety of Kossuth is of that kind which is calculated
to impress the superstitious, to satisfy the patriotic, to stimulate the revengful, to mislead the unreflecting. In the prim-

itive meaning of the language, it has ' the form of godliness, but without the power thereof.' It assumes that God is on the side of the oppressed : that is true. It assumes that he is pleased to see them engaged in deadly strife with their oppressors, and that he is the ' God of battles,' strengthening the arm of the physically weak to contend successfully in the cause of freedom against the tyrannically strong : and here is the delusion. It cannot be true, as a moral proposition, that if it is wrong to inflict injuries, it is right to retaliate when they are inflicted. It cannot be true, that He who ' causes his sun to shine on the evil and on the good, and his rain to fall on the just and on the unjust,' sanctions a bloody revenge.

What shall we say of the spirit of the Hungarian patriot? He invokes his countrymen to ' arm with axe or scythe, with clubs, with stones '—' rise in the rear, and cut down the Cossacks '—' give the enemy no rest at night, fall upon him suddenly, and hide every kind of provisions, that he may perish with hunger '—' burn the houses about their heads, so that the savage hordes may become a prey to the flames '— &c. &c.

Merciful God ! is this in accordance with thy will ? And shall he, who thus counsels the most atrocious acts, dare to offer up a prayer to Thee for succor and benediction ? Alas ! he knows not what spirit he is of.

Yet here we have as lofty and magnanimous a specimen of worldly ' patriotism ' as the age produces !

Let us be just. Let us detract nothing from the real merits of Kossuth. He abhors tyranny ; he has passed six years of his life (almost at the sacrifice of it) in a loathsome Austrian dungeon, for his love of liberty ; he is no demagogue, no selfish adventurer, but earnest in purpose, and self-sacrificing in action ; he goes for Hungarian liberty as Washington went for American independence.

Still, he is implacable, unmerciful, towards the enemies of his country, even to consuming them alive with fire !

The name of Kossuth ' rings from shore to shore.' Who among his admirers and eulogists thinks of taking any exception to his course ?

Yet what is the scope of his vision ? He is a Hungarian, as Washington was an American. His country is bounded by a few degrees of latitude and longitude, and covers a surface of some thousands of square miles. He is strictly local, territorial, national. The independence of Hungary, alone, absorbs his thoughts and inspires his efforts; and to obtain it, he feels justified in disregarding the claims of humanity, and suspending all the obligations of morality.

Contrast now with all this, the precepts, the doctrines, the example, the spirit, the life, the death, the purposes of Jesus ! — Jesus, the wronged, the calumniated, the buffeted, the hunted, the crucified ! To the injured, the oppressed, the down-trodden, he made no inflammatory appeals, but taught forbearance, long-suffering, forgiveness ; yet he also taught them to wear no yoke, and to call no man master, though a cruel martyrdom should be their lot. He counselled neither retaliation nor self-defence. He did not say, ' Arm with axes, scythes and clubs — burn the houses of your enemies about their heads ' — but soothingly declared, ' Blessed are the meek ; for they shall inherit the earth ' — ' Blessed are the merciful ; for they shall obtain mercy ' — ' Blessed are the peace-makers ; for they shall be called the children of God.' And with true nobility of soul, he gave these magnanimous injunctions : — ' I say unto you, that ye resist not evil ; but whosoever shall smite thee on the right cheek, turn to him the other also ' — ' I say unto you, love your enemies, bless them that curse you, do good to them that hate you, and pray for them that despitefully use you and persecute you. For if ye love them that love you, what reward have ye? do not even the publicans so?' 'Therefore, all things whatsoever ye would that men should do to you, do ye even so to them.' He also declared, 'All they that take the sword shall perish with the sword.' His life was in strict harmony with his precepts. He met the enmity of his persecutors with a lamb-like spirit; yet, in reproving them for their crimes, he was courageous as a lion. ' Wo unto you, scribes and Pharisees, hypocrites! ye serpents, ye generation of vipers, how can ye escape the damnation of hell?' Nothing could intimidate, subdue or enslave him. Nailed as a felon to the cross, he supplicated for the forgiveness of his enemies with his expiring breath.

Jesus was neither local nor national in his feelings or designs. The land of his birth was in bondage to the Roman power, but he exhibited no ' patriotic ' indignation, and made no appeal to Jewish pride or revenge. Abhorring oppression in every shape, his method of meeting it was to rebuke it, and to return good for evil. He would destroy tyranny, but without injury to the tyrant; by a moral regeneration, not by a physical struggle. His soul was expansive as the universe, his love for the human race impartial, his country the world.

Jesus was ever ready to be slain for his principles, but he caused no tears of misery to flow, no blood of enemies to be shed, no houses to be fired, no lands to be devastated. See the miseries and calamities brought alike upon Hungarians and Austrians by the terrible appeals of Kossuth! And how many generations must pass away, before the fierce enmities thus excited will become extinct!

Oh, Kossuth! not of thy abhorrence of Austrian oppression do I complain, but join with thee in execrating it. But the lessons of vengeance which thou art teaching thy countrymen are such as degrade and brutalize humanity. Tell the Hungarians, that a bloody warfare to maintain their nationality is incompatible with moral greatness and Christian love, and for an object which is low and selfish. Inflame them not to madness by martial appeals, but exhort them to beat their swords into ploughshares, and their spears into pruning-hooks; so, being weaponless, yet possessing a spirit determined to be free, they shall present to Austria an unconquerable front, and achieve a bloodless triumph.

O, Jesus! noblest of patriots! greatest of heroes! most glorious of all martyrs! Thine is the spirit of universal liberty and love—of uncompromising hostility to every form of injustice and wrong. But not with weapons of death dost thou assault thy enemies, that they may be vanquished or destroyed; for thou dost not wrestle against flesh and blood, but 'against principalities, against powers, against the rulers of the darkness of this world, against spiritual wickedness in high places'; therefore hast thou put on the whole armor of God, having thy loins girt about with truth, and having on the breast-plate of righteousness, and thy feet shod with the preparation of the gospel of peace, and going forth to battle with the shield of faith, the helmet of salvation, the sword of the Spirit! Worthy of all imitation art thou, in overcoming the evil that is in the world; for by the shedding of thine own blood, but not the blood even of thy bitterest foes, shalt thou at last obtain a universal victory.

'The Christian's victory alone
Hostility for ever ends;
Erects an undisputed throne,
    And turns his foes to friends.

Ye great! ye mighty of the earth!
    Ye conquerors! learn this secret true—
A secret of celestial birth—
    By suffering to subdue!

8

> Nor is the victory lost, when those
> Whom Love assails disdain to yield;
> A host of spiritual foes
> Lie vanquished on the field.
>
> All outward storms will rage in vain,
> If peace and love within abide;
> The soul each onset will sustain,
> A rock amidst the tide.'

The Practical Working of Non-Resistance.

An esteemed correspondent expresses a doubt as to the practical working of non-resistance, as applied to the case of Austrian despotism, for example. But is that despotism the result of an adoption, or of a rejection of the principle of non-resistance? Clearly the latter. Is the principle, then, to be discarded, in order to put down that which it radically condemns and utterly repudiates? Is this philosophical? Can Beelzebub cast out Beelzebub? Is evil to be overcome with evil? True, the cause of justice and liberty must eventually triumph, whether by or without a resort to murderous weapons; but it will not be because of those weapons, but because of its inherent goodness, and the transitory nature of tyranny. There will be no real freedom or security among mankind, until they beat their swords into ploughshares, and their spears into pruning-hooks, and learn war no more. We grant that every successful struggle for freedom on the part of the oppressed, even with the aid of cannon and bomb-shells, is to be hailed with rejoicing; but simply in reference to its object,

and not to the mode of its accomplishment. That a people
sufficiently enlightened to be conscious of their degradation,
yet far from being morally and spiritually regenerated,
should take up arms against their merciless oppressors, is
not surprising — nay, it is inevitable, in their condition ; but
this is no real justification of revenge or murder on their
part. If they were truly pure and good, theirs would be
the course of Jesus and his apostles, of prophets and ' the
noble army of martyrs and confessors,' in maintaining the
right and in confronting the wrong — a course attended by
no crime, stained by no blood excepting their own freely
shed for their enemies, divinely magnanimous, and ' mighty
through God to the pulling down of strong holds ' — a
course which wholly eclipses, in power and glory, any ever
pursued by blood-spilling revolutionists. Our correspondent
burns with indignation in view of Austrian tyranny ; so do
we. He rejoices to see its victims rising against it ; so do
we. He is in doubt whether the principle of non-resistance, if adopted by them, would procure for them the deliverance they seek ; we are not. A people able to adopt
that principle in theory and practice, cannot possibly be enslaved, any more than the angels of God ; and no form of
despotism can make them servile. They do not fear the
face of the tyrant, and it is their mission to ' beard the lion
in his den.' They may be burnt to ashes, but they can
never be conquered. Theirs is the ' unresistible might of
weakness,' (to borrow the expressive language of Milton,)
and no weapon used against them shall prosper. But no
people, constituting a nation, has reached this sublime state
of moral exaltation ; all are more or less brutal, eager for
revenge in case of suffering, and incapable of understanding
how they who take the sword shall perish with the sword.
This is to be lamented ; but it is history. Surely, it is no
reason why those who are ' under grace ' should abandon

their position, and discard Jesus, the non-resistant, for Moses or Joshua, the warrior.

Our correspondent is greatly in error in speaking of non-resistance as a state of ' passivity.'   On the contrary, it is a state of activity, ever fighting the good fight of faith, ever foremost to assail unjust power, ever struggling for ' liberty, equality, fraternity,' in no national sense, but in a world-wide spirit.   It is passive only in this sense, — that it will not return evil for evil, nor give blow for blow, nor resort to murderous weapons for protection or defence.   In its purity, it is the blending of the gentleness and innocency of the Lamb of God, with the courage and strength of the Lion of the tribe of Judah.

True Courage.

I BOAST no courage on the battle-field,
   Where hostile troops immix in horrid fray ;
For Love or Fame I can no weapon wield,
   With burning lust an enemy to slay : —
But test my spirit at the blazing stake,
   For advocacy of the RIGHTS OF MAN,
And TRUTH — or on the wheel my body break ;
   Let Persecution place me 'neath its ban ;
Insult, defame, proscribe my humble name ;
   Yea, put the dagger to my naked breast ;
If I recoil in terror from the flame,
   Or recreant prove when peril rears its crest,
To save a limb, or shun the public scorn —
Then write me down for aye, Weakest of woman born !

War Essentially Wrong.

THAT the history of the human race is one of progression;
that conflicting ideas of right and wrong, on many points,
have prevailed in different ages of the world; that the light
and knowledge of one age have been much inferior to those
of a succeeding age; all this is beyond controversy. 'To
whom much is given, of the same much shall be required'—
and less where less is given. But this does not prove that
God, in any age, commanded acts to be done which are in
themselves wrong, as the best method he could adopt to
educate and discipline any portion of our race for a higher
destiny. His moral attributes are absolute and immutable;
his relations to mankind, and theirs to him and to each other,
have ever been essentially the same. What is derogatory
to his character now — what is morally injurious to them —
must have always been so, whether so regarded or not.

There are certain moral propositions which need no argument or proof. God cannot lie; he cannot, therefore,
authorise lying. God cannot steal; he cannot, therefore,
enjoin theft as a duty in any case. God cannot commit
murder; he cannot, therefore, require any of his children
to be murderers. God cannot be cruel or vindictive; he
cannot, therefore, approve or enjoin acts of cruelty or
revenge. God cannot enslave; he cannot, therefore, require
or sanction slavery, under any circumstances.

Now, on what are right and wrong dependant? On
recorded declarations? on ancient parchments or modern
manuscripts? on sacred books? No. Though every parchment, manuscript and book in the world were given to the
consuming fire, the loss would not in the least affect the
right or wrong of moral actions. Truth and duty, the principles of justice and equity, the obligations of mercy and
brotherly kindness, are older than all books, and more endur-

8*

ing than tables of stone. If we find any thing contrary to
these, in any book or on any tablet, is it not to be repudiated,
even though it may claim to be divinely commanded?

The question at issue is—WAR, its nature, tendencies,
results: WAR, whether in ancient or modern times, whether
under the Jewish or Christian dispensation: is it right?
was it ever justifiable? How shall this question be settled?
Not arbitrarily by an appeal to any volume, however sacredly regarded; for every volume is of human composition,
.and therefore liable to error. Besides, if war be a *malum
in se,* it needs no other evidence than its own intrinsic character to procure for it a verdict of condemnation. In short,
we must judge of the tree by its fruits; and this we can
easily do.

War is as capable of moral analysis as slavery, intemperance, licentiousness, or idolatry. It is not an abstraction,
which admits of doubt or uncertainty, but as tangible as
bombs, cannon, mangled corpses, smouldering ruins, desolated towns and villages, rivers of blood. It is substantially
the same in all ages, and cannot change its moral features.
To trace it in all its ramifications is not a difficult matter.
In fact, nothing is more terribly distinct than its career; it
leaves its impress on every thing it touches, whether physical, mental, or moral. Why, then, not look it in the face?
Why look any where else? Is it not in this demonstrative way
that abolitionists triumphantly meet their opponents on the
subject of slavery; that the friends of total abstinence grapple with the advocates of moderate drinking; that the opponents of the gallows drive from the field the partisans of
capital punishment?

War is the antagonist of Peace, as Slavery is of Liberty,
as Sin is of Holiness. The mission of Jesus was that of
Peace. All Christians profess to believe, that when his
spirit universally prevails, mankind will sit under their own

vines and fig trees, with none to molest or make them afraid. What is this but to concede that war is opposed to his spirit? Has he come to condemn or extirpate, as morally wrong, that which his Heavenly Father expressly commanded to be done as a test of religious obedience, and to promote true piety among the idolatrous nations of old?

To this simple issue, the vindicators of the Jewish wars must be kept. They but travel in a circle when they quote from this or that portion of the Bible, passages to prove that those wars were just and holy.

"The Powers that be are ordained of God."

THERE is something not only extremely unfair, but positively slanderous, in the naked charge, so frequently preferred against non-resistants, that they 'deny the necessity of human governments.' As thus stated, without explanation or qualification, a person ignorant of their principles would be justified in supposing that they advocated the profligate doctrines of Jack Cade, were for removing all moral and legal restraints upon the people, and were a band of Jacobins and anarchists, who took delight in shedding innocent blood, crying havoc, and letting slip the dogs of war. Every such representation is something more flagrant than a broad caricature; it is both false and wicked. Non-resistants do not deny that some form of government, however arbitrary and despotic, is better than a state of anarchy; that a limited monarchy is infinitely to be preferred to

an absolute despotism ; and that a republican is far better than
a monarchical form of government.   Just as they concede
that the cholera is more dreadful than a slow fever, and
a slow fever more to be deprecated than the ague.
They also readily admit, that the abrogation of existing
laws and governmental regulations for the punishment of
evil-doers would be most calamitous, without a moral and
spiritual regeneration of the people.   But they affirm that,
under the gospel dispensation, man is no longer empowered
to take the life of man, or to demand an eye for an eye, or
a tooth for a tooth.   They maintain that, whether many or
few are willing or able to pardon their enemies, Christ
requires it of all who would be his disciples ; that the government is upon his shoulders ; that there is no foundation
in reason or scripture for incarcerating in prison, or suspending upon gibbets, domestic foes, and allowing foreign
invaders to lay waste the land and commit all manner of
excesses with impunity ; that if it is right to slay one man
in self-defence, or to save community from destruction, it is
equally right to slay two, one hundred, any number of men,
for the same reason — and, therefore, defensive war is justifiable.   They would not only disarm mankind of their
deadly weapons, but remove from their hearts all incentives
to do evil, all desire for revenge.   In short, they can use no
other weapons than those which are spiritual, in their conflict with the evil that is in the world, and believe that they
may safely treat their enemies as Jesus did his.   The Society of Friends, in approving of governments which are
upheld by the sword, and the laws of which are written in
blood, is false to its own principles.   It must either recede
from its present position, or march on to the ground of
entire non-resistance.   Its inconsistency is too glaring to
escape the observation even of those who make no pretensions to a pacific character.   An acute writer in the ' New

York Observer,' objecting to the doctrine of Friends, that war, under all circumstances, is inconsistent with the precepts of the gospel and the spirit of the Christian dispensation, says:—

'Here is the fundamental error of the English Peace Society, and also of the American, which expressly adopts the same principle as an article of its Constitution. Both Societies deny to a nation the right of *self-defence;* for they regard all war, defensive as well as offensive, as repugnant to the Christian dispensation. They would require rulers to surrender their subjects, without resistance, to every company or horde of evil-doers, coming from abroad in the shape of an army; and thus they would annihilate all government, which is nothing without the employment of physical force for the punishment of evil-doers.

'In vain do some of the peace men, whose actual principles are those of non-resistance, endeavor to escape the reproach of the non-resisting doctrines, by distinguishing between the employment of force by the magistrates against citizens, and its employment against an enemy; for it is a distinction without a difference. In all reason, the magistrate, who bears the sword for the protection of the people and the preservation of order, is bound to use it as readily against a band of pirates coming in a ship, or an invading army, as against a solitary robber or murderer.'

Surely, nothing can be more dangerous than the doctrine, that the moral obligations of men change with the latitude and longitude of a place. Surely, it is a gross paradox uttered by the Society of Friends, that if there be domestic troublers of the public peace, Christianity requires that they should be confined in prison, and deprived in some instances of their lives; but if a band of lawless invaders should throng these shores from abroad, for the purpose of ravaging the country and reducing the people to slavery, then Christianity requires that there should be no physical force arrayed against them, and the people are bound to suffer unresistingly. Such a doctrine is not less absurd than it is

unscriptural, and to state it is to refute it. If Christ has not
enjoined non-resistance to and forgiveness of all enemies,
he has to none. Why should the American people love
foreigners better than themselves? Why should they allow
Turks or Russians to inflict all possible injuries upon them
with impunity, and yet not permit any of their number to
commit the smallest offence, without subjecting them to
pains and penalties? If self-defence be not lawful in a
national, it is not in an individual capacity; for the right of
any one man cannot be more comprehensive than that of
the whole people.

The only difference, therefore, between the Society of
Friends and the Non-Resistance Society, respecting the
treatment of enemies, is, that the former goes for the pardon of those only who come from abroad, and the latter for
the pardon of all, for Christ's sake, whether they are foreign or domestic.

As to the governments of this world, all history shows that
they cannot be maintained, except by naval and military
power; that all their mandates being a dead letter without
such power to enforce them in the last extremity, are virtually written in human blood; hence, that the followers of
Jesus should instinctively shun their stations of trust, honor
and authority — at the same time, 'submitting to every
ordinance of man, for the Lord's sake,' and offering no physical resistance to any of their commands, however unjust or
tyrannical. The language of Jesus is, ' My kingdom is not
of this world, else would my servants fight.' Calling his
disciples to him, he said to them, ' Ye know that they which
are accounted to rule over the Gentiles, exercise lordship
over them; and their great ones exercise authority upon
them. But so it shall not be among you; but whosoever
will be great among you, shall be your minister; and whosoever of you will be the chiefest, shall be servant of all.

For even the Son of man came not to be ministered unto, but to minister, and to give his life a ransom for many.'

Human governments are to be viewed as judicial punishments. If a people turn the grace of God into lasciviousness, or make their liberty an occasion for anarchy — or if they refuse to belong to the 'one fold and one Shepherd' — they shall be scourged by governments of their own choosing, and burdened with taxation, and subjected to physical control, and torn by factions, and made to eat the fruit of their evil doings, until they are prepared to receive the liberty and the rest which remain, on earth as well as in heaven, for the people of God. This is in strict accordance with the arrangements of Divine Providence.

So long as men contemn the perfect government of the Most High, and will not fill up the measure of Christ's sufferings in their own persons, just so long will they desire to usurp authority over each other; just so long will they pertinaciously cling to human governments, fashioned in the likeness and administered in the spirit of their own disobedience. Now, if the prayer of our Lord be not a mockery; if the kingdom of God is to come universally, and his will to be done on earth as it is in heaven; and if, in that kingdom, no carnal weapon can be wielded, no life taken, then why are not all Christians obligated to come out now, and be separate from 'the kingdoms of this world,' which are all based upon the principle of violence, and which require their officers and servants to govern and be governed by that principle?

In almost every attempt made to justify the punishment of enemies, or uphold human government based upon brute force, it is observable that the 13th chapter of Romans is regarded as a frowning Gibraltar, inaccessible by sea and land, filled with troops and all warlike instruments, and able to vanquish every assailing force. This is an evidence of weakness, instead of strength. It shows that the whole scope of the gospel is found to be at variance with the dogma respecting governments which men entertain; else, would they not freely quote that gospel in support of their views? He who pertinaciously clings to a particular passage of scripture to uphold a favorite theory, and is always dwelling upon it, and refuses to compare scripture with scripture, so that that which is ' hard to be understood,' or is of doubtful interpretation, may be clearly apprehended, does virtually acknowledge that the mass of evidence is against him. Hence it is that so many divisions exist in the nominal church, and so many foolish heresies obtain in the world. In this manner do the advocates of slavery run to the passage, ' And they shall be your bondmen and bond-maids for ever,' to justify that atrocious system. So, also, do the lovers of wine invariably adduce the advice of Paul to Timothy, ' to take a little wine for the stomach's sake,' as authority to prove the unsoundness of the doctrine of total abstinence. In like manner have the champions of despotic governments, in various ages, urged the 13th chapter of Romans, to prove the divine authority of ' the powers that be,' and the duty of the people to obey them in all cases. So, too, is the same portion of scripture relied upon by those who cannot adopt the principles of non-resistance, to sanction the infliction of pains and penalties upon enemies.

The object of the apostle was two-fold in his allusion to ' the powers that be.' The first was, simply, to recognise their existence, as a matter of fact; and the second was, to inculcate upon Christians their obligation to lead quiet and peaceable lives,—not to be seditious, ' patriotic,' or revengeful, however cruel the despot or tyrannical the control. He recognised them as ' ministers of God for good,' in a providential sense; just as the Lord makes the wrath of man to praise him, and the remainder he restrains. But, ' let the dead bury their dead.' If the wicked will not cease from their wickedness, for self-preservation they will establish governments to rule over them, with more or less severity, according to their deserts. But, to every disciple, the language of Christ is, 'What is that to thee? Follow thou me!' Let the potsherds of the earth strive together, if they will; out of their violence good shall be educed; but be thou wise as a serpent, and harmless as a dove. The kingdom to which thou belongest is one in which no carnal weapons are allowed to be wielded, no detriment to the mind, body or estate of thine enemy is lawful. 'Be thou faithful unto death, and I will give thee a crown of life.'

It is objected, that, in the present state of the world, it would not be safe to let transgressors go without punishment. They must be punished, in order to arrest the direful progress of human guilt and disorder. But it is in the present state of the world, that Christ has enjoined the forgiveness of enemies. In a different state, there can be no opportunity for forgiveness; because all crime will have ceased, and there will be none to molest or to make afraid. The principles and obligations of Christianity belong not to a future age, but are of present and immutable application.

The existing governments of the world are the consequence of disobedience to the commands of God. But Christ came to bring men back to obedience, by a new and living way. When the cause is taken away, must not the effect cease? And in suffering and dying, that the cause might be destroyed, has He not aimed to destroy the effect? 'Governments cannot be allowed, if that which is necessary to the existence of government is prohibited.' Prisons, swords, muskets and soldiers are necessary to uphold governments which punish evil-doers by fines, imprisonment, and death. But these are prohibited by Christ; therefore, governments of force are prohibited to his followers.

9

Holy Time.

O THOU, by whom Eternal Life is given,
   Through Jesus Christ, thy well-belovèd Son ;
As is thy will obeyed by all in heaven,
   So let it now by all on earth be done !
Not by th' observance of one day in seven
   As holy time, but of ALL DAYS AS ONE ;
The soul set free — all legal fetters riven —
   Vanished the law — the reign of grace begun !
Dear is the Christian Sabbath to my heart,
   Bound by no forms — from times and seasons free ;
The whole of life absorbing — not a part ;
   Perpetual rest and perfect liberty :—
Who keeps not this steers by a Jewish chart,
   And sails in peril on a storm-tossed sea !

Penal Observance of the Sabbath.

The right of every man to worship God according to the
dictates of his own conscience is inherent, inalienable, self-
evident.   Yet it is notorious, that in all the States, excepting
Louisiana, there are laws enforcing the religious observance
of the FIRST DAY OF THE WEEK AS THE SABBATH, and
punishing as criminals such as attempt to pursue their usual
avocations on that day — avocations which even Sabbatarians recognise as innocent and laudable on all other days.
It is true, some exceptions are made to the rigorous operation of these laws, in favor of the Seventh Day Baptists,
Jews, and others, who keep the seventh day of the week as
the Sabbath ; but this freedom is granted in condescension
to the scruples of a particular sect, as a privilege, and not

recognised as a natural right. For those, (and the number is large and steadily increasing,) who believe that the Sabbath was 'exclusively a Jewish institution,— a ' shadow of good things to come,' which vanished eighteen hundred years ago before the light of the Christian Dispensation, and, therefore, that it constitutes no part of Christianity,— *there is no exemption from the penalty of the law;* but, should they venture to labor even for bread on that day, or be guilty of what is called ' Sabbath desecration,' they are liable either to fine or imprisonment ! Cases of this kind have occurred in Massachusetts, Vermont, Pennsylvania, and Ohio, within a comparatively short period, where conscientious and upright persons have been thrust into prison, for an act no more intrinsically heinous than that of gathering in a crop of hay, or selling moral or philanthropic publications. There is, therefore, no liberty of conscience allowed to the people of this country, *under the laws thereof,* in regard to the observance of a Sabbath day.

Now, I enter my solemn protest against every enactment of this kind, as at war with the genius of republicanism, and the spirit of Christianity. I believe and affirm —

That the Sabbath, according to the Jewish Scriptures, was given to ' *the children of Israel,*'— AND TO NO OTHER PEOPLE,—as ' *a sign* ' between them and God, and terminated, with all the other Mosaic rituals belonging to the ' *ministration of death,* WRITTEN AND ENGRAVEN IN STONES,' on the introduction of ' THE MINISTRATION OF THE SPIRIT,' and the substitution of ' A BETTER COVENANT, which was established upon better promises ' ; —

That Christianity knows nothing of a holy day, but only of a holy life, the possession of a spirit of love which works no ill, and is ' THE FULFILLING OF THE LAW ' ; —

That the worship of God does not pertain to any particular day—is not a special, isolated performance— and cannot ' come by observation '—but is purely spir-

itual in its nature, and comprehended in a cheerful obedience to the will of the Father, as far as it is made
known ;—

That the distinction made between sacred and secular
acts, by the advocates of Sabbath keeping,—the sacred being
the strict performance of religious observances, and the secular such as undoing heavy burdens, letting the oppressed go
free, reclaiming the drunkard, laboring in the field or in the
work-shop, public travelling, transporting the United States
mail,—is a distinction not based upon reason or Christianity,
but calculated to lower the tone of individual and public
morality, and to depress the immutable standard of moral
obligation ;—

That the Sabbath, as now recognised and enforced, is one
of the main pillars of Priestcraft and Superstition, and the
stronghold of a merely ceremonial religion ;—

That, in the hands of a Sabbatizing clergy, it is a mighty
obstacle in the way of all the reforms of the age, such as
Anti-Slavery, Peace, Temperance, Purity, Human Brotherhood, &c. &c., and rendered adamantine in its aspect towards
bleeding Humanity, whose cause must not be pleaded, but
whose cries must be stifled, on its 'sacred' recurrence ;—

That they who are for subjecting to fine or imprisonment,
such as do not receive their interpretation of the Scriptures,
in regard to the observance of the first day of the week as
the Sabbath, are actuated by a mistaken or malevolent
spirit, which is utterly at variance with the spirit of Christ—
which, in various ages, has resorted to the dungeon, the
rack, the gallows and the stake, for the accomplishment of
its purposes, and which ought to be boldly confronted and
rebuked ;—

That the penal enactments of the State Legislature, com-
pelling the observance of the first day of the week as the
Sabbath, are despotic, unconstitutional, and ought to be
immediately abrogated ; and that the interference of the

State, in matters of religious faith and ceremonies, is a usurpation which cannot be justified ; —

That, as conflicting views prevail in the community, which are cherished with equal sincerity, respecting the holiness of days, and as it is the right of every' class of citizens to be protected in the enjoyment of their religious sentiments on this and every other subject pertaining to the worship of God, all classes should be united in demanding a repeal of the enactments alluded to, on the ground of impartial justice and Christian charity ; —

That if the Legislature may rightfully determine the *day* on which the people shall abstain from labor for religious purposes, it may also determine the *place* in which they shall assemble, the *rites* and *ordinances* which they shall observe, the *doctrines* which they shall hear, the *teachers* which they shall have over them, and the peculiar *faith* which they shall embrace ; and thus entirely subvert civil and religious freedom, and enable Bigotry and Superstition, as of old, to

> ' Go to their bloody rites again — bring back
> The hall of horrors, and th' assessor's pen,
> Recording answers shriek'd upon the rack —
> Smile o'er the gaspings of spine-broken men,
> And perpetrate damnation in their den ! '

That, as it has been found safe, politic and beneficial, to allow the people to decide for themselves in all other religious observances, there is no reason to doubt that the same good results would attend their liberation from the bondage of a Sabbatical law ; —

That, under the Christian dispensation, it is a Jewish characteristic to talk of sacred days, places, rites and ceremonies ; for these, at their highest value, are only means to an end, to be used, modified or repudiated, according to cir-

9*

cumstances — and that end is, the benefit of man : hence, man is the only object that should be regarded as sacred on earth ; —

That as it is a sound rule of law, which excludes the testimony of one who is directly and strongly interested in a case on trial ; so it is equally just, when a Sabbatical institution is before the Court of Reason for adjudication, to rule out the declarations of a body of men in regard to it, who, filling clerical and priestly offices, depend on its alleged sanctity and rigid observance for their employment, remuneration, influence and power ; —

That the attempt to frighten the ignorant and unenlightened into a belief, that God frequently suspends the natural laws of the universe, and miraculously interferes to punish with blasting judgments such as engage in labor or recreation on the first day of the week — upsetting them in boats on the water, overturning them in vehicles on the land, burning their dwellings and barns, rendering barren and unproductive their farms, visiting with grievous sickness their persons, or smiting them or their cattle to the earth with a bolt from heaven — is either superstitious error or bold effrontery ; for it not only expressly contradicts the declaration of Jesus, that God ' causeth his sun to rise on the evil and on the good, and sendeth rain on the just and on the unjust ' — that we can be the ' children of our Father who is in heaven,' only by returning good for evil, and blessing for cursing — but it is disproved by universal experience and observation, as such incidents are common to every day of the week alike, and are not in any manner affected by the fact that it is the first, any more than that it is the last day of the week, on which they occur ; —

That they, who resort to such a mode of establishing their Sabbatical assumption, give indubitable proof that they are either grossly superstitious, or designedly fraudulent ;

straining at a gnat, and swallowing a camel — or, for a pretence, making long prayers, and devouring widows' houses;—

That as it is not pretended, that such extraordinary and special judgments attend the violation of other commands in the Decalogue, it follows, according to the logic of the Sabbatarians, that the fourth commandment is of more value than the other nine; so that, in the sight of God, it is incomparably more offensive to indulge in work or recreation on the Sabbath, than it is to worship idols, to dishonor father and mother, to lie, steal, commit adultery, and murder; —

That, as the duty of observing the first day of the week is not enjoined either in the second chapter of Genesis, or the twentieth chapter of Exodus, or in any other portion of the Old Testament, any reference to the Jewish scriptures, in support of such observance, is not only impertinent, but condemnatory of the present general practice; for the old Hebrew injunction runs, ' The *seventh* day is the Sabbath ';—

That the proscriptive spirit of modern Sabbatarians is the more severely to be censured, inasmuch as not an intimation is to be found in the New Testament, that the first day of the week is to be regarded as the Sabbath, instead of the seventh: nor is Sabbath-breaking, whether relating to the first or seventh day, in any instance recognised or reproved by Christ or his Apostles as a sin, nor do they inculcate any principle involving such recognition or reproof; —

That it is perfectly in character for those religious bodies, on both sides of the Atlantic, who care nothing for the desecration of *man*, to be deeply concerned for the sanctity of a *day* ; —

That a Sabbatizing clergy, in resisting, as far as practicable, every great reformatory movement, and in protesting against the advocacy of the cause of the slave, of peace, of temperance, of labor, of human brotherhood, on the first day of the week, as a desecration of the day, and injurious to the interests of religion, have revealed themselves in their true character as ' wolves in sheep's clothing,' and done more to bring their ' holy day ' into contempt than any other class of men ; —

That the innocence or criminality of any act is not to be determined by the day on which it is performed, but depends upon its intrinsic character, and the motives with which it is done; and whatever it is right to do on one day, it is right to do on any day; therefore,

That it is as innocent an act to plough in the field, to fish on the sea, to work in the shop. to ride in the railroad car, to indulge in recreation and amusement, on the first as on any other day of the week.

Of all the assumptions on the part of legislative bodies, that of interfering between a man's conscience and his God is the most insupportable, and the most inexcusable. For what purpose do we elect men to the General Court ? Is it to be our lawgivers on religious matters ? Shall we ask of that body when we may work, how we may work, or where we may work ? Is it a part of its constitutional power and prerogative to determine that point for us ? This passing a law, forbidding me or you to do on a particular day, what is in itself right, on the ground that that day, in the judgment of those who make the enactment, is more holy than another; this exercise of power, I affirm, is noth-ing better than sheer usurpation. It is the spirit which in all ages has persecuted those who have been loyal to God and their consciences. It is a war upon conscience, and no religious conclave or political assembly ever yet carried on that war successfully to the end. You cannot, by any enact-ments, bind the consciences of men, nor force men into obe-dience to what God requires.

Who wants to be persecuted on account of his own con-scientious views ? I will ask the first day Sabbatarian—do you claim a right to entertain your views, without molestation, in regard to the holiness of time? 'Most assuredly.' How do you make it out that the first day of the week is the Sabbath? 'I believe it to be so; and if it is not, to my own master I stand or fall. Under a government which avowedly tolerates all beliefs, I claim the right, as a first day Sabbatarian, to keep that day as the Sabbath.' Well, I do not assail that right. I claim the right also to have my own views of the day; the right to sanctify the first, second, or third, or all days, as I think proper. Now, I turn to the first day Sabbatarian, and ask him how he dares to assume infallible judgment against my belief; how he dares to dictate to me to keep the day which he regards as holy, and to say, 'If you do not obey me, I will put my hands into your pocket, and take out as much as I please in the shape of a fine; or if I find nothing there, I will put you in prison; or if you resist so far as to require it, I will shoot you dead'? Talk of the spirit of justice animating the bosom of the man who comes like a highwayman with, 'Do, or *die!*' Who made him a ruler over other men's consciences? In a government which is based on equality, we must have equal rights. No men, however sincere, are to wield forceful authority over others who dissent from them, in regard to religious faith and observance. The case is so plain, that it does not need an argument; and I am confident that, in the course of a few years, there will not be a Sabbatical enactment left unrepealed in the United States, if in any part of Christendom. It belongs to the tyrannical legislation which formerly sent men to the stake, in the name of God and for his glory, because they did not agree in the theological views of those who burnt them to ashes.

In this country, one pharisaical restriction after another, imposed by legislation, has been erased from the statute book, in the progress of religious freedom. We now come to this Sabbatical observance, as the last, perhaps,—a very formidable one, at any rate. If it be of God, it does not need legislation to uphold it. There is no power which can prevail against it. If it is founded in the nature of man, and in the wants of animals,—as its advocates declare,—then, of course, it is safe, and human nature will triumph. On the other hand, if it be merely a traditional usage, enforced upon us artfully, in the name of Christ, though of Jewish origin, it is for you and me, if we profess to be followers of Christ, or lovers of freedom, to speak the truth in regard to it, and deny that it has any special claim to religious veneration.

Why should we attempt to legislate upon a question of this kind? Observe how many differences of opinion prevail, honestly and sincerely, in the world, respecting it! Does any one doubt that the Seventh Day Baptists are sincere? Are they not honest, courageous, self-sacrificing men, those who stand out against the law and public sentiment, for conscience' sake? The men, even though they err, who are true to their consciences, cost what it may, are, after all, those who are ever nearest to the kingdom of God. They desire only to know what is right, and they have the spirit in them to do what is right. The great mass of first day Sabbatarians,—do they not claim to be conscientious and sincere? And the Quakers, who regard no day as in itself, or by divine appointment, more holy than another,—who will question their honesty or sincerity in this matter? Here, then, are widely conflicting sentiments; but which of these parties shall resort to the arm of violence to enforce uniformity of opinion?

By that infallible test of conscious rectitude which Jesus gave to his disciples—'Whatsoever ye would that men should do to you, do ye even so to them,'—let those who Sabbatize on the first day of the week be measured. At

present, they constitute the majority, we the minority, in this
country; hence, the legislative power is in their hands,
which they do not scruple to use for the purpose of binding
and coercing our consciences. Now, let the case be reversed. Suppose this power were in the hands of those who do
not Sabbatize, and they should proceed to enact penal laws,
forbidding the observance of any day as the Sabbath—
would not the Sabbatarians cry out against such laws as vexatious and tyrannical, destructive of the rights of conscience,
and a disgrace to the statute book?

In this country, we tolerate all religions, but must not tolerate all views with regard to a holy day! Why not? If
we tolerate the greater, why not the less? We had better
begin at the beginning. Let us tolerate none but the true
religion, and no other worship than that of a triune God.
Let us have no Jews, no Idolators, no Catholics! We are
Protestants; we are evangelical; ours is the true God, ours
the true religion; and it is all-important for the welfare of
the world, that the true religion should be promoted. Therefore, be it enacted by the Legislature, that only the Protestant religion, in its evangelical form, be allowed on the
American soil!

But we do not do this. It is not a crime, in the eye of
the law, for a man to make as many idols as he chooses,
and to worship them. It is not a crime, in the eye of the
law, to reject the doctrine of the Trinity. Time has been,
when it was a capital offence to deny the monstrous dogma
of transubstantiation as held by the Church of Rome, and
the denial carried the heretic to the stake. We tolerate
everything, excepting the opinions of men with regard to
the first day of the week! Having very successfully gone
thus far, I think we may take the next step, and finish the
whole category of religious edicts enforced by penal laws.
Many doubtless remember what a hue-and-cry was raised

by the religious press and the clergy, at the proposition
to expunge that portion of the Constitution of Massachusetts, which required persons to be taxed for the support of
public worship somewhere.   But the spirit of religious liberty came up, and said, ' That is tyranny, and the law ought
to be,—ay, must be repealed.'   What was the response of
the evangelical press ?   ' This is an infidel movement!
This is an attempt to overthrow Christianity ! '   And it
prophesied that, just as surely as the proposed amendment
should be adopted, public worship would be sadly neglected.
Well, the Constitution was altered, in this respect, notwithstanding this selfish outcry.   Is there less of public worship
than formerly ?   The clergy have never been so well sustained as they now are, and no one now laments the change.

Now, the outcry raised against the repeal of all Sabbatical laws, as an infidel movement, is as absurd, as preposterous, as libellous, as the other; and will be found so when
those laws cease to be in force.   Tie men up to the idea,
that one day is more holy than another, and enforce that
idea by the infliction of penalties in case of disobedience,
and you may make men religious hypocrites, but never
Christians.   That experiment was tried, with all exactness
and severity, under the Old Dispensation.   God has written
out that experiment in letters of fire, as it were, which shall
never go out until all men shall learn that it is not outward
observances which are required, but that spirit of the heart
and life which consecrates all things to God and humanity.

What a tremendous outcry was raised in England when
Daniel O'Connell, in behalf of plundered Ireland, demanded
the passage of the Catholic Emancipation Act by the British
Parliament !   The Protestant clergy and the Protestant press
cried out against it.   It will never do, they said ; the cause
of religion will suffer !   Where now is the Catholic test ?
Gone ! its ashes are not to be found ; but has any injury fol-

lowed from its repeal? So with regard to the unrighteous restrictions imposed upon the Jews; they were justified on the ground of Christian vigilance and security! But, during the present session of Parliament, the Jews have been admitted to equal rights with all others; and the Jew in England can now take his position any where in the government, as well as the Christian. Does any one suppose Christianity will suffer by this? Christianity, as taught by its founder, does not need any governmental safeguards; its reliance for safety and prosperity is not on the rack or the stake, the dungeon or the gibbet, unjust proscription or brutal supremacy. No—it is the only thing under heaven that is not afraid; it is the only thing that repudiates all such instruments as unholy and sinful.

Let the first day of the week stand on its own basis, as the second or third day stands, and I am satisfied that it will be much more rationally observed than it is now. Getting rid of our superstition concerning it, we shall use the day in a far more sensible and useful manner than is now done.

I desire to be clearly understood. I have no objection either to the first or the seventh day of the week, as a day of rest from bodily toil, both for man and beast. On the contrary, such rest is not only desirable, but indispensable. Neither man nor beast can long endure unmitigated labor. But I do not believe that it is in harmony with the will of God, or the physical nature of man, that mankind should be doomed to hard and wasting toil, six days out of seven, to obtain a bare subsistence. Reduced to such a pitiable condition, the rest of one day in the week is indeed grateful, and must be regarded as a blessing; but it is wholly inadequate to repair the physical injury or the moral degradation consequent on such protracted labor. It is not in accordance with the law of life, that our race should be thus worked, and only thus partially relieved from suffering and a premature death. *They need more,* AND MUST HAVE MORE, *instead of less, rest ;* and it is only for them to be enlightened and reclaimed, to put away those things which now cause them to grind in the prison-house of Toil, namely, idolatry, priest-craft, sectarianism, slavery, war, intemperance, licentious-ness, monopoly, and the like—in short, to live IN PEACE, obey the eternal law of being, strive for each other's welfare, and ' glorify God in their bodies and spirits which are his ' —and they will secure the rest, not only of one day in seven, but of a very large portion of their earthly existence.

Nor do I deny the right of any number of persons to observe a particular day of the week as holy time, by such religious rites and ceremonies as they may deem acceptable to God. To their own master, they stand or fall. In regard to all such matters, it is for every one to be fully persuaded in his own mind, and to obey the promptings of his own conscience ; conceding to others the liberty he claims for himself.

The sole and distinct issue that I make is this : — I maintain that the seventh day Sabbath was exclusively Jewish in its origin and design ; that no holiness, in any sense, attaches to the first day of the week, more than to any other ; and that the attempt to compel the observance of any day as ' THE SABBATH,' especially by penal enactments, is unauthor-ized by scripture or reason, and a shameful act of injustice and tyranny. I claim for myself, and for all mankind, the right to worship God according to the dictates of OUR OWN CONSCIENCES. This right, inherent and inalienable, is clo-ven down in the United States ; and I call upon all who desire to preserve civil and religious liberty to rally for its rescue.

See what it is that a hireling priesthood represent Chris-tianity as securing for the laboring classes ! A poor respite from brute toil of only one day in seven. Nothing more.

Why, in this view, Moses was a far more considerate and
merciful lawgiver than Jesus; and Judaism is decidedly
preferable to Christianity!   Let any man examine the
Mosaic code, and he will be surprised, I think, to find that
nearly one-third of the whole time of the people was devoted
to rest, to abstinence from labor, through the multiplication of festivals and sacred occasions.   Is there such an
exemption from toil in this boasted Christian land, eighteen
hundred years after the advent of the Messiah?   Are not
the masses driven from the earliest dawn of Monday to the
latest hour of Saturday, to enable them to keep body and
soul together?   And is this the state of society which God
has ordained, to the end of the world?   Why do not we,
under Christ and Christianity, enjoy as many rest-days as
they had under Moses and Judaism?   Nay, in this respect,
observe the difference between Catholicism and Protestantism.   The Romish church has its festivals and hallowed
days, in addition to the Sunday, and thus relief is given to
the severity of toil; but all that is conceded to us, as Protestants, is the rest of one day in seven, or fifty-two days
out of three hundred and sixty-five !

Such is not my estimate of Christianity.   As taught by
its founder, and portrayed in his life, its object is to undo
the heavy burdens of suffering humanity, not to increase
those burdens — to diminish the hours of toil, not to multiply
them; and if it cannot do this, of what value is it to mankind ?   I do not believe that God has created us under this
dire necessity to toil, like beasts, to sustain life.   I believe
it is his will that we should hold absolute mastery over time,
so as to devote it mainly to intellectual and moral improvement, domestic enjoyment, and social intercourse.   In a
rectified state of society, it will not be necessary for us to
eat our bread in the sweat of our brow.   God will work for
us, by an omnipotent and omnipresent energy, operating

upon the machinery of human invention. Our servants shall be water, fire, and air, — whatever yet remains to be drawn from the unexplored and exhaustless store-house of electricity, — to perform all servile labor, and the earth shall be filled with abundance for all.

Some of the religious journals are giving such representations of the views which are held by those who ' esteem every day,' and who allow no man to judge them in respect to a weekly Sabbath, as to make the ignorant and vicious imagine that anti-Sabbatarians are for desecrating the first day of the week by countenancing them in their evil practices — such as drinking, horse-racing, and the like. This is monstrous! They who refuse to Sabbatize are for elevating, not for depressing the standard of morality. They have done something — who have done more? — for the cause of Temperance, of Peace, of Purity, of Labor; something to redeem the slaves from their fetters; something to promulgate the doctrine of human brotherhood. What evil have they advocated? Of what crime have they been convicted? The tree is known by its fruits. I do not believe that there can be found on earth a more pure, a more unselfish, a more reformatory, a more truly Christian body. But ' if the master of the house be called Beelzebub, how much more they of his household ? ' Now, this is my reply to the charge alluded to. They who indulge in drinking, gambling and horse-racing, are not *our* disciples. They know us not, except to hate us. They do not believe in our doctrine of abstaining from all iniquity, and sanctifying all time alike. They believe what they have been taught, that the first day of the week is the Sabbath, though they desecrate it — and this is their highest idea of Christianity.

What sort of a syllogism is this — that because we deny the peculiar holiness of a certain day, therefore we are for desecrating that day by immoral conduct?

· Now, the people have an idea of only one day in seven to be given to God. On Monday morning, after Sunday is past, they absolutely look like different persons — do they not? Can you conceive a wider contrast in their mien and behavior, than is seen between Sunday and Monday? If a man did not well understand this wonderful change, and should form acquaintances on Sunday, he would have to be introduced again on the next day, such entire strangers would they be to him. They have a different look, gait, walk, and voice; they begin to breathe more freely; they once more feel and act in a natural manner; it was all un-natural before. Now, all such are assuredly deceiving themselves; they worship externally, not in the spirit; they do not yet comprehend the meaning of those pregnant de- clarations of Jesus, 'The kingdom of God cometh not by observation' — 'The hour cometh, and now is, when the true worshippers shall worship the Father in spirit and in truth.'

· I am aware that I shall inevitably be accused, by the chief priests, scribes and Pharisees of the present time, as was Jesus by the same class in his age, as 'not of God,' because I 'do not keep the Sabbath day'; but I am persuaded, that to expose the popular delusion which prevails on this subject is *to advance the cause of a pure Christianity, to promote true and acceptable worship, and to inculcate strict moral and religious accountability, in all the concerns of life,* ON ALL DAYS OF THE WEEK ALIKE. If I am an 'infidel' or a 'heretic' for this belief, I am content to stand in the same condemnation, on this point, with TYNDALE,* LUTHER,†

---

* 'As for the Sabbath, we be lords of the Sabbath, and may yet change it into Monday, or any other day, as we see need; or we may make every tenth day holy, if we see cause why.'—TYNDALE.

† 'Keep it [the first day of the week] holy, for its use sake, both to body and soul. But if any where the day is made holy for the mere

10*

CALVIN,* MELANCTHON, ROGER WILLIAMS, MILTON, FOX, PENN, PRIESTLEY, BELSHAM, PALEY, WHITBY, Archbishop WHATELY,† and a host of others, who are every where lauded, by the various sects with which they are identified, as among the brightest ornaments of the Christian Church, and who are essentially agreed in the opinion, that the Sabbath was a JEWISH INSTITUTION.

---

day's sake—if any where any one sets up its observance upon a Jewish foundation—then I order you to work on it, to ride on it, to dance on it, to do any thing that shall reprove this encroachment on the Christian spirit and liberty.' — LUTHER.

* 'Christ is the true fulfilment of the Sabbath, . . . which is contained, not in one day, but in the whole course of our life, till being wholly dead to ourselves, we be filled with the life of God. Christians, therefore, ought to depart from all superstitious observance of days.' — CALVIN.

† 'To say, that no part of the Jewish law is binding on Christians is very far from leaving them at liberty to disregard all moral duties. For, in fact, the very definition of a moral duty implies its universal obligation, independent of all enactment.   *   *   *

'Nor need it be feared, that to proclaim an exemption from the Mosaic law should leave men without any moral guide, and at a loss to distinguish right and wrong; since, after all, the light of reason is that to which every man *must* be left, in the interpretation of that very law. For Moses, it should be remembered, did not write three distinct books, one of the Ceremonial Law, one of the Civil, and a third of the Moral; nor does he hint at any such distinction. When, therefore, any one is told that a *part* of the Mosaic precepts are binding on us, viz., the *Moral* ones, if he ask *which* *are* the Moral precepts, and how to distinguish them from the Ceremonial and the Civil, with which they are mingled, the answer must be, that his conscience, if he consult it honestly, will determine that point. So far, consequently, from the moral precepts of the law being, to the Christian, necessary as a guide to his judgment in determining *what is* right and wrong, on the contrary this moral judgment is necessary to determine what *are* the Moral precepts of Moses.' — ARCHBISHOP WHATELY.

Worship.

THEY who, as worshippers, some mountain climb,
  Or to some temple, made with hands, repair,
  As though the Godhead specially dwelt there,
And absence, in Heaven's eye, would be a crime,
Have yet to comprehend this truth sublime : —
  The freeman of the Lord no chain can bear —
  His soul is free to worship every where,
Nor limited to any place or time.
No worldly sanctuary now may claim
  Man's reverence as a consecrated pile ;
Mosque, synagogue, cathedral, are the same,
  Differing in nought but architectural style : —
Avaunt, then, Superstition ! in GOD's name,
  Nor longer thy blind devotees beguile !

The True Church.

CHURCH of the living GOD ! in vain thy foes
  Make thee, in impious mirth, their laughing-stock,
  Contemn thy strength, thy radiant beauty mock :
In vain their threats, and impotent their blows —
Satan's assaults — Hell's agonizing throes !
  For thou art built upon th' Eternal Rock,
  Nor fear'st the thunder storm, the earthquake shock,
And nothing shall disturb thy calm repose.
All human combinations change and die,
  Whate'er their origin, name, form, design ;
But, firmer than the pillars of the sky,
  Thou standest ever by a power Divine :
Thou art endowed with Immortality,
  And canst not perish — GOD'S OWN LIFE IS THINE !

The American Union.

TYRANTS of the old world! contemners of the rights of man! disbelievers in human freedom and equality! enemies of mankind! console not yourselves with the delusion, that REPUBLICANISM and the AMERICAN UNION are synonymous terms — or that the downfall of the latter will be the extinction of the former, and, consequently, a proof of the incapacity of the people for self-government, and a confirmation of your own despotic claims! Your thrones must crumble to dust; your sceptre of dominion drop from your powerless hands; your rod of oppression be broken; yourselves so vilely abased, that there shall be ' none so poor to do you reverence.' The will of God, the beneficent Creator of the human family, cannot always be frustrated. It is His will that every form of usurpation, every kind of injustice, every device of tyranny, shall come to nought; that peace, and liberty, and righteousness, shall ' reign from sea to sea, and from the rivers to the ends of the earth ; ' and that, throughout the world, in the fullness of a sure redemption, there shall be ' none to molest or make afraid.' Humanity, covered with gore, cries, with a voice that pierces the heavens, ' *His will be done !* ' Justice, discrowned by the hand of violence, exclaims, in tones of deep solemnity, ' HIS WILL BE DONE ! ' Liberty, burdened with chains, and driven into exile, in thunder-tones responds, ' HIS WILL BE DONE ! '

Tyrants! know that the rights of man are inherent and inalienable, and therefore not to be forfeited by the failure of any form of government, however democratic. Let the American Union perish; let these allied States be torn with faction, or drenched in blood; let this republic realize the fate of Rome and Carthage, of Babylon and Tyre; still, those rights would remain undiminished in strength, unsul-

lied in purity, unaffected in value, and sacred as their Divine
Author. If nations perish, it is not because of their devotion
to liberty, but for their disregard of its requirements. Man
is superior to all political compacts, all governmental
arrangements, all religious institutions. As means to an
end, these may sometimes be useful, though never indispensable ; but that end must always be the freedom and happiness of man, INDIVIDUAL MAN. It can never be true, that
the public good requires the violent sacrifice of any, even the
humblest citizen; for it is absolutely dependant on his preservation, not destruction. To do evil, that good may come,
is equally absurd and criminal. The time for the overthrow
of any government, the abandonment of any alliance, the
subversion of any institution, is whenever it justifies the
immolation of the individual to secure the general welfare ;
for the welfare of the many cannot be hostile to the safety
of the few. In all agreements, in all measures, in all political or religious enterprises, in all attempts to redeem the
human race, man, as an individual, is to be held paramount.
The doctrine, that the end sanctifies the means, is the
maxim of profligates and impostors, of usurpers and tyrants.
They who, to promote the cause of truth, will sanction the
utterance of a falsehood, are to be put in the category of
liars. So, likewise, they who are for trampling on the rights
of the minority, in order to benefit the majority, are to be
registered as the monsters of their race. Might is never
right, excepting when it sees in every human being, ' a man
and a brother,' and protects him with a divine fidelity. It is
the recognition of these truths, the adoption of these principles, which alone can extirpate tyranny from the earth, perpetuate a free government, and cause the dwellers in every
clime, ' like kindred drops, to mingle into one.'

Tyrants ! confident of its overthrow, proclaim not to your
vassals, that the AMERICAN UNION is an experiment of free-

dom, which, if it fail, will for ever demonstrate the necessity
of whips for the backs, and chains for the limbs of the people.   Know that its subversion is essential to the triumph of
justice, the deliverance of the oppressed, the vindication of
the BROTHERHOOD OF THE RACE.   It was conceived in sin,
and brought forth in iniquity; and its career has been
marked by unparalleled hypocrisy, by high-handed tyranny,
by a bold defiance of the omniscience and omnipotence of
God.   Freedom indignantly disowns it, and calls for its extinction; for within its borders are three millions of slaves,
whose blood constitutes its cement, whose flesh forms a
large and flourishing branch of its commerce, and who are
ranked with four-footed beasts and creeping things.   To
secure the adoption of the Constitution of the United States,
it was agreed, first, that the African slave-trade, — till that
time a feeble, isolated, colonial traffic, — should, for at least
twenty years, be prosecuted as a national interest under the
American flag, and protected by the national arm; — secondly, that a slaveholding oligarchy, created by allowing
three-fifths of the slave population to be represented by
their taskmasters, should be allowed a permanent seat in
Congress; — thirdly, that the slave system should be secured against internal revolt and external invasion, by the
united physical force of the country; — fourthly, that not a
foot of national territory should be granted, on which the
panting fugitive from slavery might stand, and be safe from
his pursuers — thus making every citizen a slave-hunter
and slave-catcher.   To say that this ' covenant with death '
shall not be annulled — that this ' agreement with hell ' shall
continue to stand — that this ' refuge of lies ' shall not be
swept away — is to hurl defiance at the eternal throne, and
to give the lie to Him who sits thereon.   It is an attempt,
alike monstrous and impracticable, to blend the light of
heaven with the darkness of the bottomless pit, to unite the

living with the dead, to associate the Son of God with the Prince of Evil.

Accursed be the AMERICAN UNION, as a stupendous republican imposture!

Accursed be it, as the most frightful despotism, with regard to three millions of the people, ever exercised over any portion of the human family!

Accursed be it, as the most subtle and atrocious compromise ever made to gratify power and selfishness!

Accursed be it, as a libel on Democracy, and a bold assault on Christianity!

Accursed be it, stained as it is with human blood, and supported by human sacrifices!

Accursed be it, for the terrible evils it has inflicted on Africa, by burning her villages, ravaging her coast, and kidnapping her children, at an enormous expense of human life, and for a diabolical purpose!

Accursed be it, for all the crimes it has committed at home — for seeking the utter extermination of the red men of its wildernesses, and for enslaving one-sixth part of its teeming population!

Accursed be it, for its hypocrisy, its falsehood, its impudence, its lust, its cruelty, its oppression!

Accursed be it, as a mighty obstacle in the way of universal freedom and equality!

Accursed be it, from the foundation to the roof, and may there soon not be left one stone upon another, that shall not be thrown down!

Henceforth, the watchword of every uncompromising abolitionist, of every friend of God and liberty, must be, both in a religious and political sense — ' No UNION WITH SLAVE-HOLDERS!'

Persecution.

O, PERSECUTION! fearful as thou art,
　　With scowling brow, and aspect stern and rude,
　　Thy hands in blood of Innocence imbrued,
Wrung, drop by drop, from many a tortured heart, —
Why should we dread the gibbet, axe, or stake?
　　Thou dost our faith, our hope, our courage try,
　　And mak'st us valiant where we thought to fly :
Through thee, the crown of Victory we take.
Thy fires but purify our gold from dross ;
　　Once undiscerned, our value now appears,
　　Which shall, at interest, increase with years ;
So do we gain by thee, nor suffer loss :—
'T were base to sacrifice the TRUTH, to save
Our names from foul reproach — our bodies from the grave.

Liberty.

THY cause, O LIBERTY! can never fail,
　　Whether by foes o'erwhelmed or friends betray'd :
　　Then be its advocates of nought afraid !
As GOD is true, they surely shall prevail.
Let base oppressors tremble, and turn pale !
　　They, they alone, may justly be dismayed ;
　　For TRUTH and RIGHT are on thy side arrayed,
And the whole world shall yet thy triumph hail.
No blow for thee was ever struck in vain ;
　　Thy champions, martyrs, are of noble birth ;
Rare honors, blessings, praises, thanks, they gain,
　　And Time and Glory magnify their worth !
A thousand times defeated, thou shalt reign
　　Victor, O LIBERTY, o'er all the earth !

Harsh Language --- Retarding the Cause.

I AM accused of using hard language. I admit the charge.
I have not been able to find a soft word to describe villany,
or to identify the perpetrator of it. The man who makes a
chattel of his brother—what is he? The man who keeps
back the hire of his laborers by fraud—what is he? They
who prohibit the circulation of the Bible—what are they?
They who compel three millions of men and women to herd
together, like brute beasts—what are they? They who sell
mothers by the pound, and children in lots to suit purchas-
ers—what are they? I care not what terms are applied to
them, provided they do apply. If they are not thieves,
if they are not tyrants, if they are not men-stealers, I
should like to know what is their true character, and by
what names they may be called. It is as mild an epithet
to say that a thief is a thief, as it is to say that a spade
is a spade. Words are but the signs of ideas. 'A rose
by any other name would smell as sweet.' Language
may be misapplied, and so be absurd or unjust—as, for
example, to say that an abolitionist is a fanatic, or that a
slaveholder is an honest man. But to call things by their
right names is to use neither hard nor improper language.
Epithets may be rightly applied, it is true, and yet be uttered
in a bad spirit, or with a malicious design. What then?
Shall we discard all terms which are descriptive of crime,
because they are not always used with fairness and propriety?
He who, when he sees oppression, cries out against it—
who, when he beholds his equal brother trodden under foot
by the iron hoof of despotism, rushes to his rescue—who,
when he sees the weak overborne by the strong, takes sides
with the former, at the imminent peril of his own safety—
such a man needs no certificate to the excellence of his

11

temper, or the sincerity of his heart, or the disinterestedness of his conduct. It is the apologist of slavery—he who can see the victim of thieves lying bleeding and helpless on the cold earth, and yet turn aside, like the callous-hearted priest and Levite—who needs absolution.

The Anti-Slavery cause is beset by many dangers. But there is one which we have special reason to apprehend. It is, that this hollow cant and senseless clamor about ' hard language,' will insensibly check that free utterance of thought, and close application of the truth, which have characterized abolitionists from the beginning. As that cause is becoming popular, and many may be induced to espouse it from motives of policy, rather than from any reverence for principle, let us beware how we soften our just severity of speech, or emasculate a single epithet. The whole scope of the English language is inadequate to describe the horrors and impieties of slavery, and the transcendent wickedness of those who sustain this bloody system. Instead, therefore, of repudiating any of its strong terms, we rather need a new and stronger dialect. Hard language! Let us mark those who complain of its use. In ninety-nine cases out of a hundred, they will be found to be the most unscrupulous in their allegations, the most bitter in their spirit, the most vituperative in their manner of expression, when alluding to abolitionists. The cry of ' hard language ' has become stale in my ears. The faithful utterance of that language has, by the blessing of God, made the Anti-Slavery cause what it is— ample in resources, strong in numbers, victorious in conflict. Like the hand-writing upon the wall of the palace, it has caused the knees of the American Belshazzar to smite together in terror, and filled with dismay all who follow in his train. Soft phrases and honeyed accents were tried in vain for many a year:—they had no adaptation to the subject. ' Canst thou draw out the leviathan, SLAVERY, with a hook ?

or his tongue with a cord which thou lettest down? Canst
thou put a hook into his nose? or bore his jaw through with
a thorn? Will he make many supplications unto thee?
wilt thou take him for a servant for ever? Shall not one be
cast down at the sight of him? Out of his nostrils goeth
smoke, as out of a seething pot or caldron. His breath
kindleth coals, and a flame goeth out of his mouth. His
heart is as firm as a stone; yea, as hard as a piece of the
nether mill-stone. When he raiseth up himself, even the
mighty are afraid. He esteemeth iron as straw, and brass as
rotten wood.' O the surpassing folly of those 'wise and
prudent' men, who think he may be coaxed into a willingness to be destroyed, and who regard him as the gentlest of
all fish — provided he be let alone! They say it will irritate
him to charge him with being a leviathan; he will cause the
deep to boil like a pot. Call him a dolphin, and he will not
get angry! If I should call these sage advisers by their
proper names, no doubt they would be irritated too.

Strong denunciatory language is consistent with gentleness
of spirit, long-suffering, and perfect charity. It was the God
whose name was LOVE, who could speak, even to his chosen
people, in the following terms, by the mouth of his prophet
Ezekiel: —' An end, the end has come upon the four corners
of the land. I will send mine anger upon thee, and will
judge thee according to thy ways, and will recompense upon
thee all thy abominations. And mine eye shall not spare,
neither will I have pity.' 'A third part of thee shall die
with the pestilence, and with famine shall they be consumed
in the midst of thee: and a third part shall fall by the sword,
round about thee, and I will scatter a third part into all the
winds, and I will draw out a sword after them.' It was the
Lamb of God who could exclaim, —' Wo unto you, scribes
and Pharisees, hypocrites! for ye devour widows' houses,
and for a pretence make long prayers: therefore ye shall

receive the greater damnation. Ye blind guides! which strain at a gnat, and swallow a camel. Ye serpents, ye generation of vipers, how can ye escape the damnation of hell?' It was the martyr Stephen, who, though in his dying agonies, supplicated forgiveness for his enemies, and, a few moments before his cruel death, could address his countrymen in the following strain:—'Ye stiff-necked, and uncircumcised in heart and ears, ye do always resist the Holy Ghost: as your fathers did, so do ye. Which of the prophets have not your fathers persecuted? and ye have slain them which showed before of the coming of the Just One; of whom ye have been now the betrayers and murderers.'

My accusers impudently assert, that I have seriously injured the sacred cause of liberty. Much do they care for the speedy triumph of that cause! Rather, they care nothing, fear nothing about it, except that the abolitionists will succeed in putting the slave-system down. Will any man say, that I have overrated the rights, privileges, enjoyments of liberty?—that I have eulogized it too strongly, painted its beauties in too glowing colors, represented it above its true value, advocated its universal prevalence too earnestly, defended it too vigorously against the assaults of its enemies? Who and where is that man? Is he a man? Is he an American, a Republican, a Christian? Why, I have been taught from childhood to consider liberty an inestimable boon,—as something worth contending for, worth dying for, above all price, above all earthly considerations! It has been instilled into me, that

> 'A day, an hour of virtuous liberty
> Is worth a whole eternity of bondage!'

and I shall be slow to unlearn a lesson that so perfectly harmonises with all the instincts and aspirations of the soul.

I thought American freemen subscribed to the affirmation, that it is :

'Better to sit in Freedom's hall,
With a cold damp floor and mouldering wall,
Than to bend the neck, or bow the knee,
In the proudest palace of slavery !'

I thought it was the earnest inquiry in 1776, — 'the times that tried men's souls,' —

'O, where's the slave, so lowly,
Condemned to chains unholy,
Who, could he burst his bonds at first,
Would pine beneath them slowly?
What soul, whose wrongs degrade it,
Would wait till time decayed it,
When thus its wing at once might spring
To the throne of HIM who made it?'

'O LIBERTY! O sound once delightful to every AMERICAN ear! Once sacred, but now trampled upon!' Arise from the dust, armed with immortal energy, and scatter thy foes as chaff is driven before the whirlwind! Knowest thou not that thou art destined to be the conqueror of the world, and that no weapon against thee can prosper? O, sublime is the conflict before thee, and right royally shalt thou triumph, to the joy of all heaven and earth!

That I have estimated a state of freedom too highly is impossible! The difficulty is, to appreciate it, in all its grandeur and glory. Never, never can I be too thankful to God, that I was not born a slave; that my wife and little ones are secure from the clutches of the kidnapper; that my hearth-stone is sacred to purity and love; that it is not the horrible fate of myself and family, to be prized as goods and chattels, and herded with four-footed beasts and creeping things. O, to be free as the winds of heaven; to be

11*

restrained by nothing but love to God and love to man; to
go and come, rise up or lie down, labor or rest, just as the
free spirit shall elect; to stand up in the dignity of manhood,
almost on a level with the angels of God, and find no superior on earth; to understand, all knowledge, and know the
why and wherefore of ' the brave o'erhanging sky,' and the
outstretched earth, and pry into the mysteries of creation;
above all, to be instructed from those Scriptures which
are able to make the seeker wise unto salvation, and which
show what is the perfect will of God, and how we may
become free indeed in Christ Jesus; this is to make life a
blessing, and the reverse of it a curse. I have not, then, at
any time, extolled liberty too highly.

Still, the popular cry against me is, that have I spoken of
slavery, and slaveholders, and the apologists of slavery, in
harsh, denunciatory language, so as greatly to injure the
cause I profess to love. This is not only hypercritical, but,
I fear, hypocritical, on the part of my accusers. Who ever
knew men induced to love freedom less, because they were
urged to hate slavery more? I scoff at such a conclusion!
That my language has been rough, vehement, denunciatory,
is true: but why? Because the exigency of the times
demanded it; because any other language would have been
inappropriate and ineffectual; because my theme was not a
gentle one, about buds, and blossoms, and flowers, and gentle
zephyrs, and starry skies; but about a nation of boasting republicans and Christians, ruthlessly consigning to chains and
slavery every sixth person born in the land—about a land,

'Where the image of God is accounted as base,
And the image of Cæsar set up in its place'—

about one vast system of crime and blood, and all imaginable
lewdness and villany—about the robbers of God's poor,

those who keep back the hire of their laborers by fraud,
those who sin against the clearest light, and in the most
awful manner.   Now, what words shall I use to express the
convictions of an honest soul, in view of such atrocious
impiety, and such unequalled meanness and baseness?
Shall they be gentle, and carefully selected, and cautiously
expressed?   Away with such counsel; it is treason against
the throne of God!   Call things by their right names, and
let the indignant spirit find free utterance.

> 'On such a theme 't were impious to be calm!
> Passion is reason, transport temper here!',

It may be said, this is all declamation,— why not argue
the matter?   Argue, indeed!   What is the proposition to
be discussed?   It is this: whether all men are created free
and equal, and have an inalienable right to liberty!   I am
urged to argue this with a people, who declare it to be a
self-evident truth!   Why, such folly belongs to Bedlam.
When my countrymen shall burn their Bibles, and rescind
their famous Declaration of Independence, and reduce
themselves to colonial dependence upon the mother country,
I will find both time and patience to reason with them on the
subject of human rights.   Argument is demanded — to prove
what?   Why, that one man has no right to make a chattel
of another! that he is a thief who picks another man's
pockets, and kidnaps his body and soul! that an American
citizen, who is a slave-master, and yet pretends to be a
republican or Christian, is an arrant hypocrite! that to sell
families at auction, like cattle or swine, in lots to suit purchas-
ers, is a crime! that to forbid the instruction of almost one
half of the Southern population, and also the circulation of
the Bible, under terrible pains and penalties, is to incur the
displeasure of Heaven! that it would be right, safe, expedient, to pay a laborer wages, recognise and treat him as a

man, place him under the protection of equal laws, and
cease brutalizing him without a cause! Are these propositions to be gravely discussed in the United States, in the
nineteenth century? Not by me, whatever others may think
proper to do. For there is not a slaveholder in all the land,
who does not as certainly know that he is a thief and a
tyrant, as that he exists, — whether he claims to be a titled
divine, or a Senator in Congress. How do I make good the
assertion? By condemning him out of his own mouth: for
he acknowledges, that the sentiments contained in his country's Declaration are true, yet dares to put an equal brother
under his feet! By appealing to his own nature : for, sooner
than he would suffer himself to be placed in the condition
of his slave, he would choose to encounter death in any
form. No man ever yet hated his own flesh. Therefore,
' thou shalt love thy neighbor as thyself,' — and ' whatsoever
ye would that men should do to you, do ye even so to them.'
' He that hath ears to hear, let him hear.' The day for
admitting excuses has gone by! No man may now plead
ignorance of his duty. The motives for immediate action
are overwhelming. More than three millions of men, women
and children already in chains in our midst; seventy thousand infants, the offspring of slave parents, annually kidnapped from their birth; the right of petition trampled in
the dust; freedom of speech no longer tolerated; the slave
system defended as a divine institution by the rulers in Church
and State; and the whole country filled with pollution, violence, and blood; behold out situation, and what is to be our
fate, as a people, if we will not amend our ways and our
doings!

   Still, envy, and effrontery, and falsehood, and jesuitism,
accuse me of hindering the work of emancipation! The
Southern advocates of perpetual slavery, who fear and hate
me exceedingly, make oath that I have prolonged the bond-

age of their slaves at least one century. The same charge is (inconsistently enough!) brought against me by the Northern supporters of the bloody slave-system, who dread nothing so much as the liberation of the slaves. They who fear not God and regard not the black man, who riotously assemble together to destroy freedom of speech and of the press, whose only arguments are curses, brickbats and rotten eggs, who are anxious to give a coat of tar and feathers to every man who pities the oppressed, who offer rewards for my abduction and murder; these publicly howl and mourn because I am an insurmountable obstacle to the deliverance of their oppressed colored brethren and sisters! The men of wolf-like ferocity, who are multiplying the stripes upon the bodies of their victims, and making their yokes heavier and their chains more galling, and revelling in their blood, and basely withholding their wages, and excluding every ray of knowledge from their minds, and claiming a heaven-derived title to their bodies and souls, — these eagerly and unitedly affirm, that I am not only accountable for this new infliction of their cruelty, but positively rivetting those fetters which they themselves would gladly break, — at a more convenient season, — were I out of the way! In short, all who swear eternal hostility to the colored population; all who impiously maintain that the prejudices against them are natural, invincible, and beyond the power of religion to subdue; all who aim to banish them to a strange and barbarous land; all who implore that they may have a little more sleep and a little more slumber; all who are greedy of the gains of oppression; and all who fear the threats of the oppressor more than they do the judgments of the Almighty; whatever may be their other differences of opinion, are singularly agreed upon this one thing — that I am greatly hindering the emancipation, elevation and happiness of my enslaved countrymen! Aside from other evidence, these declarations furnish conclusive proofs that my course is straight and direct, and that I am successfully doing the very thing that ought to be done for the overthrow of ' that most execrable villany,' American slavery.   When such men, continuing in their prejudices or oppressions, shall begin to approve of my course, and to recognise me as a co-worker, I shall then know to a certainty that I am as corrupt, as cruel, and as dishonest as they would fain make me appear.   As rationally might it be said, that Fulton, by his application of steam power, has injured navigation ; or that the multiplication of rail-roads obstructs the transportation of goods, and diminishes the public travel.   When the Prince of Evil vociferously declares, that you are not fighting to advantage against him, that you are wasting your powder and balls, and that you do not manage aright to dethrone him ; nay, that by your labors you are only building up, instead of subverting his dark kingdom ; and when he offers to show you how to lie in ambush, how to place your cannon, and how to carry on the siege against him, rely upon it, that he is still ' a liar from the beginning,' and that he feels his supremacy to be in danger.

But let the unparalleled and glorious change wrought in public sentiment, since the establishment of the Liberator, through the potency of truth, determine whether my labors have been injurious or beneficial.   Before the review is commenced, let it be premised, that the slave-system is one of the strongholds of the devil — perhaps the strongest ; that it has been strengthening and enlarging itself for more than two hundred years ; that it is a combination of almost every conceivable crime against God or man — such as robbery, cruelty, lewdness, adultery, blasphemy, oppression, soul-murder, &c. &c. ; and that the necessary consequences of a righteous and vigorous attack upon it must be a stirring up of the fury and resistance of the oppressors,

and a shaking of the nation that has so long tolerated it.
A few years ago, was not the land slumbering in the lap of
moral death, upon this subject? Who did not deride or
oppose the doctrines that I then promulgated? Where was
there one society organized with the doctrine of 'immediate
emancipation' as its basis? Who wished me God-speed?
How many stood by me,—how many encouraged me,—
how many patronized the Liberator? What agents occupied the field, and dispensed light to the people? Look
back only two years ago, and see how mighty has been the
growth of our cause during that brief period! Since the
days of Luther, has the world witnessed so rapid a transformation in public sentiment, amidst equal difficulties, trials
and sacrifices? It was with difficulty that a small body of
men could then defray their expenses to Philadelphia, to
form an Anti-Slavery Convention! They were opulent in
faith, but without money in their purse. Yet they assembled
together, and were a gazing-stock to the nation. They
prayed, and pleaded, and resolved, as did they of old, of
whom the world was not worthy ; and they enunciated truths
that have shaken the system of slavery to its foundation.
Where now is that other monster, who lifted his proud crest
to heaven, seemingly invincible in his strength,—the American Colonization Society? Struggling in the agonies of
dissolution! Look, now, at that powerful association, the
American Anti-Slavery Society! Look at seven flourishing
State Societies! Look at one thousand auxiliary societies,
and see them multiplying daily! Look at the flood of our
publications sweeping through the land, and carrying joy,
and hope, and life, and fertility, wherever they go! See
how many presses have espoused our cause! See how
many agents are in the field, how many pens employed, how
many tongues loosed, how many prayers offered! And the
stream of sympathy still rolls on—its impetus is increasing;

and it must ere long sweep away the pollutions of slavery.
What then? Do I boast of this as *my* work? God forbid!
To Him be all the glory and renown. But, as an instrument,
he has honored my labors; he has induced a great multitude
of wise and good men, and holy women, to adopt my views
and principles; and he has thus confounded those who would
fain make it appear, that I have labored worse than in vain.
The work is his—the cause is his—and his shall be the victory. ' Not unto us, not unto us, but unto thy name, O Lord,
be the glory!'

The sins of abolitionists are those of omission, rather than
of commission. We do not yet reason, and feel, and act,
precisely as if our wives and daughters were given over to
the tender mercies of lewd and brutal wretches, or our children were liable to be sold to the slave speculators at any
moment, or the chains were about to be fastened upon our
own free limbs. They who accuse us of being uncharitable
in spirit, harsh in speech, personal in denunciation, have no
sympathy with the oppressed, and therefore are disqualified
to sit in judgment upon our conduct. They do not regard
the negro race as equal to the Anglo-Saxon; hence it is
impossible for them to resent a wrong or an outrage done to
a black man as they would to a white. In regard to their
own rights and enjoyments, they are sensitively alive to the
slightest encroachments upon them. Touch but their interests, however lightly, conflict with their prerogatives, however gently, injure their persons, however triflingly, and see
how they will flame, and denounce, and threaten! Such
men are condemned out of their own mouths. Let no heed
be given to what they say of our principles and measures.
Their criticism is as false as their philanthropy is spurious.
They make great pretensions to prudence, which means
moral cowardice; to gentleness of spirit, which means
total insensibility; to moderation, which means stony-heart-

edness; to candor and impartiality, which mean favoritism
and spleen; to evangelical piety, which means cant and
bigotry.

But I will not enlarge upon this point. If Southern slaveholders, and their apologists, cannot endure our rebukes,
how will they be able to bear the awful retributions of
Heaven, which must inevitably overwhelm them, unless they
speedily repent? I am ready to make a truce with the
South: if she will give up her stolen property, I will no
longer brand her as a thief; if she will desist from driving
woman into the field, like a beast, under the lash of a brutal
overseer,—from stealing infants, from trafficking in human
flesh, from keeping back the hire of the laborer by fraud—
I will agree not to call her a monster; if she will honor the
marriage institution, and sacredly respect the relations of
life, and no longer license incest, pollution and adultery, I
will not represent her as Sodomitish in spirit and practice;
if she will no longer prevent the unobstructed circulation of
the Scriptures, and the intellectual and religious education of her benighted population, I will not stigmatize her
as practically atheistical. In short, if she will abolish her
cruel slave-system, root and branch, at once and for ever,
we will instantly disband all our anti-slavery societies, and
no longer agitate the land. But, until she thus act, we shall
increase, instead of relaxing our efforts — multiply, instead of
diminishing our associations — and make our rebukes more
terrible than ever!

> 'If we have whispered truth,
>   Whisper no longer;
>   But speak as the tempest does,
>   Sterner and stronger!'

12

Song of the Abolitionist.

I.

I AM an Abolitionist!
  I glory in the name;
Though now by SLAVERY's minions hissed,
  And covered o'er with shame:
It is a spell of light and power—
  The watchword of the free:—
Who spurns it in the trial-hour,
  A craven soul is he!

II.

I am an Abolitionist!
  Then urge me not to pause;
For joyfully do I enlist
  In FREEDOM's sacred cause:
A nobler strife the world ne'er saw,
  Th' enslaved to disenthral;
I am a soldier for the war,
  Whatever may befall!

III.

I am an Abolitionist!
  Oppression's deadly foe;
In God's great strength will I resist,
  And lay the monster low;
In God's great name do I demand,
  To all be freedom given,
That peace and joy may fill the land,
  And songs go up to heaven!

IV.

I am an Abolitionist!
  No threats shall awe my soul—
No perils cause me to desist—
  No bribes my acts control;

A freeman will I live and die,
In sunshine and in shade,
And raise my voice for liberty,
Of nought on earth afraid.

V.

I am an Abolitionist —
The tyrant's hate and dread —
The friend of all who are oppressed —
A price is on my head!
My country is the wide, wide world,
My countrymen mankind : —
Down to the dust be Slavery hurled!
All servile chains unbind!

Sonnet to Liberty.

THEY tell me, LIBERTY! that, in thy name,
I may not plead for all the human race;
That some are born to bondage and disgrace,
Some to a heritage of wo and shame,
And some to power supreme, and glorious fame.
With my whole soul, I spurn the doctrine base,
And, as an equal brotherhood, embrace
All people, and for all fair freedom claim!
Know this, O man! whate'er thy earthly fate —
GOD NEVER MADE A TYRANT, NOR A SLAVE:
Wo, then, to those who dare to desecrate
His glorious image! — for to all He gave
Eternal rights, which none may violate;
And by a mighty hand, th' oppressed He yet shall save.

No Compromise with Slavery.

Cost what it may, every slave on the American soil must
be liberated from his chains. Nothing is to be put in com-
petition, on the score of value, with the price of his liberty ;
for whatever conflicts with the rights of man must be evil,
and therefore intrinsically worthless. Are we to be intimidated from defending his cause by the fear of consequences? Is it, then, safe to do wrong? Has a just God so
ordered it, that the strong may oppress the weak, the rich
defraud the poor, the merciless torture the innocent, not only
without guilt, but with benefit to mankind? Is there no
similitude between the seed that is sown, and the harvest
which it brings forth? Have cause and effect ceased to
retain an indissoluble connection with each other? On such
a plea, what crime may not be committed with impunity?
what deed of villany may not demand exemption from
rebuke? what system of depravity may not claim protection
against the assaults of virtue?

Let not those who say, that the path of obedience is a
dangerous one, claim to believe in the living and true God.
They deny his omniscience, omnipresence, omnipotence. It
is his will, that the bands of wickedness should be loosed, the
heavy burdens of tyranny undone, the oppressed set free.
They reject it as absurd, impracticable, dangerous. It is his
promise, that the results of emancipation shall be noon-day
light for darkness, health for disease, fertility for barrenness,
prosperity like a spring of water whose waters fail not, the
building up of old waste places, the restoring of paths to dwell
in, the glory of the Lord for a rereward, and his guidance
continually ! They affirm, that the promise is worthless, and
to disregard it is a duty. They exalt the Spirit of Evil above
all that is called God, and raise an Ephesian clamor against

those who will not fall down and worship it. Yet they put on the garb of religion; they extol faith, hope, charity; they build and dedicate temples of worship, in the name of Christ; they profess to be the disciples of Him who came to proclaim liberty to the captives, and the opening of the prison to them that are bound. Unblushing hypocrites! think not, by your pious dissembling, to hide your iniquity from the pure in heart, or to 'circumvent God'! Impious contemners of Divine wisdom and goodness! from your companionship, the spirits of the free shrink with horror!

For more than two centuries, slavery has polluted the American soil. It has grown with the growth, and strengthened with the strength of the republic. Its victims have multiplied, from a single cargo of stolen Africans, to three millions of native-born inhabitants. In our colonial state, it was deemed compatible with loyalty to the mother country. In our revolutionary struggle for independence, it exchanged the sceptre of monarchy for the star-spangled banner of republicanism, under the folds of which it has found ample encouragement and protection. From the days of the Puritans down to the present time, it has been sanctified by the religion, and upheld by the patriotism of the nation. From the adoption of the American Constitution, it has declared war and made peace, instituted and destroyed national banks and tariffs, controlled the army and navy, prescribed the policy of the government, ruled in both houses of Congress, occupied the Presidential chair, governed the political parties, distributed offices of trust and emolument among its worshippers, fettered Northern industry and enterprise, and trampled liberty of speech and of conscience in the dust.

It has exercised absolute mastery over the American Church. In her skirts is found 'the blood of the souls of the poor innocents.' With the Bible in their hands, her priesthood have attempted to prove that slavery came down

12*

from God out of heaven. They have become slave-owners and dealers in human flesh. They have justified robbery, adultery, barbarity, man-stealing and murder, on a frightful scale. They have been among the foremost to crush the sacred cause of emancipation, to cover its advocates with infamy, to oppose the purification of the Church. They have become possessors of the flock, whom they slay, ' and hold themselves not guilty ; and they that sell them say, Blessed be the Lord, for I am rich : and their own shepherds pity them not.'

If slavery be thus entwined around the civil, social, and pecuniary interests of the republic — if the religious sects and political parties are banded together for its safety from internal revolt and external opposition — if the people, awed by its power and corrupted by its influence, are basely bending their knees at its footstool — is it wonderful that Church and State are shaken to their foundations by the rallying cry of Liberty, ' To the rescue ! ' in behalf of imbruted humanity ? Or should it be accounted marvellous, that they who have sternly resolved to effect the utter overthrow of this frightful usurpation are subjected to persecution, reproach, loss of character, and the hazard of life ? Constituting the ' forlorn hope ' in the struggling cause of freedom, they must be prepared to meet all the vicissitudes of the conflict, and to make whatever sacrifices may be needed to achieve the victory. Hereafter, when the song of jubilee shall be sung by those for whose deliverance they toiled so devotedly, their deeds and their memories shall be covered with a halo of glory, and held in grateful remembrance by enfranchised millions.

Slavery must be overthrown. No matter how numerous the difficulties, how formidable the obstacles, how strong the foes to be vanquished — slavery must cease to pollute the land. No matter, whether the event be near or remote, whether the taskmaster willingly or unwillingly relinquish his arbitrary power, whether by a peaceful or a bloody process—slavery must die. No matter, though, to effect it, every party should be torn by dissensions, every sect dashed into fragments, the national compact dissolved, the land filled with the horrors of a civil and a servile war—still, slavery must be buried in the grave of infamy, beyond the possibility of a resurrection. If the State cannot survive the anti-slavery agitation, then let the State perish. If the Church must be cast down by the strugglings of Humanity to be free, then let the Church fall, and its fragments be scattered to the four winds of heaven, never more to curse the earth. If the American Union cannot be maintained, except by immolating human freedom on the altar of tyranny, then let the American Union be consumed by a living thunderbolt, and no tear be shed over its ashes. If the Republic must be blotted out from the roll of nations, by proclaiming liberty to the captives, then let the Republic sink beneath the waves of oblivion, and a shout of joy, louder than the voice of many waters, fill the universe at its extinction.

Against this declaration, none but traitors and tyrants will raise an outcry. It is the mandate of Heaven, and the voice of God. It has righteousness for its foundation, reason for its authority, and truth for its support. It is not vindictive but merciful, not violent but pacific, not destructive but preservative. It is simply asserting the supremacy of right over wrong, of liberty over slavery, of God over man. It is only raising the standard of rectitude from the dust, and placing it on the eternal throne.

The Party or Sect that will suffer by the triumph of justice cannot exist with safety to mankind. The State that cannot tolerate universal freedom must be despotic; and no valid reason can be given why despotism should not at once be hurled to the dust. The Church that is endangered by

the proclamation of eternal truth, and that trades in slaves
and souls of men, is ' the habitation of devils, and the hold
of every foul spirit, and a cage of every unclean and hateful bird ; therefore shall her plagues come in one day, death,
and mourning, and famine ; and she shall be utterly burned
with fire : for strong is the Lord God who judgeth her.'
The Union that can be perpetuated only by enslaving a portion of the people is ' a covenant with death, and an agreement with hell,' and destined to be broken in pieces as a
potter's vessel.   When judgment is laid to the line, and
righteousness to the plummet, the hail shall sweep away the
refuge of lies, and the waters shall overflow the hiding-place.
The Republic that depends for its stability on making war
against the government of God and the rights of man, though
it exalt itself as the eagle, and set its nest among the stars,
shall be cast into the bottomless deep, and the loss of it shall
be a gain to the world.

There must be no compromise with slavery—none
whatever.   Nothing is gained, every thing is lost, by subor-
dinating principle to expediency.   The spirit of freedom
must be inexorable in its demand for the instant release of
all who are sighing in bondage, nor abate one jot or tittle of
its righteous claims.   By one remorseless grasp, the rights
of humanity have been taken away ; and by one strong blow,
the iron hand of usurpation must be made to relinquish its
hold.   The apologist for oppression becomes himself the
oppressor.   To palliate crime is to be guilty of its perpetration.   To ask for a postponement of the case, till a more
convenient season, is to call for a suspension of the moral
law, and to assume that it is right to do wrong, under present
circumstances.   Talk not of other questions to be settled,
of other interests to be secured, of other objects to be attained, before the slave can have his fetters broken.   Nothing
can take precedence of the question of liberty.   No interest

is so momentous as that which involves ' the life of the soul ; ' no object so glorious as the restoration of a man to himself. It is idle to talk of human concerns, where there are not human beings. Slavery annihilates manhood, and puts down in its crimson ledger as chattels personal, those who are created in the image of God. Hence, it tramples under foot whatever pertains to human safety, human prosperity, human happiness. Hence, too, its overthrow is the primary object to be sought, in order to secure private advantage and promote the public weal.

In the present struggle, the test of character is as infallible as it is simple. He that is with the slaveholder is against the slave : he that is with the slave is against the slaveholder. He that thinks, speaks, acts, on the subject of slavery, in accordance with the feelings and wishes of the tyrant, does every thing to perpetuate the thraldom of his victims. When was it ever known for tyranny to devise and execute effective measures for its own overthrow ? Or for the oppressor and the oppressed to be agreed on the great question of equal rights ? Who talks of occupying neutral ground between these hostile parties ? of reconciling them, by prolonging the sufferings of the one, and the cruelty of the other ? of mutually satisfying them as to the means and the plan by which the rod and the chain shall be broken ? I tell such vain babbler, or crafty hypocrite, that he is acting the part of a fool or a knave. Impossibilities are impossibilities ; and to propose their adoption, as the only rational methods by which to dethrone injustice, is an insult to human intelligence. Slavery cannot be conquered by flattery or stratagem. Its dying throes will convulse the land and sea.

Abolitionists ! friends of liberty ! remember that the foe with whom you are in conflict is full ' of all deceivableness of unrighteousness,' and will resort to every artifice to make you quit the field. Put on the whole armor of God; so shall you be invulnerable and invincible ; so shall no weapon against you prosper. The war admits of no parley. No flag of truce must be sent or received by you ; you must neither give nor take any quarters.   As Samuel hewed Agag in pieces, so, with the battle-axe of Truth, you must cleave Slavery to the ground, and give its carcass to the fowls of the air.   May Heaven reinspire your hearts, give new vigor to your arms, direct you blows aright, fill the breast of the enemy with dismay, and grant you a splendid victory !

On completing my Thirty-Fifth Year,

DECEMBER 10, 1840.

IF, to the age of threescore years and ten,
   God of my life ! thou shalt my term prolong,
   Still be it mine to reprobate all wrong,
And save from wo my suffering fellow-men.
Whether, in Freedom's cause, my voice or pen
   Be used by thee, who art my joy and song,
   To vindicate the weak against the strong,
Upon my labors rest thy benison !
O ! not for Afric's sons alone I plead,
   Or her descendants; but for all who sigh
In servile chains, whate'er their caste or creed :
   They not in vain to Heaven send up their cry ;
For all mankind from bondage shall be freed,
And from the earth be chased all forms of tyranny.

Letter to Hon. Peleg Sprague.*

SIR — Whatever respect I have cherished, hitherto, for your character as a patriot and statesman, has fled on perusing your late speech in Faneuil Hall. In my opinion, there is not more of moral turpitude in firing a whole city, than in the delivery of such a speech, in such a place, on such an occasion, and under such circumstances. There seems to be no flesh in your heart. You are a man — and yet the eulogist of those tyrants, who are trampling your brother in the dust! You are a husband — a parent — and yet join in upholding a traffic and a system, which ruthlessly sunder the holiest ties of life! You are an American — and yet can look complacently, nay, approvingly, upon the brutal enslavement of more than one-sixth portion of YOUR OWN COUNTRYMEN! I was about to add, you are a Christian — but I dare not thus libel Christianity. ' He that saith he is in the light, and hateth his brother, is in

---

* The speech which elicited this Letter was made at the great Anti-Abolition Meeting which was held in Faneuil Hall, August 21, 1835. Among other speakers on that occasion were Hon. HARRISON GRAY OTIS and RICHARD FLETCHER, Esq. The period was one of the hottest excitement against the abolitionists, in Boston, and in all parts of the country. Among the evil consequences of this meeting was the memorable mob, boastingly composed of 'five thousand gentlemen of property and standing,' on the 21st of October, which, in broad daylight, assailed a meeting of the Female Anti-Slavery Society, held at 46 Washington Street, violently dispersed it, overawed the city authorities, and seized Mr. GARRISON, for the purpose of wreaking their fury upon him, who, after being nearly stripped of his clothing, was with difficulty rescued out of their hands, and had to be temporarily committed to the jail in Leverett Street, to save his life! [SEE APPENDIX.]

darkness even until now.' 'If a man say, I love God, and
hateth his brother, he is a liar. For he that loveth not his
brother whom he hath seen, how can he love God whom he
hath not seen?' You have dared to stand up, even in the
OLD CRADLE OF LIBERTY, hostile to human freedom; you
have sought to base the pillars of your popularity upon the
necks of down-trodden millions; and you have uttered sentiments, which elicit thunders of applause from all that is
loathsome in impurity, hateful in revenge, base in extortion,
dastardly in oppression. You are in amicable companionship and popular repute with thieves and adulterers; with
slave-holders, slave-breeders, slave-dealers, slave-destroyers;
with those who trample law and order beneath their feet;
with the plunderers of the public mail; with ruffians who
insult, pollute and lacerate helpless women; and with con-
spirators against the lives and liberties of New England
citizens. These facts are undeniable. Talk not of more
honorable associates: none are honorable, who throw the
weight of their influence into the scale of oppression.

You affect to think that the abolitionists are laboring in
the wrong section of the Union. You insinuate, that, while
they preach the doctrine, ' We must do right, regardless of
consequences,' none are more craven in spirit; and add —

'They insist, that it is right that they should urge their doctrines
for the conviction of the South. Ask them why they do not go
and preach them there, where they most desire to make converts —
they reply, Why! we should be in danger of our lives! Then
they begin to think of consequences. So that the practical result
of that proposition, which sounds so well in the abstract, is, that
they are to go on regardless of consequences to others, but not
without a due regard to themselves.'

Sir, there may be wit, but there is little truth, in the above
extract. To do right, is always to regard consequences,
both to ourselves and to others. Since you are pleased to

banter us for prosecuting our labors at the North, I will take for my text the interrogation that is so constantly, either by ignorance or impudence, propounded to us. It is this: —

'WHY DON'T YOU GO TO THE SOUTH?'

I proudly answer — Not because we are afraid to go there. Not because we are not prepared for danger, persecution, outrage, and death. Not because the dungeon or the halter, the rack or the stake, appals us. Yet the question is sneeringly put, and sometimes with murder evidently in the heart, as if we were deficient in fortitude and courage, with all our seeming boldness. 'O, forsooth! it is very safe and convenient for Mr. Garrison to denounce the holders of slaves a thousand miles off, in Boston! A great deal of heroism is required to do this! But he is very careful to keep out of the slave States. Why don't he go to the South? Let him go there, and denounce slavery, and we will then believe that he is sincere.' This is the language which is constantly uttered — by men, too, permit me to say, who have never peculiarly signalized themselves in any hazardous enterprise, whether moral or physical. I am vain enough to believe, that those who bring this charge of cowardice against me do not doubt my readiness to go wherever duty requires. Will they give me no credit for having published an anti-slavery publication in Maryland, as long as it could be sustained by a meagre patronage? — a publication in which my denunciations of slavery and slaveholders were as severe as any to be found in the Liberator. Did my spirit quail under my imprisonment in a Southern cell? Is it true, that I am hazarding nothing by my advocacy of the cause of emancipation, even in Boston? Has no endurance, no unusual courage, been required to oppose all classes of society, and to sustain the odium, derision and hatred of a slaveholding nation? Is it nothing to have large rewards offered by a Southern legislature, and by private combina-

13

tions, for my seizure and destruction? Sir, the slaveholders of the South may call me a fanatic — they may call
me a madman, or an incendiary, or an agitator, and believe
me to be such; but to call me a coward — that is an epithet
which they have too much good sense to apply to me.
They regard me in any other light than that of a craven:
all the trembling, and shrinking, and alarm, is felt and manifested on their part — not on mine. I may be rash — I
may be obstinate — but no fear of man shall deter me from
a faithful discharge of my duty to the oppressed. As for
mere animal courage, it is nothing to excel in it — no proof
of true bravery.

'Why don't you go to the South?'

Why, Sir, when we denounce the tyranny exercised over
the miserable Poles, do we not go into the dominions of the
Russian autocrat, and beard him to his face? Why not go
to Constantinople, and protest against the oppression of the
Greeks? Why assail the despotic governments of Europe
here in the United States? Why, then, should we go into
the slaveholding States, to assail their towering wickedness,
at a time when we are sure that we should be gagged, or
imprisoned, or put to death, if we went thither? Why
rashly throw ourselves into the ocean, or commit ourselves
to the flames, or cast ourselves into the jaws of the lion?
Understand me, Sir. I do not mean to say, that even the
certainty of destruction is, in itself, a valid reason for our
refusing to go to the South; for we are bound to take up
any cross, or incur any peril, in the discharge of our duty
to God and our suffering brother. Prove to me that it is
imperatively my duty, in view of all the circumstances of
the case, to locate myself among slaveholders, and I will
not hesitate to do so, though (to borrow the strong language
of Martin Luther) every tile upon their houses were a
devil. Moral courage — duty — self-consecration — all have

their proper limits. When He who knew no fear — the immaculate Redeemer — saw that his enemies intended to cast him down from the brow of a hill, he prudently withdrew from their midst. When he sent forth his apostles, he said unto them, ' When they persecute you in one city, flee ye into another.' Was there any cowardice in this conduct, or in this advice ?

' WHY DON'T YOU GO TO THE SOUTH ? '

If we should go there, and fall — as fall we certainly should — martyrs to our zeal, our enemies would still call us, what we then should deserve to be called, fanatics and madmen. Pointing at our mangled bodies, they would commence their derisions afresh. ' Poor fools !' they would exclaim — ' insane enthusiasts! thus to rush into the cage of the tiger, with the certain knowledge that he would tear them in pieces !' And this, Sir, would be the eulogy which they would pronounce over us !

' WHY DON'T YOU GO TO THE SOUTH ? '

Because it is essential that the beam should first be cast out of the eyes of the people of the free States, before they attempt to cast out the mote in the eyes of the people of the slave States. Because they who denounce fraud, and cruelty, and oppression, should first become honest, and merciful, and free, themselves. ' Thou that sayest, a man should not steal — dost thou steal ? ' Thou that preachest, a man should not be a slaveholder — art thou a slaveholder? ' Physician, heal thyself !'

' WHY DON'T YOU GO TO THE SOUTH ? '

Have I answered the question satisfactorily ? If not, Sir, you will help me to additional reasons for our staying here at the North, in my answer to another question, which is iterated on all occasions, as if it for ever ended the controversy — viz. :

' WHAT HAVE WE TO DO WITH SOUTHERN SLAVERY ? '

This question is put, sometimes with reference to legislation — at other times, it refers to moral obligation. I answer, then, that WE, THE PEOPLE OF THE UNITED STATES, have legislated on the subject of slavery, and we have a right to legislate upon it, within certain limits. As to our moral obligation, it belongs to our nature, and is a part of our accountability, of which neither time nor distance, neither climate nor location, neither republican nor monarchical government, can divest us. Let there be but one slave on the face of the globe — let him stand on one extremity of the globe, and place me on the other — let every people, and tribe, and clime, and nation, stand as barriers between him and myself : still, I am bound to sympathise with him — to pray, and toil, and plead for his deliverance — to make known his wrongs, and vindicate his rights. It may not be in my power, it may not be my duty, directly to emancipate him ; for the power rests in the hands of the tyrant who keeps him in chains, and it is his duty to break them asunder. But it matters not, except to demand an increase of zeal and activity, if every interposing tribe or nation, if the whole world is to be changed, before that solitary slave can go free.   Then I will begin with him who stands next by my side, and with my associates, and with my country ; and if the impulse must be sent by proxy, if every man, woman and child must be abolitionised by detail, before the captive can be disenthralled, I am nevertheless bound to commence the work, if no others will, and to co-operate with them if they have begun it.   Why ?   Because he is my neighbor, though occupying the remotest point of the earth ; and I am charged by Him, ' who spake as never man spake,' to love my neighbor as myself.   Because he is my brother, for whom Christ died ; and if Christ estimated him so highly as to die for him, then, surely, he is an object worthy of my sympathy and regard.   Because by his enslavement, man is no longer recognised as man, but as a brute, and our whole species is degraded. Because by it the laws of nature and of spirit are violated, the moral government of the universe is rebelled against, and God is insulted and dethroned, by the usurpation of his power and authority. Because by it an example is set, which, if passively submitted to, may lead to the enslavement of others — of a community — of a people — of myself. Enslave but a single human being, and the liberty of the world is put in peril. Nay, all the slavery that exists — all the tyranny of past ages — originated from a single act of oppression, committed upon some helpless and degraded being. Hence it is, that, whether I contemplate slavery singly or in the aggregate, my soul kindles within me — the entire man is moved with indignation and abhorrence — I cannot pause, I cannot slumber — I am ready for attack, and will admit of no truce, and of no compromise. The war is a war of extermination; and I will perish before an inch shall be surrendered, seeing that the liberties of mankind, the happiness and harmony of the universe, and the authority and majesty of Almighty God, are involved in the issue.

If, Sir, I am again asked, ‘ What have we to do with slavery ? ’ I answer by a retort — ‘ What have we to do with heathenism ? ’ And yet —

‘ From Greenland’s icy mountains,
To India’s coral strand ’ —

from frozen Labrador to the sunny plains of Palestine — from the rivers to the ends of the earth — from the rising of the sun to its going down — our missionary line is extended, and we are continually sending out fresh troops to invade the dominions, and destroy the supremacy of the Man of Sin, and of the false Prophet — and Juggernaut is tottering to his fall; we are disregarding institutions and laws, cus-

13*

toms and ceremonies, governments and rulers, prohibitions and penalties ; we are setting ' a man at variance against his father, and the daughter against her mother, and the daughter-in-law against her mother-in-law ; ' and we make a man's foes to be they of his own household ; we are troubling the peace of Africa, of Asia, of the isles of the sea, and seeking to turn the world upside down, that He may come whose right it is to reign.

What have we to do with intemperance in England and France ? And yet, Sir, we sent out to those countries the Apostle of Temperance, to scatter light, to reveal iniquity, to prick the consciences of men, to preach of righteousness, temperance, and a judgment to come — and to sow the seeds of holy strife between the distillers, the importers, the rum-sellers and the rum-drinkers, on the one hand, in those countries, and the friends of sobriety, mercy and good will, on the other.

What have we to do with Southern slavery ? What has England to do with it ? And yet, a few years since, the American Colonization Society (of which, Mr. Sprague, you are a champion) sent out an agent to that country, to procure the charities of her philanthropists, in order to undermine and abolish American slavery — this being the great object of the Society, as stated to the British public by that agent. Now, if Old England may meddle with this ' delicate ' subject, surely New England may venture to do so likewise. If that which is remote, is or ought to be interested in the abolition of American slavery, how much more that which is near !

Sir, what have we — what has Congress — to do with the oppression of the Greeks and Poles ? And yet, as a people, how have we prayed for their deliverance ! how warmly have we denounced Russia and Turkey ! how cheerfully have we taxed ourselves to send food and raiment, men and

money, banners and arms, in aid of the brave and struggling champions of liberty! how have we lifted up our
voices to cheer them onward in the strife of blood! how
have we taken them to our arms, when they were crushed
and scattered abroad, and given them an asylum, and bound
up their wounds, and comforted their souls! what speeches
have been made in their behalf upon the floor of Congress!
Now, Sir, have we so much to do with foreign, and nothing
to do with domestic oppression — an oppression far more
dreadful than that which the Greek or Pole has ever suffered?

What had the South to do with the 'three days' in Paris —
the overthrow of tyranny in France? And yet, in honor
of that sanguinary event, the patriotic slaveholders of Baltimore, and Richmond, and Charleston, kindled bonfires,
illuminated their dwellings, rung the bells, fired cannon,
formed processions, made orations, devoured dinners, and
ingurgitated toasts, even to ebriety!

What had Lafayette to do with the quarrel about liberty
between us and the mother country? Shall we apply to
him the infamous epithets which you have cast upon our
moral Lafayette? Shall we call him 'a foreign emissary,'
'a professed agitator,' and talk of his 'audacious interference'? Should he have been sent back to 'prostrate the
triple power of the Priesthood, the Aristocracy, and the
Throne?' Sir, will you answer these questions?

You venture the assertion, 'that the agitators here are
few, and that even the whole number of those who have
permitted their names to be enrolled in these societies is
small.' Perhaps this conviction furnishes the principal reason why you are found in opposition to them; for, to borrow
the classical language of your admirer, the Richmond Whig,
politicians 'know too well which side their bread is buttered
on,' ever to be caught supporting the cause of moral reform

in its unpopular stages. Let New England become thoroughly abolitionised, and you, our distinguished opponents
who now tower so loftily, will at once ' hide your diminished
heads,' and become the obsequious followers of public sentiment! Not one of you will be found in the minority!
About once in every six months, the abolitionists are scattered to the winds of heaven by their spasmodic opponents,
who rush upon them like a hurricane, fill the air with feathers, brickbats, and all sorts of argumentative. missiles, and
burn and destroy all before them! Semi-annually, too, the
Constitution is triumphant! Still, the ghost of murdered
Banquo ' will not down.' In a short time, the abolitionists
are seen in mulitudinous array every where, marching from
village to village, from city to city, from State to State,
augmenting their number at every step, and evidently invig-
orated by the respite from their labors which the storm
enabled them to take. Once more, however, they have
been utterly annihilated — and again has the Constitution
been rescued from the hand of treason! It is more than
probable, that the world will soon witness another miracle of
restoration; for Truth, like our Savior, may be scourged,
and crucified, and buried — and the tomb may be sealed,
and a watch set — but it has a divine energy in itself, that
will burst the cerements of the grave, and reign triumphant
over death. Nay, even the Courier and Enquirer begins
already to despond! Hear it — ' It is dreadful to contemplate the short period of time which has elapsed since these
abolitionists were a mere handful, to the MULTITUDE they
have since become.' So, then, we derive from our opponents these instructive but paradoxical facts — that without
numbers, we are multitudinous; without power, we are sap-
ping the foundation of the confederacy; without a plan, we
are hastening the abolition of slavery; and without wealth
or talent, we are rapidly converting the nation!

Sir, the success of any great moral enterprise does not depend upon numbers. Slavery will be overthrown long before a majority of all the people shall have called, voluntarily and on the score of principle, for its abolition. Ten righteous men would have saved Sodom. Even in a physical campaign, how often is a subordinate force victorious! What, then, is the promise to those who engage in a moral contest, that God may be glorified, and a rebellious world subdued? ' One shall chase a thousand, and two put ten thousand to flight.' This has recently been fulfilled before our eyes, in the cause of temperance — and its faithfulness is continually verified in the strife of Truth with Error. Cowardice, shame and irresolution are the treacherous companions of wickedness, and they readily yield to courage, virtue and integrity. Sir, we may be branded with opprobrious epithets — we may be called ' agitators,' or ' fanatics,' or ' incendiaries ' — but we deem it a very small thing to be judged of man's, and especially of a politician's judgment. Ours is that fanaticism which listens to the voice of God, which believes his promises and obeys his commandments, which remembers those in bonds as bound with them. Ours is the agitation of humanity in view of cruelty — of virtue in opposition to pollution — of holiness against impiety. It is the agitation of thunder and lightning, to purify a corrupt atmosphere — of the storm, to give new vigor and freshness to field and forest. Ours is the incendiary spirit of truth, that burns up error — of freedom, that melts the fetters of the bondman — of impartial love, that warms every breast with the sacred fire of heaven. Could any men but those of extraordinary moral courage and endurance sustain, unflinchingly, a contest which requires such loss of reputation, and such hazard of property and life? They are the winnowing of the nation. Indeed, a perfect analogy is seen in the history of the abolition of the foreign slave-trade, as contrasted with the present anti-slavery struggle. The venerable CLARKSON, at the close of his instructive History, makes the following remarkable statement — remarkable, because it exactly applies to the moral separation which is now taking place in our land on the great question of emancipation. Of the conflict in Great Britain, he says —

'It has been useful, also, in the discrimination of moral character. In private life, it has enabled us to distinguish the virtuous from the more vicious part of the community. I have had occasion to know many thousand persons in the course of my travels on this subject; and I can truly say, that the part which these took on this great question was always a true criterion of their moral character. It has shown the general philanthropist. It has unmasked the vicious, in spite of his pretension to virtue. It has separated the moral statesman from the wicked politician. It has shown us who, in the legislative and executive offices of our country, are fit to save, and who to destroy a nation.'

Sir, the ground that you and your colleagues maintain is, that the free States are not involved in the guilt of slavery; that we have no right, morally, (for as to our political right, there is no difference of opinion,) to meddle with it; that the slave States alone are criminal, if there be any criminality attaching to the system; that the doctrine of immediate emancipation is impracticable and dangerous; and that anti-slavery associations are unwarrantable and seditious. Abolitionists hold that the North and the South are alike involved in guilt, whether past, present or prospective; that, therefore, it is the right and the duty of the people, every where, to seek the overthrow of slavery by moral means, and to wash the blood from their hands individually; that it is unjust and pharisaical for one portion of the country to say to another, — 'Stand by, for I am holier than thou;' and that the doctrine of immediate emancipation is the doctrine of common sense, common honesty, and the Bible.

Sir, you have a strange method of proving that we of the North are not involved in the guilt of slavery. You expressly declare —

1. 'The Constitution provides for the suppressing of insurrections; we should rally under the Constitution, we should respond to its call: nay, we should not wait for such a requisition, but on the instant should rush forward with fraternal emotions to defend our brethren from desolation and massacre.' That is, we have agreed to keep the slaves in bondage, and to crush or exterminate them if they should rise, as did our fathers, to obtain their freedom by violence: therefore, we are guiltless of their oppression!

2. 'The Constitution recognises and provides for the continuance of slavery:' therefore, we are not guilty!

3. 'It does sanction, it does UPHOLD slavery:' therefore, we are not responsible!

4. 'Few parts of the Constitution were more carefully and deliberately weighed:' therefore, we are sinless!

Now, Sir, in presenting these facts to prove the innocence of the North, it seems to me that you must really believe that 'justice has fled to brutish beasts, and men have lost their reason.' Or do you mean to mock us, as those who cannot discriminate between honesty and knavery — liberty and oppression? What would you think, if an associate of thieves should be arrested and brought up for trial, and, to prove his own and their innocence, should begin to specify what robberies they had perpetrated, what more they meant to effect, and what part each had to perform in plundering the community? You are a lawyer, Sir, and can readily decide how this testimony would operate. Your plea is just as rational: as well might the assassin bring the body of his victim into court, and brandish the reeking knife over his head, to prove that he ought not to be accused of murder! 'As for our iniquities, we know them.'

Oh, Sir, when has a nation sinned so perversely, so under-
standingly, against so much light, as our own ?   Say not, as
did certain transgressors of old, ' We are delivered to do all
these abominations.'   The whole world must see, that, for
our own aggrandizement, we have most basely sacrificed the
rights and liberties of an immense multitude of our fellow-
creatures — consigning them to a bondage, ' one hour of
which is fraught with more misery than ages of that which
our fathers rose in rebellion to oppose.'

' Go, look through the kingdoms of earth,
   From Indus, all round to the Pole,
And something of goodness, of honor and worth,
   Shall brighten the sins of the soul :—
But we are alone in our shame,
   The world cannot liken us there ;
Oppression and vice have disfigured our name,
   Beyond the low reach of compare ;
Stupendous in guilt, we shall lend them through time
A proverb, a bye-word, for treach'ry and crime ! '

Now that space for repentance is yet mercifully granted
to us, let us abase ourselves, as did the inhabitants of Nine-
veh, and God will rebuke the destroyer for our sake, and
open the windows of heaven, and pour upon us such blessings that there shall not be room to receive them.

' Thus saith the Lord of hosts, the God of Israel, If ye
thoroughly amend your ways and your doings; if ye thoroughly execute judgment between a man and his neighbor ;
if ye oppress not the stranger, the fatherless, and the widow,
and shed not innocent blood ; then will I cause you to dwell
in the land that I gave to your fathers, for ever and ever.

Departure of George Thompson for England.

He has gone! The paragon of modern eloquence — the benefactor of two nations — the universal philanthropist — is no longer in our midst! Abandoning the field of his well-deserved and ever increasing popularity — bidding adieu to his native shores, and to a vast multitude of as dear and estimable friends as one man ever possessed — he committed himself, with his family, to the perils of the deep, and fearlessly ventured, in the cause of the bound and bleeding slave, to encounter the still greater perils which he was conscious awaited him upon these shores. It was no ordinary sacrifice of ease, preferment, interest and popularity, that he made, when he resolved to plead the heaven-originated cause of universal emancipation in a land of republican despots and Christian kidnappers. He exchanged comfort for severe hardship; he sought abasement rather than exaltation; for safety, he substituted peril; he sacrificed his interest for the pleasure of doing good; and he consented to leave his popularity among good men at home, that he might be honored with the abuse and proscription of wicked men abroad. His departure from England was viewed with regret, yet admiration, by a noble and philanthropic people. They would have gladly retained him in their midst, had they not been convinced that Providence had a great work for him to perform in this hemisphere: they did not love themselves less, but they loved the perishing slaves more. Wherever he went to bid them farewell, they rushed in crowds to hang upon the thrilling accents of his lips, to pay him the respect of grateful hearts, and to bestow on him the testimonials of their love. Never, perhaps, did man break through stronger ties to make himself an exile, and a by-word and gazing-stock among the

14

plunderers and oppressors of the human race. A physical Lafayette had come to these shores on an errand of patriotism, and the applause was universal. A moral Lafayette came hither on a mission of peaceful liberty and holy love, and the hosts of heaven rejoiced, and gave glory to God. Both excited the fear and hatred of tyrants: the former was dreaded for his rank and influence — the latter for his Christian courage and spiritual might. The former came equipped with carnal weapons, to sunder the chains of political oppression by the arm of violence: the latter came with the whole armor of God, having his loins girt about with truth, and having on the breast-plate of righteousness, and his feet shod with the preparation of the gospel of peace, and taking the shield of faith, the helmet of salvation, and the sword of the Spirit, to effect a two-fold emancipation, both of the body and the soul. The former slaughtered opposing forces, to vindicate the rights of man: the latter toiled unceasingly to maintain the justice of God in the peaceful deliverance of the captive, through conviction of sin and the spirit of repentance. The former aimed to overthrow an unjust exercise of monarchical power; the latter, to extirpate the most dreadful form of despotism that the world had ever witnessed — chattel slavery.

He has gone! And with him will go the prayers and blessings, the gratitude and love, the respect and admiration, of all those who cherish an innate and holy hatred of oppression, and who hold no fellowship with the unfruitful works of darkness. Around the hearts of thousands in this country, his memory is entwined with the ties of a deathless affection; for they have known him, and can testify of his extraordinary worth. What a rich freight of gratitude would accompany him, more to be desired than the treasures of royal argosies, from millions who yet pine in slavery, if they could understand how much he has suffered and hazarded to loose their fetters! But their emancipated descendants will not forget the debt!

He has gone! But not in vain did he come hither. By his presence, and the power of his victorious eloquence, and the resistless energy of his movements, he has shaken the land from side to side. In one year, he has accomplished the work of many. At the mention of his name, republican tyrants stand aghast, and their knees smite violently against each other. Unable to hide the bloody stains that disfigure their polluted garments — conscious of their full exposure to the detestation and rebuke of a horror-stricken world — despairing of ever regaining an honorable reputation, until they emancipate the victims of their lust and avarice — they have sought to destroy the advocates of righteous liberty, with wolf-like ferocity and fiendish hate. Especially have they planned to abduct and murder the man, who, having been signally instrumental in breaking the fetters of eight hundred thousand slaves in the British Colonies, heroically came to these shores to assist in emancipating a still larger number of bleeding captives. But, thanks be to God, he has walked unharmed through the fire which they kindled to consume him, and the smell thereof has not passed upon his garments.

He has gone! But not to cease from his labors in the cause of mercy. He has a mighty work to perform in England, and there he will toil like an unbound giant. With the materials which he has industriously accumulated in this country, and which he has carried with him, he cannot fail to rouse up and concentrate the entire sympathies and energies of the people of Great Britain, in opposition to American slavery; and it is by the pressure of popular opinion abroad, as well as at home, that the bloody system is to be tumbled into ruins. Let the same withering public sentiment prevail throughout Christendom respecting the guilt of slaveholding, as now obtains in opposition to the diabolical slave trade, and the day of jubilee will be ushered in without delay. Our pride, as a nation, will not be able much longer to bear the taunts and jeers of the world, in view of our hypocrisy, falsehood and oppression ; and our consciences, seared though they be as with a hot iron, will yet be awakened to remorse and repentance by the thunders of Sinai and the melting accents of Calvary. The Christians of Great Britain, of all denominations, will multiply their warnings, rebukes and exhortations to their brethren in this country, and they cannot speak in vain.

He has gone ! The dagger of a murderous nation has been pointed at his heart, and he has been hunted like a partridge upon the mountains. He came to us on an errand of mercy, drawn by the ties of Christ, and spared no pains to bring us to repentance for our manifold transgressions. To flatter us was easy — but he loved the truth, and hated falsehood ; and for declaring the truth, his life was placed in continual jeopardy !

He has gone ! But the foreign MAN-MONKEY * remains behind, to show us how exactly he can grin like an ape, look like an ape, climb and chatter like an ape, and finally die like an ape — and his popularity is increasing daily !

---

* Allusion is here made to a foreign mountebank, who was at that time (the fall of 1835) peregrinating through the country, and exhibiting himself as ' THE MAN-MONKEY.'

Song of Welcome.*

I.

Our noble advocate and friend,
 Thy presence here we hail!
But, O! our feelings to express,
 The strongest words must fail!
  Yet still accept a gateful song—
   Our blessings on thee rest—
  For thou hast pleaded well the cause
   Of all who are oppressed.

II.

Thy love of liberty extends
 To every race and clime;
Thy hatred of oppression burns
 To the remotest time:
  In thee the slave a champion finds,
   Intrepid, faithful, strong,
  Though scorn and wrath assail thy course,
   And perils round thee throng.

III.

While traffickers in human flesh
 Their teeth upon thee gnash;
While for thy precious life they hunt,
 Who wield the gory lash;
  While their abettors here conspire
   To howl and mob thee down;
  Thou need'st no higher meed of praise—
   Can'st wear no brighter crown!

---

* After an absence of fifteen years, GEORGE THOMPSON again visited the United States, and on the evening of Nov. 18th, 1850, was enthusiastically welcomed by a crowded assembly of the colored citizens of Boston, for which occasion this Song was written.

14*

IV.

All noble spirits of the past —
 Saints, martyrs, heroes true —
All of the present, loving God
 And man, the wide earth through —
  Are with thee in this trial-hour,*
   To strengthen and applaud —
  And angel voices cheer thee on,
   In th' name of Christ, our Lord!

V.

The ransomed bondmen of the isles
 Thy name shall shout with pride;
And India's plundered millions bless
 Their champion, true and tried;
  And England's crushed and toiling poor, —
   Columbia's fettered race, —
  Thy memory ever shall revere,
   Thy brow with laurels grace.

VI.

Once more we greet thee with delight,
 Remembering ' auld lang syne,'
And pray kind Heaven may richly smile,
 Through life, on thee and thine!
  We offer thee a grateful song —
   Our blessings on thee rest —
  For thou hast pleaded well the cause
   Of all who are oppressed!

---

* Notwithstanding so long a period had elapsed since Mr. THOMPSON first came to the United States, the pro-slavery spirit of the land was exceedingly alarmed and terrified at his presence; and, during his sojourn of seven months, constantly endeavored to prevent his being heard, by mobocratic violence; but he triumphed over all opposition, and returned home, carrying with him the benedictions of a host of admiring friends.

Words of Encouragement to the Oppressed.

I never rise to address a colored audience, without feeling ashamed of my own color; ashamed of being identified with a race of men, who have done you so much injustice, and who yet retain so large a portion of your brethren in servile chains. To make atonement, in part, for this conduct, I have solemnly dedicated my health, and strength, and life, to your service. I love to plan and to work for your social, intellectual, and spiritual advancement. My happiness is augmented with yours: in your sufferings I participate.

Henceforth I am ready, on all days, on all convenient occasions, in all suitable places, before any sect or party, at whatever peril to my person, character or interest, to plead the cause of my colored countrymen in particular, or of human rights in general. For this purpose, there is no day too holy, no place improper, no body of men too inconsiderable to address. For this purpose, I ask no church to grant me authority to speak—I require no ordination—I am not careful to consult Martin Luther, or John Calvin, or His Holiness the Pope. It is a duty, which, as a lover of justice, I am bound to discharge; as a lover of my fellow-men, I ought not to shun; as a lover of Jesus Christ, and of his equalizing, republican and benevolent precepts, I rejoice to perform.

Your condition, as a people, has long attracted my attention, secured my efforts, and awakened in my breast a flame of sympathy, which neither the winds nor waves of opposition can ever extinguish. It is the lowness of your estate, in the estimation of the world, which exalts you in my eyes. It is the distance that separates you from the blessings and privileges of society, which brings you so closely to my

affections.   It is the unmerited scorn, reproach and persecution of your persons, by those whose complexion is colored
like my own, which command for you my sympathy and
respect.   It is the fewness of your friends—the multitude of your enemies—that induces me to stand forth in
your defence.

Countrymen and Friends !   I wish to gladden your hearts,
and to invigorate your hopes.   Be assured, your cause is
going onward, right onward.   The signs of the times do
indeed show forth great and glorious and sudden changes in
the condition of the oppressed.   The whole firmament is
tremulous with an excess of light; the earth is moved out
of its place; the wave of revolution is dashing in pieces
ancient and mighty empires ; the hearts of tyrants are beginning to fail them for fear, and for looking forward to those
things which are to come upon the earth.   There is

> 'A voice on every wave,
> A sound on every sea !
> The watchword of the brave,
> The anthem of the free !
> Where'er a wind is rushing,
> Where'er a stream is gushing,
> The swelling sounds are heard,
> Of man to freeman calling,
> Of broken fetters falling—
> And, like the carol of a cageless bird,
> The bursting shout of Freedom's rallying word !'

Let this be an occasion of joy.   Why should it not be so ?
Is not the heaven over your heads, which has so long been
clothed in sackcloth, beginning to disclose its starry principalities, and illumine your pathway ?   Do you not see the pitiless
storm, which has so long been pouring its rage upon you,
breaking away, and a bow of promise, as glorious as that
which succeeded the ancient deluge, spanning the sky,—a

token that, to the end of time, the billows of prejudice and oppression shall no more cover the earth, to the destruction of your race; but seed-time and harvest shall never fail, and the laborer shall eat the fruit of his hands? Is not your cause developing like the spring? Yours has been a long and rigorous winter. The chill of contempt, the frost of adversity, the blast of persecution, the storm of oppression—all have been yours. There was no sustenance to be found—no prospect to delight the eye, or inspire the drooping heart—no golden ray to dissipate the gloom. The waves of derision were stayed by no barrier, but made a clear breach over you. But, now—thanks be to God! that dreary winter is rapidly hastening away. The sun of humanity is going steadily up, from the horizon to its zenith, growing larger and brighter, and melting the frozen earth beneath its powerful rays. The genial showers of repentance are softly falling upon the barren plain; the wilderness is budding like the rose; the voice of joy succeeds the notes of wo; and hope, like the lark, is soaring upwards, and warbling hymns at the gate of heaven.

And this is but the outbursting of spring. What, think you, shall be the summer and autumn?

> 'Then shall the trembling mourner come,
> And bind his sheaves, and bear them home;
> The voice, long broke with sighs, shall sing,
> And heaven with hallelujahs ring!'

This is but 'the twilight, the dim dawn' of day. What, then, shall be the brightness of the day itself? These are but a few drops of mercy. What shall be the full shower, the rolling tide? These are but crumbs of comfort, to prevent you wholly from perishing. What shall be the bountiful table?

Why should this not be an occasion of joy, instead of

sorrow? Listen to those trumpet tones which come swelling on the winds of the Atlantic, and which shall bring an
echo from every harp in heaven! If there is joy in that
blissful abode over one sinner that repenteth, how mighty
and thrilling must it be over a repentant nation! And Great
Britain is that nation. Her people are humbling themselves
before God, and before those whom they have so long held
in bondage. Their voices are breaking, in peals of thunder,
upon the ear of Parliament, demanding the immediate and
utter overthrow of slavery in all the colonies; and in obedience to their will, the mandate is about being issued by Parliament, which shall sever at a blow the chains of eight
hundred thousand slaves! What heart can conceive, what
pen or tongue describe, the happiness which must flow
from the consummation of this act? That cruel lash, which
has torn so many tender bodies, and is dripping with innocent blood; that lash, which has driven so many human victims, like beasts, to their unrequited toil; that lash, whose
sounds are heard from the rising of the sun to its decline,
mingled with the shrieks of bleeding sufferers; that lash is
soon to be cast away, never again to wound the flesh, or
degrade those who are made in the image of God. And
those fetters of iron, which have bound so many in ignominious servitude, and wasted their bodies, and borne them down
to an untimely grave, shall be shivered in pieces, as the
lightning rends the pine, and the victims of tyranny leap
forth, ' redeemed, regenerated, and disenthralled, by the irresistible genius of universal emancipation.' And that darkness, which has for so many generations shrouded the minds
of the slaves—making them like the brutes that perish—
shall give way to the light of freedom and religion. O, how
transforming the change! In contemplating it, my imagination overpowers the serenity of my soul, and makes language seem poor and despicable.

Cheers for Great Britain! cheers for her noble men and women! cheers for the bright example which they are setting to the world! cheers for their generous sympathy in the cause of the oppressed in our own country!

Why should we not rejoice this evening, brethren? Find we nothing at home to raise our drooping spirits, to invigorate our hopes, and to engage our efforts? Have we made no progress, either in self-improvement, or in the cause of bleeding humanity? Are there no cheering signs of the times, in our moral sky, upon which we may fix our joyful gaze?

Look, in the first place, at the abolition standard—more gorgeous and spirit-stirring than the star-spangled banner—floating high in the air! Fresh is the breeze that meets it! bright are the sunny rays which adorn it! Around it thousands are gathering, with high and holy courage, to contend, not with carnal but spiritual weapons, against the powers of darkness. O, the loftiness of that spirit which animates them! It towers above the Alps, it pierces beyond the clouds. O, the intensity of that flame of brotherly love which burns within their breasts! It never can burn out— nor can many waters extinguish it. O, the stability of that faith which sustains them under all their toils and trials! It is firmer than the foundations of the earth—it is strong as the throne of God. O, the generous daring of that moral principle which inspires their hearts and governs their actions! Neither reproach nor persecution, neither wealth nor power, neither bolts nor bars, neither the gibbet nor the stake, shall be able to subdue it. Yes, my colored countrymen, these are the men—ay, and the women, too, who have espoused your cause. And they will stand by it, until life be extinct. They will not fail in strength, or faith, or courage, or zeal, or action. Loud as the tempest of oppression may rage around them, above it shall their rally-

ing cry be heard in the thunder-tone of heaven. Dark as
their pathway may be, it shall blaze with the light of truth
in their possession. Numberless as may be the enemies
who surround them, they will not retreat from the field; for
He who is mightier than legions of men and devils is the
captain of their salvation, and will give them the victory. I
know your advocates well — I know the spirit which actuates
them. Whether they reside in the East, or West, or North,
they have but one object — their hearts are stirred with the
same pulsation; their eye is single, their motives are pure.
Tell me not of the bravery and devotedness of those whose
life-blood reddened the plains of Marathon, poured out in
defence of liberty. Tell me not of the Spartan band, with
Leonidas at their head, who defended the pass of Thermopylæ against a Persian host. I award to them the meed of
animal courage; but the heroism of blood and carnage is as
much below the patient endurance of wrong, and the cheerful forgiveness of injury, as the earth is below the sky — it
is as often displayed by brute animals as by men. With
infinitely higher satisfaction, with a warmer glow of emula-
tion, with more intense admiration, do I contemplate the
abolition phalanx in the United States, who are maintaining
your cause, unflinchingly, through evil report — for the good
report is yet to come — and at the imminent peril of their
lives; and, what is dearer than life, the sacrifice of their
reputation. If ever there was a cause which established the
disinterestedness and integrity of its supporters, yours is
that cause. They who are contending for the immediate
abolition of slavery, the destruction of its ally, the American Colonization Society, and the bestowal of equal rights
and privileges upon the whole colored population, well knew
what would be the consequences of their advocacy to themselves. They knew that slander would blacken their characters with infamy; that their pleadings would be received

with ridicule and reproach; that persecution would assail
them on the right hand and on the left; that the dungeon
would yawn for their bodies; that the dagger of the assassin would gleam behind them; that the arm of power would
be raised to crush them to the earth; that they would be
branded as disturbers of the peace, as fanatics, madmen and
incendiaries; that the heel of friendship would be lifted
against them, and love be turned into hatred, and confidence
into suspicion, and respect into derision; that their worldly
interests would be jeoparded, and the honor and emoluments
of office would be withheld from their enjoyment. Knowing
all this, still they dare all things, in order to save their
country by seeking its purification from blood. Will the
base and the servile accuse them of being actuated by a
hope of reward? Reward! It is the reward which calumny gives to virtue — the reward which selfishness bestows
upon benevolence; but nothing of worldly applause, or
fame, or promotion. Yet they have a reward — and who
will blame them for coveting it? It is the gratitude of the
suffering and the oppressed — the approbation of a good conscience — the blessing of the Most High.

> 'Tempt them with bribes, you tempt in vain;
> Try them with fire, you'll find them true.'

To deter such souls from their purposes, or vanquish
them in combat, is as impossible as to stop the rush of the
ocean when the spirit of the storm rides upon its mountain
billows. They are hourly increasing in number and strength,
and going on from conquering to conquer. Convert after
convert, press after press, pulpit after pulpit, is subdued, and
enlisted on the side of justice and freedom.

A grave charge is brought against me, that I am exciting
your rage against the whites, and filling your minds with
revengful feelings? Is this true? Have not all my addresses

15

and appeals to you had just the contrary effect upon your minds? Have they not been calculated to make you bear all your trials and difficulties in the spirit of Christian resignation, and to induce you to return good for evil? Where is the calumniator who dares to affirm that you have been turbulent and quarrelsome since I began my labors in your behalf? Where is the man who is so ignorant as not to know or perceive that, as a people, you are constantly improving in knowledge and virtue? No, brethren; you will bear me a unanimous testimony, that I have not implanted in your minds any malice towards your persecutors, but, on the contrary, forgiveness of injuries. And I can as truly aver that, in all my intercourse with you as a people, I have not seen or heard any thing of a malignant or revengeful spirit. No: yours has been eminently a spirit of resignation and faith, under the most aggravating circumstances.

I will notice but one other charge which the enemies of our cause have brought against me. It is, that I am unduly exciting your hopes, and holding out to your view prospects of future happiness and respectability which can never be realized in this country. Pitiful complaint! Because I have planted a solitary rose, as it were, in the wilderness of suffering in which your race has so long wandered, to cheer your drooping hearts, I am sharply reproved for giving even this little token of good things to come — by those, too, who make loud professions of friendship for you, that is, if you will go to Liberia, but who are constantly strewing in your path briars and thorns, and digging pits into which you may stumble to rise no more. These querulous complainants, who begrudge every drop of comfort which falls upon your thirsty lips, as a miser mourns the loss of a penny, seem to forget or discard the promise of Jehovah, that 'the wilderness shall bud and blossom like the rose.' I have faith to believe that this promise will ultimately be fulfilled, even in this land of republicanism and Christianity. Surely I may be pardoned, when so many are endeavoring to break down all your rising hopes and noble aspirations, if I urge you not to despair, for the day of redemption will assuredly come. Nay, I may still be forgiven, if I transcend the limits of probability, and suffer my imagination to paint in too glowing colors the recompense which is to be yours; since, strive as I may, I can scarcely hope to equalize the heart-crushing discouragements and assaults made by your enemies.

All things considered, you have certainly done well, as a body. There are many colored men whom I am proud to rank among my friends; whose native vigor of mind is remarkable; whose morals are unexceptionable; whose homes are the abode of contentment, plenty and refinement. For my own part, when I reflect upon the peculiarities of your situation; what indignities have been heaped upon your heads; in what utter dislike you are generally held even by those who profess to be the ministers and disciples of Christ; and how difficult has been your chance to arrive at respectability and affluence, I marvel greatly, not that you are no more enlightened and virtuous, but that you are not like wild beasts of the forests. I fully coincide with the sentiment of Mr. Jefferson, that the men must be prodigies who can retain their manners and morals under such circumstances. Surely, you have a right to demand an equal position among mankind.

O, if those whose prejudices against color are deeply rooted—if the asserters of the natural inferiority of the people of color, would but even casually associate with the victims of their injustice, and be candid enough to give merit its due, they could not long feel and act as they now do. Their prejudices would melt like frost-work before the blazing sun; their unbelief would vanish away, their contempt be turned

into admiration, their indifference be roused to benevolent
activity, and their dislike give place to friendship. Keeping
aloof from your society, ignorant of the progress which you
are making in virtue, knowledge and competence, and
believing all the aspersions of malice which are cast upon
your character, they at length persuade themselves that you
are utterly worthless, and nearly akin to the brute creation.
Cruel men! cruel women! thus hastily and blindly to pass
condemnation upon those who deserve your compassion, and
are worthy of your respect!

Be this your encouragement, in view of our separation.
Although absent from you in body, I shall still be with you
in spirit. I go away, not to escape from toil, but to labor
more abundantly in your cause. If I may do something for
your good at home, I hope to do more abroad. In the mean
time, I beseech you fail not, on your part, to lead quiet and
orderly lives. Let there be no ground whatever for the
charge which is brought against you by your enemies, that
you are turbulent and rude. Let all quarrelling, all dram-
drinking, all profanity, all violence, all division, be confined
to the white people. Imitate them in nothing but what is
clearly good, and carefully shun even the appearance of
evil. Let them, if they will, follow the devices and perform
the drudgery of the devil; but be ye perfect, even as your
heavenly Father is perfect. Conquer their aversion by moral
excellence; their proud spirit by love; their evil acts by acts
of goodness; their animosity by forgiveness. Keep in your
hearts the fear of God, and rejoice even in tribulation; for
the promise is sure, that all things shall work together for
good to those who love His name.

As for myself, whatever may be my fate — whether I fall
in the spring-time of manhood by the hand of the assassin,
or be immured in a Georgia cell, or be permitted to live to
a ripe old age — I know that the success of your cause is

not dependant upon my existence. I am but as a drop in the ocean, which, if it be separated, cannot be missed.

My own faith is strong—my vision, clear—my consolation, great. 'Who art thou, O great mountain? Before Zerubbabel thou shalt become a plain: and he shall bring forth the headstone thereof with shoutings, crying, Grace, grace unto it.' Let us confidently hope, that the day is at hand, when we shall be enabled to celebrate not merely the abolition of the slave trade by law but in fact, and the liberation of every descendant of Africa, wherever one exists in bondage under the whole heavens.

To My Birth-Place.

WHETHER a persecuted child of thine
   Thou deign to own, my lovely native place,*
   In characters that Time cannot efface,
Thy worth is graved upon this heart of mine.
Forsake me not in anger, nor repine
   That with this nation I am in disgrace:
   From ruthless bondage to redeem my race,
And save my country, is my great design.
How much soe'er my conduct thou dost blame,
   (For Hate and Calumny belie my course,)
My labors shall not sully thy fair fame;
   But they shall be to thee a fountain-source
Of joyfulness hereafter—when my name
   Shall e'en from tyrants a just tribute force.

* NEWBURYPORT, MASS.

15*

Tribute to Clarkson and Wilberforce.

THE names of CLARKSON and WILBERFORCE will, to the end of time, be watchwords in the mouths of the friends of bleeding humanity. Venerable men! they live, as yet, to receive the benedictions of a grateful people! Would they were present on this occasion, to receive our individual thanks and gratulations! How would their dim eyes rekindle with light, and their feeble pulse rise to a strong vibration, and their almost passive hearts beat joyfully with emotion, could they see a portion of that persecuted people, for whom they have toiled for so long a period, assembled together under such happy auspices, presenting such an appearance of comfort, safety and pleasure, to celebrate a deed which they, under God, successfully consummated! Were they before me, I would address them after this manner: —

Benefactors of mankind! thrice welcome to the shores of America! welcome to the land in which the infant Liberty was born, whose tread is now shaking the nations! welcome to a seat with those for whose improvement and protection you have spent a long life, enduring shame and reproach, perilling your health and reputation and lives, seeking no reward but the approbation of your consciences and the smiles of Heaven, never tiring in your arduous labors, never faltering in feebleness of faith, never diverted from the object of your pursuit! Suffer me to present to you a worthy portion of my down-trodden colored countrymen. Others may shun their presence, and pour contempt upon them, but I am sure that CLARKSON and WILBERFORCE are too noble to treat them with indignity. To you the color of their skin is nothing: it is enough that they have souls — that they are rational beings — that they belong to the same common family, and are the children of one com-

mon Parent. The scorn which separates them from society
but serves to increase your attachment for them. Venerable
men! they appreciate your goodness — your toils to effect
their deliverance — all that you have done and suffered in
behalf of their race. Forgive the feebleness of language,
the imperfection of speech. They feel the poverty of words;
they can give you nothing but the pressure of the hand, the
tear of gratitude, the broken benediction of a full heart.
Their prayers for your preservation and happiness are constantly ascending to the God of the needy. Encouraged by
your example and countenance, they have risen up from the
dust, and are making rapid progress in virtue, in knowledge,
and in piety. The evidence is before you, and you will not
desire a richer reward for your labors.

   Your fame is broader than the Atlantic, and shall be as
enduring. It shall blossom and bear fruit in every clime,
among every tribe and nation, to the latest posterity. It
shall be a living impulse to move the moral world. It is not
founded upon rapine and conquest, like an Alexander's or
Napoleon's, but upon benevolence and equity. You have
not, like them, desolated the earth, and sacrificed thousands
of human beings upon the altar of your ambition, but have
actively sought to stop the shedding of blood, break the yoke
of oppression, and prevent the destruction of human life.
You have not, like the priest and the Levite, passed by on
the other side, and left the victim of thieves — poor, bleeding Africa — to perish; but, like the good Samaritan, have
endeavored to heal her wounds and restore her to health.
As yet, your names are not familiar to the lips of her
benighted children; but when the light of civilization and
Christianity shall illumine her vast empire, and a river of
knowledge, deeper and more fruitful than the Niger or
the Nile, shall flow throughout her borders, then shall they
recognize you as their noblest benefactors, and offer up

incense to God for having raised you up to vindicate their cause.

These things I say, not because you court the applause of men, nor because I hope to gratify your vanity, or thereby secure your esteem. Praise to a good man is scarcely less painful than censure. They are reflections which are naturally suggested in tracing the relation of cause and effect — an active and laborious career of philanthropy and piety.

To you, respected sirs, I am personally, and, doubtless, by reputation, unknown. Cherishing, however, the same abhorrence to oppression, the same love of justice, the same attachment to freedom, the same desire to extricate the enslaved from their terrible condition, as yourselves; I have resolved, through divine assistance, and stimulated by your example, to dedicate my life — all that I have, all that I hope to be, to the cause of human liberty. Humble as have been my efforts, I have thus early drawn upon me the maledictions of a large portion of my countrymen, and, like yourselves, been misunderstood, calumniated, threatened — branded as a madman and fanatic, and deemed worthy of death. If I have not yet experienced enough to put my sincerity and endurance to the test, I feel no desire to shrink from any additional trials or perils. In your patient submission under reproach, your perseverance through every obstacle, your fearless avowal of the truth, your uncompromising spirit of justice, your willingness to lay down your lives in this great cause, your final and glorious triumph over the enemies of injured Africa; and above all, in the examples of the Son of God, and the apostles and prophets, and the martyrs to truth in all ages, I derive all the encouragement and confidence I can need in any situation or under any trials in which I may be placed; and if I prove recreant to my pledge, if I swerve for a moment from the path of duty to avoid reproach or conciliate the ill-will of any living being, I shall deserve the curse of mankind, as I surely shall receive the retribution of Heaven. No reproaches, no dangers shall deter me. Wherever Providence may call me, my voice shall be heard in behalf of the perishing slave, and against the claims of his oppressor. With you I feel that, in such a task, it is impossible to tire : it fills my mind with complacency and peace. At night, I lie down with composure, and rise to it in the morning with alacrity. I never will desist from this blessed work.

Sonnet to Thomas Clarkson.

CLARKSON! among the wise, the great, the good,
   The friend of MAN, whate'er his caste or clime,
Thy memory shall be hailed with gratitude—
   Thy labors honored to the end of time !
Thine was a soul with sympathy imbued,
   Broad as the earth, and as the heavens sublime;
Thy godlike object, steadfastly pursued,
   To save thy race from misery and crime.
Mourn, England ! for the loss thou hast sustained,
   And let the nations of the earth lament,
With spirit broken, and with grief unfeigned;
   And to her tears let LIBERTY give vent;
A star of glory has in darkness waned—
   No more on earth survives the good man eloquent.

Vindication of the Liberator.

BITTER enemies and lukewarm friends represent the Liberator as an incendiary publication. I am willing to admit the propriety of the designation. It is, unquestionably, kindling a great fire; but it is the fire of sympathy and holy indignation against the most oppressive system on earth, and will burn up nothing but the chaff. That fire is spreading from house to house, from village to village, from city to city, from State to State. The East is glowing, as if a new sun had risen in splendid radiance; and the West has caught its beams, and is kindling with new intensity. Even the dark Atlantic, as far as the shores of old England, shows a luminous path of light, and the philanthropists of that country are rejoicing as they gaze upon it. Like a vestal fire, may this never cease to burn. Let those throw water upon it, who will—love to God and man shall feed it, and prevent its extinguishment.

But the Liberator is said to be destructive in its character and tendency. That charge, also, I admit is true. It is putting whole magazines of truth under the slave system, and I trust in God will blow it into countless fragments, so that not the remnant of a whip or chain can be found in all the South,—so that upon its ruins may be erected the beautiful temple of freedom. I will not waste my strength in foolishly endeavoring to beat down this great Bastile with a feather. I will not commence at the roof, and throw off its tiles by piecemeal. I am for adopting a more summary method of demolishing it. I am for digging under its foundations, and springing a mine that shall not leave one stone upon another. I leave colonizationists to pick up the leaves which are annually shed by the Bohon Upas of our land, with the vain hope of exterminating it; but as for myself, I

choose rather to assail its trunk with the axe of justice, and
strike with all my nerve such blows as shall cause 'this
great poison-tree of lust and blood, and of all abominable
and heartless iniquity, to fall before it; and law and love,
and God and man, to shout victory over its ruin.'

But the Liberator uses very harsh language, and calls a
great many bad names, and is very personal and abusive.
Precious cant, indeed! And what has been so efficacious
as this harsh language? Now, I am satisfied that its strength
of denunciation bears no proportion to the enormous guilt
of the slave system. The English language is lamentably
weak and deficient, in regard to this matter. I wish its epithets were heavier—I wish it would not break so easily—I
wish I could denounce slavery, and all its abettors, in terms
equal to their infamy. But, shame to tell! I can apply to
him who steals the liberties of hundreds of his fellow-creatures, and lacerates their bodies, and plunders them of all
their hard earnings, only the same epithet that is applied by
all to a man who steals a shilling in this community. I call
the slaveholder a thief, because he steals human beings,
and reduces them to the condition of brutes; and I am
thought to be very abusive! I call the man a thief who
takes my handkerchief from my pocket, and all the people
shout, 'Right! right! so he is!' and the court seizes him,
and throws him into prison. Wonderful consistency!

I am anxious to please the people; but if, in order to do
so, I must violate the plainest precepts of the gospel, and
disregard the most solemn obligations, will the people see
that my name is written in the Book of Life, and that my
sins are 'blotted out of the Book of Remembrance? If I
put out my eyes, and stop my ears, and petrify my heart,
and become insensible as a marble statue, to please the community, will the community rescue me from the charge of
inhumanity, selfishness and cowardice, which will be pre-

ferred against me at the bar of God? If they cannot, I must boldly declare the truth, ' whether men will hear, or whether they will forbear.'

A man who should be seen whipping a post in the street would doubtless excite the mirth of the passing throng. For them to be indignant at such treatment would be a perversion of sympathy, and clearly ridiculous. But if it were a dog or a horse, instead of a senseless post, which the man was beating so unmercifully, their feelings ought to be, and would be, far different. They would warmly denounce such conduct as inhuman, and exhibit much vehemence in their manner. But if it were a man, or woman, or child, instead of a dog or horse, thus suffering under the lash, how the spectators would flame! how their indignation would kindle! how strong would be their denunciations! how liberally would they apply the ungracious epithets—' a brute! a wretch! a monster!'

How, then, ought I to feel, and speak, and write, in view of a system which is red with innocent blood, drawn from the bodies of millions of my countrymen by the scourge of brutal drivers; which is full of all uncleanness and licentiousness; which destroys the ' life of the soul;' and which is too horrible for the mind to imagine, or the pen to declare? How ought I to feel and speak? As a man! as a patriot! as a philanthropist! as a Christian! My soul should be, as it is, on fire. I should thunder—I should lighten. I should blow the trumpet of alarm, long and loud. I should use just such language as is most descriptive of the crime. I should imitate the example of Christ, who, when he had to do with people of like manners, called them sharply by their proper names—such as, an adulterous and perverse generation, a brood of vipers, hypocrites, children of the devil, who could not escape the damnation of hell. Moderation under such circumstances is deliberate barbarity, both to the oppressor and the oppressed — calmness is marble indifference. No! no! I never will dilute or modify my language against slavery — against the plunderers of my fellow-men — against American kidnappers. They shall have my honest opinions of their conduct.

What the Liberator has been, is a matter of history; what it now is, every reader can determine; what it is yet to be, time must unfold. 'The past, at least, is secure.' Since the commencement of the paper, many thousands of persons have been enrolled on its list of subscribers, and multitudes have been in the habit of perusing it gratuitously. Its general effect upon their minds and character must be the surest evidence of its good or evil tendency. The rule is a good one, that a tree is known by its fruits. It is also a dictate of reason, that whatever enlarges the spirit of human sympathy, opposes tyranny in every form, inculcates love and good will to mankind, and seeks to reconcile a hostile world, must be in consonance with the Divine Mind.

In the long, dark struggle with national injustice, through which I have been called to pass, I have been cheered and strengthened by the knowledge of the reformatory change which has taken place in the sentiments of thousands, through the instrumentality of the Liberator. To this they gratefully testify : — that it has given them more exalted views of God, a more just appreciation of man, a truer conception of Christianity; that it has emancipated them from the bondage of party and sect, dispelled from their minds the mists of superstition, and made them courageous in the investigation of truth; that it has enlarged the limits of their country, and multiplied the number of their countrymen, so that they no longer regard geographical boundaries, but truly esteem every one as ' a man and a brother,' whether he be near or remote; that, instead of lowering the standard of moral obligation, or lessening the sphere of human duty, it has quick-

16

ened their moral sense, and given unlimited scope to their sympathies, and supplied them with more objects of benevolent concern than they can readily discharge. This testimony has been borne by its patrons on both sides of the Atlantic. Among those patrons are some of the best intellects, the purest spirits, the most devoted Christians, to be found in Europe or America. With them, the abolition of slavery is not ' the end of the law for righteousness ; ' nor is it a solitary or barren idea, but a principle of action as wide as the universe, and comprehensive as universal and impartial love.

How much the Liberator has accomplished, directly and indirectly, in the distinctive enterprise to which it is pledged, (the liberation of an appalling number of the human family from a horrid servitude,) by giving to it a vital tone and an unconquerable energy, by arousing multitudes from their guilty slumbers, by an uncompromising adherence to principle, by a fearless assault on the fierce spirit of complexional caste, and by sending dismay into the ranks of the enemies of emancipation, it is not for me to proclaim. On this subject, it is for candid and upright men to determine, in accordance with the facts.

The enemies of the Liberator are ever at work for its suppression. Are its friends as resolutely determined that it shall be sustained, ' a terror to evil-doers, and a praise to them that do well ' ? If so, they must not merely resolve — they must act ; for never has it been called to stem such a flood of opposition as is now swelling and dashing against it. Those who have seceded from the anti-slavery platform are peculiarly hostile to it. The clergy, as a body, spare no pains to cripple its circulation ; and their influence is very powerful. The radical reforms of the day have exhibited them in their true character, as blind leaders of the blind — as those who love the praises of men more than the praise of

God — as the most faithless and skeptical of men. Hence
their fierce opposition to the Liberator, which has been the
principal instrument of their exposure, and their ceaseless
efforts to silence its warning voice. For them to be addressed like other men — to be examined, impeached and
censured, as though they were no better than others — to
be placed on the dead level of our common humanity, without any regard to their claims to superior sanctity — is an
outrage not to be endured! In order to shield themselves
from utter condemnation, to avoid the necessity of repentance and confession of sin, and to intimidate such as are
under their domination from searching for the truth, they
have artfully raised the odious cry of ‘ INFIDELITY ’ against
those who have been called to unmask them, and misrepre-
sented their religious sentiments in the most flagrant manner.
In too many instances, this artifice has been successful ; and
there are not a few, who ‘ ran well for a time ’ as abolitionists, and who once rejoiced to mingle with persons of every
shade of religion on the anti-slavery platform; but who have
been frightened into a withdrawal from the ranks, in consequence of this appeal to sectarian exclusiveness. But the
cunning shall yet be caught in their own craftiness.

Not having been dismayed by the cry of ‘ madman! fanatic! incendiary !’ at the commencement of my anti-
slavery career, I shall not allow my peace to be disturbed
by this cry of ‘ infidelity.’ My infidelity consists in this :
I do not happen to agree with the majority in regard to
certain outward forms and observances ; — I have refused
to connect myself with any religious sect, and to adopt a
human creed as the standard of my faith ; — I do not
believe that the clergy are impeccable — nay, I have dared
to affirm that, as a body, they love the fleece better than
they do their flocks, as their treatment of every righteous
but unpopular reform plainly indicates ; — I do not believe

that men can have the spirit of Christ, who hold their fellow-creatures in bondage; — I do not believe it is right or
consistent for abolitionists to support a pro-slavery priesthood, or recognise a pro-slavery church as a religious
body; — I do not believe that it is right for Christians to
imprison, hang or butcher their enemies; — I do not believe
that governments of human contrivance, upheld by military
power, and administered by wicked rulers, are divine; — I
do not believe in the necessity of sinning against God, or
being always more or less in bondage to the devil — I do
not believe that Christ is unable to save his people from
their sins in the present life, or that the world may not be
overcome, through faith, by those who dwell in it; — I do
not believe in holiness of time, but in holiness of heart; —
I do not believe in a worldly sanctuary and ordinances of
divine service, but in the true tabernacle which the Lord
pitched, and not man, and in spiritual worship and communion, without the intervention of any types or figures; —
and, finally, I do not believe in making religion a thing of
circumstance, time or place — something distinct from the
every-day pursuits and avocations of life — but earnestly
maintain, with Him who was ranked among the offscouring
of all things, that, whether we eat or drink, or whatsoever
we do, we should do all to the glory of God.   This is the
head and front of my ' infidelity.'   How far it is dishonorable to God, or hostile to the temporal or eternal interests of
man, I leave the reader to decide, according to the light
that is in him.

Before the Liberator was established, I doubt whether, on
either side of the Atlantic, there existed a newspaper or
periodical that admitted its opponents to be freely and impartially heard through its columns — as freely as its friends.
Without boasting, I claim to have set an example of fairness
and magnanimity, in this respect, such as had never been

set before; cheerfully conceding to those who were hostile to my views, on any subject discussed in the Liberator, not only as much space as I, or as others agreeing with me, might occupy, but even more, if they desired it. From this course, I have never deviated. Nay, more; I have not waited for opponents to send in their original contributions, but, in the absence of these, have constantly transferred their articles, published in other periodicals, to my own paper, without prompting from any quarter. In this manner, I have laid before my readers thousands of columns of matter, strongly denunciatory of my sentiments, crowded with sweeping misrepresentations of my designs, and bitterly unjust in regard to the anti-slavery enterprise. To these, I have seldom appended a word of comment, to show their folly or malignity. Can any other editor in the world say as much?

For the hundredth time I repeat it, — the Liberator is an independent journal, devoted to the abolition of slavery in particular, and the cause of humanity in general; that it is not, never has been, and, while it is mine, I am quite sure, never will be, the organ of any anti-slavery society, or any other organization whatever; that, for its support, it is solely dependent on its subscription list; that its aim is to reform, not merely to please; and that it claims to be animated by the apostolic injunction, 'Prove all things—hold fast that which is good.' Hence it is not only unjust, but extremely base, to make any anti-slavery society responsible for what appears in its columns, and equally absurd and unreasonable to complain that it is open to the discussion of other questions besides that of chattel slavery; and most unjust is it to hold me responsible for the views of my correspondents, any further than they are approved by me. Those who do not want, or cannot tolerate such a paper, have a very simple remedy at hand, so far as they are concerned —

16 *

either not to subscribe for it, or, if they are subscribers, to discontinue it whenever they think proper. I mean that the Liberator shall be a FREE PRESS, in a comprehensive and manly sense; and I advise those who cannot endure free discussion to beware how they give it any countenance. But to those who believe with JEFFERSON, that 'error of opinion may be safely tolerated where reason is left free to combat it,' I present the Liberator as a journal conducted in the spirit of absolute independence and entire impartiality. It is as free to those who believe in eternizing slavery, as it is to the friends of immediate emancipation; as free to the advocates of war, as it is to those of peace ; as free to the believers in the necessity of the gallows, as it is to those who plead for the entire abolition of capital punishment; as free to those who maintain the holiness of the first or seventh day of the week, as it is to those who esteem every day alike; as free to those who believe in the plenary inspiration of the Bible, as it is to those who do not; as free to those who regard woman as subordinate to man, as to those who believe that the rights of the sexes are equal ; and so on to the end of the catalogue. Now, then, whenever any person withdraws his subscription, or refuses any longer to contribute to the National Anti-Slavery Bazaar, or the funds of the American Anti-Slavery Society, on account of both sides of every question being allowed an impartial hearing in the Liberator, or because he discovers in the paper sentiments which he deems heretical, I find no difficulty in reading the mind and spirit of that person, like an open book, printed in very legible characters; and at once come to the conclusion, that his mind is narrow, or his spirit cowardly, or his confidence in the truth weaker than a bulrush, or his regard for the perishing bondman of a very superficial stamp. For whoever is strong in the truth, never runs from the advocate of error ; whoever delights in progress, believes in probing and testing all things; whoever admires freedom, likes equally well free discussion; whoever 're-members them that are in bonds as bound with them,' will never sacrifice their cause to gratify a sectarian spirit.

I sincerely pity all bigots, pharisees, formalists, time-servers, and the like; for they are ever querulous, uncom-fortable, suspicious, cowardly, and proscriptive of the true and good. These I expect to anathematise the Liberator, and to be utterly unable to read its pages with composure. To my ears, their mingled outcries against me of 'infi-delity, incendiarism, treason, fanaticism,' are like strains of melody; and so long as these fill the air, I shall neither ask nor desire better evidences of the rectitude of my course, or the efficacy of my labors.

Sonnet to the New Year.

Now let there be on earth an end of sin,
  And all oppression cease throughout the world;
The glorious reign of HOLINESS begin,
  And Satan's empire to the dust be hurled!
Let heavenly PEACE her final victory win!
  Let WAR's red banner be for ever furled! —
Resolve, Mankind! to love and bless each other;
  Forget each hateful caste, each jarring creed;
Behold in every man a friend and brother,
  And minister to him as he hath need.
Are ye not children of a common Father?
  Then to His will implicitly give heed:—
So Crime and Poverty shall disappear,
And perfect bliss shall crown each new-born Year.

Extracts from a Fourth of July Oration.

I PRESENT myself as the advocate of my enslaved countrymen, at a time when their claims cannot be shuffled out
of sight, and on an occasion which entitles me to a respect-
ful hearing in their behalf. If I am asked to prove their
title to liberty, my answer is, that the Fourth of July is not
a day to be wasted in establishing ' self-evident truths.' In
the name of the God, who has made us of one blood, and
in whose image we are created; in the name of the Messiah, who came to bind up the broken-hearted, to proclaim
liberty to the captives, and the opening of the prison to them
that are bound; I demand the immediate emancipation
of those who are pining in slavery on the American soil,
whether they are fattening for the shambles in Maryland and
Virginia, or are wasting, as with a pestilent disease, on the
cotton and sugar plantations of Alabama and Louisiana;
whether they are male or female, young or old, vigorous
or infirm. I make this demand, not for the children merely,
but the parents also; not for one, but for all; not with restrictions and limitations, but unconditionally. I assert their
perfect equality with ourselves, as a part of the human race,
and their inalienable right to liberty and the pursuit of happiness. That this demand is founded in justice, and is
therefore irresistible, the whole nation is this day acknowledging, as upon oath at the bar of the world. And not
until, by a formal vote, the people repudiate the Declaration
of Independence as a false and dangerous instrument, and
cease to keep this festival in honor of liberty, as unworthy
of note or remembrance; not until they spike every cannon,
and muffle every bell, and disband every procession, and
quench every bonfire, and gag every orator; not until they
brand Washington, and Adams, and Jefferson, and Hancock,

as fanatics and madmen; not until they place themselves again in the condition of colonial subserviency to Great Britain, or transform this republic into an imperial government; not until they cease pointing exultingly to Bunker Hill, and the plains of Concord and Lexington; not, in fine, until they deny the authority of God, and proclaim themselves to be destitute of principle and humanity, will I argue the question, as one of doubtful disputation, on an occasion like this, whether our slaves are entitled to the rights and privileges of freemen. That question is settled irrevocably. There is no man to be found, unless he has a brow of brass and a heart of stone, who will dare to contest it on a day like this. A state of vassalage is pronounced, by universal acclamation, to be such as no man, or body of men, ought to submit to for one moment. I therefore tell the American slaves, that the time for their emancipation is come; that, their own taskmasters being witnesses, they are created equal to the rest of mankind, and possess an inalienable right to liberty; and that no man has a right to hold them in bondage. I counsel them not to fight for their freedom, both on account of the hopelessness of the effort, and because it is rendering evil for evil; but I tell them, not less emphatically, it is not wrong in them to refuse to wear the yoke of slavery any longer. Let them shed no blood — enter into no conspiracies — raise no murderous revolts; but, whenever and wherever they can break their fetters, God give them the courage to do so! And should they attempt to elope from their house of bondage, and come to the North, may each of them find a covert from the search of the spoiler, and an invincible public sentiment to shield them from the grasp of the kidnapper! Success attend them in their flight to Canada, to touch whose monarchical soil ensures freedom to every republican slave!

Is this preaching sedition? Sedition against what? Not

the lives of Southern oppressors for — I renew the solemn injunction, ' Shed no blood ! ' — but against unlawful authority, and barbarous usage, and unrequited toil. If slaveholders are still obstinately bent upon plundering and starving their long-suffering victims, why, let them look well to consequences ! To save them from danger, I am not obligated to suppress the truth, or to stop proclaiming liberty ' throughout all the land, unto all the inhabitants thereof.' No, indeed. There are two important truths, which, as far as practicable, I mean every slave shall be made to understand. The first is, that he has a right to his freedom now ; the other is, that this is recognised as a self-evident truth in the Declaration of American Independence. Sedition, forsooth ! Why, what are the American people doing this day ? In theory, maintaining the freedom and equality of the human race ; and in practice, declaring that all tyrants ought to be extirpated from the face of the earth ! We are giving to our slaves the following easy sums for solution : — If the principle involved in a three-penny tax on tea justified a seven years' war, how much blood may be lawfully spilt in resisting the principle, that one human being has a right to the body and soul of another, on account of the color of his skin ? Again : — If the impressment of six thousand American seamen, by Great Britain, furnished sufficient cause for a bloody struggle with that nation, and the sacrifice of hundreds of millions of capital, in self-defence, how many lives may be taken, by way of retribution, on account of the enslavement, as chattels, of more than two millions of American laborers ?

Oppression and insurrection go hand in hand, as cause and effect are allied together. In what age of the world have tyrants reigned with impunity, or the victims of tyranny not resisted unto blood ? Besides our own grand insurrection against the authority of the mother country,

there have been many insurrections, during the last two
hundred years, in various sections of the land, on the part
of the victims of our tyranny, but without the success that
attended our own struggle.   The last was the memorable
one in Southampton, Virginia, headed by a black patriot,
nicknamed, in the contemptuous nomenclature of slavery,
Nat Turner.   The name does not strike the ear so harmoniously as that of Washington, or Lafayette, or Hancock,
or Warren ; but the name is nothing.   It is not in the power
of all the slaveholders upon earth, to render odious the
memory of that sable chieftain.   ' Resistance to tyrants is
obedience to God,' was our revolutionary motto.   We acted
upon that motto — what more did Nat Turner ?   Says
George McDuffie, ' A people who deliberately submit to
oppression, with a full knowledge that they are oppressed,
are fit only to be slaves.   No tyrant ever made a slave —
no community, however small, having the spirit of freemen,
ever yet had a master.   It does not belong to men to count
the costs, and calculate the hazards of vindicating their
rights, and defending their liberties.'   So reasoned Nat
Turner, and acted accordingly.   Was he a patriot, or a
monster ?   Do we mean to say to the oppressed of all
nations, in the 62d year of our independence, and on the
4th of July, that our example in 1776 was a bad one, and
ought not to be followed ?   As a Christian non-resistant, I, for
one, am prepared to say so ; but are the people ready to
say, no chains ought to be broken by the hand of violence,
and no blood spilt in defence of inalienable human rights,
in any quarter of the globe ?   If not, then our slaves will
peradventure take us at our word, and there will be given
unto us blood to drink, for we are worthy.   Why accuse abolitionists of stirring them up to insurrection ?   The charge
is false ; but what if it were true ?   If any man has a right
to fight for liberty, this right equally extends to all men

subjected to bondage.   In claiming this right for themselves,
the American people necessarily concede it to all mankind.
If, therefore, they are found tyrannizing over any part of
the human race, they voluntarily seal their own death-war-
rant, and confess that they deserve to perish.

> ‘ What are the banners ye exalt ? — the deeds
>   That raised your fathers’ pyramid of fame ?
> Ye show the wound that still in history bleeds,
>   And talk exulting of the patriot’s name —
> Then, when your words have waked a kindred flame,
>   And slaves behold the freedom ye adore,
> And deeper feel their sorrow and their shame,
>   Ye double all the fetters that they wore,
> And press them down to earth, till hope exults no more ! ’

But, it seems, abolitionists have the audacity to tell the
slaves, not only of their rights, but also of their wrongs !
That must be a rare piece of information to them, truly !
Tell a man who has just had his back flayed by the lash,
till a pool of blood is at his feet, that somebody has flogged
him ! Tell him who wears an iron collar upon his neck,
and a chain upon his heels, that his limbs are fettered, as if
he knew it not ! Tell those who receive no compensation
for their toil, that they are unrighteously defrauded ! In
spite of all their whippings, and deprivations, and forcible
separations, like cattle in the market, it seems that the
poor slaves realized a heaven of blissful ignorance, until
their halcyon dreams were disturbed by the pictorial representations and exciting descriptions of the abolitionists !
What ! have not the slaves eyes ? have they not hands,
organs, dimensions, senses, affections, passions ? Are they
not fed with the same food, hurt with the same weapons,
subject to the same diseases, healed by the same means,
warmed and cooled by the same winter and summer, as
freemen are ? ‘ If we prick them, do they not bleed ? if

we tickle them, do they not laugh? if we poison them, do they not die? and if we wrong them, will they not be revenged?'

'For the slaveholders,' we are told, 'there is no peace, by night or day; but every moment is a moment of alarm, and their enemies are of their own household!' It is the hand of a friendly vindicator, moreover, that rolls up the curtain! What but the most atrocious tyranny on the part of the masters, and the most terrible sufferings on the part of the slaves, can account for such alarm, such insecurity, such apprehensions that 'even a more horrible catastrophe' than that of arson and murder may transpire nightly? It requires all the villany that has ever been charged upon Southern oppressors, and all the wretchedness that has ever been ascribed to the oppressed, to work out so fearful a result;—and that the statement is true, the most distinguished slaveholders have more than once certified. That it is true, the entire code of slave laws—whips and yokes and fetters—the nightly patrol—restriction of locomotion on the part of the slaves, except with passes—muskets, pistols and bowie knives in the bed chambers during the hours of rest—the fear of the intercommunication of colored freemen and the slaves—the prohibition of even alphabetical instruction, under pains and penalties, to the victims of wrong—the refusal to admit their testimony against persons of a white complexion—the wild consternation and furious gnashing of teeth exhibited by the chivalric oppressors, at the sight of an anti-slavery publication—the rewards offered for the persons of abolitionists—the whipping of Dresser and the murder of Lovejoy—the plundering of the U. S. mail—the application of lynch law to all who are found sympathizing with the slave population as men, south of the Potomac—the reign of mobocracy in place of constitutional law—and, finally, the Pharaoh-like conduct of the

17

masters, in imposing new burdens and heavier fetters upon
their down-trodden vassals — all these things, together with
a long catalogue of others, prove that the abolitionists
have not 'set down aught in malice' against the South —
that they have exaggerated nothing. They warn us, as
with miraculous speech, that, unless justice be speedily done,
a bloody catastrophe is to come, which will roll a gory tide
of desolation .through the land, and may peradventure blot
out the memory of the scenes of St. Domingo. They are the
premonitory rumblings of a great earthquake — the lava
tokens of a heaving volcano! God grant, that while there
is time and a way to escape, we may give heed to these
signals of impending retribution !

One thing I know full well. Calumniated, abhorred, persecuted as the abolitionists have been, they constitute the
body-guard of the slaveholders, not to strengthen their oppression, but to shield them from the vengeance of their
slaves. Instead of seeking their destruction, abolitionists
are endeavoring to save them from midnight conflagration
and sudden death, by beseeching them to remove the cause
of insurrection ; and by holding out to their slaves the hope
of a peaceful deliverance. We do not desire that any
should perish. Having a conscience void of offence in this
matter, and cherishing a love for our race which is 'without
partiality and without hypocrisy,' no impeachment of our
motives, or assault upon our character, can disturb the
serenity of our minds ; nor can any threats of violence, or
prospect of suffering, deter us from our purpose. That we
manifest a bad spirit, is not to be decided on the testimony
of the Southern slave driver, or his Northern apologist.
That our philanthropy is exclusive, in favor of but one
party, is not proved by our denouncing the oppressor, and
sympathizing with his victim. That we are seeking popularity, is not apparent from our advocating an odious and

unpopular cause, and vindicating, at the loss of our reputation, the rights of a people who are reckoned among the
offscouring of all things. That our motives are not disinterested, they who swim with the popular current, and
partake of the gains of unrighteousness, and plunder the
laborers of their wages, are not competent to determine.
That our language is uncharitable and unchristian, they who
revile us as madmen, fanatics, incendiaries, traitors, cut-
throats, &c., &c., cannot be allowed to testify. That our
measures are violent, is not demonstrated by the fact, that
we wield no physical weapons, pledge ourselves not to countenance insurrection, and present the peaceful front of non-
resistance to those who put our lives in peril. That our
object is chimerical or unrighteous, is not substantiated by
the fact of its being commended by Almighty God, and
supported by his omnipotence, as well as approved by the
wise and good in every age and in all countries. If the
charge, so often brought against us, be true, that our temper
is rancorous and our spirit turbulent, how has it happened,
that, during so long a conflict with slavery, not a single instance can be found in which an abolitionist has committed
a breach of the peace, or violated any law of his country? If
it be true, that we are not actuated by the highest principles
of rectitude, nor governed by the spirit of forbearance, I ask,
once more, how it has come to pass, that when our meetings
have been repeatedly broken up by lawless men, our property burnt in the streets, our dwellings sacked, our persons
brutally assailed, and our lives put in imminent peril, we
have refused to lift a finger in self-defence, or to maintain
our rights in the spirit of worldly patriotism?

Will it be retorted, that we dare not resist — that we are
cowards? Cowards! No man believes it. They are the
dastards, who maintain MIGHT makes RIGHT; whose arguments are brickbats and rotten-eggs; whose weapons are

dirks and bowie-knives ; and whose code of justice is lynch law. A love of liberty, instead of unnerving men, makes them intrepid, heroic, invincible. It was so at Thermopylæ — it was so on Bunker Hill. Who so tranquil, who so little agitated, in storm or sunshine, as the abolitionists ? But what consternation, what running to and fro like men at their wits' end, what trepidation, what anguish of spirit, on the part of their enemies! How Southern slave-mongers quake and tremble at the faintest whisperings of an abolitionist! For, truly, ' the thief doth fear each bush an officer.' O, the great poet of Nature is right —

> 'Thrice is he armed who hath his quarrel just —
> And he but naked, though locked up in steel,
> Whose conscience with injustice is corrupted ! '

A greater than Shakspeare certifies, that ' the wicked flee when no man pursueth; but the righteous are bold as a lion.' In this great contest of Right against Wrong, of Liberty against Slavery, who are the wicked, if they be not those, who, like vultures and vampyres, are gorging themselves with human blood ? if they be not the plunderers of the poor, the spoilers of the defenceless, the traffickers in ' slaves and the souls of men ' ? Who are the cowards, if not those who shrink from manly argumentation, the light of truth, the concussion of mind, and a fair field ? if not those whose prowess, stimulated by whiskey potations or the spirit of murder, grows rampant as the darkness of night approaches ; whose shouts and yells are savage and fiend-like ; who furiously exclaim, ' Down with free discussion ! down with the liberty of the press !. down with the right of petition ! down with constitutional law ! ' — who rifle mail-bags, throw types and printing presses into the river, burn public halls dedicated to ' Virtue, Liberty and Independence,' and assassinate the defenders of inalienable human

rights? And who are the righteous, in this case, if they be
not those who will ' have no fellowship with the unfruitful
works of darkness, but rather reprove them ; ' who maintain
that the laborer is worthy of his hire, that the marriage institution is sacred, that slavery is a system accursed of God,
that tyrants are the enemies of mankind, and that immediate
emancipation should be given to all who are pining in bondage? Who are the truly brave, if not those who demand
for truth and error alike, free speech, a free press, an open
arena, the right of petition, and no quarters? if not those,
who, instead of skulking from the light, stand forth in the
noontide blaze of day, and challenge their opponents to
emerge from their wolf-like dens, that, by a rigid examination, it may be seen who has stolen the wedge of gold, in
whose pocket are the thirty pieces of silver, and whose garments are stained with the blood of innocence?

The charge, then, that we are beside ourselves, that we
are both violent and cowardly, is demonstrated to be false,
in a signal manner. I thank God, that ' the weapons of our
warfare are not carnal,' but spiritual. I thank him, that by
his grace, and by our deep concern for the oppressed, we
have been enabled, in Christian magnanimity, to pity and
pray for our enemies, and to overcome their evil with good.
Overcome, I say : not merely suffered unresistingly, but
conquered gloriously.

If it must be so, let the defenders of slavery still have
all the brickbats, bowie-knives and pistols, which the land
can furnish ; but let us still possess all the arguments, facts,
warnings and promises, which insure the final triumph of
our holy cause.

Nothing is easier than for the abolitionists, if they were
so disposed, as it were in the twinkling of an eye, to ' cry
havoc and let slip the dogs of war,' and fill this whole land
with the horrors of a civil and servile commotion. It is

17*

only for them to hoist but one signal, to kindle but a single torch, to give but a single bugle-call, and the three millions of colored victims of oppression, both bond and free, would start up as one man, and make the American soil drunk with the blood of the slain. How fearful and tremendous is the power, for good or evil, thus lodged in their hands! Besides being stimulated by a desire to redress the wrongs of their enslaved countrymen, they could plead, in extenuation of their conduct for resorting to arms, (and their plea would be valid, according to the theory and practice of republicanism,) that they had cruel wrongs of their own to avenge, and sacred rights to secure, inasmuch as they are thrust out beyond the pale of the Constitution, excluded from one half of the Union by the fiat of the lynch code, deprived of the protection of law, and branded as traitors, because they dare to assert that GOD WILLS ALL MEN TO BE FREE! Now, I frankly put it to the understandings of Southern men, whether, in view of these considerations, it is adding any thing to their safety, or postponing the much dreaded catastrophe a single hour,— whether, in fact, it is not increasing their peril, and rendering an early explosion more probable,— for them to persevere in aggravating the condition of their slaves by tightening their chains and increasing the heavy burdens — or in wreaking their malice upon the free people of color — or in adopting every base and unlawful measure to wound the character, destroy the property, and jeopard the lives of abolitionists, and thus leaving no stone unturned to inflame them to desperation? All this, Southern men have done, and are still doing, as if animated by an insane desire to be destroyed.

The object of the Anti-Slavery association is not to destroy men's lives, — despots though they be, — but to prevent the spilling of human blood. It is to enlighten the understanding, arouse the conscience, affect the heart. We

rely upon moral power alone for success. The ground
upon which we stand belongs to no sect or party — it is holy
ground. Whatever else may divide us in opinion, in this
one thing we are agreed — that slaveholding is a crime
under all circumstances, and ought to be immediately and
unconditionally abandoned. We enforce upon no man
either a political or a religious test, as a condition of mem-
bership ; but, at the same time, we expect every abolitionist
to carry out his principles consistently, impartially, faithfully, in whatever station he may be called to act, or
wherever conscience may lead him to go. I hail this union
of hearts as a bright omen, that all is not lost. To the
slaveholding South, it is more terrible than a military army
with banners. It is indeed a sublime spectacle to see men
forgetting their jarring creeds and party affinities, and embracing each other as one and indivisible, in a struggle in
behalf of our common Christianity and our common nature.
God grant that no root of bitterness may spring up to divide
us asunder! 'United we stand, divided we fall' — and if
we fall, what remains for our country but a fearful looking
for of judgment and of fiery indignation, that shall consume it? Fall we cannot, if our trust be in the Lord of
hosts, and in the power of his might — not in man, nor any
body of men. Divided we cannot be, if we truly 'remember them that are in bonds as bound with them,' and love
our neighbors as ourselves.

Genuine abolitionism is not a hobby, got up for personal or
associated aggrandizement; it is not a political ruse; it is
not a spasm of sympathy, which lasts but for a moment,
leaving the system weak and worn; it is not a fever of en-
thusiasm; it is not the fruit of fanaticism; it is not a spirit
of faction. It is of heaven, not of men. It lives in the
heart as a vital principle. It is an essential part of Christianity, and aside from it there can be no humanity. Its

scope is not confined to the slave population of the United States, but embraces mankind. Opposition cannot weary it out, force cannot put it down, fire cannot consume it. It is the spirit of Jesus, who was sent ' to bind up the broken-hearted, to proclaim liberty to the captives, and the opening of the prison to them that are bound; to proclaim the acceptable year of the Lord, and the day of vengeance of our God.' Its principles are self-evident, its measures rational, its purposes merciful and just. It cannot be diverted from the path of duty, though all earth and hell oppose; for it is lifted far above all earth-born fear. When it fairly takes possession of the soul, you may trust the soul-carrier any where, that he will not be recreant to humanity. In short, it is a life, not an impulse — a quenchless flame of philanthropy, not a transient spark of sentimentalism.

To Samuel J. May.

FRIEND of mankind! for thee I fondly cherish
   Th' exuberance of a brother's glowing love;
And never in my memory shall perish
   Thy name or worth — so time shall truly prove !
   Thy spirit is more gentle than a dove,
Yet hath an angel's energy and scope;
   Its flight is towering as the heaven above,
And with the outstretched earth doth bravely cope.
Thou standest on an eminence so high,
   All nations congregate around its base;
There, with a kindling soul and piercing eye,
   The wrongs and sufferings of thy kind dost trace:
Thy country is the world — thou know'st no other —
And every man, in every clime, thy brother !

The Great Apostate.

In a speech delivered in Niblo's Garden, New York, in 1837, DANIEL WEBSTER said, with an emphasis which elicited from the vast assembly almost deafening cheers,—' On the general question of slavery, a great portion of the community is already strongly excited. The question has not only attracted attention as a question of politics, but it has struck a far deeper chord. IT HAS ARRESTED THE RELIGIOUS FEELING OF THE COUNTRY; IT HAS TAKEN STRONG HOLD OF THE CONSCIENCES OF MEN. *He is a rash man, indeed, little conversant with human nature, and especially has he a very erroneous estimate of the character of the people of this country, who supposes that a feeling of this kind is to be trifled with or despised.* IT WILL ASSUREDLY CAUSE ITSELF TO BE RESPECTED. It may be reasoned with; it may be made willing—I believe it is entirely willing—to fulfil all existing engagements and all existing duties; to uphold and defend the Constitution as it is established, with whatever regrets about some provisions which it does actually contain. But, *to coerce it into silence—to endeavor to restrain its free expression—to seek to compress and confine it, warm as it is, and more heated as such endeavors would inevitably render it*—should all this be attempted, I KNOW NOTHING IN THE CONSTITUTION, OR EVEN IN THE UNION ITSELF, WHICH WOULD NOT BE ENDANGERED BY THE EXPLOSION WHICH MIGHT FOLLOW.' .

This estimate of the spirit which animates and controls the Anti-Slavery movement is justified by all the facts connected with the rise and progress of that movement.

Slavery is not only inhuman and anti-christian, but ATHEISTICAL, in the most depraved sense of that term. Indeed, there has never been any other form of atheism, as a system, known to the world. This is none the less true, because slaveholders profess to revere God, to believe in Christ, and to receive the Bible as an inspired volume. Their religious profession only deepens their condemnation, and makes their daily practice all the more appalling. In respect to those whom they have chattelized, their conduct is thoroughly atheistical.

Exalting themselves ' above all that is called God,' they claim and exercise absolute authority over their victims, to the annihilation of all personality. A slave is one who must have no other God than his master—no higher law than the will of him who claims him as his property ; whose intellect must not be developed ; whose conscience is not to be governed by moral considerations ; whose soul may lay no claim to immortality. In slavery, all human ties are abrogated ; the parent has no child, the child no parent ; there is neither father nor mother, neither husband nor wife, neither brother nor sister ; no genealogical descent or relationship is recognised. Hence the appearance in the Southern journals of advertisements like the following :—' Will be sold, on Monday and Tuesday, the second and third day of December next, · · . all the right, title, and interest of the subscriber, in and to the contents of a Country Store, consisting of a quantity of Dry Goods, Shoes, Umbrellas, Medicines, Hardware, Wines, Champaign Cider, and a variety of other articles. *Also, three Negroes, Levinia and her two children.* Also, a Horse, Carriage, Dray and Cart.' What is this but a bold denial of the accountability and immortality of those who are created ' in the image of God ' ?

Now, if Christianity has any work to accomplish, surely it is the utter subversion of an atheistical system like this ; if the religious sentiment is to be arrayed against any form of iniquity, it must be against this, which is unparalleled for its enormity.

Since the advent of the Founder of Christianity, no effort for the melioration of the condition of man has been more largely imbued with the religious element, in its purest and most vital form, than the Anti-Slavery movement. This declaration may astonish, and even shock, some who have been taught by their religious teachers to regard this movement as disorganizing in its tendencies and infidel in its spirit. Are not the abolitionists every where stigmatized as infidels, fanatics, incendiaries, madmen — equally hostile to the peace of the nation and the stability of the Christian Church? Yes — but this stigma is not less malignant than was the accusation brought against Jesus — ' He casteth out devils through Beelzebub, the chief of the devils . . . We found this fellow perverting the nation, and forbidding to give tribute to Cæsar . . . . He stirreth up the people, teaching throughout all Jewry, beginning from Galilee to this place.' In what manner, in any age, is true piety best authenticated? Not by professions of reverence for dead saints or heroes; not by conformity to the usages of popular religion; not by the observance of rites and ceremonies, or of times and seasons; not by the surrender of reason to arbitrary authority, or of conscience to ecclesiastical dictation; not by a dread of dissent, or fear of change, or dislike of investigation; not by making public opinion the standard of action, or what is customary the rule of duty; not by exclaiming, ' Lord, Lord, have we not prophesied in thy name, and in thy name done many wonderful works? ' These things are easily said and done. The test is in regarding principles more than persons, the present more than the past, truth more than tradition, humanity more than parchment; in refusing to go with the multitude in any evil way; in letting the dead bury their dead; in stemming the tide of popular corruption, arraigning unjust laws, exciting the fury of the oppressor, returning good for evil, and living above that

' fear of man which bringeth a snare ; ' in being willing to be
made of no reputation, and to suffer the loss of all things,
for righteousness' sake.

Consider, now, the actual condition of the colored population of this country ; despised, shunned, insulted, outraged,
enslaved, by common consent, with deliberate purpose, sys-
tematically and perseveringly, by all that is respectable,
wealthy, and powerful—by all that is vulgar, brutal, and
fiendish !   They are universally treated as a leprous race on
account of their complexion ; so that to such of them as are
nominally free, every avenue to political and social equality,
to wealth and station, to learning and improvement, is closed ;
and it is deemed ridiculous and impudent for them to aspire
to be any thing else than hewers of wood and drawers of
water for their white contemners.   The great body of them
registered with cattle and swine, and stripped of all their
rights as human beings, to interpose for their deliverance is
to come into collision with a spirit more unrelenting, murderous and God-defying than any other that ever assumed
the despotic form, and which rules this whole nation ' with a
rod of iron.'

Again, consider the degradation, helplessness, and utter
destitution of these oppressed millions.   They are ignorant,
and cannot read ; in a hopeless minority as to physical
strength ; cut off from all correspondence, even with those
who desire to befriend them ; without any thing in the world
that they may call their own ; hence the espousal of their
cause requires rare disinterestedness, as well as great moral
courage.

Consider, moreover, that in the immediate presence of the
Slave Power, no one can demand the liberation of its victims, or enter his protest against their enslavement, except
at the imminent peril of his life.   So dreadful is that power,
that, of a thousand pulpits on its soil, not one has the martyr-

spirit to confront it—of a thousand churches, whether Catholic, Episcopal, Presbyterian, Baptist, or Methodist, not one
has the courage to unchristianize it.   No meetings can be
held to discuss the question of human rights, in relation to
the slave population; no press is tolerated to speak out
boldly and uncompromisingly against making man the property of man; a dead silence is everywhere enforced, a gag
is put into every mouth, except when slavery is to be defend--
ed, or the friends of impartial liberty are to be denounced.
Not only are there the severest legal penalties to be incurred
by agitating the subject, but outrage and death in their most
appalling forms, by what is called the ' lynch ' process.   No
parallel to this state of society can be found in any despotic
government on earth.
     Consider, finally, that by its professed expounders and
teachers in this country, generally, Christianity has been
made to sanction the right to ' trade in slaves and the souls
of men,' to any extent !   Yes, in the Law given by Moses,
in the Gospel as promulgated by Christ, they maintain that
divine authority is given to one portion of the human family
to enslave another !   Hence to own a thousand slaves is no
barrier to religious fellowship, no stain upon the Christian
profession, no cause for church discipline.   Hence it is common for ministers and church members at the South to be
slaveholders; and none are more angry than they at any
proposition for emancipation, or more ready to instigate to the
infliction of summary and cruel punishment on any one
suspected of being an abolitionist.
     It is under such circumstances, that slavery must be assail-
ed—with the certainty of no reward on the part of its victims, as they have nothing to give, and know not when or
by whom their claims are advocated—with the certainty of
being derided, caricatured, hated, calumniated, in the North,
and tarred and feathered, or hung, at the South—with the
                         18

certainty of being branded with 'infidelity,' and charged
with rejecting the Bible, in all parts of the country!

Now, then, when was it ever known that bad men became
the advocates of suffering humanity, in the midst of fiery
trials like these? Never! If an unfaltering faith in the
promises of God—the deepest sympathy with Christ, and
love for his character—were ever demanded or exemplified,
it has been in the prosecution of the Anti-Slavery movement,
from its commencement to the present hour. As, on the
other side of the Atlantic, in the struggle for the abolition of
British West India slavery, the purest, the most disinterested,
the most philanthropic, the most truly pious, rallied together;
so, on this side, the same elements have mingled for the
deliverance of a much larger number from bondage, but
through tribulation and peril unknown abroad. The men
and the women whom God has inspired to demand liberty
for the enslaved in this land are worthy of the apostolic age.
They need no defence. The position which they serenely
maintain in the midst of a scoffing and merciless nation;
feared, abhorred, proscribed by the pharisaical, the powerful, and the despotic; howled at and hunted by the lewd,
the profane, and the riotous; honored and blest by the suffering and the oppressed, is their noblest eulogy. They are
neither fanatical nor mad, neither foolish nor ignorant, neither
violent nor impracticable, but speak 'the words of truth and
soberness,' plainly and unequivocally. They ask nothing
more than that liberty may be 'proclaimed throughout all
the land, unto all the inhabitants thereof.' As friends, neighbors, citizens, in all the relations and duties of life, they have
no cause to shrink from a comparison with their traducers.
In their company, the ungodly take no delight. It is their
aim to keep their consciences void of offence towards God
and towards man. Nor is the abolition of slavery the only
enterprise in which their sympathies are enlisted. The tem-

perance cause has no more thorough and reliable supporters ; they constitute the backbone of the peace enterprise, in its radical form ; in all the reform movements of the age, they feel a friendly interest. For the last twenty years, they have been ' a spectacle to angels and to men '—but where is the evidence of their misconduct to be found, except in opening their mouths for the suffering and the dumb ? The cry of ' fanaticism ' and ' infidelity ' against them is raised to divert attention from the true issue, to excite popular odium, and to hide conscious guilt. Their fanaticism is all embraced in the American Declaration of Independence ; they are infidel to the Slave Power, and will not bow down to a corrupt public sentiment. What motive, but reverence for God and love for man, could have induced them to take their position by the side of the imbruted slave ? Were they not connected with the various religious sects and political parties—clinging to these with characteristic tenacity, and highly esteemed for their zeal and fidelity ? And what have they not yielded to their convictions of duty, their regard for principle, their love of right ? The ties of sect and of party, reputation, the hope of worldly preferment, pecuniary interest, personal safety, in some instances, life itself. They are intelligently and deeply religious, without cant or pre- tence ; but neither expect nor desire any recognition of their Christian character on the part of a people ' whose feet run to evil, and who make haste to shed innocent blood.'

When, therefore, Mr. Webster, thirteen years ago, con- fessed that the subject of slavery had ' taken strong hold on the consciences of men,' and ' arrested the religious feeling of the country,' his vision was clear, his understanding sound, his testimony true ; when he admonished those who listened to him, that ' a feeling of this kind was not to be trifled with or despised,' but would ' assuredly cause itself

to be respected,' he uttered a sentiment which cannot be
too deeply impressed upon the public mind, and especially
upon the legislation of the country, at the present time;
when he declared, as his conviction, that ' to coerce it into
silence, to endeavor to restrain its free expression, to seek to
repress and confine it, there is nothing even in the Constitution, or in the Union itself, which would not be endangered
by the explosion that might follow,' he evinced a familiar
acquaintance with the martyr-history of the ages, and showed a deep insight into human nature.   For as the Anti-Slavery movement rests on an eternal basis, and challenges the
support of all those who fear God, it is sure in the end to
triumph; and in proportion to the resistance made against it
will be the convulsion attending its irresistible progress.
Nothing can overturn it; nothing hold it back.   Governmental edicts for its suppression will be as chaff before the
whirlwind; compromises and combinations to deceive or
crush it will all be in vain.   If American slavery can be
perpetuated, then there is no essential difference between a
man and a beast; then every form of despotism may continue to the end of time; then Christ has died in vain;
then the Creator is weaker than the creature whom he has
made.

Within the last twelve months, a radical change appears
to have taken place in the feelings and sentiments of Mr.
Webster on the subject of slavery.   No case of apostacy is
comparable to it since the days of Judas Iscariot.   In view
of it, conscientious and enlightened men of all sects and
parties are filled with sadness and amazement.   There is
nothing to mitigate its turpitude — no assignable cause for it,
except the desperate hope of filling the Presidential Chair
as the reward of the blackest treachery to the cause of Liberty.

On the 7th of March, 1850, in his place in the Senate of

the United States, at a crisis when every blow struck for
freedom was of incalculable importance — when the slightest defection from the path of rectitude was pregnant with
momentous consequences — Mr. Webster threw off the mask,
turned his back upon the free North, humbled himself even
to the dust in the presence of the Slave Power, and has ever
since been prostituting his great powers to the work of
crushing the Anti-Slavery spirit of the age! It is not for
him any longer to exclaim, 'Where shall I go?' He has
reached the lowest depths of moral depravity. He may
boast that he 'takes no steps backwards'— his strides from
Plymouth Rock to Carolina lead as surely to perdition. There
are steps downwards as well as backwards.

> 'Since he, miscalled the Morning Star,
> Nor man, nor fiend, hath fallen so far.'

To sustain this grave impeachment, a brief reference to
the sentiments avowed in his recent speeches and letters must
suffice, the limits necessarily assigned to this article forbidding an extended review.

There is no man, who has professed higher veneration for
the memories and deeds of our Pilgrim Fathers and Revolutionary Sires, than Mr. Webster. The names of Carver,
and Standish, and Bradford — of Washington, and Hancock,
and Warren — are ever on his lips. He was the chosen
Orator of Liberty at the laying of the Monumental Corner-
Stone on Bunker Hill. He is one of twenty millions of
people, who are never weary of extolling the Declaration of
Independence. Yet, to reconcile the whole country to the
most hideous system of oppression attainable, he says — as
though ancient villany were time-honored virtue — 'We all
know that slavery has existed in the world from time imme-
morial.' And it is not less certain that the spirit of violence
and murder has prevailed ever since Cain slew his brother

18*

Abel! Ought all efforts therefore to be frowned upon, which aim to promote peace on earth and good will among men? 'There was slavery,' he continues, 'in the earliest periods of history, in the Oriental nations.' The best of all reasons why it should no longer be suffered to curse any portion of the earth. 'There was slavery among the Jews; the theocratic government of that people made no injunction against it.' As Mr. Webster doubtless regards that form of government as having proceeded directly from God, he means to be understood as saying, that God regarded with approbation the act of his chosen people in reducing others to chattel bondage! What, then, becomes of free agency, conscience, reason, accountability? Where are the inalienable rights of man? At what period did it become a 'self-evident truth, that all men are created equal'? The imputation thus cast upon Him 'who has made of one blood all nations of men,' and 'whose tender mercies are over all the works of His hand,' is ever to be repelled as in the highest degree impious. The nature of man has been the same in all ages, and it has ever rebelled against oppression. God never yet made a human being for the chains and stripes of servitude. Over the head of the oppressor, the clouds of divine retribution are constantly impending, and his doom is sealed.

To the assertion, that 'there was slavery among the Jews,' we reply that, if so, it was because they forsook 'the ordinances of justice,' and 'built high the places of Tophet.' Why did Mr. Webster forget to inform the Senatorial body whom he was addressing, that these Jewish oppressors were admonished and rebuked by their prophets, (the abolitionists of their times,) in the following style:—'Seek judgment, relieve the oppressed, judge the fatherless, plead for the widow'—'Loose the bands of wickedness, undo the heavy burdens, let the oppressed go free, break every yoke.'

Not satisfied with staining the Law with cruel injustice,

Mr. Webster proceeds to sully the Gospel. He says :—
' At the introduction of Christianity into the world, the Roman
world was full of slaves; and I suppose there is to be found
no injunction against that relation between man and man,
(i. e. the relation of one man as a piece of property to
another man as the owner of it!) in the teachings of the
Gospel of Jesus Christ, or any of his Apostles.' The meaning of this language is, that Christianity lays no prohibition
upon the strong enslaving the weak; and the object of this
reference is, to soothe the troubled conscience of this nation
by making slavery and the Gospel compatible with each
other ! No marvel, therefore, that, in this besotted state of
mind, Mr. Webster denies that there is any such thing as
absolute justice, and sneeringly says —' There are men who
are of opinion, that human duties may be ascertained with
the exactness of mathematics. They deal with morals as
with mathematics, and they think what is right may be distinguished from what is wrong with the precision of an alge-
braic question.' Hence, there are no natural relations of
life, no permanent rules of justice, no fixed and immutable
laws of God ! Morality is a shifting sand-bar, which makes
safe navigation at all times difficult ! Right differs so little
from Wrong, in its spirit, aspect and claims, that it is
extremely difficult to determine wherein they conflict ! This
is a very convenient doctrine for one who has put principle
under his feet, and thrown away his manhood to gratify a
wicked ambition ; but in theory it is atheistical, in practice
profligate, and in its consequences appalling.

However perplexing in casuistry some questions may be,
there are such things as ' self-evident truths ; ' there are some
human duties too plain to be mistaken. THE SLAVE IS A
MAN !

> ' Though by his brother bought and sold,
>   And beat, and scourged, and a' that,

> His wrongs can ne'er be felt nor told,
> - Yet he's a man, for a' that !
> For a' that, and a' that,
>   His body chained, and a' that,
> *The image of his God remains —*
>   THE SLAVE'S A MAN, FOR A' THAT !'

In him, therefore, the Divine image is to be revered, not des-
ecrated ; his rights are all that pertain to any human being ;
to enslave him is to be guilty of man-stealing.

But, in the estimation of Mr. Webster, the slave is nothing — three millions of slaves are nothing — nothing, certainly, humanly considered — nothing but personal property,
and only as such worthy of any solicitude — nothing deserving of prayer or effort for their deliverance ! His sympathies, affinities, energies, associations, are wholly with their
remorseless oppressors. He sees nothing in slavery reproachful to the character, injurious to the prosperity, or
dangerous to the stability of the Republic ; it is the effort
making to abolish it that alarms and inflames him ! Of the
Anti-Slavery societies he says, without qualification — 'I do
not think them useful. I think their operations for the last
twenty years have produced nothing good or valuable . . . I
cannot but see what mischiefs their interference with the
South has produced . . . The result of it has been, not to
enlarge, but to restrain, not to set free, but to bind faster the
slave population of the South. That is my judgment.' The
very language of the dealers in human flesh, who are aiming
to eternize slavery on the American soil ; who are eager to
imbrue their hands in the blood of the abolitionists ; who
turn pale whenever they hear their crimes alluded to, and
become frantic at the sight of an Anti-Slavery publication !
The charge is alike absurd and monstrous.

It is in this cool, oracular and audacious manner, that Mr.
Webster, from his high position, pours contempt and scorn

upon the tears of the sympathizing, the prayers of the afflicted, the labors of the philanthropic. If it were in his power,
he would disband every Anti-Slavery Society, and suppress
all discussion of the subject of slavery. According to his
miserable logic, to demand justice for the wronged, liberty
for the enslaved, is the very way to perpetuate injustice and
to prolong human servitude. How, then, would he abolish
the slave system? Let him answer:—'As it has existed
in the country, and as it now exists, I have expressed no
opinion of the mode of its extinguishment or ameliora-
tion . . . I have nothing to propose on that subject.' Profound statesman!   But on one point he feels himself
competent to act:—'If any gentleman from the South shall
propose a scheme of COLONIZATION, to be carried on by this
government upon a large scale, for the transportation of FREE
colored people to any colony or any place in the world, I
should be quite disposed to incur almost any degree of
expense to accomplish that object'!!—an object dastardly,
unjust, inhuman, to the last degree—an object which the
slaveholding perpetualists have for more than thirty years
sought to accomplish, through deception, violence, and persecution, for the purpose of holding their slaves more securely in bondage!   Mr. Webster prides himself upon his title
of 'Defender of the Constitution.'   In what article or clause
of that instrument can he find any warrant, on the part of
Congress, to expend any portion of the national revenue in
transporting to other lands citizens of this country, on
account of their freedom and the hue of their skin? Accumulated shame upon him for such a proposition!

'New England, it is well known,' says Mr. Webster, 'is
the chosen seat of the abolition presses and the abolition
societies.' Why should it not be? The struggle for the
abolition of slavery is a moral one, and the moral power of
this nation lies chiefly in New England. 'Here it is, princi-

pally,' continues this distinguished scoffer, ' that the former cheer the morning by full columns of lamentations over the fate of human beings free by nature, and by a law above the Constitution — but sent back, nevertheless, chained and manacled, to slavery and to stripes ; and the latter refresh themselves from daily toil by orgies of the night, devoted to the same outpourings of philanthropy — mingling all the while their anathemas at what they call ' man-catching,' *with the most horrid and profane abjurations of the Christian Sabbath,* and, indeed, *of the whole of Divine Revelation.* They sanctify their philanthropy *by irreligion and profanity ;* they manifest their charity *by contempt of God and his commandments.*'

Examine this whole extract.   Can its parallel be found on the score of insensibility to human degradation and suffering, as experienced by the poor imbruted slave — of misrepresentation and calumny of thousands of as intelligent, virtuous, humane and Christian men and women as were ever united to extend the reign of justice and mercy — and, at the same time, of affected regard for the cause of religion ? Where has so much of barbarity, malice, falsehood, and cant, ever been compressed into so small a compass ?   There is Satanic skill in the grouping of its several parts.   *He* talk of the ' Christian Sabbath,' of reverencing a day, who looks with complacency upon the desecration of the image of God, and mocks at the ' lamentations ' which are raised by the pure and tender-hearted over lacerated bodies, and darkened minds, and ruined souls !   *He* talk of ' Divine Revelation,' who affirms that the Gospel of Jesus Christ contains no injunction against turning men, women and children into chattels personal !   *He* concerned for the honor of God and keeping his commandments, who laughs at the idea of a ' higher law ' than that enacted at the last session of Congress for the re-capture of fugitive slaves, and with whom allegiance to a blood-stained compact is the end of the law for righteousness! Marvellous assurance!

As for the charge, that the Abolition Societies of New England indulge in ' the most horrid and profane abjurations of the Christian Sabbath,' it is utterly and inexcusably false. Mr. Webster is challenged to produce a particle of evidence to substantiate it. Let him show when or where any one of those societies ever used the abjurations alleged, or stand before the world a convicted libeller. In regard to their members, they are composed of persons differing more or less as to their religious opinions, (like 'the temperance and peace societies,) but united for one common object—the liberation of the fettered bondman. They have never entertained for discussion, they have never adopted, any other question than that which relates legitimately to their enterprise. Without attempting to determine any extraneous subject—whether the first, or seventh, or any other day, is peculiarly holy time—they unite in sentiment with the Great Teacher, that ' it is lawful to do well on the Sabbath day,' and therefore commendable in the sight of God to endeavor to extricate, on that day, the millions of our countrymen who are perishing in the pit of slavery. As for ' horrid and profane abjurations,' they leave all such to be made by those, who, like Mr. Webster, ' strike hands with thieves, and consent with adulterers'; who, being on the side of tyranny, have neither argument nor fact wherewith to justify themselves; whose weapons of defence are lies and forgeries, sophistries and shams, tar and feathers, brickbats and rotten eggs, pistols and bowie knives; who hunt for the life of him who pleads for those who are appointed to destruction, and riotously trample all law and order under their feet. It is this wicked accuser and his man-stealing confederates—not abolitionists nor Abolition Societies—who manifest ' contempt of God and his commandments,' and whose 'irreligion and profanity,' intemperance and lewd-ness, are corrupting the nation.

In 1837, when his vision was clear and his judgment sound, Mr. Webster could testify that it 'was the religious feeling of this country' that was struggling for the overthrow of slavery, and could do homage to it. In 1850, now that he has wholly apostatized from the cause of freedom, he brands that feeling as irreligious and profane, makes its 'lamenta-tions' over the woes of the slave a subject of merriment, treats it as 'a spirit of faction and disunion, of discord, crimination and recrimination,' and stigmatizes those who are animated by its spirit as 'shallow, ignorant, and factious men'! Nay, more — as for the general excitement against slavery, it is utterly inexplicable to him! 'I suspect all this,' he says, with feigned ignorance of its cause and aim, 'to be the effect of that wandering and vagrant philanthropy which disturbs and annoys all that is present, in time or place, by heating the imagination on subjects distant, remote, and uncertain (!) . . . A spirit should prevail, which shall look to things important and real, 'and less to things ideal and abstract (!) . . . I shall support no agitations having their foundations in unreal, ghostly abstractions (!) . . . May my tongue cleave to the roof of my mouth, before it may utter any sentiment which shall increase the agitation in the public mind on such a subject!'

'The wandering and vagrant philanthropy,' which so 'dis-turbs and annoys' Mr. Webster, is kindred to that which was manifested by Jesus and his disciples, eighteen hundred years ago, to the consternation and displeasure of scribe, pharisee, and ruler; for which the memories of HOWARD, OBERLIN, WILBERFORCE, CLARKSON, and other illustrious benefactors of their race, are now venerated; and which makes human redemption the absorbing object of its solici-tude. It does not 'heat the imagination'—it warms the heart. It ' wanders' only to save—it is 'vagrant' only as it is persecuted from city to city. It is not, (as is foolishly alleged by Mr. Webster,) that it looks to 'things ideal and abstract,' that it creates general uneasiness; it is, that it deals with 'things important and real,' and calls for the suppression of all abuses.

What can be more preposterous than the assertion, that the Anti-Slavery agitation has its foundations in 'unreal, ghostly abstractions'? Is the slave system or the slave code an abstraction? Are whips and chains, padlocks and thumb-screws, branding-irons and blood-hounds, 'unreal abstractions'? Are slave-holders, slave-breeders, slave-buyers, overseers and drivers, only 'ghostly' illusions? It would be much to his credit, if Mr. Webster should let his tongue cleave to the roof of his mouth, rather than to use it so absurdly and basely.

In one breath, he asserts that 'the slavery question New England can interfere with only as a meddler: she has no more to do with it than she has to do with the municipal government of a city on the island of Cuba'! In the next, he insists that constitutional safeguards should be thrown around that system as much by Massachusetts as by Georgia; that no fugitive slave should receive food or raiment, or any protection whatever, in all the free North; that such as have escaped from the Southern house of bondage ought to have long since been arrested, and returned to their masters; and that to be the abettors and allies of the traffickers in human flesh should be regarded by the people of the Free States as 'a duty, an affair of high morals and high principles'! This incoherency of the brain is the consequence of depravity of the heart.

How Mr. Webster stands in Southern estimation is not a doubtful matter. Where on that blood-stained soil a true, out-spoken friend of freedom would be instantly lynched, he

19

is regarded with favor, and greeted with applause. At the present time, the South relies on him for the protection of her ' peculiar institution' more than on any other man in the nation—not excepting Henry Clay.

At the North, the supporters and admirers of Mr. Webster are those who have bought him with a price—those who pay that homage to rare intellect, however perverted, which is essentially devil-worship—those who bow down to the shrine of Mammon, and believe in the trinity made up of ' the gold eagle, the silver dollar, and the copper cent '— those who have ' stolen the livery of the court of heaven ' wherein to serve the great Adversary — those who are profane, drunken, lewd, riotous.

In May last, the American Anti-Slavery Society attempted to hold its sixteenth anniversary in New York. Its meetings were invaded and broken up by a band of rioters utterly lost to shame, led on by the notorious ruffian, ' Captain Isaiah Rynders,' and connived at by the city authorities. In the midst of their profanity, obscenity and violence, they repeatedly gave three cheers—for. whom ? For DANIEL WEBSTER !

On the fifteenth of November, 1850, an immense meeting of the friends of international amity and universal emancipation, drawn together spontaneously from all parts of New England, was held in Faneuil Hall, Boston, to welcome the arrival to these shores, after an absence of fifteen years, of GEORGE THOMPSON, the noble advocate of impartial liberty, the present distinguished member of the British Parliament for the Tower Hamlets, London. That meeting, at an early period of the evening, was invaded by an organized body of rioters, who, for the space of two hours, (like their lawless predecessors at Ephesus,) by their groans and yells, prevented any speaker from being heard—the city authorities interposing no restraint whatever. ' We never heard,' said one of the city journals of the next morning; 'such unearthly, inhuman, strange, uncouth, hideous noises, in all our born days. One would have thought Babel was let loose, and all the black fiends of the lower region out on a frolic.' Another journal, equally in favor of this dastardly outrage, testified as follows:—'Rings were formed in the centre of the floor, in which individual and general fights took place; hats were smashed, and ivory-headed canes flew briskly; then came a series of dances, with Indian war-hoop accompaniments. IT WAS HELL LET LOOSE, AND NO MISTAKE!'

For whom did these miscreants send up cheer after cheer, throughout the entire evening? Who was the recreant and fallen man whom, on that occasion, they were proud to recognise and eager to applaud, as one with him in spirit and fellowship? DANIEL WEBSTER!

Where shall we look in history for a more melancholy instance of human degradation?

> 'So fallen, so lost! the light withdrawn
>   Which once he wore!
> The glory from his gray hairs gone
>   Forevermore!
>
> Of all we loved and honored, nought
>   Save power remains —
> A fallen angel's pride of thought,
>   Still strong in chains.
>
> All else is gone: from those great eyes
>   The soul has fled:
> When faith is lost, when honor dies,
>   The man is dead!'

𝕿𝖍𝖊 𝕮𝖗𝖎𝖘𝖎𝖘.

SOUTHERN AGGRESSIONS UPON NORTHERN RIGHTS — THE EXPULSION
OF HON. SAMUEL HOAR FROM SOUTH CAROLINA — THE IMPRISON-
MENT OF WALKER IN FLORIDA, AND TORREY IN MARYLAND — ETC.

I.

WHY, like a sluggard, sleeps the BAY STATE now,
   As lost to hope, and dead to scorn and shame?
   A blot is on th' escutcheon of her fame;
Dishonor stamps its brand upon her brow;
Forgotten is her old and solemn vow,
   To keep for ever burning FREEDOM's flame,
   Maintain her rights, and vindicate her name,
And never at the shrine of SLAVERY bow.
Insensate as the shaft on Bunker's Hill,
   And harder than its granite, seems her breast;
The tyrannous South her sons enslave and kill,
   Yet moves she not to have their wrongs redressed : —
Then let her of oppression have her fill,
   And be, henceforth, the Southron's mock and jest!

II.

Hold! give not up, as lost, this free-born State!
   For Pilgrim blood yet courses in her veins;
   The Pilgrim spirit brooks no servile chains,
As they shall find, her rights who violate!
Slow unto wrath, magnanimously great,
   Nor fear, nor lack of might, her hand restrains;
   Cool, firm, resolved — to bluster she disdains;
But when she acts, 'tis with the force of fate!
In this great trial-hour she will not blench,
   But, single-handed, should all others flee,
The ruffian hosts of SLAVERY meet, and wrench
   All chains asunder, and th' oppressed set free:
Nought shall her courage daunt, her ardor quench,
   In battling for thy cause, O LIBERTY!

Divine Authority of the Bible.

It cannot be denied, that the question of the divine authority of the Bible is one of grave importance, and therefore
worthy of searching investigation. The right of private
judgment is, theoretically, the cardinal doctrine of Protestantism; and it is a doctrine fatal to every form of spiritual
infallibility. It allows no man, no conclave of men, to
determine arbitrarily, whether the Bible is of heaven or of
men; how much of it is in accordance with the truth, or
how much mixed with error; what portion of it is genuine,
or what spurious; how this precept is to be understood, or
that declaration interpreted. It leaves the human mind (as
it should be left) free to judge of the origin, authenticity,
inspiration, authority, value of the Bible, according to its
own perception of right, its own conviction of duty. The
natural result is, a wide diversity of opinions respecting the
book, and the duties it inculcates. Men equally sincere
arrive at diametrically opposite views as to its teachings.
Some find in it the doctrine of the trinity, of total depravity,
of the atonement, of eternal reprobation, in the Calvinistic
sense. Others find no such doctrines. Some derive from
it divine sanctions for polygamy, war, slavery, wine-bibbing,
capital punishment, the *lex talionis*, governments upheld by
military and naval power, aristocracy, monarchy, autocracy.
Others construe it in direct opposition to all such views·
Some believe in its plenary, some in its partial inspiration ;
others reject the popular notion of inspiration, whether
plenary or partial. Some reverence the volume as holy
and divine, and with superstitious awe; others esteem it as
of incomparable worth ; while others treat it with contempt,
and pronounce it a pernicious book. A multitude of rival
sects find in its pages any quantity of proof-texts in support

19*

of their own peculiar faith, and each one makes out at least
a plausible case for itself. In this Babel confusion of
tongues,.the questions arise — Who is right? what is truth?
who is it that believes in the Bible? Is it the Episcopalian,
or the Presbyterian, or the Baptist, or the Methodist, or the
Swedenborgian, or the Unitarian, or the Universalist, or the
Quaker? If any of these, which — and how do you prove
it? If all of them, who, then, rejects the Bible? To what
does it all amount, in the last analysis, except that the Bible
is variously interpreted by the various readers of it? But
whose interpretation is to be oracular, absolute, final, in this
matter? Who shall play the Pope among us? or coolly
accuse another of rejecting the Bible, merely because of a
difference of opinion respecting some particular passages?
There are plenty of such, and a very ludicrous and con-
temptible appearance they make, in the guise of Protestants.
They are swollen with conceit, stultified through superstition, contracted by ignorance. For one, I shall not heed
their fulminations, nor submit to their rule, for one moment.
When I am prepared to give up my own independent judgment, and to pin my faith upon any man's sleeve, I will
repudiate Protestantism, turn Catholic, and do homage to
the genuine, unadulterated Pope at Rome.

It is to use language in a very loose sense to talk of any
one rejecting the Bible, for there is an immense amount of
truth in it, which no one has ever sought to invalidate. It is
true, some parts of it are deemed incongruous, inaccurate,
spurious, or doubtful ; other parts clearly impossible to understand or interpret ; other parts obsolete, exclusive,
Jewish — deemed so by eminent theologians, devout schol-
ars, enlightened Christians. They neither accept nor reject
the book, as such; but they study it as a compilation of
books, written in different ages of the world ; and each one
claims and exercises the right to decide for himself what

he finds therein compatible with his sense of justice, humanity, and right. True, they often accuse each other of rejecting the Bible; but it amounts only to this, that, in some of their interpretations of Scriptural language, they differ very widely.

Much of this confusion arises from the common error of regarding the Bible as a unit—a work prepared by one mind, (and that a divine one,) consecutively, for the guidance of all mankind; instead of realizing the fact, that it is a compilation of Jewish and Christian manuscripts, written in different parts of the world, in ages more or less remote from each other — written nobody knows by whom, beyond what supposition and probability may suggest. As it is not one production, but many productions — as it is neither exclusively Jewish nor wholly Christian, but a mixture of both — as it relates to different people, under different laws and usages, possessing various degrees of light and knowledge — it is easy to see why it is that, treating it as a unit, and every portion of it as alike sacred, so many jarring sentiments and so many conflicting practices are attempted to be justified from its pages. A dexterous theologian, having full liberty to range, in the name of God, from Genesis to Revelation, finds it an easy matter to cull out such passages as seem to substantiate the doctrine, or defend the practice, that he is zealous to maintain. It is true, he may be beaten with his own weapons, and yet neither the victor nor the vanquished be enlightened as to the truth.

The Bible, then, is the product of many minds, and was never designed to be a single volume, to be received as of infallible authority or divine origin. The Jewish portion of it is supposed to have been collated by Ezra. The Christian portion was decreed to be canonical by the Council of Nice. ' What is writ, is writ,' and it must stand or fall by the test of just criticism, by its reasonableness and utility, by the probabilities of the case, by historical confirmation, by human experience and observation, by the facts of science, by the intuition of the spirit. Truth is older than any parchment, and would still exist, though a universal conflagration should consume all the books in the world. To discard a portion of Scripture is not necessarily to reject the truth, but may be the highest evidence that one can give of his love of the truth.

As yet, mankind are not governed by reason; they do not reason, particularly in regard to matters of religion; they are taught by their crafty leaders to be afraid of reason, and hence dare not give heed to its voice. As a general fact, they are wholly influenced by imitation, by tradition, by education, by custom. They believe or disbelieve, not from the results of their own independent investigation, but because it is the fashion to do so in the community or nation in which they happen to reside. No wonder the earth is covered with mental darkness, and crowded with all forms of superstition, and groaning under the dominion of religious and political tyranny. Of the millions who profess to believe in the Bible as the inspired word of God, how few there are who have had the wish or the courage to know on what ground they have formed their opinion! They have been taught that, to allow a doubt to arise in their minds on this point, would be sacrilegious, and to put in peril their salvation. They must believe in the plenary inspiration of the ‘ sacred volume,’ or they are ‘ infidels,’ who will justly deserve to be ‘ cast into the lake of fire and brimstone.’ Imposture may always be suspected when reason is commanded to abdicate the throne; when investigation is made a criminal act; when the bodies or spirits of men are threatened with pains and penalties, if they do not subscribe to the popular belief; when appeals are made to human credulity, and not to the understanding.

Now, nothing can be more consonant to reason than that the more valuable a thing is, the more it will bear to be examined. If the Bible be, from Genesis to Revelation, divinely inspired, its warmest partisans need not be concerned as to its fate. It is to be examined with the same freedom as any other book, and taken precisely for what it is worth. It must stand or fall on its own inherent qualities, like any other volume. To know what it teaches, men must not stultify themselves, nor be made irrational by a blind homage. Their reason must be absolute in judgment, and act freely, or they cannot know the truth. They are not to object to what is simply incomprehensible, — because no man can comprehend how it is that the sun gives light, or the acorn produces the oak; but what is clearly monstrous, or absurd, or impossible, cannot be endorsed by reason, and can never properly be made a test of religious faith, or an evidence of moral character.

To say that every thing contained within the lids of the Bible is divinely inspired, and to insist upon this dogma as fundamentally important, is to give utterance to a bold fiction, and to require the suspension of the reasoning faculties. To say that every thing in the Bible is to be believed, simply because it is found in that volume, is equally absurd and pernicious. It is the province of reason to ' search the Scriptures,' and determine what in them is true, and what false — what is probable, and what incredible — what is historically true, and what fabulous — what is compatible with the happiness of mankind, and what ought to be rejected as an example or rule of action — what is the letter that killeth, and what the spirit that maketh alive.

There are two dogmas which the priesthood have attempted to enforce, respecting the Bible, from which has resulted great mischief. The first is — its plenary inspiration: in other words, that the writers of it were, in fact,

only machines, operated upon by a divine power, to com-
municate to the world, in an infallible manner, the contents
of the book: so that it is free from all error. This is
already rejected by many enlightened minds as a monstrous
absurdity, and will be utterly exploded at last. What miraculous endowment was needed to record the fact, that unto
Job were born seven sons and three daughters ; or that Paul
left his cloak at Troas ; or that he was shipwrecked at
Melita ; or that Solomon had six hundred wives and concu-
bines ; or that Samson ' caught three hundred foxes, and
took firebrands, and turned tail to tail, and put a firebrand
in the midst between two tails'?   And so of a thousand
other occurrences.

The other dogma is — the Bible is the only rule of faith
and practice ; so that whatever it teaches or allows must
be right, and whatever it forbids must be wrong, independent
of all other considerations.   Thus, there is no right principle or action, in itself; and, but for the parchment, there
would be no test of morality, — no evidence of piety.
Hence, if slavery or war is allowed in the book, it cannot
be wrong; if a certain number of texts can be found to
sanction a particular crime, then it is no longer a crime, but
a virtuous act, because God has sanctioned it! What controversies have been held over the book, as to whether it is in
favor of this or that form of government ; whether it advocates human liberty, or permits human enslavement ;
whether it is opposed to all war, or only to wars of aggression; whether it maintains the inviolability of human life,
or requires the execution of the murderer ; whether it approves of the moderate use of intoxicating liquor, or enjoins
the duty of total abstinence! As if monarchy, republicanism, slavery, war, the gallows, and alcoholic drink, could
not be settled on their own merits, without an appeal to any
book!   As if God himself could make a lie the truth,

wrong right, cruelty mercy, or poison an innocent beverage! Can they who appeal to the Bible, as to an infallible authority, for the rectitude of their conduct, have any belief in absolute justice?

It is proverbial, that one extreme is very apt to beget another. The priesthood have imposed on the people the belief, that the entire Bible is divinely inspired, even every chapter and verse; that they are to submit their reason to its teachings, not its teachings to their reason; and whatever it inculcates or allows, in any portion of it, must be from God, and therefore right. On the other hand, there are those who have discarded the Bible as a pious imposture, and denounced it as evil, and only evil. They have not been satisfied with refuting the foolish dogma of priestcraft, as to the plenary inspiration of the volume; but they have manifested toward it exceeding bitterness and contempt of spirit, and blinded their eyes as to its real excellence, and the estimate in which it should be justly held. They seem unwilling to recognise any thing good in its pages, and treat it as profanely as the priesthood do idolatrously. Generally, they have very little acquaintance with it, and have no disposition to take it at its true value. They find in it historical inaccuracies and things incredible, and on that account condemn the whole work. They are flippant in their talk about the adultery of David, and the concubinage of Solomon, and affect to be shocked at what they call the obscenity of the book, — though an investigation into their private character would, in many cases, show them to be any thing but patterns of virtue. As to those portions of the Bible which inculcate the most stringent morality, the noblest sentiments, the most expansive benevolence, the purest life — and which contain the wisest admonitions, the best instructions, the brightest examples, the most cheering prophecies, and the richest promises — they seldom refer to them, and take no pleasure in selecting the wheat from the chaff. To avoid Scylla, they have perished on Charybdis.

The objection is sometimes raised — ' The Bible is like a fiddle ; you can play any tune on it you please.' Then, if the tune be discordant to the ear of humanity, the fault must be in the player, rather than in the instrument. Shall the instrument therefore be broken in pieces ? Let those pervert it, to vile uses, who are so inclined ; on them rest the responsibility. I believe it can be made to discourse most excellent music, and therefore set a high value upon it.

The Bible does not change, but the interpretations of the Bible are constantly fluctuating. Those interpretations are generally in accordance with popular opinion and the spirit of the interpreters. Men who are warlike, — men who deem it no sin to enslave their fellow-men, — men who are for retaliating injuries done to them, — men who are fond of a ceremonial religion, — naturally interpret the Bible in accordance with their views ; while men of an opposite spirit construe its language in favor of perfect goodness and universal love. Even if we admit the plenary inspiration of the volume, nothing is gained by the admission ; for, after all, it remains an open question, what does this inspired book teach ? — and, in answering the question, those who most devoutly believe in its inspiration, disagree as widely, even on points of practical morality, as do those who reject the doctrine.

I have lost my traditional and educational notions of the holiness of the Bible, but I have gained greatly, I think, in my estimation of it. As a divine book, I never could understand it ; as a human composition, I can fathom it to the bottom. Whoever receives it as his master, will necessarily be in bondage to it ; but he who makes it his servant, under the guidance of truth, will find it truly serviceable. It must be examined, criticised, accepted or rejected, like any other 'book, without fear and without favor. Whatever excellence there is in it will be fire-proof; and if any portion of it be obsolete or spurious, let that portion be treated accordingly.

Why should any wonder that some minds, keenly sensitive to the slightest outrage to humanity, and receiving the pulpit interpretations of the book as sound, grow morbidly averse to the Bible? Think of identifying the Cross of Christ, the Prince of Peace, with the Sword of the blood-stained Warrior, who, though an Orthodox clergyman, could make wadding of Watts's Psalms and Hymns, and seize an opponent by his whiskers with one hand, while he 'pommelled him soundly with the other'!—and then in his pulpit attempt to justify the act from this text—' And I contended with them, and cursed them, and smote certain of them, and plucked off their hair, and made them swear by God'!!—[Nehemiah xiii. 23.] ' From this very applicable passage,' says his eulogist, and the writer of his memoir, (Rev. Dr. Murray, of Elizabethtown, N. J.,) ' he preached a serious, exculpatory discourse, placing himself right before his people, and silencing all opposition to his proceedings'!! ' He was one day preaching to the battalion—the next, marching with them to battle'!! A Soldier of the Cross!

I am fully aware how grievously the priesthood have perverted the Bible, and wielded it both as an instrument of spiritual despotism and in opposition to the sacred cause of humanity; still, to no other volume do I turn with so much interest, no other do I consult or refer to so frequently, to no other am I so indebted for light and strength, no other is so identified with the growth of human freedom and progress, no other have I appealed to so effectively in aid of the various reformatory movements which I have espoused; and it embodies an amount of excellence so great as to make it, in my estimation, THE BOOK OF BOOKS.

20

The Guiltless Prisoner.

PRISONER! within these gloomy walls close pent —
  Guiltless of horrid crime or venial wrong —
Bear nobly up against thy punishment,
  And in thy innocence be great and strong!
Perchance thy fault was love to all mankind;
  Thou didst oppose some vile, oppressive law;
Or strive all human fetters to unbind;
  Or wouldst not bear the implements of war: —
What then? Dost thou so soon repent the deed?
  A martyr's crown is richer than a king's!
Think it an honor with thy Lord to bleed,
  And glory 'midst intensest sufferings!
Though beat — imprisoned — put to open shame —
Time shall embalm and magnify thy name.

Freedom of the Mind.

HIGH walls and huge the BODY may confine,
  And iron grates obstruct the prisoner's gaze,
And massive bolts may baffle his design,
  And vigilant keepers watch his devious ways:
Yet scorns th' immortal MIND this base control!
  No chains can bind it, and no cell enclose:
Swifter than light, it flies from pole to pole,
  And, in a flash, from earth to heaven it goes!
It leaps from mount to mount — from vale to vale
  It wanders, plucking honeyed fruits and flowers;
It visits home, to hear the fireside tale,
  Or in sweet converse pass the joyous hours:
'Tis up before the sun, roaming afar,
And, in its watches, wearies every star!

Claims and Position of the Clergy.

I VENERATE such preachers as Paul, and Peter, and others of the apostolic school, who were the ' fanatics ' and ' disorganizers ' of their times ; who bargained with no body of men when, where, how, or for what pecuniary inducement, they should utter their testimonies against sin and sinners ; who never consulted a corrupt public sentiment, in order to avoid persecution ; who had no salary to lose or to be diminished by a too plain utterance of the truth ; who never claimed to be above or distinct from the laity in the congregation of believers, but every one prayed or prophesied in order, all standing on the same platform of equality. But the modern clergy are not their successors, and may urge no apostolic claim to private veneration or popular respect. Dr. GANNETT extracts all the ' divinity ' from them, in putting them into the same category with lawyers and physicians. He says, with an air of satisfaction that is almost ludicrous—' There are as many poor lawyers and poor physicians, as there are poor preachers.' Possibly ; but of what benefit are they, as classes, to mankind ? ' We expect that only a few will be eminent in their several employments. The ministry need not dread a comparison, in this respect, with other professions.' Indeed! But the ' other professions ' claim to be human, not divine. The clergyman talks of being the ' sent of God,' an ambassador of Christ—of being filled with the Spirit, and delivering what he has had communicated to him from above ; but neither the lawyer nor physician lays claim to any thing beyond what he himself can originate and perform. Hence, on the ground of special inspiration, the clergy ought to throw into the shade all other professions. To say that ' there are more merchants who fail in their business, than there are ministers who fail in their ser-

mons,' is a queer defence—a very secular one, at least, for
' a heavenly calling.' But the defence ends not here :—
' Many of our preachers are obliged to prepare at least one
sermon a week, and some of them two, or even more, the
year through. Now, I ask the man whose flippancy is ever
berating the pulpit, if he would lay the same requisition on
the public orator or legal advocate ? . . . No, he would be
ashamed to make such a demand of any one but a minister.
Why, then, in the name of justice, should he make it of the
minister, who is but a man, at best, and not often made of
finer mould than other men ? ' What does the reader think
of this ? The minister is but a man, at best. Remember
that! Next, he is no more divinely assisted than the lawyer
or the physician, and therefore is to be measured by the
same standard. Remember that! It is a ' doctor of divinity ' who voluntarily takes the witness's stand. But the witness has a very short memory; for he proceeds to affirm
that ' preaching is the highest exercise of the human powers .. . . Enter the pulpit as if it were the loftiest position
you could take on earth . . . If you would choose the most
honorable service, if you would exercise the highest function
within the reach of man, if you desire to place yourselves
in the most enviable position on earth, enter the ministry.'
And so it becomes a divine calling again, and is no longer
secular, like that of the lawyer or physician. Now, this
shuffling from one standard to another cannot be allowed.
If the clergy are to be judged simply as men, let them claim
nothing of divinity; if they are superhuman, heaven-inspired, let them be tried by a superhuman test.

As to the loftiness of the pulpit, though the old-fashioned
mode of erecting it was somewhat elevated, the weather-
cock on the spire finds a more lofty position than the pulpit
occupant, but both commonly indicate which way the wind
blows.

The preacher, we are told, ' must apply Christianity to the habits and practices of the age in which he lives, even as the guager applies his rule to the vessel he would measure, or the assayer his test to the metal he would prove.' Very good; but where is the clergyman, in regular standing, who dares to be thus faithful? And where one Abdiel is found, are there not scores of the fraternity, who, to avoid difficulty, refuse to say aught about ' the habits and practices of the age,' except to uphold them?

Dr. GANNETT thinks otherwise. He says, ' it is an old slander, that the clergy always oppose social advancement, and it is a slander which every popular movement since the Reformation has refuted ' ! To this general assertion, I enter a general denial, and wait for the proof. With much assurance, he says—' Look at the relation they sustain to the reforms of the day, moral, political, or social; always ready to examine their claims, (!) sometimes compelled to pronounce the schemes of ardent philanthropists unsound or dangerous, but more often prompt to give their assistance, (!) and not seldom found among the foremost and firmest friends of the enterprise ' ! Now, these assertions are as far removed from the facts in the case, as the North is from the South pole. Take the question of slavery, for example. The reducing of three millions of the inhabitants of this country to the awful condition of chattels is an' act of impiety and cruelty so monstrous, that the clergy should have needed no solicitation to induce them to cry out against it in thunder tones. Yet, to this hour, as a class, their sympathy and co-operation are notoriously with the slaveholders, with whom they are in religious fellowship; they seek to cover the abolitionists with shame and infamy; their meeting-houses are closed against those who wish to inculcate the doctrine, that slaveholding is, under all circumstances, a sin against God. Indeed, the history of the anti-slavery movement will prove

20 *

the struggle for the overthrow of slavery to have been as directly with the clergy of the land, as with the actual hold-ers of slaves at the South. The facts are on record, and can never be effaced. I admit that there have been, and that there are, exceptions to the general rule — clergymen who have done, and are doing, much toward liberating those who are in bondage ; but these only serve to confirm the rule. The manner in which they have been treated by their cleri-cal brethren generally, of the same denomination, and by the churches, has been contemptuous and most unchristian. Will the successor of WILLIAM ELLERY CHANNING pretend that he, or the Unitarian clergy, countenanced Dr. CHAN-NING in his efforts to awaken pity for the slave, and shame for the existence of slavery ? When and where has he uttered a single word of encouragement to those who have borne the heat and burden of the day in the cause of the oppressed ? When has he allowed an abolitionist to occupy his pulpit ? What Unitarian clerical man-stealer from the South would he exclude from it ? How was the lamented FOLLEN treated in his day ? How has JOHN PIERPONT been treated ? What approbation has THEODORE PARKER receiv-ed from the clergy for his faithful anti-slavery testimonies — his apostolic boldness in grappling with popular sins ? For how many years did not SAMUEL J. MAY stand up among the Unitarian clergy almost alone, in his earnest and Christ-like advocacy of the cause of negro emancipation — being deem-ed an intolerable troubler of Israel ?

I appeal to those who are struggling to carry forward the reforms of the day, as to their experience and knowledge of clerical influence. Friends of peace, of moral reform, of non-resistance, of the abolition of the gallows, of woman's rights, of land reform, of social reorganization, &c. &c., are you not ready to testify, that you find the clergy hindrances rather than helps ?

Practical righteousness is what the age needs, and what should most deeply concern those who are qualified to act the part of instructors and guides. This is not within the pale of polemic divinity. At least, religious controversies are well nigh interminable, and seldom of any value, because they generally relate to the past, rather than to the present, to an orthodox creed, rather than to a pure life, to 'words, words, words,' rather than to ideas and practices. Doctrinal assaults, however vigorously made, are easily parried or returned; but, when judgment is laid to the line, and righteousness to the plummet, and the church, of whatever name, is convicted of immorality, then her power is broken, and every blow of the reformer is felt. If I had arraigned the clergy or the church on account of their peculiar tenets, they would have rejoiced to meet me in a polemic encounter, and text for text would they have hurled at me with spirit and skill. But I measured them by the unerring standard—'By their fruits shall ye know them.' I demonstrated their position, in regard to slavery, war and other crimes, to be time-serving and corrupt—convicted them of 'striking hands with thieves, and consenting with adulterers'—showed their identity with those of old, who were full of their sabbaths and solemn assemblies, their fastings and prayers, their tithing of mint, anise and cummin, while they were strengthening the bands of oppression, binding heavy burdens upon men's shoulders, shedding innocent blood, and stoning the faithful witnesses for God. In this manner they have been humbled; on this ground they cannot stand. A free platform is offered to them, but they shrink from an encounter before the people, conscious that they are justly accused.

Representing no society or body of people on earth—speaking only my own sentiments, on my own responsibility, on the platform of free discussion, not of technical anti-

slavery—I am free to declare, that my objections are not
to the 'abuses' of the priestly order. It has no abuses;
it is, in itself, an abuse. Mankind cannot tolerate it
safely. It is the sworn foe of Progress, a mountainous
obstacle in the pathway of Humanity. It was unknown to
primitive Christianity; it derives no authority from the
gospel.

For as cogent reasons, I seek the overthrow of every
church, which, simply by virtue of its organization, or its
creed, claims to be divinely instituted — the church of Christ,
and thus makes the evidence of piety to consist in joining it,
or acknowledging the validity of its claims. There never
yet was a divine human organization. Associations are not
of heaven, but of men. They are no positive test of character. To join them is no certain proof of piety; to refuse
to be connected with them, nay, to advocate their dissolution, is no evidence of an irreligious or heretical state of
mind. 'A breath can make them as a breath has made '—
and unmake them too. Men shape them as they do their
coats, their hats, or their dwellings, according to their own
taste and convenience. None may say to another, without
daring presumption, 'You must connect yourself with our
church, or with some other, or you are not a Christian.'
The Church of Christ is not mutable but permanent, and
therefore not a formal organization. No one can be voted
into it, no one expelled from it, by human suffrages. They
are grossly deceived, who imagine that, because they have
joined a body calling itself the church of Christ, therefore
they are members of the true church. Our Protestant
churches are nearly all based on a false foundation—the
foundation of Rome itself — and with Rome are destined to
perish.

For these views, however, no Anti-Slavery society in the
land is responsible; nor is it the purpose of any such society

to promulgate or sanction any doctrine or sentiment which does not relate strictly to the abolition of slavery. The American Anti-Slavery Society has sacredly adhered to its one great object, leaving all other question, whether relating to Church or State, to be settled by its members on another platform, on their individual responsibility. It arraigns no man for his religious or political opinions, beyond insisting on the duty of giving no countenance to slaveholding. With a ministry, or church, or government, or party, that is faithful to the cause of the slave, it has no controversy, but is ever ready to give credit to whom credit is due.

On the Death of a Friend.

THE grave, dear sufferer, had for thee no gloom,
   And Death no terrors when his summons came :
   Unto the dust returns the mortal frame,
But the SOUL spurns the bondage of the tomb,
And soars to flourish in immortal bloom !
  Thou hast attained, at last, thy glorious aim —
   Heaven and its joys — through faith in Christ's dear name.
Why should we grieve, then, at thy early doom ?
If thy freed spirit be indeed at rest,
   And singing sweetly in another sphere ;
If, as we trust, thou art among the blest,
   Redeemed from all that made life painful here ;
Songs of rejoicing far become us best,
   For light resplendent beams around thy bier !

Free Speech and Free Inquiry.

SINCE the commencement of the nineteenth century, the Spirit of Reform has been developed in a shape, and to an extent, unknown to all preceding ages — Reform, not pertaining merely to local abuses or wrongs, not marked by degrees of latitude or longitude, but making man the object of universal solicitude, aside from all considerations of party, sect, education, condition, and clime — Reform, not for the overthrow of any one particular evil, but for the removal of all those burdens and disabilities under which mankind are groaning in agony of spirit — Reform, not animated by the spirit of revenge, not armed with weapons of steel with which to cleave down tyrants and usurpers, but relying for its success on the utterance of truth, and the enforcement of right, on the weakness of injustice, and the cowardice of crime — Reform, to the conservative, timid and faithless, never so daring in its aspect, and unhallowed in its purposes, as now ; to the believing, the true-hearted and clear-sighted, never so serene in its spirit, disinterested in its design, and beneficent in its operations.

> ' The poor crushed bondman hears it, and upspringeth
>   To burst his shackles, and once more be free ;
> And shouts aloud, until the echo ringeth
>   O'er the far islands of the Eastern sea.
> The faithful lover of his race rejoices —
>   The champion girds his gleaming armor on —
> The seer saith, ' GOD speaks in those earnest voices;
>   Earth's fearful battle-field shall yet be won ! '
> O'er every radiant island of creation
>   The music of that swelling peal is borne ;
> Land bears to land, and nation shouts to nation,
>   The war-cry of the age — REFORM ! REFORM ! '

All things are interrogated as to their origin, intent, tendency, and lawfulness, without much regard to their antiquity, or the authority with which they are clothed. The cry is everywhere heard for free speech and free inquiry, that Right may prevail, and Imposture be put to flight. It is beginning to be seen, that not only are these the best weapons, but that no others may be innocently used against Wrong. Revolutions are to be wrought out by reason, not by brute force.

It was a bold act when the divine right of kings to rule over the people was questioned and denied ; it was a bolder act when it was declared, (as it was by our revolutionary fathers,) that even the toleration of a king was not compatible with the liberty of the people. But other voices are heard, not only protesting against monarchical governments, but demanding that even republican governments, as now constituted, be dispensed with, for something more just, protective, and beneficent. The political views of 1776 have been greatly transcended ; and the doctrine, that might is right, when the majority obtain the reins of power, is seen by many to be as essentially despotic in principle, as that of the divine right of kings. Religiously, there are those who go much further than did Luther, when he attacked the Romish Church as inherently corrupt and anti-christian; for they maintain that the Protestant Church rests on no better foundation than the Romish, and is as false in its claims. All the winds of controversy are freshly blowing, and well may they tremble, whose houses are built upon the sand ; but those whose cause is just, who are earnest seekers after truth, who are in the right, may join in the song of the royal singer of Israel — ' God is our refuge and strength, a very present help in trouble. Therefore will not we fear, though the earth be removed, and though the mountains be carried into the midst of the sea; though the waters thereof roar

and be troubled, though the mountains shake with the swelling thereof'—'They that trust in the Lord shall be as
Mount Zion, that cannot be moved.'

If we had not innumerable facts to prove the general
corruption of the times, the prevalent fear of free speech
and free inquiry would prove it ; for where the mind and
tongue are fettered, either by imperial edicts, by ecclesiastical bulls, by statutory enactments, by the terrors of summary
punishment, by popular sentiment, by the fear of suffering,
or by the prospect of beggary, it indicates an evil state of
society, and the supremacy of a false and sanguinary religion. It is under such circumstances that hypocrisy and
superstition flourish like briars and thorns on an uncultivated
soil.

Talk not of this or that subject being too sacred for investigation ! Is it too much to assert, that there is but one
object beneath the skies that is sacred — and that is, MAN ?
Surely, there is no government, no institution, no order, no
rite, no day, no place, no building, no creed, no book, so
sacred as he who was before every government, institution,
order, rite, day, place, building, creed, and book, and by
whom all these things are to be regarded as nothing higher
or better than means to an end, and that end his own elevation and happiness ; and he is to discard each and all of
them, when they fail to do him service, or minister unto
his necessities. They are not of heaven, but of men, and
may not, therefore, receive the homage of any human being.
Be assured, that whatever cannot bear the test of the closest
scrutiny, has no claim to human respect or confidence, even
though it assume to be sacred in its orgin, or given by
inspiration of God, but must be treated as spurious, profane,
dangerous.

Let, then, the mind, and tongue, and press, be free. Let
free discussion not only be tolerated, but encouraged and

asserted, as indispensable to the freedom and welfare of mankind. A forcible suppression of error is no aid to the cause of truth; and to allow only just such views and sentiments to be spoken and circulated as we think are correct, is to combine bigotry and cowardice in equal proportion. If I give my children no other precept — if I leave them no other example — it shall be, a fearless, impartial, thorough investigation of every subject to which their attention may be called, and a hearty adoption of the principles which to them may seem true, whether those principles agree or conflict with my own, or with those of any other person. The best protection which I can give them is to secure the unrestricted exercise of their reason, and to inspire them with true self-reliance. I will not arbitrarily determine for them what are orthodox or what heretical sentiments, on any subject. I have no wish, no authority, no right to do so. I desire them to see, hear, and weigh, both sides of every question. For example: — I wish them to examine whatever may be advanced in opposition to the doctrine of the divine inspiration of the Bible, as freely as they do whatever they find in support of it; to hear what may be urged against the doctrines, precepts, miracles, or life of Jesus, as readily as they do any thing in their defence; to see what arguments are adduced for a belief in the non-existence of God, as unreservedly as they do the evidence in favor of his existence. I shall teach them to regard no subject as too holy for examination; to make their own convictions paramount to all human authority; to reject whatever conflicts with their reason, no matter by whomsoever enforced; and to prefer that which is clearly demonstrative to mere theory. And why do I intend to pursue such a course? Because I am not infallible, and therefore dare not put on the robes of infallibility. Because I think free inquiry is essential to the life of truth among mankind.

21

Because I believe that right will prevail over wrong, and all the sooner in a fair conflict. Because,

> 'Truth, crushed to earth, shall rise again;
> Th' eternal years of God are hers;
> But Error, wounded, writhes in pain,
> And dies among her worshippers!'

'It is a pleasure to stand upon the shore,' says Lord Bacon, ' and to watch the ships tossed upon the sea ; but no pleasure is comparable to the standing upon the vantage ground of truth — a hill not to be commanded, and where the air is always clear and serene — and to see the errors, and wanderings, and mists, and tempests, in the vale below : so always that this prospect be with pity, and not with pride. Certainly, it is heaven upon earth to have a man's mind move in Charity, rest in Providence, and turn upon the poles of Truth.'

' Whoever is afraid,' says Bishop Watson, ' of submitting any question, civil or religious, to the test of free discussion, seems to me. to be more in love with his own opinion than with the truth.' A noble sentiment for a man,—much more for a prelate !

No sentiment has been more greatly admired, or more frequently quoted, since it was uttered, than that of Jefferson —'Error of opinion may be safely tolerated, where Reason is left free to combat it.'

'Philosophy, wisdom, and liberty,' says Sir W. Drummond, ' support each other. He who will not reason is a bigot ; he who cannot is a fool ; and he who dares not is a slave.'

' The imputation of novelty,' says John Locke, ' is a terrible charge amongst those who judge of men's heads as they do of their perukes, by the fashion — and can allow none to be right but received doctrines.'

Coleridge tersely says—'He who begins with loving Christianity better than Truth, will end by loving himself better than either.'

'There is nothing more unreasonable,' says Lord Mansfield, 'more inconsistent with the rights of human nature, more contrary to the spirit and precepts of the Christian religion, than persecution for opinion.'

It was the complaint of Cicero—'Most men—alas! I know not why—prefer to rest in error, and defend with pertinacity their cherished dogmas, than to examine without bigotry, and seek out what is rational and most consistent.'

'A theological system,' says Dr. Jortin, 'is too often a temple consecrated to implicit faith; and he who enters in there to worship, instead of leaving his shoes, after the Eastern fashion, must leave his understanding at the door; and it will be well if he find it when he comes out again.'

What can be more brave than the words, what more sublime than the front of M. Antoninus, when he exclaimed—'I seek after Truth, by which no man ever yet was injured!'

'I am in the place,' said the intrepid John Knox, on one occasion, 'where I am demanded of conscience to speak the truth, and therefore the truth I speak, impugn it whoso list.'

It is 'Truth that results from discussion and from controversy,' says Paley—not confusion and error.

Among all the noble sayings that fell from the lips of that great champion of English freedom, John Milton, none deserves to be eternized more than this:—'Let Truth and Falsehood grapple: who ever knew Truth put to the worse in a free and open encounter?'

'The spirit of Jesus,' says the amiable and courageous Abbe de la Mennais, 'is a spirit of peace, of compassion, and of love. They who persecute in his name, and who search men's consciences with the sword; who torture the body to convert the soul; who cause tears to flow, instead

of drying them up ; — these men have not the spirit of
Christ, and are none of His.'

The craven, unintelligent, superstitious state of the times
led Byron to write —

  ' What from this barren being do we reap ?
     Our senses narrow, and our reason frail,
   Life short, and TRUTH a gem that loves the deep,
     And all things weighed in CUSTOM's falsest scale ;
   OPINION an omnipotence, whose veil
     Mantles the earth with darkness, until right
  And wrong are accidents ; and men grow pale,
     Lest their own judgments should become too bright,
And their free thoughts be crimes, and earth have too much light ! '

It is never for the people to be afraid of light, or willing
to be tongue-tied.   They cannot think too much, or talk too
freely.   They never lead, but have always been led — why
should they not move forward independently ?   They have
for long ages been burdened and oppressed — what have
they to lose by the growth of freedom ?   They have been
kept in the darkness of ignorance — what have they to fear
from the prevalence of knowledge ?   Let tyrants cry, ' Put
out the light ! '   Good reason have they to do so !

    ' Tyrants are but the spawn of Ignorance,
     Begotten by the slaves they trample on,
     Who, could they win a glimmer of the light,
     And see that Tyranny is always weakness,
     Or Fear with its own bosom ill at ease,
     Would laugh away in scorn the sand-wove chain,
     Which their own blindness feigned for adamant.
     Wrong ever builds on quicksands, but the Right
     To the firm centre lays its moveless base.
     The tyrant trembles, if the air but stirs
     The innocent ringlets of a child's free hair,
     And crouches when the thought of some great spirit,
     With world-wide murmur, like a rising gale,

Over men's hearts, as over standing corn,
Rushes, and bends them to its own strong will.'

So testifies one of the youngest, yet ripening to be the greatest of all our American poets, (J. R. LOWELL,) and even now unsurpassed in the freedom of his muse, and the moral grandeur of his genius. Hear him again, in a strain of which Milton himself would have been proud : —

'My soul is not a palace of the past,
Where outworn creeds, like Rome's grey senate, quake,
Hearing afar the Vandal's trumpet hoarse,
That shakes old systems with a thunder-fit.
The time is ripe, and rotten-ripe, for change :
Then let it come! I have no dread of what
Is called for by the instinct of mankind ;
Nor think I that God's world will fall apart,
Because we tear a parchment more or less.
Truth is eternal, but her effluence,
With endless change, is fitted to the hour ;
Her mirror is turned forward, to reflect
The promise of the future, not the past.'

Again :

'Get but the Truth once uttered, and 'tis like
A star new-born, that drops into its place,
And which, once circling in its placid round,
Not all the tumult of the earth can shake.'

What serenity of mind, what deliverance from the power of tradition, what depth of moral philosophy, what faith in man, what trust in God, have we here compressed into a few lines!

My conviction of the weakness and mutability of error is such, that the free utterance of any opinions, however contrary to my own, has long since ceased to give me any uneasiness as to the final triumph of Right. My confidence

21*

in the unconquerable energy of Truth is absolute ; and therefore I ask for it, what only it requires, ' a fair field and no
quarters.' It never shuns the light, but always rejoices in it.
It never forbids, but ever encourages freedom of thought,
speech and inquiry. It is never afraid to be examined, but
challenges the severest scrutiny. It commends itself to the
human understanding by its own inherent excellence, and
discards all factitious props. It is not a miracle, but a fact.
It belongs to the human race, not to a sect or party. It may
be called an exact science, by the application of which, all
falsehood and imposture shall finally be detected, and exiled
from the earth.

But what is Truth, and how shall it be discovered ?

As to what it is, let this answer suffice — it is not error ;
and error is that which is not true. The ignorance of men
concerning Truth does not touch its reality, nor invalidate its
authenticity ; neither do their conflicting speculations in relation to it render it equivocal or uncertain. It was the same
in the days of Adam, of Noah, of Abraham, of Moses, of
Jesus, however dimly revealed or imperfectly understood in
the procession of ages. It is as old as the sun, moon, and
stars — yea, ' from everlasting to everlasting.'

As to the discovery of it, I know of no safer, higher, or
better way, than to leave the human mind perfectly untrammelled, to contend for unlimited investigation, to vindicate
the supremacy of reason, to plead for unfettered speech, to
argue from analogy, to decide upon evidence, to be governed by facts, to disclaim infallibility, to believe in eternal
growth and progress, to repudiate all arbitrary authority, to
make no man or body of men oracular, to learn from the
teachings of history, to see with our own eyes and hear with
our own ears — in one sentence, to ' prove all things, and
hold fast that which is good.' The fact, that men are more
or less ignorant — that they misapprehend the truth, and

conflict in their views of it—demonstrates the absolute need of freedom of conscience and speech on the part of every individual, as also the absurdity and cruelty of putting reason under the ban, or of affixing pains and penalties to heretical opinions; for who shall dogmatically assume to decide what is heresy, or inflict vengeance upon the heretic?

'Free inquiry' is an expression which has become a terror to multitudes, who claim to have God, Christ, and his gospel, reason and common sense, on their side! It has become odious by being the watchword of a certain class, popularly styled 'infidels.' Now this I am free to declare, that I am against that religion which discountenances free inquiry, and in favor of that infidelity which is for it. This was the infidelity of Paul. He was a 'free inquirer,' and among his injunctions was this—'Prove ALL things,'—in other words, take nothing for granted; whatever is true will bear handling; whatever you find to be good, that receive and cherish for its own sake, though, for so doing, you be denounced as a pestilent and seditious fellow, and ranked among the offscouring of all things.

Is it worthy of us, as rational beings, to be stultified by ghostly authority, or intimidated from hearing, searching, trying all things, in consequence of the outcries of a bigoted intolerance? Is it impossible for us to be mistaken? Have we never detected ourselves in error, or changed in opinion? Can we grow no more? Who that is in the right, or that honestly believes that he has truth on his side, is afraid?

True, it does not follow that a man is in the right, because he is ready to engage in controversy; for he may be devoid of sense, or disgustingly presumptuous, or extremely vain, or annoyingly combative, or incurably perverse. But this is certain:—he who is for forcibly stopping the mouth of his opponent, or for burning any man at the stake, or thrusting him into prison, or exacting a pecuniary fine from him, or impairing his means of procuring an honest livelihood, or treating him scornfully, on account of his peculiar views on any subject, whether relating to God or man, to time or eternity, is either under the dominion of a spirit of ruffian-ism or cowardice, or animated by that fierce intolerance which characterized Saul of Tarsus, in his zeal to extermi-nate the heresy of Christianity.   On the other hand, he who forms his opinions from the dictates of enlightened reason, and sincerely desires to be led into all truth, dreads nothing so much as the suppression of free inquiry — is at all times ready to give a reason for the hope that is in him — calmly listens to the objections of others — and feels nothing of anger or alarm, lest his foundation shall be swept away by the waves of opposition.   It is impossible, therefore, for him to be a persecutor, or to call upon the strong arm of vio-lence to put a gag into the mouth of any one, however heret-ical in his sentiments.   In proportion as we perceive and embrace the truth, do we become meek, heroic, magnani-mous, divine.   They may not talk of faith in God, or of standing on the eternal rock, who turn pale with fear or are flushed with anger when their cherished convictions are call-ed in question, or who cry out, ' If we let this man alone, the people will believe on him, and the Romans will come, and take away our place and nation.'   They know not what spirit they are of; the light that is in them is darkness, and ' how great is that darkness '!   It was not Jesus who was filled with consternation, but his enemies, on account of the heresy of untrammelled thought and free utterance :— ' Then the high priest rent his clothes, saying, He hath spoken blasphemy : what further need have we of wit-nesses?   Behold, now ye have heard his blasphemy.   What think ye?   They answered and said, He is guilty of death. Then did they spit in his face, and buffet him ; and others smote him with the palms of their hands.'   So have ever behaved the ' pious ' advocates of Error ; such has ever been the treatment of the ' blasphemous ' defender of Truth.

> ' Let us speak plain : there is more force in names
> Than most men dream of ; and a lie may keep
> Its throne a whole age longer, if it skulk
> Behind the shield of some fair-seeming name.
> Let us call tyrants, TYRANTS, and maintain
> That only freedom comes by grace of God,
> And all that comes not by his grace must fall ;
> For men in earnest have no time to waste
> In patching fig-leaves for the naked truth.'

' Let us call tyrants, TYRANTS.' Not to do so is to misuse language, to deal treacherously with freedom, to consent to the enslavement of mankind. It is neither an amiable nor a virtuous, but a foolish and pernicious thing, not to call things by their right names. John Knox, when he was reprimanded for his severity of speech, with much significance and great good sense declared that he would call a fig a fig, and a spade a spade. ' Wo unto them,' says one of the world's great prophets, ' that call evil good, and good evil ; that put darkness for light, and light for darkness ; that put bitter for sweet, and sweet for bitter.'

Popular sins are never regarded by the people as sins ; they are never called sins. Terms are invented to describe them, which fall upon the ear without harshness, and which, whenever uttered, give no alarm to the moral sense. This is what is called in Scripture, the transformation of Satan into an angel of light. Thus, they who are engaged in upbuilding the horrid slave system in this country — a system which presents no single feature of decency or utility, and which John Wesley comprehensively and justly called ' the sum of all villanies ' — the Southern slaveholders and their abettors, designate it as ' the peculiar institution,' as ' the corner-stone of our republican edifice.' This descrip-

tion of it conveys no idea to the mind that is revolting or
disagreeable, but quite the contrary — and yet it means
theft and robbery; it means assault and battery; it means
nakedness and penury; it means yokes, fetters, branding-
irons, drivers and bloodhounds; it means cruelty and murder,
concubinage and adultery; it means the denial of all chances
of intellectual and moral culture, gross mental darkness, and
utter moral depravation; it means the transformation of
those, who, in the scale of creation, are but a little lower
than the angels, to the condition of brutes and the fate of
perishable property; in one sentence, it means the denial of
God as the common Father of us all, and of Christ as our
common Savior and Redeemer. Still, we wrap it up in the
fine linen of a deceitful phraseology — we call it ' the peculiar institution ' — outwardly, we garnish this sepulchre, and
make it pleasant to the eye, but carefully hide the bones,
the uncleanness, and the pollution, which are festering
beneath. The terrible exclamation which Milton puts into
the mouth of Satan seems to be our great national motto —
' Evil, be thou my good ! '

Thus, in the formation of our national Constitution, we
carefully eschewed every word that might shock the ear of
the most fastidious lover of liberty; and yet, by words,
phrases and clauses therein inserted, we intentionally and
deliberately became partners in the capital crime of slaveholding; we agreed to prosecute the African slave trade, with
national energy and enterprise, for at least twenty years;
we admitted a slaveholding oligarchy (incomparably more
oppressive and dangerous than an hereditary nobility) into
Congress; we made it lawful to hunt and recapture fugitive
slaves in every part of our national domains; we pledged our
entire naval and military force to keep the slave population
securely in their chains. And having thus involved ourselves in blood-guiltiness, we fall down and worship the

instrument that we have made, with the same infatuation as
that which characterizes the worshippers of Juggernaut. And
we say, as did the murderous and oppressive Jews of old,
who broke in pieces the people of God, and afflicted his
heritage,—who slew the widow, the stranger, and the fatherless—'The Lord shall not see, neither shall the God of
Jacob regard it.' But the admonition that was given to
them may be addressed to us, with even greater force and
solemnity—' Understand, ye brutish among the people ; and
ye fools, when will ye be wise ? He that planted the ear,
shall he not hear ? he that formed the eye, shall he not see ?
he that chastiseth the heathen, shall not he correct ? he that
teacheth man knowledge, shall not he know ? '

'Once to every man and nation comes the moment to decide,
In the strife of Truth with Falsehood, for the good or evil side;
Some great cause, God's new Messiah, offering each the bloom or
blight,
Parts the goats upon the left hand, and the sheep upon the right;
And the choice goes by for ever 'twixt that darkness and that light.

'Have ye chosen, O my people, on whose party ye shall stand,
Ere the Doom from its worn sandals shakes its dust against our
land?
Though the cause of evil prosper, yet the Truth alone is strong,
And, albeit she wander outcast now, I see around her throng
Troops of beautiful, tall angels, to enshield her from all wrong.'

Of all the reformers who have appeared in the world—
whether they were prophets, the Son of God, apostles, martyrs or confessors; whether assailing one form of popular
iniquity or another; whether impeaching the rulers in the
State, or the teachers in the Church; not one of them has
been exempt from the charge of dealing in abusive language,
of indulging in coarse personalities, of libelling the characters of great and good men, of aiming to subvert time-hon-

ored and glorious institutions, of striking at the foundations
of the social fabric, of being actuated by an irreligious spirit.
The charge has ever been false, malicious, the very reverse
of the truth; and it is only the reformer himself who has
been the victim of calumny, hatred and persecution.   His
accusations are denied, his impeachments are pronounced
libellous, simply because the giant iniquity which he assails
has subdued to its own evil purposes all the religious and
political elements of the land, and everywhere passes current as both necessary and reputable.   Of Jesus it was said,
' This man is not of God ; he keepeth not the Sabbath day.'
' He is a blasphemer ; he hath a devil.'   Of the Apostles it
was said, ' They are pestilent and seditious fellows, who go
about seeking to turn the world upside down.'   And Paul
declares that they were treated as the offscouring of all
things.   Luther and his coadjutors were represented as the
monsters of their times.   Those excellent and wonderful
men, Penn, Fox, Barclay, with the early Friends, suffered
every kind of reproach, and experienced great tribulation,
as infidel emissaries and fanatical disorganizers.   Before the
abolition of the African slave trade, Wilberforce and Clarkson were vehemently denounced as interfering with vested
rights, and seeking to cripple the prosperity of England ;
and a murderous attempt was made to drown the latter in
the river Mersey, at Liverpool.   It is needless to ask how
those heroic and unfaltering pioneers of our race are now
regarded.   The mid-day sun, shining in the fullness of its
strength, is not brighter — the firm-set earth is not more
solid, than their fame ; and down through all coming time
shall they be hailed by countless processions of new-born
generations as among the saviors of their race.   There will
be none to distrust their disinterestedness, none to question
their sanity, none to scoff at their testimony.

'For Humanity sweeps onward; where to-day the martyr stands,
On the morrow crouches Judas with the silver in his hands;
Far in front the Cross stands ready, and the crackling faggots burn,
While the hooting mob of yesterday in silent awe return
To glean up the scattered ashes into History's golden urn.

'Careless seems the great Avenger; history's pages but record
One death-grapple in the darkness 'twixt old systems and the
    Word;
Truth for ever on the scaffold, Wrong for ever on the throne, —
Yet that scaffold sways the future, and, behind the dim unknown,.
Standeth God within the shadow, keeping watch above his own.'

In taking a retrospect of the past, the present stands ostensibly amazed and shocked at the treatment of those glorious
old reformers. It sees nothing in the sternest language of
the prophets to condemn; it hails Jesus as the true Messiah,
and weeps over his crucifixion; it venerates the memories
of the apostles and martyrs; it places Luther, Calvin, Penn,.
in the calendar of saints. It mourns that all these were
beyond its countenance and succor, and takes infinite credit
to itself, that it is animated by a far higher and nobler spirit.
All this is spurious virtue and mock piety; it is a cheap
mode of being heroic and good, for it costs nothing. The
corrupt rulers, false prophets, and cunning priests, whom
Isaiah and Jeremiah rebuked, and who visited upon the
heads of these martyr-witnesses a terrible retribution, are all
in their graves, and can neither bribe nor overawe us; nor
have we any interests in common with them; and we therefore sit in judgment between them and their accusers with a
clear vision, a steady pulse, and an unbiased judgment.
The chief priests, scribes and pharisees, with the rabble who
cried out, 'Release not this man, but Barrabbas,' and ended
by crucifying Jesus between two thieves, are gone, with all
their official splendor; their religious authority, their brutal
ruffianism, their power to kill. We fear them not; we read
22

the woes pronounced against them by the faithful Nazarene, and feel no indignation at his strong language; we regard that generation with abhorrence.   So, too, they who hunted, like wild beasts, the reformers of the 15th and 16th centuries, are crumbled to dust, and we stand upon their ashes, and brand them freely and bravely as a band of cowards and persecutors.   Why should we not?   We have no trade at stake; our reputation is not in peril; the fires of Smithfield are quenched; we are living in the nineteenth century; and dead men cannot harm us.   But what are we doing in regard to the impostures, the crimes, the wrongs of our own times, and our own country?   Are we grappling with them, with any thing like the boldness of those whose sepulchres we are proud to build, whose memories we almost adore?   Are we striving to do for posterity what they did for us, and thus honestly discharging that great debt?   Or are we basely bowing the knee to a corrupt public sentiment, hurrying with the multitude to do evil, and leaving those responsibilities which God has imposed upon us, to be met by those who shall come after us?   If not ourselves acting as the moral pioneers of our times, what are we saying of those who are willing to be made of no reputation for Truth's sake, and who are receiving a share of the persecution that was meted out to Jesus and his disciples?   Are we joining with the enslavers of their fellow-men, with designing priests and profligate demagogues, with the infuriated and lawless mob, in raising the cry, 'Fanatics! traitors! infidels!'

If so, how much better, then, are we, than those old Jewish murderers of our Lord, who built the tombs of the prophets, and garnished the sepulchres of the righteous, and said, 'If we had been in the days of our fathers, we would not have been partakers with them in the blood of the prophets?'   To them the language of Jesus was, 'Wherefore ye be witnesses unto yourselves, that ye are children of them which killed the prophets, and of you shall be required all the blood that has been shed, from the blood of Abel unto the blood of Zacharias.' If we are treading in their foot-steps; if we are as recreant to truth, as false to right, as hostile to liberty, in our day, as they were in theirs; if we are unwilling to suffer in our reputation or worldly prosperity, to look tyrants and impostors serenely in the face, and bid them defiance while we unmask them; if we ask, concerning those who are perishing, or grinding in the prison-house of bondage, ' Are we our brother's keepers? '— then may we not sing the praises of Christ as our exemplar and guide, nor profess to honor his apostles, nor pretend to be animated by the love of God. We must be associated — nay, if we persevere in such a course, we shall be associated hereafter, by posterity — with those whom we now admit were the enemies of their race.

But let it not be so with us. Let us prove ourselves worthy of the great and good who have gone before us. Truth needs our help; let her have it. Right is cloven down in the land; let us come to the rescue. Liberty is hunted with bloodhounds, and lynch law is threatened to her advocates; let us form a body-guard around her, and bare our bosom to the shafts that are aimed at her. Christianity, as exemplified in the life of its great Founder, is tarnished, modified, perverted to the sanctioning of enormous crimes, to the justification of sinners of the first rank; let us endeavor to remove its stain, to hold it up in its pristine purity, as against all wrong, all injustice, all tyranny, and embracing all mankind in one common brotherhood. Millions of our countrymen are in chains, crying to us for deliverance; on the side of their oppressors there is power; let us rally for their emancipation, and never retire from the conflict, until victory or death be ours. The demon spirit of War is driving his chariot-wheels over the bodies of pros-

trate thousands, and kindling the flames of hell throughout
our borders; let us be volunteers in the cause of peace, and
give no countenance whatever to the spirit of violence. To
do all this, it will cost us something; we must think no more
of the bubble reputation of the hour than did Jesus; we
must have entire faith in God, and be baptized into the divine
spirit of love; we must see of the travail of our souls, and
be satisfied; we must be strengthened and consoled by the
thought, that, in addition to the sweet approval of our own
consciences, we shall secure the gratitude of a redeemed
posterity, and the smiles of God; we must possess that
indomitable spirit which led John Adams to exclaim, on
signing the Declaration of Independence, 'Sink or swim,
live or die, I give my hand and my heart to this Declaration!'

'Then to side with Truth is noble, when we share her wretched
        crust,
Ere her cause bring fame and profit, and 'tis prosperous to be just;
Then it is the brave man chooses, while the coward stands aside,
Doubting in his abject spirit till his Lord is crucified,
And the multitude make virtue of the faith they had denied.'

No amount of homage paid to the past is a sure indica-
tion of living virtue. On the contrary, the more profusely
it is bestowed, the more clearly it will be seen that it is designed as a cloak to cover moral cowardice or arrant apostacy. Nothing is easier, nothing more common, than to
honor 'Abraham, Isaac and Jacob'; to build and garnish
the tombs of the old prophets; to celebrate the deeds of
Jesus and his Apostles. Nothing is more difficult, nothing
more rare, than to walk in their footsteps and imitate their
example; to live, in our day, as they did in theirs, without
reputation, hated, despised, persecuted, for righteousness'
sake. Generally speaking, I care not how highly any one

praises the dead, or how great may be his professed veneration for Luther or Calvin, for Whitefield or Wesley, for
David or Moses, for Jesus or Paul. As, at this day, all this
is popular, and is everywhere well received, it gives me
no evidence of any vital appreciation of the character of
those intrepid reformers, on the part of the encomiast. The
cowardly and time-serving, the hypocritical and pharisaical,
are always prompt to appear as the special champions of all
departed, canonized worth. The last persons in the world
who ought to profess admiration of the bold dissenter, the
upright heretic, the righteous agitator, the heaven-inspired
fanatic of the past, are they who dread to be found in a
minority; who are ever consulting the vane of public opinion; who shrink from grappling with prevailing iniquity;
who tremble at the thought of perilling their reputation;
and whose aim is to pass through life without the slightest
connection with any thing deemed extravagant or fanatical.
Heaven save me from the folly of descanting about the
merits and sacrifices of the dead, unless my own life bear
some little resemblance to theirs, in manly contempt of what
is merely fashionable, in cheerful readiness to endure
reproach, in bold aggression upon systematic wrong, in
wrestling against ' principalities, and powers, and spiritual
wickedness in high places.'

To every great reform, the same objections, substantially,
are urged, until it triumphs. First — That it is against
the Scriptures. Second — That it disturbs the peace and
endangers the safety of the Church. . Third — That it is
generally discarded by the priesthood, who, being divinely
appointed, must know all about it. Fourth — That it is
contrary to long-established precedent and venerated authority. Fifth — That it lacks respectability and character;
those who espouse it are generally obscure, uninfluential,
and none of the rulers believe on it. Sixth — It is sheer

22 *

fanaticism; and its triumph would be the overthrow of all
order in society, and chaos would come again. Lastly —
Its advocates are vulgar in speech, irreverent in spirit, personal in attack, seeking their own base ends by bad means,
and presumptuously attempting to dictate to the wise, the
learned, and the powerful.

Be not intimidated by any of these outcries. They are
'full of sound and fury, signifying nothing.' Or, rather,
they indicate the standard around which it is your duty and
my duty to rally ; and that is, the standard of Right, whether
storm or sunshine is to be our portion, or whatever may be
the consequences.

First of all, let us maintain freedom of speech; let us
encourage honest and fearless inquiry in all things. Let us
recognise no higher standard than that of Reason, and dare
to summon to its bar all books, customs, governments, institutions and laws, that we may prove them, and render our
verdict accordingly. Whatever in this great universe is
above our reason, with that we need have no controversy,
nor should it give us any anxiety ; whatever is contrary to
our reason, that let us promptly reject, though a thousand
books deemed sacred should declare it to be true — though
ten thousand councils should affirm it to be right — though
all nations should pronounce us to be guilty of a terrible
heresy in rejecting it. If God does not address us as reasonable beings, he cannot address us as accountable beings,
and hence we are absolved from every moral obligation to
him : we take our place with the beasts of the field, with
the fowls of the air, with stocks and stones. But he has
created us in his great and glorious image : and

> 'In our spirit doth His spirit shine,
> As shines the sunbeam in a drop of dew.'

'Come, now, let us reason together, saith the Lord.' To

resort to reason, then, is godlike; to discard it, to be afraid
of it, to set something else above it, is to make ourselves
weak and foolish, as well as criminal and worthless. 'Why
judge ye not of yourselves what is right?' said Jesus to
the Jews. He appealed to their reason, and by so doing,
implied that he could make no higher appeal. 'It is a small
thing to be judged of man's judgment,' said Paul. 'Let
every man be fully persuaded in his own mind.' 'Prove all
things; hold fast that which is good.'

Such are not the injunctions given us by modern teachers.
They beg us not to be inquisitive; they attempt to frighten
us from a searching investigation of the things which they
assume to be sacred; they desire us to be satisfied with the
discoveries of the past; they point us to the interpretations,
readings and decisions of the ancient fathers; they declare
dissent to be a heresy that will endanger the eternal safety
of the soul; they cry—'Prove nothing'—it has been
already proved by others; they enjoin us to 'hold fast that
which *is*,' whether it be good or bad. Such are moral
cowards, false teachers, or wolves in sheep's clothing;
from such, turn away.

Thank God, the Past is not the Present. For its opportunities and deeds, we are not responsible. It is for us to
discharge the high duties that devolve on us, and carry our
race onward. To be no better, no wiser, no greater than
the Past, is to be little, and foolish, and bad; it is to misap-
ply noble means, to sacrifice glorious opportunities for the
performance of sublime deeds, to become cumberers of the
ground. We can and must transcend our predecessors, in
their efforts to give peace, joy, liberty to the world.

'New occasions teach new duties; Time makes ancient good
　　uncouth;
They must upward, still, and onward, who would keep abreast of
　　Truth:—

Lo! before us gleam her camp-fires! we ourselves must Pilgrims be,
Launch our Mayflower, and steer boldly through the desperate
      winter sea,
Nor attempt the FUTURE's portal with the PAST's blood-rusted key.'

The history of the world presents no period so interesting
or so sublime as the one in which we are called to be actors.
It furnishes scope for the noblest ambition, for the exercise
of the mightiest intellect, for the indulgence of the most
philanthropic spirit, for the achievement of the most beneficent purposes.

The extremity in which we find our country, at the present crisis, should induce us to forget our party feuds, our
sectarian rivalries, and our personal variances. A common
danger should make us *one*, to conspire for our safety, and
the maintenance of the Right. We have in our midst,
occupying two thirds of our national territory, a system,
which, in all that vast section, allows no man to examine it,
to speak his mind freely in regard to it, — especially, to
labor for its overthrow. The very fact, that it will not
submit to examination, strikes down freedom of speech
and of the press, and the right of petition, demonstrates it
to be incurably wicked and horribly offensive. That system
is slavery; and, like a cancer, it is eating out the vitals of
the republic. We are under the absolute dominion of the
Slave Power—a Power, which, like the grave, is never
satisfied—and, like the horse-leech, is ever crying, ' Give!
give!' It is ruling us with a rod of iron; and it is constantly lengthening its cords and strengthening its stakes.
Before we ourselves can know what freedom is, and what
it can do for us, — before freedom of speech and free inquiry can be safely enjoyed on our soil,—we have, first of all,
to grapple with that unhallowed Power, and to decree its
annihilation.

To My First-Born.

I.

HEAVEN's long-desired gift! my first-born child!
  Pledge of the purest love! my darling son!
  Now do I feel a father's bliss begun, —
A father's hopes and fears, — babe undefiled!
Shouldst thou be spared, I could be reconciled
  Better to martyrdom, — so may be won
  Freedom for all, and servile chains undone.
For if, amid this conflict, fierce and wild,
With the stout foes of God and man, I fall,
  Then shalt thou early fill my vacant post,.
And, pouring on the winds a trumpet-call,
  Charge valiantly OPPRESSION's mighty host;;
So captive millions thou shalt disenthral,
  And, through the mighty God, of victory boast..

II.

Remember, when thou com'st to riper years,
  That unto GOD, from earliest infancy,
  Thy grateful father dedicated thee,
And sought HIS guidance through this vale of tears.
Fear GOD — then disregard all other fears;
  Be, in HIS Truth, erect, majestic, free;
  Abhor OPPRESSION — cling to LIBERTY —
Nor recreant prove, though horrid Death appears.
I charge thee, in the name of HIM who died
  On Calvary's cross, — an ignominious fate, —
If thou wouldst reign with the GREAT CRUCIFIED,.
  Thy reputation and thy life to hate.:.
Thus shalt thou save them both, nor be denied
  A glittering crown and throne of heavenly state! .

III.

Flesh of my flesh! now that I see thy form,
  And catch the starry brilliance of thine eyes,
  And hear — sweet music! thy infantile cries,

And feel in thee the life-blood beating warm,
Strange thoughts within me generate and swarm;
  Streams of emotion, overflowing, rise;
  Such joy thy birth affords, and glad surprise,
O nursling of the sunshine and the storm !
Bear witness, Heaven ! do I hate Slavery less, —
  Do I not hate it more, intensely more, —
Now this dear babe I to my bosom press ?
  My soul is stirred within me — ne'er before
Have horrors filled it with such dire excess,
  Nor pangs so deep pierced to its inmost core !

IV.

Bone of my bone ! not all Golconda's gold
  Is worth the value of a hair of thine !
  Yet is the Negro's babe as dear as mine —
Formed in as pure and glorious a mould :
But, ah ! inhumanly 'tis seized and sold !
  Thou hast a soul immortal and divine,
  My priceless jewel ! — In a sable shrine
Lies a bright gem, ' bought with a price ' untold !
A little lower than th' angelic train
  Art thou created, and a monarch's power,
My potent infant ! with a wide domain,
  O'er beast, bird, fish, and insect, is thy dower :
The Negro's babe with thee was made to reign —
  As high in dignity and worth to tower !

V.

O, dearest child of all this populous earth !
  Yet no more precious than the meanest slave !
  To rescue thee from bondage, I would brave
All dangers, and count life of little worth,
And make of stakes and gibbets scornful mirth !
  Am I not perilling as much to save,
  E'en now, from bonds, a race who freedom crave ?
To bless the sable infant from its birth ?
Yet I am covered with reproach and scorn,
  And branded as a madman through the land !

But, loving thee, FREE ONE, my own first-born,
 I feel for all who wear an iron band : —
So Heaven regard my son when I am gone,
 And bless and aid him with a liberal hand !

Oaths and Affirmations.

A SHORT time since, I was summoned as a witness in a civil suit, in the Court of Common Pleas.   On being told to hold up my hand and take the oath, I declined doing so, as a matter of conscience.   Fortunately for me, my testimony was not indispensably necessary ; but, if it had been, or if the Court had chosen to inflict the penalty, I might have been torn from my family, and confined like a felon in jail. Every hour, I am living under this distressing liability ; and there are many others, who, on account of conscientious scruples, are placed in similar peril.   I am fully persuaded that the people only need to have their attention called to this subject, to make them demand the abolition of all oaths and affirmations, at least, in all cases where there are conscientious scruples against taking them.

If, in one instance, conscience may be trampled upon, it may be in all others.   It is not a more arbitrary stretch of power to make it penal to believe in one God, than it is to punish, as a crime, an unwillingness to testify in a manner which the conscience believes is contrary to the will of God. It is in vain to pretend, that the safety of property or the welfare of society requires this legal form of giving testimony ; for this is to say, in other words, that the enjoyment of individual liberty is not compatible with the public good,

and, therefore, that the rights of the minority are not absolute but conditional — dependant upon the sovereign will
and pleasure of the majority. It is yet to be proved, that
legal forms are of any real benefit to society. That, in a
multitude of cases, they are useless, vexatious, oppressive,
is a fact too notorious to need any proof.

Every judge is bound to see that the laws of the State are
duly enforced. Whether those laws are right or wrong, it
is not for him to set them aside. If convinced that they
are barbarous or unchristian, he can only say, 'I am very
sorry that the laws are so made ' — ' The only remedy is to
apply to the Legislature — that is a matter for them, not for
me ' — ' If the courts of law are not conformable to Christianity, it may be proper to bring the subject before the Legislature.' He does not know, and it would be treason for
him to know, any higher power than the Legislature of
Massachusetts, subordinate to the Constitution. He is bound
to know and obey no other God. The enactments of the
Legislature are his standard of justice and mercy, and
beyond these he must not go one hair's breadth, at the peril
of impeachment. He must be ever ready to change with
the vacillating legislation of the Commonwealth. If, to-day,
it makes that a criminal act, which yesterday was innocent, he must expound and enforce the law accordingly,
be its absurdity or its profligacy what it may. Thus, he
surrenders his understanding, conscience and heart to the
will of men, and, consequently, deems it his duty to obey
men rather than God. He knows not, from one session of
the Legislature to another, what he may be called to do.
If, by a decree of that body, he must now send a person to
prison, who will not give his testimony on oath or affirmation, for conscience sake ; by another decree, he may be
called to send to the stake, any one who refuses, in time of
war, to march to the battle-field, for conscience sake. He

may plead, that he is not responsible for the laws ; that it is his duty simply to expound them ; that the legislative and judicial departments of the government are not identical ; — but the plea is worthless. He holds to the doctrine, that might makes right ; that the majority have a right to rule over the minority, and to make such laws and to affix such penalties to them as they please ; that the laws must be obeyed and executed ; that the legislature may properly enact those laws ; that the judicial station which he fills is indispensable to the administration of the government. Hence, he is to be held responsible for the legitimate results of his own principles, and cannot shield himself from condemnation, on the plea that it is not for him, as a judge, to decide on the moral character of the laws.

Why should the custom of administering and taking oaths be universally abandoned ? For the following, among other reasons : —

1. Those who profess to have ' put on Christ,' and to be governed by the Christian law, are assuredly prohibited from taking oaths. In his Sermon on the Mount, Jesus taught nothing more explicitly or more emphatically than the criminality of this practice. Mark his language : — ' Ye have heard that it hath been said by them of old time, Thou shalt not forswear thyself, but shalt perform unto the Lord thy oaths. But I say unto you, SWEAR NOT AT ALL : neither by heaven ; for it is God's throne : nor by the earth ; for it is his footstool : neither by Jerusalem ; for it is the city of the great King. Neither shalt thou swear by thy head, because thou canst not make one hair white or black.' It will be observed, that the prohibition covers the whole ground. It does not merely refer to what is sometimes called unnecessary or profane swearing, nor to swearing falsely, but to swearing at any time, or for any purpose, even truly. It reads, ' Swear not AT ALL ' — but before he

23

lays it down, Jesus quotes the passage, 'Thou shalt not forswear thyself, but shalt perform unto the Lord thine oaths' — (see Leviticus 19 : 12 ; Numbers 30 :2 ; Deuteronomy 23 : 23) — and then repudiates each and all of them, however sacredly they might be performed unto the Lord. 'For it is manifest, that if truth may not be attested by an oath, no oath may be taken.'

But Jesus did not stop here. He proceeded as follows: — 'But let your communication be, Yea, yea ; Nay, nay.' 'This,' says DYMOND, in his able essays on this subject, 'is remarkable : it is positive superadded to negative commands. We are told not only what we ought not, but what we ought to do. It has indeed been said, the expression, "your communication," fixes the meaning to apply to the ordinary course of life. But to this there is a fatal objection : the whole prohibition sets out with a reference, not to conversational language, but to solemn declarations on solemn occasions. Oaths "to the Lord" are placed at the head of the passage ; and it is too manifest to be insisted upon, that solemn declarations, and not every-day talk, were the subject of the prohibition.'

The grand reason for this prohibition is given in the declaration — 'Whatsoever is more than these, COMETH OF EVIL.' Evil, then, is the foundation of oaths ; and that which is built upon evil cannot be good.

Similar were the views of the early Christians. 'The old law,' says Basil, 'is satisfied with the honest keeping of the oath, but Christ cuts off the opportunity of perjury.' 'I say nothing of perjury,' says Tertullian, 'since swearing itself is unlawful to Christians.' Chrysostom says, 'Do not say to me, I swear for a just purpose ; it is no longer lawful for thee to swear, either justly or unjustly.' 'He who,' says Gregory of Nysse, 'has precluded murder by taking away anger, and who has driven away the pollution of adultery by subduing desire, has expelled from our life the cause of perjury by forbidding us to swear; for where there is no oath, there can be no infringement of it.'

2. It is an irreverent act for a court, or any other body of men, to summon God as a witness to their dealings, for purposes of vengeance, as though he could be made a party in the case at their bidding, and could know nothing of the matter without their calling upon him! The obligation to speak the truth cannot be enhanced by any form or device, however 'legally' resorted to.

3. Good men — the honest and truthful — do not need to be put under oath. Bad men — the immoral and abandoned — will not regard an oath, and can never be trusted in giving evidence, beyond the probabilities of the case. Besides: when was it ever known that the latter objected to taking an oath, for conscience sake? They are always ready to be sworn! It is invariably men of true self-respect, of deep conscientiousness, of strong religious principle, who object to this degrading and unchristian practice.

4. To take an oath implies that, were it not administered, it would not be so wicked to testify falsely. But this is to strike at the basis of moral rectitude, and to make the duty of probity dependant upon circumstances. What can be more pernicious than the prevalence of this idea in society?

5. It is wrong to make a man swear that he will tell ' the truth, the whole truth, and nothing but the truth,' while on the stand; because he may be at a loss to know how much is implied by that promise; because his memory may be seriously defective, so as to involve him in apparent and even real contradiction, while his intentions are perfectly upright; because his position, as a witness, may be to him embarrassing beyond expression, questioned and cross-questioned as he is liable to be in the most jesuitical and merciless manner by the counsel employed, so that he is not in a

calm and rational state of mind, but feels bewildered, often alarmed, at the extraordinary array that meets his troubled gaze; because his anxiety to be literally correct in his testimony may be the very cause of his giving it in an incoherent manner. Now, it is wrong to cause any man's memory, veracity or self-possession to pass through this terrible ordeal, ' under the pains and penalties of perjury.' The practice, moreover, is as useless as it is pernicious — no possible good resulting from it to any one, but much positive evil — and therefore it ought no longer to be tolerated among a people claiming to be civilized, to say nothing of ' the Christian law.'

But as, in this Commonwealth, the Legislature has not made it imperative that the oath shall be taken, where there are conscientious scruples against taking it, but allows an affirmation to be given in its place, it is not necessary to dwell any longer on this question of oaths, as though the consciences of good men were not regarded on that particular point. For a long time, however, I have felt some scruples in regard to affirming in the manner required by law, — not for all the reasons which influence me to refuse to take an oath, but because it seems to me equally at war with the spirit of Christ's prohibition, and equally derogatory to the character of every honest man. I have no doubt that there are many others who cherish the same objections, and that their number is steadily increasing. All these, be it remembered, are constantly liable to be summoned as witnesses, in which case, as the law now is, they may be sent to prison for constructive ' contempt of Court.' Is there any necessity for such a law?

It may be argued, that as there is a wide difference between the act of taking an oath and that of affirming — as the former is an appeal to God, and the latter nothing more than a promise to tell the truth, ' under the pains and penalties of perjury '— as the Quakers, who have always borne a faithful testimony against oaths, do not object to the form of affirmation legally prescribed — it is absurd to have any conscientious scruples respecting the latter, and therefore the law ought not to be abrogated to gratify the religious whims of individuals as to what constitutes ' the Christian law.'

To this mode of reasoning it is sufficient to reply, that though there is a difference between the oath and the affirmation, as alleged, it is a difference more in the form than in the substance or design — they being regarded by the government and the people as equally essential to the procuring of true evidence, equally binding upon the conscience of the witness, equally safe for the Commonwealth. The one keeps in countenance and perpetuates the other — just as the moderate use of intoxicating liquor perpetuates intemperance.

Again : there are those who conscientiously believe, that the same Christian law which prohibits swearing, also forbids the inflicting of ' pains and penalties ' on the wrongdoer. It is as explicit in the one case as in the other. ' Ye have heard that it hath been said, An eye for an eye, and a tooth for a tooth. But I say unto you, that ye resist not evil: but whosoever shall smite thee on thy right cheek, turn to him the other also,' &c. Now, to affirm as the law requires, implies something more than a passive acquiescence in the infliction threatened, in case of being detected in testifying falsely: it is virtually sanctioning that infliction as just and right on the part of the government, which many good men cannot do: hence, to compel them to affirm, on peril of imprisonment — nay, more, to force them to invoke that punishment upon themselves — is palpably an oppressive act.

The fact, that the Quakers do not object to taking an
23*

affirmation, proves nothing more than that they have no conscientious scruples in the case. I am not yet convinced that their conscience is to be the guide of my own, or that it is necessarily innocent to perform that which they see no evil in doing. To their own Master they stand or fall. I honor them greatly for the many noble testimonies which they have borne against moral and legal wrong; and I have no doubt that they will be led to see that, in consenting to be put under affirmation, they have departed from the simplicity of the law of Christ — ' Let your communication be, Yea, yea : Nay, nay : for whatsoever is more than these, [whether oath or affirmation,] cometh of evil.'

To say, that it is a religious whim to object to affirming, is to say that conscience is to be governed by the statute book, and punished severely whenever it interferes with popular usage. Hence, that it must not bow to its own conviction of the will of God, and has no higher duty to perform than to obey the State.

Many think the Quakers unnecessarily squeamish in refusing to be sworn ; but no one now thinks they ought to be imprisoned on that account. The Constitution very properly respects their conscientious feelings, and provides a remedy. Let that body go one step further, and allow all those to testify who are scrupulously unwilling to take an oath or to affirm, without any legal form.

This is indeed a serious matter. By an absurd requirement, eminently conscientious persons are now prevented from giving testimony in cases where human life and property are at stake, and placed on a level with felons.

But I argue for the abolition of oaths and affirmations, not only for conscience sake, but BECAUSE THEY ARE WHOLLY USELESS. Of what avail is the plea of the prisoner, ' Not guilty,' in determining his criminality ? None. Neither the judge nor the jury are influenced by it. They proceed to ascertain the facts as carefully as though he had not made any response. It is a mere form, but one not less pernicious than it is useless; for it tempts the guilty to lie, that he may have a chance to escape through some legal technicalities, or defect in the evidence. It ought to be abolished, for its iniquity and folly.

Of what avail is it that the witnesses have affirmed or taken the oath? Is their testimony rendered more credible on that account? No. The court proceeds to try the case precisely as though they had complied with no such requisition. The verdict is rendered, not upon the fact that they testified under oath or affirmation, but upon the coherency of the evidence, the probabilities of the case, and the general character of the witnesses for probity. By no other standard could there ever be a verdict rendered! For, if the fact, that the witnesses on the one side have been sworn, makes their evidence decisive, then the fact, that the witnesses on the other side have been sworn, proves them to have testified truly; and as they utterly contradict each other, it proves that both the plaintiff and defendant are in the right! Such are some of the absurdities of the law.

If, then, the administering or taking of oaths and affirmations fails to elicit or determine the truth; if it conflicts with the consciences of many enlightened and upright persons, and exposes them, through contumacy, to the punishment of felons; if it implies (as it does) that man may impose upon his brother man, by the enforcement of a particular ceremony, a higher obligation to speak the truth than his Creator has affixed to his moral nature; if its tendency is to demoralize rather than to elevate society; and if it is not necessary for private security or the public good; then let it be at once and for ever abrogated.

Harriet Martineau.

ENGLAND! I grant that thou dost justly boast
  Of splendid Geniuses beyond compare;
    Men great and gallant — Women good and fair —
Skilled in all arts, and filling every post
Of learning, science, fame — a mighty host;
  Poets divine, and Benefactors rare —
    Statesmen — Philosophers — and they who dare
Boldly to explore Heaven's vast and boundless coast.
To one alone I dedicate this rhyme,
  Whose virtues with a starry lustre glow;
Whose heart is large, whose spirit is sublime,
  The friend of Liberty, of Wrong the foe:
Long be inscribed upon the roll of Time,
  The name, the worth, the works of HARRIET MARTINEAU!

To Elizabeth Pease,

OF DARLINGTON, ENGLAND.

A NATIVE dignity and gentle mien;
  An intellect expansive, clear and strong;
  A spirit that can tolerate no wrong;
A heart as large as ever yet was seen;
A soul in every exigence serene,
  In which all virtuous excellencies throng;
    These, best of women! all to thee belong:
What more of Royalty has England's Queen?
Thy being is absorbed in doing good,
  As was thy LORD's, to all the human race;
With courage, faith, hope, charity endued,
  All forms of wretchedness thou dost embrace: —
Still be thy work of light and love pursued,
  And thy career shall angels joy to trace.

Mr. Webster's Speech on Bunker Hill.

It is not possible that the late celebration on Bunker Hill can have been either pleasing to God, or honorable to the people of the United States. Failing in these particulars, it is to be regarded as an exhibition of national hypocrisy, only faintly illustrated by the conduct of the Jewish people, who, at the very moment they were pretending to seek God daily, ' as a nation that did righteousness, and were asking of him the ordinances of justice, and affectedly taking delight in approaching to God,' were smiting with the fist of wickedness, and tightening the bands of oppression. Surely, it would not be more absurd than monstrous, for a people, given over to all uncleanness of mind and body, to erect a monument in honor of Purity, and to join in celebrating its completion. Not less absurd, not less monstrous, was the pageant witnessed on Bunker Hill, on the 17th of June ; for in that pageant were embodied all forms of national dissimulation, cant, bombast, effrontery. The festivity was general — the commemoration a universal act. It is to constitute a part of the history of these United States ; not simply of Massachusetts. The leading participants in it were the President and his Cabinet, and other distinguished officers of the Government. All parts of the republic were represented by accredited delegates. An ' uncounted multitude' came from the broad savannas of the South, from the newer regions of the West, from the rich valley of the Genesee, and along the chain of the Lakes, from the mountains of Pennsylvania, and the thronged cities of the coast. The battle of June 17, 1775, was for a national object, involved national consequences, and led to national deliverance from a foreign yoke. The erection of a monument was made an affair of national importance, interest and honor.

If there be any trait of character specially detestable in the sight of God or men, it is that of hypocrisy. It is the wolf in sheep's clothing—it is Satan in the garb of an angel of light. This nation is infected with it. How, in words, it recognises the freedom, the equality, the inalienable rights of mankind! How, in acts, it annihilates those rights, denies that equality, and scoffs at that freedom! How great, in profession, is its reverence for liberty! How strong, in practice, is its attachment to slavery! The celebration on Bunker Hill constitutes the climax of its inconsistency.

I turn to the Address of Mr. Webster, delivered on that memorable occasion. It is not for an intellect so vigorous and a mind so capacious as his own, to make a feeble effort under circumstances so spirit-stirring. Yet I am disappointed, on a careful perusal of it. It contains few passages of robust thought, or expansive love, or rhetorical power. Marked by his usual simplicity of style, it yet lacks the declamatory fire, the axiomatic form of speech, the over-powering unction of feeling, that have characterized some of his other productions. Its exordium, though certainly pertinent in any account of the origin, progress and completion of the monument, is common-place, occupied as it is with the petty details of individual merit, in relation to the building of this stupendous granite pile. What strikes me as somewhat singular is, that more space is given to record the death and worth of George Blake, 'a man of wit and talent,' and twenty times as much to emblazon the virtues of Thomas H. Perkins, an eminent merchant of Boston, than is conceded to a notice of the life and death of Lafayette! Indeed, all that is said by the orator, respecting the latter, is—'Lafayette sleeps in his native land.' Strange that, in view of the fact that this distinguished champion of American freedom was present at the laying of the corner-stone of the monument, and that the project for building it was conceived and announced to the people during his last sojourn among us — strange, I say, that Mr. Webster should have left wholly unimproved so rare and apposite an opportunity to bestow an elaborate eulogium on his revolutionary services and eventful life !

The Address is too purely historical for such an occasion. It is an effort to please, rather than to benefit the people ; it distributes praise with a liberal hand, but finds nothing to censure in our past or present career. Acting as the historian of the country, justice and verity demanded of Mr. Webster, that he should record its evil, as well as its good deeds. But to do this requires moral courage, insensibility to public anger, reverence for truth, and deep solicitude for the welfare of the republic. These traits are not perceptible in the character of Mr. Webster. He knows well how to play the flatterer, but in him are seen none of the elements of a reformer. Morally, he is a colossal coward. In the light of reason, the selection of such a man to be the orator on Bunker Hill was a biting satire on republican liberty, and a shameful insult to the memories of those who perished in ' the first great battle of the revolution.' He, the man of men, the first choice of a nation of freemen — the one pre-eminently qualified, among seventeen millions of people, to deliver the Address on such an occasion ! The man who travelled to Richmond, Virginia, on an electioneering tour in 1840, and then and there, ' in the face of an October sun,' and in the presence of a great crowd of cradle-plunderers and men-stealers, basely gave a pledge, in behalf of himself and the people of New England, to stand by the Southern slave system, and to frown on the Anti-Slavery enterprise ! The man, who, as the leading Senator in Congress from Massachusetts, saw the sacred right of petition cloven down, session after session, and raised no note of remonstrance, no voice of warning, against

the tyrannous deed !   The man who has seen millions of his
countrymen chained, enslaved, without any hope or prospect
of redemption ; and yet has never shed one tear of sympathy for their fate, never felt one throb of indignation in view
of their terrible treatment, never once opened his mouth to
plead their cause !   The man who has prostituted his great
talents in negotiating with the British government, to cause
the self-emancipated, heroic slaves of the Creole to be given
up to our own government, that they may be put to an ignominious death, as rebels and murderers, merely for imitat-
ing the example of Washington, Hancock and Warren !
He, the chosen orator for the 17th of June, 1843, on Bunker
Hill, to expatiate on the blessings of civil and religious liberty, and to eulogize those who resisted unto death ' a three-
penny tax on tea ' !   Assuredly, if the people of New
England, of Massachusetts, had been true to themselves,
and loyal to the cause of liberty, they never would have
consented to the appointment of DANIEL WEBSTER as the
orator on the occasion alluded to.   But the whole affair was
a sublime mockery, and it was perfectly in character to place
him at the head of it.

What the occasion demanded was, not merely a retrospect
of the past, but a sober, careful, faithful survey of the present condition of the country ; not only a picture of what
had been achieved by revolutionary valor and self-sacrifice,
but a description of what remained to be done by other and
higher instrumentalities, to give peace, security, permanency
to the republic.   Nothing can be more dangerous than to
administer compliments to national vanity ; for every nation
had an abundance of this commodity, even for exporta-
tion, and none appears to be so well supplied with it as our
own.   It is true, in the peroration of his discourse, Mr.
Webster speaks of duties and obligations to be performed ;
bids us remember ' the sacred trust, attaching to the rich in-

heritance which we have received from our fathers'; tells us
to feel our personal responsibility for the preservation of our
institutions of civil and religious liberty; invokes us to
' remember that it is only religion, and morals, and knowledge, that can make men respectable and happy, under any
form of government'; and reminds us of ' the great truth,
that communities are responsible, as well as individuals.'
But a homily like this defines nothing, and is not intended
to be applied to any thing. It is nothing more than a sop to
the religious sentiment, and an unsuccessful effort to appear
virtuous. Neither the man who gave utterance to it, nor the
people who heard it, comprehended its actual meaning.
' No government,' said Mr. Webster, ' is respectable, which
is not just.' Did he mean to say that the American government is unjust, and therefore degraded? Not he! Did the
assembled multitude understand him as impeaching the integrity and honor of the country? Not they! Had he so
meant, had they so understood him, his praise had been
small on that day; their tumult had been great. Yet, that
injustice is the distinguishing feature of our government, all
men know. For what is implied in the fact, that, under it,
three millions of people lie crushed and bleeding, if it be
not injustice in its most dreadful form? There was no sincerity, therefore, in the words of the orator; no self-convic-
tion in the minds of his hearers.

Be it conceded, that this was an occasion that justified
praise — even high-wrought panegyric. It also called for
solemn warning, stern rebuke, strong condemnation. These
being omitted, the praise becomes no less dangerous than
flattery. ' Credit to whom credit,' but also censure to whom
censure is due. ' We may praise what we cannot equal,'
says Mr. Webster, ' and celebrate actions which we were
not born to perform.' This is true; but when he avers that
' Heaven has not allotted to this generation an opportunity of

24

rendering high services, and manifesting strong personal
devotion, such as they [the patriots of the Revolution] rendered and manifested, and in such a cause as roused the
patriotic fires of their youthful breasts, and nerved the
strength of their arms,' he shows that, while he is able to
describe the past, he is unable to appreciate the present, or
to take a large survey of the future. These are more
solemn, more eventful, far more grand and sublime times—
times requiring a more self-sacrificing spirit, a higher and
better kind of courage, a holier zeal, a loftier devotion—
times incomparably more trying to the souls of men—than
those which our revolutionary fathers were called to experience. But, having eyes, the boasted ' Defender of the Constitution ' is blind; having ears, he hears not. What to him
is the present? Nothing. What is he doing to advance
the welfare of the future? Nothing. The past—the
past—the past! On that he can dwell with exultation,
expatiate eloquently, and flourish abundantly. The giant in
intellect is a pigmy in heart. His courage is of the most
craven character; his regard for human rights incomparably less than for his own popularity; his estimation of the
cause of freedom low, partial, false, *American*. Another
struggle, mightier than of old, for the emancipation of three
millions of people from servile chains, is going on in the
land; but in the eyes of the *purchased* Webster, it is as
despicable, as unjustifiable, as treasonable, as was the revolutionary war, for a time, in the eyes of the tories of England. It is a struggle on the part of the few against the
many—the weak against the mighty—the poor against the
rich—the friends of universal liberty against the supporters
of a worse than absolute despotism. It is a struggle to
secure to all the full enjoyment of those rights, which the
patriots of 1776 fought and bled in vain to establish; not
limited by any geographical boundaries, nor actuated by any

local considerations, nor animated by any vindictive feelings
towards those who are enacting the part of tyrants; waged
with ethereal weapons, stained with no other blood than that
of its own martyrs, full of stirring incident, rich prospect-
ively in historic renown, glorious in its object, magnanimous
in its spirit, sublime in its moral majesty, on the speedy triumph of which, the prosperity, the harmony, the very existence of the republic depend! In every one of its features,
it wears a nobler aspect than any of those which characterised the revolutionary war. Laurels are to be gathered in
it, that never fade; a name and a fame, that shall survive
those ever obtained by diplomatic skill or political success,
or on the battle-field of blood-spilling war. Yet Mr. Webster has the fatuity to declare, that 'Heaven has not allotted
to this generation an opportunity of rendering high services,
and manifesting strong personal devotion,' such as they rendered and manifested, who rushed to the strife of blood sixty
years ago! O, this is a melancholy exhibition of mingled
cowardice and slothfulness, under circumstances which admit of no palliation! Yet, how all tongues are extolling the
'godlike' intellect and spirit of DANIEL WEBSTER! 'How
great, wide-spread, enduring is his reputation!' they exclaim.
'The pride of America! a prodigy among mankind!' It
is on such flatteries that he is attempting to feed his immortal nature, while he rejects the bread and water of life.
The greatness of his intellect cannot save his memory from
the corruption of mortality. Nothing can perpetuate that
memory, but its connection with every righteous reform,
every virtuous struggle for liberty, every just testimony
against wrong-doing, during the remainder of his life. For
politicians and time-servers, for warriors and chieftains, there
remains no honorable place on the scroll of fame, or in the
annals of time. Their memories shall fade away in the

pure, noon-tide light of a new dispensation, as the stars of night retire before the blaze of day.

Thus it shall be with the name even of WASHINGTON, who, in the remembrance, affection and gratitude of the American people, has been made by them more than a rival of Christ, and practically exalted ' above all that is called God.' The language of panegyric has long since been exhausted to describe his merits; but, as if emulous of surpassing all panegyrists who have gone before him, and of drawing a portraiture that should immortalize the artist as well as the subject, Mr. Webster has tasked his genius and imagination to the utmost, adequately to represent the heroic glory and moral grandeur of the character of Washington. Vain, though brilliant attempt! From the low eminence on which he stood to survey that character, looking at it through the disordered medium of a carnal vision, and measuring it by the imperfect rule of worldly patriotism, Mr. Webster has given utterance to sentiments that challenge the assent and admiration of all who are subjects of ' the kingdoms of this world.' From the high eminence of Christianity, and in the light of universal and perfect love, the character of Washington is seen to be radically defective. See what has long been proudly claimed for him! ' First in war, first in peace, and first in the hearts of his countrymen!' First in war! The first to give the blow, to spill human blood, to lead others to the conflict of death! What a eulogy! How incongruous, how impious it would sound to apply it to the Son of God! ' First in war!' Can that which is degrading to the character of Christ, be worthy of praise and homage in that of Washington? But let us be just. It is also claimed for the latter, that he was ' first in peace.' Absurd paradox! At best, it amounts only to this — that, having the disposition to be the first to resort to arms in defence of

his own rights, he was also disposed to be first in effecting a
truce; but only on this condition:—'If you will let me
alone, I will let you alone. If you will not strike me, I will
not strike you. If you will not attack the liberties of my
country, I will not kill and destroy by way of retaliation. If
you will be peaceable, I will; if not, remember I am FIRST
IN WAR.' How different the spirit of Him, ' who left us an
example, that we should follow his steps; who, when he was
reviled, reviled not again; when he suffered, he threatened
not; but committed himself to him that judgeth righteously!' Either Jesus or Washington must be rejected, as
unworthy to receive the homage of mankind; for their traits
of character were utterly dissimilar. ' First in the hearts of
his countrymen.' . This is a terrible fact. It is far more
unpopular and hazardous to arraign the conduct of Washington, than to speak against Jesus. He is incomparably before Jesus in the esteem of the American people;
and they regard his ' Farewell Address ' with far higher
reverence than they do ' the glorious gospel of the blessed
God.' They are patriotic idolators. No matter who comes
next—Washington must stand ' first.' I know how angry
my countrymen will be with me, for presuming to dispute
the right of Washington to be first in their hearts; but will
they do well to be angry? I readily concede to him all that
worldly patriotism claims in his behalf; but I say that worldly
patriotism, though it is something preferable to cowardice
and a slavish spirit, is not Christianity, and, therefore, not to
be applauded as worthy of imitation. It may be said, that
Washington was a pious man. In a popular sense, this is
true; but his piety was made compatible with oppressive and
sanguinary acts.

Mr. Webster vauntingly says of Washington—He is all,
all our own. I claim him for America.' The boast and the
claim are equally derogatory. Washington gave himself for

his country, not for the world.   He was strictly 'an American production.'   His philanthropy was not expansive ; his
regard for the rights of man was not founded on principle ;
for while he would not submit to wear even a political yoke
himself, and was inciting his countrymen to throw off that
yoke by physical force, and was professedly the champion
of the Declaration of Independence, he was basely enslaving men, women and children, and living on the fruits of
their unrequited toil !   Nor did he release his grasp upon
them, till he felt that of death on himself.   And he is the
paragon, the idol of America ! the ' first in the hearts of his
countrymen ' !

What shall be said of the example of Washington as a
warrior and slaveholder ?   Say, ye friends of peace — say,
ye friends of impartial liberty — is it worthy of imitation ?
Has it not been disastrous to the cause of Humanity, as
sanctioning war and slavery ?   Is it not time to exhibit it in
its true light — to assert its utter incompatibility with a great
soul, a true life, a Christian disposition ?   Shall a stain be
cast on the character of Jesus, in order to screen the reputation of Washington ? ' The gospel requires us to suppress
every angry emotion, to forgive every injury, to revenge
none.   Shall we forgive as individuals, and retaliate as communities ?   Shall we turn the other cheek as individuals, and
plunge a dagger into the heart of our enemy, as nations ?
We might as well be sober as individuals, and drunk as
nations.   We might as well be merciful as individuals, and
rob as patriots.   We must not deceive ourselves.   To be a
patriot is one thing ; to be a Christian, another.   The characters are irreconcilable.   They demand conflicting duties.
We cannot serve our country in war, and serve God in
peace.   We cannot love our enemies, and kill them.'

To Benjamin Lundy,

THE EARLY, STEADFAST, INTREPID ADVOCATE OF EMANCIPATION.

SELF-TAUGHT, unaided, poor, reviled, contemned —
  Beset with enemies, by friends betrayed ;
As madman and fanatic oft condemned,
  Yet in thy noble cause still undismayed !
Leonidas could not thy courage boast ;
  Less num'rous were his foes, his band more strong ;
Alone, unto a more than Persian host,
  Thou hast undauntedly given battle long.
Nor shalt thou singly wage th' unequal strife ;
  Unto thy aid, with spear and shield, I rush,
And freely do I offer up my life,
  And bid my heart's blood find a wound to gush !
New volunteers are trooping to the field —
To die they are prepared — but NOT AN INCH TO YIELD !

To the Memory of the Same.

THANK God, that though thy body Death has slain,
  Thy quenchless spirit nothing could subdue ;
  That though thou art removed from mortal view,
Thou livest ever more — and not in vain !
Our loss is but thine everlasting gain !
  Of FREEDOM's friends, the truest of the true
  Wast thou, as all her deadly foes well knew !
For bravely her good cause thou didst maintain.
No threats could move, no perils could appal,
  No bribes seduce thee, in thy high career :
O, many a fettered slave shall mourn thy fall,
  And many a ransomed one let drop the tear ;
A nation wakened by thy trumpet-call —
  The world itself — thy memory shall revere !

Forgiveness of Injuries.

THE first great step in aid of the prisoner was taken by John Howard. It was his mission to explore the prisons of his own country and of Europe, and to reveal their horrors to the world — to demand, in the name of justice, and by the claims of our common humanity, a change in their structure, discipline and administration. For this, he has immortalized his memory. The effect of his example, and the result of his labors, have been prodigious.

To take the convict by the hand, in the spirit of goodwill, and to lead him back to virtue and respectability, as soon as he is discharged from his confinement, is the second step in the march of criminal reform ; and it is essential to secure the object aimed at by the first.

But there is another, a more comprehensive, and a far more radical step yet to be taken, not in disparagement or neglect of the others, but as a truly philosophical and Christian corollary. It is, for those who are injured not to call upon the State, with its inexorable, arbitrary and murderous power, to punish the criminal, but for themselves to forgive him, with all the magnanimity and long-suffering of Christ, and promptly to return good for the evil that may have been done. If this course were pursued, in an overwhelming majority of cases, the immediate result would be reconciliation, and the reclamation of the offender ; and few indeed would be the instances, in which it would be found necessary to exercise even the slightest bodily restraint. It constitutes no part of the mission of Christ to incarcerate men in cells and dungeons, as a punishment for their crimes. He came to open prison-doors, not to bolt and bar them. He has left those who would be his followers a plain an glorious example as to the manner in which he would have

even the vilest offenders treated. (II. Peter, 2 : 19 – 25.)
See his Sermon on the Mount. See his entire life, his
affecting death. The forgiveness (which certainly is not
the punishment) of enemies, or of those who are criminally
disposed, is the hinge on which turns the door of admission
into the kingdom of God, wherein is no violence, no retaliation, no reliance upon brute force for safety or redress. O,
it is pitiable to see the eagerness with which the professed
disciples of Christ rush to the criminal courts, to have
arrested and thrust into horrid places of confinement, those
who have injured them in person, reputation or property,
however slightly ! In this particular, between them and the
most unblushing worldlings, there is no perceptible difference. If a debt be withheld, if an article be stolen from
them, if an assault be made upon them, if they be defamed
in their character, straightway they cry out for the intervention of the murderous power of the State, and exact all that
the law allows in such cases, however sanguinary or de-
moralizing ! And then they will get down on their knees,
and pray to the God whose laws they so frequently
violate—'Forgive us our trespasses, *as* we forgive those
who trespass against us' ! They will gravely talk about
filling up the measure of Christ's sufferings, bearing the
cross, overcoming evil with good, and counting all things as
dross that they may win Christ ! There cannot be a greater
mockery than this. What the magnanimous Paul thought
of all this is plainly indicated by his sharp admonition to
his Corinthian brethren : —' Dare any of you, having a
matter against another, go to law before the unjust, and not
before the saints? . . . Now, therefore, there is utterly
a fault among you, because ye go to law one with another.
Why do ye not rather take wrong? WHY DO YE NOT
RATHER SUFFER YOURSELVES TO BE DEFRAUDED? Nay, ye
do wrong.'

Sonnet.

Who talks of weariness in Freedom's cause,
  Knows nothing of its life-sustaining power;
Who in the conflict for the right would pause,
  Beneath a tyrant's rod was made to cower;
Who something loves more than his brother man, —
  Holds it more sacred, at a higher price, —
Fails to discern Redemption's glorious plan,
  Or in what sense Christ is our sacrifice;
Who stands aloof from those who are agreed
  In charity to aid and bless mankind,
Because they walk not by his narrow creed,
  Himself among the fallen spirits shall find;
Who would show loyalty to God must be
At all times true in man's extremity.

Complexional Prejudice.

THERE is nothing which excites more unfeigned astonishment in the old world, than the prejudice which dogs the footsteps of the man of color in this pseudo republic. True, there are many absurd, criminal, aristocratic distinctions abroad, which ought to cease; but these are also found, to a great extent, in the United States, and have been common to all countries, and in every age. They originate in the pride of wealth, in successful enterprise, in educational superiority, in official rank, in civil, military, and ecclesiastical rule. For these, there may be framed some plausible excuses. But to scorn, insult, brutalize and enslave human beings, solely on account of the hue of the skin which it has pleased God to bestow on them; to pronounce them accursed, for no crime on their part; to treat them substantially alike, whether they are virtuous or vicious, refined or vulgar, rich or poor, aspiring or grovelling; to be inflamed with madness against them in proportion as they rise in self-respect, and improve in their manners and morals; this is an act so unnatural, that it throws into the shade all other distinctions known among mankind. Thank God, it is confined to a very small portion of the globe; though, strange to tell, it is perpetrated the most grossly, and in a spirit the most ferocious and inexorable, in a land claiming to be the pattern-land of the world — the most enlightened, the most democratic, the most Christian. Complexional caste is tolerated no where, excepting in the immediate vicinage of slavery. It has no foundation in nature, reason, or universal custom. But, as the origin of it is to be traced to the existence of slavery, so its utter eradication is not to be expected until that hideous system be overthrown. Nothing but the removal of the cause can destroy the effect. That, with all its desperate efforts to lengthen its cords and strengthen its stakes, the Slave Power is continually growing weaker, is most clearly demonstrated in the gradual abatement of the prejudice which we have been deploring; for strong and terrible as that prejudice now is, it has received a very perceptible check within the last ten years, especially in New England.

No one can blame the intelligent and virtuous colored American for turning his back upon the land of his nativity, and escaping from it with the precipitancy that marked the flight of Lot out of Sodom. To remain in it is to subject himself to continual annoyance, persecution, and outrage. In fifteen or twenty days, he can place his feet on the shores of Europe — in Great Britain and Ireland — where, if he cannot obtain more food or better clothing, he can surely find that his complexion is not regarded as a crime,

and constitutes no barrier to his social, intellectual, or political advancement. He who, with this powerful temptation
to˙become an exile before him, is resolved to remain at
home, and take his lot and portion with his down-trodden
brethren — to lay his comfort, reputation and hopes on the
altar of freedom — exhibits the true martyr spirit, and is
deserving of a world's sympathy and applause. Such a
man, in an eminent degree, is FREDERICK DOUGLASS.
Abroad, beloved, honored, admitted to the most refined cir-
cles, and eulogised by the Jerrolds, the Howitts, and a host
of Britain's brightest intellects ; — at home, not without
numerous friends and admirers, it is true, yet made the
object of popular contumely, denied the customary rights
and privileges of a man, and surrounded by an atmosphere
of prejudice which is enough to appal the stoutest heart,
and to depress the most elastic spirit. Such is the difference
between England and America ! — O what crimes are perpetrated under the mask of democratic liberty ! what outrages are consummated under the profession of Christianity !

> ' Fleecy locks and dark complexion
>   Cannot forfeit Nature's claim ;
> Skins may differ, but affection
>   Dwells in white and black the same.'

It is a very disgusting fact, that they who cannot tolerate
the company or presence of educated and refined colored
men, are quite willing to be surrounded by ignorant and
imbruted slaves, and never think of objecting to the closest
contact with them, on account of their complexion ! The
more of such the better ! Their ' odor ' is more coveted
than the perfume wafted by ' the gales from Araby, the
blest ' ! It is only as they are free, educated, enlightened,
that they become a nuisance, between whom and their white
despisers the broad Atlantic should for ever interpose !

A Short Catechism,

ADAPTED TO ALL PARTS OF THE UNITED STATES.

1. Why is American slaveholding not in all cases sinful?
Because its victims are black.

2. Why is gradual emancipation right?
Because the slaves are black.

3. Why is immediate emancipation wrong, dangerous, impracticable?
Because the slaves are black.

4. Why ought one-sixth portion of the American population to be exiled from their native soil?
Because they are black.

5. Why would the slaves, if emancipated, cut the throats of their masters?
Because they are black.

6. Why are our slaves not fit for freedom?
Because they are black.

7. Why are American slaveholders not thieves, tyrants and men-stealers?
Because their victims are black.

8. Why does the Bible justify American slavery?
Because its victims are black.

9. Why ought not the Priest and the Levite, ' passing by on the other side,' to be sternly rebuked?
Because the man who has fallen among thieves, and lies weltering in his blood, is black.

10. Why are abolitionists fanatics, madmen and incendiaries?
Because those for whom they plead are black.

11. Why are they wrong in their principles and measures?
Because the slaves are black.

25

12. Why is all the prudence, moderation, judiciousness, philanthropy, piety, on the side of their opponents?

Because the slaves are black.

13. Why ought not the free discussion of slavery to be tolerated?

Because its victims are black.

14. Why is Lynch law, as applied to abolitionists, better than common law?

Because those, whom they seek to emancipate, are black.

15. Why are the slaves contented and happy?

Because they are black.

16. Why don't they want to be free?

Because they are black.

17. Why are they not created in the image of God?

Because they are black.

18. Why are they not cruelly treated, but enjoy unusual comforts and privileges?

Because they are black.

19. Why are they not our brethren and countrymen?

Because they are black.

20. Why is it unconstitutional to plead their cause?

Because they are black.

21. Why is it a violation of the national compact to rebuke their masters?

Because they are black.

22. Why will they be lazy, improvident, and worthless, if set free?

Because they are black.

23. Why will the whites wish to amalgamate with them in a state of freedom?

Because they are black.

24. Why must the Union be dissolved, should Congress abolish slavery in the District of Columbia?

Because the slaves in that District are black.

25. Why are abolitionists justly treated as outlaws in one half of the Union?

Because those whose cause they espouse are black.

26. Why is slavery 'the corner-stone of our republican edifice'?

Because its victims are black.

27. Why ought the slaves to be obedient to their masters, and never to attempt to emancipate themselves by violence?

Because they are black.

28. Why, though reduced to the level of brutes, are they, when emancipated, the best qualified to go as missionaries to Africa?

Because they are black.

29. Why are the slaveholders the best judges of the time and mode of emancipation?

Because they, upon whose necks they are standing, are black.

30. Why ought the North to mind its own business, and cease interfering with the question of Southern slavery?

Because the slaves are black.

31. Why has the cause of emancipation been 'thrown back at least a century' by the rash intermeddling of the abolitionists?

Because the victims are black.

We have thus given thirty-one replies to those who assail our principles and measures — that is, one reply, unanswerable and all-comprehensive, to all the cavils, complaints, criticisms, objections and difficulties which swarm in each State in the Union, against our holy enterprise. The victims are BLACK! 'That alters the case!' There is not an individual in all this country, who is not conscious before God, that if the slaves at the South should be to-day miraculously transformed into men of white complexion, to-mor-

row the abolitionists would be recognised and cheered as
the best friends of their race ; their principles would be
eulogised as sound and incontrovertible, and their measures
as rational and indispensable! Then, indeed, immediate
emancipation would be the right of the slaves, and the duty
of the masters!

Is it not so? Who has ever heard any complaints made
against those who have denounced Turkish oppression,
Russian oppression, or the oppression of the mother country 'in the times that tried men's souls'? Every thing may
be said and done against those who enslave white men, and
it is all very proper. But wo to those, who, in relation to
human rights, will imitate God, and be no respecter of
men's complexions and persons! What does all this prove,
but that the men who are so furiously assailing abolitionists
and their sacred cause, (making all due allowances for those
who know not what they do,) are the basest of all hypocrites — the shameless enemies of men on account of their
color — the libellers of the wisdom and goodness of God in
the creation of man?

* * *

Farewell Address to George Thompson.[*]

In behalf of this large and brilliant assembly — of a
host of ardent friends and advocates of universal emancipation, unavoidably absent on this occasion — I proffer to
you, our honored guest, GEORGE THOMPSON, the strongest

---

[*] Delivered at the Farewell Soiree, in Assembly Hall, Boston,
June 16, 1851.

expressions of personal regard, and the warmest aspirations for your health and happiness.

On the eve of embarking for your native land, after a sojourn of more than eight months among us, it will prove equally gratifying and instructive to take a brief survey of the object and result of your visit to the United States, characterised, as it has been, by so many anomalous circumstances and remarkable events.

Your object has been one of disinterested and godlike philanthropy — to assist, by all righteous instrumentalities, in the extirpation of the most comprehensively cruel and detestable system of slavery that ever defied the living God, or reduced man to the condition of a brute. In this you have shown a regard for the honor, prosperity, perpetuity and glory of this republic, deserving of its eternal gratitude, but of which an overwhelming majority of our native population seem to be utterly destitute. Instead of being inimical to our theory or form of government, or to the institutions which generally exist among us, you have constantly enforced the radical truths which are embodied in the Declaration of Independence, and fairly awarded to us all that justice and truth warrant. Your single purpose has been to exhibit the guilt of man claiming property in man; to open your mouth in the cause of all such as are appointed to destruction; to vindicate the right of man to be free; and to assert the Fatherhood of God, and the Brotherhood of the Human Race. If you have arraigned the political parties of the country, or the government itself, or the leaders of the people, or the popular religion, it has been solely on the ground of their pro-slavery character and position. You have raised no other issue; and in no instance have you had any respect unto persons, or manifested any party or sectarian bias, or evinced any foreign prejudice or predilection.

25*

You came to us without solicitation, moved by your own benevolent and noble impulses, on your own responsibility, at your own hazard, representing no organization at home or abroad, in the spirit of an apostle, with the fidelity of a prophet, with the courage of a martyr.

On your part, it was no untried experiment. A former visit,— never to be forgotten in the history of this slave-holding republic,— fully revealed to you the terrible su-premacy of the Slave Power over the whole extent of our national domains — the insults, outrages, perils, to which the uncompromising friend of the slave must be subjected. You had ' counted the cost' once and again. Instead of being received as a friend, you knew you would be treated as an enemy. All that a venal press and a time-serving pulpit could do to make you an object of detestation, you anticipated they would do. You came to us with your life in your hands; and it is by the help of God, not by the protection of men, that you continue to this day. An example of such moral heroism is of more service to the world than all the gold of California.

In a variety of aspects, your visit has been of immense service. It has served as a probe to test the comparative soundness or corruption of the body politic. It has proved that the guilt of this country is colossal, and equalled only by its cowardice. Your presence has terrified the nation far more than an invading army could have done, because

 ' 'T is conscience that makes cowards of them all.'

Many have been your assailants behind your back, but no one has ventured to confront you, face to face. A CLAY, a CASS, a DICKINSON, have not deemed you unworthy of their notice, on the floor of the Senate chamber, and have done what they could, by their malicious attacks and great influence, to cause your life to be forfeited, if you could not be driven from the country. Cowardice is ever the companion of ruffianism. Such conduct is a confession of guilt. You are but one; but then you represent that cause, in the service of which, ' one can chase a thousand, and two put ten thousand to flight.' You are but one; and yet twenty millions of people are disquieted because of your sojourn among them. It is not that you are the bravest, the strongest, or the most eloquent of men; they can match you in power of persuasion, power of argument, power of appeal, in a good cause; but with the foul, inhuman, detestable system of slavery to vindicate on principle, they can do nothing better than to call for the suppression of speech, and deny the right of investigation.

Your visit has been warranted by the missionary enterprise from the apostolic age to the present time. If it is right to assail idolatry in India, it cannot be wrong to denounce slavery in America. If, by foreign interference, it is laudable to seek the suppression of cannibalism in New Zealand, then, by foreign interference, similarly evinced, it is equally praiseworthy to seek the abolition of the traffic in human flesh in Carolina or Georgia. The popular objection to your course, that you are a foreigner, and therefore have no right to meddle with any thing in this country, is alone sufficient to stamp with hypocrisy the religious professions of the people. Christ is the Universal Reformer. With him and his disciples, ' the field is the world.' In him ' there is neither Jew nor Gentile, neither Barbarian nor Scythian, neither male nor female, neither bond nor free, but all are one.' It is his mission to overturn, and overturn, and overturn,—to put down all rule and all authority,—and to break in pieces and consume all the kingdoms of the earth. Against him are still arrayed ' principalities and powers, and spiritual wickedness in high places.' You have vindicated the universality of Christianity, by asserting and maintaining your right, in the name of Christ, to arraign injustice and tyranny wherever they exist in the world. Whoever denies that right, or interferes with its freest exercise, is not a Christian.   Whoever taunts another with being a foreigner, or seeks to render him odious on account of his foreign birth, is not a Christian.   No government has a right to claim exemption from foreign criticism; and none will claim such exemption, unless it be tainted with corruption or stained with blood.   It is the natural prerogative of every human being to circumnavigate the globe, and interrogate evil customs, wicked laws, despotic governments, a spurious religion, and denounce them, in the name of God the Creator, Christ the Redeemer, and Man the Sufferer.   It may be attended with odium, persecution, and all the terrors of martyrdom ; but it is a prerogative none the less inherent and sacred.   Take it away, and the redemption of the world becomes impracticable.   ' Go ye into all the world,' — not excepting the United States of America, — ' and preach the gospel to every creature,' is still a Christian obligation.

To show that you are desirous that your own country should be rebuked for its injustice, as well as the United States, I quote your own words, from a lecture delivered by you in Manchester, in 1841, in opposition to the Corn Laws : —

'The people of America are fully justified in uttering their loud complaints against our present system.   They have just ground for accusation and recrimination.   It is with peculiar appropriateness that our friend from America, wearing the complexion of millions who are in bondage, appears before us to-night, and tells us, "if we would emancipate the slave, abolish the Corn Laws."   I WELCOME THE REBUKES OF AMERICA.   *If we have a free trade in nothing else, let us have one in mutual and wholesome remonstrances.*   I would that every packet that sets sail from the bay of Boston, or New York, or the mouth of the Mississippi, should bear over the billows *a solemn protest and a faithful rebuke, on the subject of our inconsistency and our guilt.* The monopolists of freedom in the slave States may well taunt us with being monopolists of food in our own country, When we cry, "Abolish your slavery!" they may well cry, "Abolish your Corn Laws!" When we send them from Lancashire a memorial praying for mercy to the slave, they may justly utter the voice of rebuke, and say, "Base hypocrites! keep your remonstrance at home; your cotton smells of blood!" (Loud cheers.) Welcome, then, every voice, *every note of warning and recrimination.* I trust the time is coming when both systems shall fall; when liberty shall be proclaimed in America, and cheap food be the portion of our own starving children. Let the cause of food and freedom go together. From this time forth, let the Anti-Corn Law cause and the Anti-Slavery cause be indissolubly united. (Cheers.) They are both founded in justice; alike, they have respect to the happiness and well-being of millions, and to the honor of the two great nations whose crying abuses they are intended to extirpate: I rejoiced when I heard Mr. Remond give his solemn pledge, thus publicly, that he would discuss the question of slavery in his own country upon Anti-Corn Law grounds. He returns, therefore, to the land of his birth, as our missionary. Let him lift up his voice boldly, and it is no uninfluential one ; and *let him tell his countrymen to give us no peace, until we have swept away our own domestic abomination.* And let him tell his countrymen, also, that they shall enjoy no rest, until the abomination which maketh desolate the plains of the South is exterminated, and there breathes not a captive within the limits of their proud republic.' (Loud cheers.)

Your visit has helped to redeem Christianity from the stains that have been cast upon it, in this country, by its treacherous professors. They have made it subservient to the most infamous purposes. They have taken its sacred mantle, and spread it over 'the abomination that maketh desolate.' You have exhibited it in its primitive purity, loveliness and grandeur, as utterly and eternally opposed to every form of oppression.

Your visit has given a new and powerful impulse to the anti-slavery movement, and thus has shortened the period of bondage for the millions who are waiting for deliverance. The knowledge of it has been carried to the remotest hamlets : it has shaken the nation. If it has excited afresh the fury of the oppressor, it has quickened the zeal of the advocate of the oppressed. If it has led, in a few instances, to disgraceful disturbances, it has almost uniformly been attended with brilliant omens and signal victories. Wherever you have had an opportunity to speak for yourself, — to vindicate your right to be heard, and the glorious cause you have espoused — you have uniformly secured the esteem, respect, confidence and assent of your auditors. The base attempts of satanic presses to prevent your being listened to, have served as a powerful stimulant to public curiosity : and the more the people have been told to stay away from your meetings, the more they have resolved not to do so, but to hear impartially for themselves. The understandings you have enlightened, the hearts you have affected, the prejudices you have overcome, the obstacles you have surmounted, the triumphs you have won, constitute an aggregation of influences and results that cannot be measured.

Your visit and labors, though geographical and specific, have had a world-wide bearing. Slavery in this republic obscures its otherwise glorious characteristics, gives to despotism throughout the globe its most formidable weapon, obstructs the progress of freedom universally, strengthens every throne, and sanctions every act of governmental usurpation. The oppressed and starving millions in Europe have cause to bestow upon you their benediction for what you have done here, not less than the millions of chattel slaves at the South. Instead of forgetting their claims, you have never labored more effectually in their behalf. They will never accuse you of being indifferent to their deliverance. The accusation comes from those, and those only, who justify the enslavement of the colored population in America, and care nothing for the degradation of the laboring population of Europe, except as a matter of cant and hypocrisy. Such are ever ready to strain at a gnat, while they readily swallow ' a whole caravan of camels.'

We address you in the language of commendation, not as a matter of form or in the spirit of flattery, but because you have been 'among the faithless, faithful found.' Of the tens of thousands of your own countrymen who have come to these shores, either as visitors or residents, scarcely one in a thousand, whatever his anti-slavery pretensions at home, has failed to do homage to the all-prevailing pro-slavery sentiment of the land. You have been, here, every thing you claimed to be at home; you have said to our faces severer things than you have ever uttered behind our backs; you have despised all threats, rejected all overtures, trampled on all temptations, spurned all bribes. In this, it is true, you have only done your duty; but, contrasted with the cowardly, time-serving course of nearly all who come to us from the old world, your conduct is calculated to excite the joy of angels and the admiration of all the inflexibly good in the universe. And for such conduct is the award to be given in the day of final account — 'Well done, good and faithful servant!'

On your return home, if you are asked, whether the American Union will stand or fall in this conflict, answer, it is not for you to prophesy. If they ask you, whether slavery is destined to be abolished, answer, on the veracity of God, YES! By the undying wants and irresistible impulses of nature, YES! By the instincts and aspirations of the human soul, YES!

'The end will come— it will not wait —
Chains, yokes and scourges have their date;
Slavery itself shall pass away,
And be a tale of yesterday!'

Proclaim to the people of England, that as Slavery and Christianity were found incompatible together in the West India Islands, it is equally true in America, that they are utterly irreconcilable ; that as the missionaries were either banished from Jamaica or cast into prison, and their chapels torn down, so, in the slave States of America, every faithful witness for God against slavery is subjected to the Lynch code, and compelled to flee for his life ; in the immediate presence of the Slave Power, no man can testify against it in the name of Christ, without risk of martyrdom.

Conjure, therefore, all Christian denominations, as one, in Great Britain, to renew and multiply their testimonies against our gigantic slave system ; to declare that a church which sanctions or connives at the existence of chattel slavery cannot be the church of Christ, but is apostate in spirit and practice ; and to refuse to give the right hand of Christian fellowship to those who claim or justify property in man. Tell them this is the infidelity, all the infidelity, of the American abolitionists.

' And now, in giving you our farewell benediction, we cherish the hope that our separation is for a very brief season. Come to us again, in the spirit of peace and of liberty, as the way shall be opened to you by the guidings of Providence. Long may your life be preserved, to be the terror of tyrants and the hope of the oppressed. The blessings of those who are perishing are resting upon your head : with these are mingled the best wishes and warmest aspirations of every true lover of liberty, whose motto is —

> 'Patient, firm and persevering —
> God speed the right!
> Ne'er th' event nor danger fearing —
> God speed the right!
> Pains, nor toils, nor trials heeding,
> And in Heaven's own time succeeding —
> God speed the right !'

To a Distinguished Advocate of Peace.

THE conquerors of the earth have had their day —
 Their fame lies weltering in a bloody shroud ;
As Crime and Desolation haste away,
 So fade their glory and their triumphs proud.
Great advocate ! a fairer wreath is thine,
 Base Envy cannot soil, nor Time destroy ;
Thou art enlisted in a cause divine,
 Which yet shall fill all earth and heaven with joy.
To calm the passions of a hostile world ;
 To make content and happiness increase ;
In every clime to see that flag unfurled,
 Long since uplifted by the Prince of Peace ;
This is thy soul's desire, thy being's aim,
No barrier can impede, no opposition tame.

Earthly Fame.

How fall FAME's pillars at the touch of Time !
 How fade, like flowers, the memories of the dead !
How vast the grave that swallows up a clime !
 How dim the light by ancient glory shed !
One generation's clay enwraps the next,
 And dead men are the aliment of earth ;
'Passing away !' is Nature's funeral text,
 Uttered coeval with Creation's birth.
I mourn not, care not, if my humble name,
 With my frail body, perish in the tomb ;
It courts a heavenly, not an earthly fame,
 That through eternity shall brightly bloom ; —
Write it within thy Book of Life, O Lord,
And, in 'the last great day,' a golden crown award !
26

The United States Constitution.

THERE are some very worthy men, who are gravely try-ing to convince this slaveholding and slave-trading nation, that it has an Anti-Slavery Constitution, if it did but know it — always has had it since it was a nation — and so design-ed it to be from the beginning! Hence, all slaveholding under it is illegal, and ought in virtue of it to be forthwith abolished by act of Congress. As rationally attempt to con-vince the American people that they inhabit the moon, and ' run upon all fours,' as that they have not intelligently, deliberately and purposely entered into a covenant, by which three millions of slaves are now held securely in bond-age! They are not to be let off so easily, either by indig-nant Heaven or outraged Earth! To tell them that, for three score years, they have misunderstood and misinter-preted their own Constitution, in a manner gross and dis-torted beyond any thing known in human history; that Washington, Jefferson, Adams, all who framed that Consti-tution — the Supreme Court of the United States, and all its branches, and all other Courts — the national Congress and all State Legislatures — have utterly perverted its scope and meaning — is the coolest and absurdest thing ever heard of beneath the stars! No, not thus are they to be allowed to escape hot censure and unsparing condemnation. They have committed no blunder; they have not erred through stupidity; they have not been misled by any legal sophis-try. They are verily guilty of the most atrocious crimes, and have sinned against the clearest light ever vouchsafed to any people. They have designedly ' framed mischief by a law,' and consigned to chains and infamy an inoffensive and helpless race. Hence, it is not an error in legal interpre-tation that they are to correct, but they are to be arraigned as criminals of the deepest dye, warned of the wrath to come, and urged to the immediate confession and abandonment of this great ' besetting sin.' ' Now, therefore, go to, speak to the men of Judah, and to the inhabitants of Jerusalem, saying, Thus saith the Lord, Behold, I frame evil against you, and devise a device against you; return ye now every one from his evil way, and make your ways and your doings good.'

Some are unwilling to admit the possibility of legalizing slavery, because of its foul and monstrous character. But what iniquity may not men commit by agreement? and what obligations so diabolical, that men may not promise to perform them to the letter? To say that men have no right to do wrong is a truism; to intimate that they have not the power to do so is an absurdity. If they have the power, it is possible for them to use it; and no where do they use it with more alacrity, or on a more gigantic scale, than in the United States.

' To ascertain the meaning of the Constitution,' we are told, ' we are to subject it, as we do any other law, to the strict rules of legal interpretation. It seems to us that this statement is extremely fallacious. The Constitution is not a statute, but a UNION, a COMPACT formed between separate and independent colonies, with conflicting interests and diverse sentiments, to be reconciled in the best manner possible, by concession and compromise, for the attainment of a common object—their own safety and welfare against a common enemy. What those concessions and compromises were, all knew when the compact was framed and adopted : they related to the prosecution of the foreign slave trade for twenty years, to the allowance of a slave representation in Congress, to the hunting of fugitive slaves, and to the suppression of domestic insurrections, for the special benefit of the slave States ; and to direct taxation and the navigation laws, in

.behalf of the free States. The Constitution of the United
States, then, is a form of government, having special powers and prerogatives of its own — created under great emer-
gencies and with peculiar features — unlike any thing in
ancient or modern times; a form of government, we reite-
rate, not a legislative enactment, but under which, and by
authority of which, laws are to be passed, but never to
be interpreted to the subversion of the government, or by a
higher standard! The people of this country have bound
themselves by an oath to have no other God before them
than a CONSTITUTIONAL GOD, which their own hands have
made, and to which they demand homage of every one born
or resident on the American soil, on peril of imprisonment
or death! His fiat is ' the supreme law of the land.'

It is said, that with the intention of the framers of the
Constitution, we do not need to concern ourselves, ' any
more than with the intention of the scrivener whom we
employ to write the deed of a parcel of land.' We see no
pertinency in the illustration: the analogy is defective. A
scrivener employed to write a deed — to write as ordered by
us — to write according to an approved and established form;
in the name of common sense, is he, or his avocation, or
his deed, or all together, to be compared with a deliberative
assembly, chosen by popular suffrage, and invested with
powers to frame a new government, in some shape or other
endurable, if not every thing desirable! Now, historically
and legally, it is a matter of great moment to know what the
framers of the Constitution understood and meant by every
article, section and clause of it; what they expressed in
plain and unequivocal language, there being no necessity for
using any other; what they embodied in equivocal or collu-
sive phraseology, to meet a disagreeable necessity; what
they implied by circumlocution, to cover up positive wickedness; and what they asserted in direct terms. It was given

to them to frame the instrument, as, representing conflicting interests and opposite parts of the country, they could best agree ; but after its adoption, the nation became responsible for it, as made in good faith by their authorized representatives.

Again it is said, we are to look after the intention of the adopters, not that of the framers of the Constitution. We do not see that any thing is gained by this distinction. That the adopters and framers of that instrument understood its conditions and requirements in precisely the same manner is historically certain ; and especially as to whatever is in it relating to slavery and the slave trade. The law of Congress, providing for the recapture of fugitive slaves, was passed almost immediately after the adoption of the Constitution : who cried out against it as unconstitutional ? When Southern representatives of the slave population (on the three-fifths basis) first made their appearance in Congress, who raised his voice against them in the name of the Constitution ? The foreign slave traffic was prosecuted under our star-spangled banner more vigorously after than before the adoption of that instrument : who dreamed of its being an illegal trade ? There were at least six hundred thousand slaves in the country, at the adoption of the Constitution : who thought, believed, or proclaimed, that they were made free by it ? If, then, they who adopted it so understood and so designed it, how came the slaveholding South to vote for it ? and how came it to pass, that, under the ' supreme law of the land,' not a single slave thereby became free ? When was the will, yes, the very purpose of a people, so instantly nullified before ? ' The slave system, it was supposed, (!) could not extend beyond that generation '; but though the Constitution demanded its abolition, neither during that generation was it applied, nor has it been at any subsequent period, in any other manner than to extend

26 *

and perpetuate what it was framed to suppress! All logi-
cal gravity terminates here in loud and long-protracted
laughter.

But this is not the height of this folly. We are told, that
it was thought better to let slavery live on in sufferance
through that generation, at least, than to disturb the infant
and unconsolidated nation by putting an immediate stop to
it! So, then, even at that period, an attempt to give the
slaves the benefit of the Anti-Slavery Constitution aforesaid
would have convulsed the land, and blown the Union sky
high! Undoubtedly; because no such Constitution was
ever adopted, and for no other reason! And is any one so
infatuated as to believe, that what could not be done sixty
years ago, with only six hundred thousand slaves to be liberated, without convulsing the country, can now be done
' by the strict rules of legal interpretation,' in utter disregard
of all the facts and all the precedents in our national history,
with fifteen instead of six slave States, and three millions of
slaves, without filling the land with a deluge of blood? Supposing—what is not within the scope of probabilities—that
we could win over to their view of the Constitution a majority, ay, the entire body of the people of the North, so that
they could control the action of Congress through their representatives, and in this manner decree the abolition of
slavery throughout the South—could we hope to witness
even the enactment of such a decree, (to say nothing of its
enforcement,) without its being accompanied by the most
fearful consequences? Does any reply, that a fear of consequences should not deter us from doing right? This is cheerfully granted: but are these Anti-Slavery interpreters ready
for a civil war, as the inevitable result of their construction
of the Constitution? What reason have they to believe,
from the past, that a civil war would not immediately follow,
in the case supposed? Why, even a Wilmot proviso is

shaking this Union to its foundation, so that ' men's hearts are failing them for fear.' Where, then, and what is to be the Union, under this new constitutional interpretation ?

Away with all verbal casuistry, all legal quibbling, the idle parade of Lord Mansfield's decision in the case of Somerset, the useless appeals to Blackstone's Commentaries, and the like, to prove that the United States Constitution is an Anti-Slavery instrument! It is worse than labor lost, and, as a false issue, cannot advance, but must rather retard, the Anti-Slavery movement. Let there be no dodging, no shuffling, no evasion. Let us confess the sin of our fathers, and our own sin as a people, in conspiring for the degradation and enslavement of the colored race among us. Let us be honest with the facts of history, and acknowledge the compromises that were made to secure the adoption of the Constitution, and the consequent establishment of the Union. Let us, who profess to abhor slavery, and who claim to be freemen indeed, dissolve the bands that connect us with the Slave Power, religiously and politically ; not doubting that a faithful adherence to principle will be the wisest policy, the highest expediency, for ourselves and our posterity, for the miserable victims of Southern oppression, and for the cause of liberty throughout the world.

We regard this as indeed a solemn crisis, which requires of every man sobriety of thought, prophetic forecast, independent judgment, invincible determination, and a sound heart. A revolutionary step is one that should not be taken hastily, nor followed under the influence of impulsive imitation. To know what spirits they are of—whether they have counted the cost of the warfare—what are the principles they advocate—and how they are to achieve their object—is the first duty of revolutionists.

But, while circumspection and prudence are excellent qualities in every great emergency, they become the allies of tyranny whenever they restrain prompt, bold and decisive action against it.

We charge upon the present national compact, that it was formed at the expense of human liberty, by a profligate surrender of principle, and to this hour is cemented with human blood.

We charge upon the American Constitution, that it contains provisions, and enjoins duties, which make it unlawful for freemen to take the oath of allegiance to it, because they are expressly designed to favor a slaveholding oligarchy, and, consequently, to make one portion of the people a prey to another.

It was pleaded at the time of its adoption, it is pleaded now, that, without such a compromise, there could have been no union; that, without union, the colonies would have become an easy prey to the mother country; and, hence, that it was an act of necessity, deplorable indeed when viewed alone, but absolutely indispensable to the safety of the republic.

To this we reply: The plea is as profligate as the act was tyrannical. It is the jesuitical doctrine, that the end sanctifies the means. It is a confession of sin, but the denial of any guilt in its perpetration. This plea is sufficiently broad to cover all the oppression and villany that the sun has witnessed in his circuit, since God said, ' Let there be light.' It assumes that to be practicable which is impossible, namely, that there can be freedom with slavery, union with injustice, and safety with bloodguiltiness. A union of virtue with pollution is the triumph of licentiousness. A partnership between right and wrong is wholly wrong. A compromise of the principles of justice is the deification of crime.

Better that the American Union had never been formed, than that it should have been obtained at such a frightful cost! If they were guilty who fashioned it, but who could not foresee all its frightful consequences, how much more guilty are they, who, in full view of all that has resulted from it, clamor for its perpetuity! If it was sinful at the commencement to adopt it, on the ground of escaping a greater evil, is it not equally sinful to swear to support it for the same reason, or until, in process of time, it be purged from its corruption?

The fact is, the compromise alluded to, instead of effecting a union, rendered it impracticable; unless by the term union we are to understand the absolute reign of the slave-holding power over the whole country, to the prostration of Northern rights. It is not certain, it is not even probable, that if the present Constitution had not been adopted, the mother country would have reconquered the colonies. The spirit that would have chosen danger in preference to crime, to perish with justice rather than live with dishonor, to dare and suffer whatever might betide, rather than sacrifice the rights of one human being, could never have been subjugated by any mortal power. Surely, it is paying a poor tribute to the valor and devotion of our revolutionary fathers in the cause of liberty, to say that, if they had sternly refused to sacrifice their principles, they would have fallen an easy prey to the despotic power of England.

To the argument, that the words 'slaves' and 'slavery' are not to be found in the Constitution, and therefore that it was never intended to give any protection or countenance to the slave system, it is sufficient to reply, that though no such words are contained in the instrument, other words were used, intelligently and specifically, to meet the necessities of slavery; and that these were adopted in good faith, to be observed until a constitutional change could be effected. On this point, as to the design of certain provisions, no intelligent man can honestly entertain a doubt. If it be objected, that though these provisions were meant to cover slavery, yet, as they can fairly be interpreted to mean something exactly the reverse, it is allowable to give to them such an interpretation, especially as the cause of freedom will thereby be promoted — we reply, that this is to advocate fraud and violence toward one of the contracting parties, whose co-operation was secured only by an express agreement and understanding between them both, in regard to the clauses alluded to; and that such a construction, if enforced by pains and penalties, would unquestionably lead to a civil war, in which the aggrieved party would justly claim to have been betrayed, and robbed of their constitutional rights.

Again, if it be said, that those clauses, being immoral, are null and void — we reply, it is true they are not to be observed; but it is also true, that they are portions of an instrument, the support of which, as a whole, is required by oath or affirmation; and, therefore, because they are immoral, and because of this obligation to enforce immorality, no one can innocently swear to support the Constitution.

Again, if it be objected, that the Constitution was formed by the people of the United States, in order to establish justice, to promote the general welfare, and secure the blessings of liberty to themselves and their posterity; and, therefore, it is to be so construed as to harmonize with these objects; we reply, again, that its language is not to be interpreted in a sense which neither of the contracting parties understood, and which would frustrate every design of their alliance — to wit, union at the expense of the colored population of the country. Moreover, nothing is more certain than that the preamble alluded to never included, in the minds of those who framed it, those who were then pining in bondage — for, in that case, a general emancipation of the slaves would have instantly been proclaimed throughout the United States. The words, ' secure the blessings of liberty to ourselves and our posterity,' assuredly did not mean to include the slave population. 'To promote the general welfare,' referred to their own welfare exclusively. 'To establish justice,' was understood to be for their sole benefit as slaveholders, and the guilty abettors of slavery. This is demonstrated by other parts of the same instrument, and by their own prac- tice under it.

We would not detract aught from what is justly their due; but it is as reprehensible to give them credit for what they did not possess, as it is to rob them of what is theirs. It is absurd, it is false, it is an insult to the common sense of mankind, to pretend that the Constitution was intended to embrace the entire population of the country under its shel- tering wings; or that the parties to it were actuated by a sense of justice and the spirit of impartial liberty; or that it needs no alteration, but only a new interpretation, to make it harmonize with the object aimed at by its adoption. As truly might it be argued, that because it is asserted in the Declaration of Independence, that all men are created equal, and endowed with an inalienable right to liberty, therefore none of its signers were slaveholders, and since its adoption slavery-has been banished from the American soil! The truth is, our fathers were intent on securing liberty to them- selves, without being very scrupulous as to the means they used to accomplish their purpose. They were not actuated by the spirit of universal philanthropy; and though in words they recognised occasionally the brotherhood of the human race, in practice they continually denied it. They did not blush to enslave a portion of their fellow-men, and to buy and sell them as cattle in the market, while they were fighting against the oppression of the mother country, and boasting of their regard for the rights of man. Why, then, concede to them virtues which they did not possess? Why

cling to the falsehood, that they were no respecters of persons in the formation of the government?

Alas! that they had no more fear of God, no more regard
for man, in their hearts! 'The iniquity of the house of
Israel and Judah (the North and South) is exceeding great,
and the land is full of blood, and the city full of perverse-
ness; for they say, the Lord hath forsaken the earth, and
the Lord seeth not.'

If, in utter disregard of all historical facts, it is still
asserted, that the Constitution needs no amendment to make
it a free instrument, adapted to all the exigencies of a free
people, and was never intended to give any strength or countenance to the slave system — the indignant spirit of insulted
Liberty replies: — ' What though the assertion be true?   Of
what avail is a mere piece of parchment?   In itself, though
it be written all over with words of truth and freedom —
though its provisions be as impartial and just as words can
express, or the imagination paint — though it be as pure as
the gospel, and breathe only the spirit of Heaven — it is
powerless; it has no executive vitality; it is a lifeless corpse,
even though beautiful in death.   I am famishing for lack of
bread!   How is my appetite relieved by holding up to my
gaze a painted loaf?   I am manacled, wounded, bleeding,
dying!   What consolation is it to know, that they who are
seeking to destroy my life, profess in words to be my
friends?   If the liberties of the people have been betrayed — if judgment has been turned away backward, and justice standeth afar off, and truth has fallen in the streets, and
equity cannot enter — if the princes of the land are roar-
ing lions, the judges evening wolves, the people light and
treacherous persons, the priests covered with pollution — if
we are living under a frightful despotism, which scoffs at all
constitutional restraints, and wields the resources of the

nation to promote its own bloody purposes — tell us not that the forms of freedom are still left to us! 'Would such tameness and submission have freighted the May Flower for Plymouth Rock? Would it have resisted the Stamp Act, the Tea Tax, or any of those entering wedges of tyranny with which the British government sought to rive the liberties of America? The wheel of the Revolution would have rusted on its axle, if a spirit so weak had been the only power to give it motion. Did our fathers say, when their rights and liberties were infringed — "Why, what is done cannot be undone! That is the first thought!" No, it was the last thing they thought of: or, rather, it never entered their minds at all. They sprang to the conclusion at once — "What is done shall be undone! That is our first and only thought!"''

'Is water running in our veins? Do we remember still
Old Plymouth Rock, and Lexington, and famous Bunker Hill?
The debt we owe our fathers' graves? and to the yet unborn,
Whose heritage ourselves must make a thing of pride or scorn?

Gray Plymouth Rock hath yet a tongue, and Concord is not dumb;
And voices from our fathers' graves and from the future come:
They call on us to stand our ground — they charge us still to be
Not only free from chains ourselves, but foremost to make free!'

It is of little consequence who is on the throne, if there be behind it a power mightier than the throne. It matters not what is the theory of the government, if the practice of the government be unjust and tyrannical. We rise in rebellion against a despotism incomparably more dreadful than that which induced the colonists to take up arms against the mother country; not on account of a three-penny tax on tea, but because fetters of living iron are fastened on the limbs of millions of our countrymen, and our most sacred rights are trampled in the dust. As citizens of the State, we

27

appeal to the State in vain for protection and redress. As citizens of the United States, we are treated as outlaws in one half of the country, and the national government consents to our destruction. We are denied the right of locomotion, freedom of speech, the right of petition, the liberty of the press, the right peaceably to assemble together to protest against oppression and plead for liberty — at least, in fifteen States of the Union. If we venture, as avowed and unflinching abolitionists, to travel South of Mason and Dixon's line, we do so at the peril of our lives. If we would escape torture and death, on visiting any of the slave States, we must stifle our conscientious convictions, bear no testimony against cruelty and tyranny, suppress the struggling emotions of humanity, divest ourselves of all letters and papers of an anti-slavery character, and do homage to the slaveholding power — or run the risk of a cruel martyrdom! These are appalling and undeniable facts.

Three millions of the American people are crushed under the American Union! They are held as slaves, trafficked as merchandise, registered as goods and chattels! The government gives them no protection — the government is their enemy, the government keeps them in chains! Where they lie bleeding, we are prostrate by their side — in their sorrows and sufferings we participate — their stripes are inflicted on our bodies, their shackles are fastened on our limbs, their cause is ours! The Union which grinds them to the dust rests upon us, and with them we will struggle to overthrow it! The Constitution which subjects them to hopeless bondage is one that we cannot swear to support. Our motto is, 'No UNION WITH SLAVEHOLDERS,' either religious or political. They are the fiercest enemies of mankind, and the bitterest foes of God! We separate from them, not in anger, not in malice, not for a selfish purpose, not to do them an injury, not to cease warning, exhorting, reproving them for their crimes, not to leave the perishing bondman to his fate — O no! But to clear our skirts of innocent blood — to give the oppressor no countenance — and to hasten the downfall of slavery in America, and throughout the world!

Do you ask what can be done if you abandon the ballot-box? What did the crucified Nazarene do without the elective franchise? What did the apostles do? What did the glorious army of martyrs and confessors do? What did Luther and his intrepid associates do?

'If thou must stand alone, what then? The honor shall be more!
But thou canst never stand alone while Heaven still arches o'er —
While there's a God to worship, a devil to be denied —
The good and true of every age stand with thee, side by side!'

The form of government that shall succeed the present government of the United States, let time determine. It would be a waste of time to argue that question, until the people are regenerated and turned from their iniquity. Ours is no anarchical movement, but one of order and obedience. In ceasing from oppression, we establish liberty. What is now fragmentary shall in due time be crystalized, and shine like a gem set in the heavens, for a light to all coming ages.

---

* 'When the powers of government came to be delegated to the Union, the South — that is, South Carolina and Georgia — refused their subscription to the parchment, till it should be saturated with the infection of slavery, which no fumigation could purify, no quarantine could extinguish. The freemen of the North gave way, and the deadly venom of slavery was infused into the Constitution of freedom. Its first consequence has been to invert the first principle of Democracy, that the will of the majority of numbers shall rule the land. By means of the double representation, the minority command the whole, and a knot of slaveholders give the law and prescribe the policy of the country.' — JOHN QUINCY ADAMS.

The Triumph of Freedom.

God speed the year of jubilee,
  The wide world o'er!
When from their galling chains set free,
Th' oppressed shall vilely bend the knee,
And wear the yoke of tyranny,
  Like brutes, no more : —
That year will come, and Freedom's reign
To man his plundered rights again
  Restore.

God speed the day when human blood
  Shall cease to flow!
In every clime be understood
The claims of human brotherhood,
And each return for evil, good —
  Not blow for blow : —
That day will come, all feuds to end,
And change into a faithful friend
  Each foe.

God speed the hour, the glorious hour,
  When none on earth
Shall exercise a lordly power,
Nor in a tyrant's presence cower,
But all to Manhood's stature tower,
  By equal birth ! —
That hour will come, to each, to all,
And from his prison-house the thrall
  Go forth.

Until that year, day, hour arrive, —
  If life be given, —
With head and heart and hand I'll strive
To break the rod, and rend the gyve, —
The spoiler of his prey deprive, —
  So witness Heaven !
And never from my chosen post,
Whate'er the peril or the cost,
  Be driven.

The Anti-Slavery Platform.

IT is the strength and glory of the Anti-Slavery cause, that its principles are so simple and elementary, and yet so vital to freedom, morality and religion, as to commend themselves to the understandings and consciences of men of every sect and party, every creed and persuasion, every caste and color. They are self-evident truths — fixed stars in the moral firmament — blazing suns in the great universe of mind, dispensing light and heat over the whole surface of humanity, and around which all social and moral affinities revolve in harmony. They are to be denied, only as the existence of a God, or the immortality of the soul, is denied. Unlike human theories, they can never lead astray; unlike human devices, they can never be made subservient to ambition or selfishness. When Jesus gave this rule of action to a Jewish lawyer, who interrogated him, 'Thou shalt love thy neighbor as thyself,' and illustrated its meaning by the case of the man fallen among thieves, aided by one with whom he was at mortal variance because of sectarian and national antipathies, the Great Teacher evidently intended to inculcate this among other truths, that all men are bound to rally upon the broad ground of a common humanity, to succor the distressed, without reference to the caste, the creed, the country, or the name of the sufferer;—or, in other words, that when a victim of robbers lies weltering in his blood, he only is 'neighbor to him,' who pours wine and oil into his wounds, forgetful of all other considerations; while he who passes by on the other side does but act the priest and the Levite. We repeat it, therefore, that it is the strength and glory of the Anti-Slavery cause, that men of all sects not only ought to unite, but are united in one common phalanx, to break every yoke, and let the oppressed go free. Why

27*

should it not be so ?   It is a reproach to the name of Christianity, that while its professors, however widely differing in
their religious or political sentiments, eagerly associate
together for the purpose of MONEY-GETTING — to establish
banks, build railroads, dig canals, and erect manufactories —
they are slow, almost reluctant, to give each other the right
hand of fellowship in carrying on an enterprise of mercy.
When they themselves are thirsty, they ask not who it is
that proffers them a cup of cold water ; when they are
oppressed, they care not who it is that breaks their fetters ;
when they are threatened with death, they demand not in a
cavilling spirit, who it is that comes to their rescue.   When
the mother country attempted to bind the chains of civil despotism upon the limbs of our fathers, how ineffectual would
have been their struggle for emancipation, if they had stood
aloof from each other on account of sectarian or political
disagreements, and refused to coöperate *en masse* for a common object, to effect a common deliverance !   Would the
war have been finished in seven years ?   Would it not have
been ended, disastrously, in less than seven months ?   If
each religious sect, if each political party, had resolved to
prosecute the war *per se*, in an invidious and antagonistical
form, would England have lost the brightest gem that was
ever set in her regal crown ?   Never.   And what were they
styled, who, in those ' times that tried men's souls,' for any
pretext whatever, refused to stand shoulder to shoulder in
breasting the tide of British despotism ?   Tories — traitors
to their country — the enemies of liberty.   Why were they
bound to forget their creeds and their names, and to throw
themselves, as one man, into ' the imminent deadly breach,'
for the preservation of their liberty ?   First, because it was
a common good which was to be secured ; secondly, because
it was a common ground to be occupied by all who were
not willing to wear the yoke of bondage ; thirdly, because

disunion would have been inevitable defeat; and lastly, and for the all-conclusive reason, that all sects and parties in England, the government, the people, were united together for the subjugation of the colonies, and nothing but a similar union of the people of the colonies could have procured their independence.

The moral conflict now waging against American slavery is, in many of its aspects, a parallel case. Its object, like the love of God, consults the happiness of all men: it is a common one, in which all sects and all parties have an equal, the deepest interest. The ground on which it is fought is a common one, broad enough to contain all who would occupy it. Disunion in the ranks is defeat—no true friend to the cause will seek to foment it. Those who refuse to enlist, because they are not agreed upon other and minor points with the gallant band who are struggling against the opposing hosts of despotism—what are they? Are they the friends of emancipation? No. What are they? Neutrals? Neutrality in such a struggle is the abhorrence of God, and active rebellion against his government. The Moloch of slavery finds worshippers and defenders among all classes of society throughout the land; and it is to be remarked—it is a fact too alarming and too important to be forgotten, that, wherever they are, at the East or West, the North or South—whatever the party they espouse, or to whatever denomination they belong, their sympathies, feelings, interests, opinions, blend together like the drops of the ocean, to sink the victims of oppression beyond the fathom line of humanity. Their language is one; their shibboleth the same; their grand hailing sign of distress the same; their grip and knock the same. In their spirit, they are alike; in their purpose, identical; in their fellowship, undivided. Upon almost every other subject, they differ wide as the poles asunder; but upon the duty of paying

homage to the bloody idol set up in our land, their agreement is perfect.   Are the children of this world to be always
wiser than the children of light?   If Episcopalians, Metho-
dists, Baptists, Presbyterians, Unitarians, &c. &c., are joined
hand to hand, and heart to heart, in earnest defence of slavery; if they associate together, plot together, co-operate
together, to uphold that execrable system; shall not, may
not, cannot members of the same religious persuasions, who
desire the utter extirpation of slavery, and will not bow down
to the image of Baal, nor pass through the fire to Moloch,
be as united, as forgetful of their other variances, as ready
to act in concert?   If the friends and the opponents of the
national administration are found in the same phalanx, fighting in defence of the worst oppressors; shall they not
also be found leagued together for the rescue of the oppressed?   When the standard of HUMANITY is unfurled to the
breeze, in the sunshine of heaven, who that is created in
the image of God, who that is human, will not rally under
its folds?   Let us suppose a case.   In the progress of the
revolutionary struggle, there were many dark periods, when
the cause of liberty seemed to be at its last gasp; when its
champions began to fear, that the night of despotism must
inevitably settle over the land, with no hope that there would
ever be another dawn of Freedom's day.   Let us suppose,
that, in the darkest hour, when Washington and his bare-
footed followers, in the midst of winter, were retreating
before their victorious enemy, and tracking their snowy
path with blood, some of them had suddenly thrown down
their arms, and declared that they could no longer be associated with men whose religious or political creed differed
from their own, or who refused to subscribe to any creed.
Suppose they had attempted to seduce others from the cause,
by inflaming their suspicions and alienating their affections,
by artful appeals and slanderous representations.   Suppose

they had tried to cut off the supplies which were sent to enable the tried and faithful few to carry on the war, until victory perched upon their standard, or the last drop of blood had oozed from their veins. And suppose that these factious individuals had boasted of their patriotism, and professed that they were actuated by love of country, and gave as one reason for their mutinous conduct, that, in withdrawing themselves from the army, they believed they should be able to do more execution, inasmuch as a large portion of the enemy coincided with them in religious profession, and would certainly be more willing to be shot down or taken captive by them, than by those who held to a different creed. What would have been thought, what said of conduct like this? Would not the whole world, civilized and savage, have cried out, 'Shame! shame!' But suppose, in addition to all this, that they had eulogized the conduct of those tories, who had refused to join the little patriotic army, as 'men who had a quick sense of propriety, and were not willing to be identified with their movements;' whose hearts bled for the oppressed colonists, but who were beaten off from active exertion in their behalf, in consequence of the character and measures of those who were carrying on the war. Suppose they had declared, that their feelings had often been exceedingly pained by the abuse which was heaped upon tory ministers and other excellent tory Christians, who did not feel prepared to enter fully into the efforts of the revolutionists. Suppose, further, they had carried on a secret correspondence with the disaffected in various parts of the land, as well as made their appeals to them in public, urging them to come forward in a body, take the cause into their own hands, and carry it on in a manner to suit themselves. Suppose, finally, that, in view of this mutiny, shouts should be heard in all the enemy's camps, rending the very heavens with their exultation. In what

light would the conduct of those disorganizers have appeared to the friends of American liberty throughout the world?
As dictated by a superior regard, a more holy concern for
the success of the Right? Impossible. Nay, they would
have been viewed, despite all their flaming professions of
attachment to the cause, as recreant to it.

This supposition will serve to illustrate a similar defection which has taken place in the Anti-Slavery ranks, in this
Commonwealth, and in other parts of the country, during
the past year, through clerical chicanery and the spirit of
sectarian narrowness; yet pretending to be animated by the
deepest solicitude for the integrity and welfare of our great
movement.

  *   *   *   *   *   *

Whilst we should watchfully see to it, that nothing of
human passion, or personal hatred, or sectarian bitterness,
or party policy, enters into our feelings in assailing the
execrable system of American slavery, and in rebuking
the transcendent wickedness of American slaveholders, we
should be equally on our guard not to give heed to the suggestions of a false charity, or to dilute the pure word of
liberty. Let our single purpose be—regardless whom it
may please or offend among men—to speak the truth of
God in its simplicity and power—not to conceal danger, or
gild over crime, or screen the wrong-doer. It is not light
that is needed on this subject, so much as a heart of flesh.
While the chains of millions of our enslaved countrymen
are clanking in our ears, and their cries are piercing the
heavens, and we know that their bodies and spirits (which
are God's) are daily sold under the hammer of the auctioneer
as household goods or working cattle, we need no nice
adjustment of abstractions, no metaphysical reasonings, to
convince us that such scenes are dreadful, and such practices
impious. All the nobility of our manhood, all that is nature

within us, all the instincts and faculties of our souls, settle
the question instantly. With the indignation that fired the
bosom of a Brougham, each of us exclaims—' Tell me not
of rights! talk not of the property of the planter in his
slaves! I deny the right, I acknowledge not the property!
The principles, the feelings of our nature rise in rebellion
against it. Be the appeal made to the understanding or the
heart, the sentence is the same that rejects it.' O, the
odious inconsistency of the American people! When the
iron heel of Turkish despotism was planted upon the necks
of the Greeks; when the Autocrat of Russia was sending
his barbarian hordes to conquer the unconquerable Poles;
when the incensed populace of Paris contended for the
space of three days with the National Guards, and drove
Charles the Tenth from his throne; when the news of the
passage of the Stamp Act, and the tax on tea, by the mother
country, was received by our fathers, and insurrections for
liberty broke out in all parts of the colonies; when, at a
subsequent period, the tidings came that American citizens
had been captured by the Algerines, and were pining in
bondage; when, at a still later period, the rights of American seamen ceased to be respected by Great Britain, and
some six or seven thousand were said to have been impressed; on each and on all of those memorable occasions, no
denunciation against the oppressors was regarded as too
strong, no impeachment of motives too sweeping, no agitation too great, no zeal too burning, no sacrifice too dear, no
peril too imminent to be encountered. O, no! Then weakness became strength; prudence, noble daring; moderation,
impetuosity; caution, a generous disdain of consequences
charity, righteous indignation! Then the cold blood
philosophy, congealed by icy frigidness, was changed into
the warm fluid of patriotic life; then the abstractions of
metaphysics became practical realities, affecting life, liberty,

and the pursuit of happiness; then halting expediency was transformed into high, immutable, eternal principle. Then the man, who, at such a crisis, had dared to mock the agony of men's minds, and to insult their understandings, by giving them grave and severe homilies upon the duty of being cautious, and prudent, and charitable, and upon the propriety of exercising moderation and being dumb—such a man would have been deemed and treated as recreant to God and liberty. Then the land trembled as Freedom went forth to battle. Then words, however huge, expostulations, however earnest, petitions, however importunate, assertions of rights, however bold and uncompromising in language, were deemed wholly inadequate to such a crisis. Paving-stones in the streets were taken up, and hurled at the heads of the myrmidons of tyranny; human blood was poured out like water, and the dead bodies of the friends and foes of liberty were piled up in hecatombs round about. Then the press spoke out in thunder-tones—the public halls and churches rang with the shouts of victory, or resounded with heart-stirring appeals to arms; and even 'ministers of the gospel' felt that, in a strife for the rights of man, carnal weapons were not less efficacious than spiritual weapons, and hence it is recorded that some of them carried loaded muskets into the pulpit on the Sabbath day. Now, we do not say that all this conduct was justifiable—God forbid! We have not so learned duty. But, in the name of justice and mercy, we protest against being condemned for our zeal or language, our principles or measures, by the men who eulogize such deeds and such excitements as we have just recited. The only lesson they can teach us is, that our zeal is tame, our sensibility obtuse, our language weak, our self-sacrifice nothing, compared to the wrongs to be redressed, the evils to be overcome.

To an Eloquent Advocate of Indian Rights.

I.

If unto marble statues thou hadst spoken,
  Or icy hearts congealed by polar years,
The strength of thy pure eloquence had broken —
  Its generous heat had melted them to tears;
Which pearly drops had been a rainbow token,
  Bidding the red men sooth their gloomy fears.

II.

If Honor, Justice, Truth, had not forsaken
  The place once hallowed as their bright abode,
The faith of Treaties never had been shaken,
  Our country would have kept the trust she owed;
Nor Violence nor Treachery had taken
  Away those rights which Nature's God bestowed.

III.

Fruitless thy mighty efforts — vain appealing
  To grasping Avarice, that ne'er relents;
To Party Power, that shamelessly is stealing,
  Banditti-like, whatever spoil it scents;
To base Intrigue, his cloven foot revealing,
  That struts in Honesty's habiliments.

IV.

Our land, once green as Paradise, is hoary,
  E'en in its youth, with tyranny and crime;
Its soil with blood of Afric's sons is gory,
  Whose wrongs Eternity can tell — not Time;
The red man's woes shall swell the damning story,
  To be rehearsed in every age and clime!

28

West India Emancipation.

'JEHOVAH hath triumphed—his people are free!' 'Alleluia! for the Lord God omnipotent reigneth!' Such is the choral song of praise thundering heavenward, this day, from millions of voices in the islands of the sea, and on the shores of Great Britain, in view of the most wonderful transition, the most sublime achievement, and the noblest experiment, recorded in the world's history. Of all lands, (excepting, indeed, the emancipated colonies,) our own republic should be the most joyfully affected, and present the most animating spectacle, from its eastern extremity to its last great western barrier—from its chainless lakes to the topmost height of the Rocky Mountains; for the trump of jubilee is sounding across the waters, above the roar of the Atlantic, giving freedom to half a million of slaves, and elevating them from among cattle and creeping things to the privileges and rights of an immortal existence! And so it would, if it were not a republic of tyrants and slaves—if it were not basely recreant to all its professions—if it recognized man as man universally. Of all people, (excepting, again, the mighty host who only last night lay entombed in the cold, damp sepulchre of slavery, but at the earliest dawn of day obtained a glorious resurrection,) the American people should be foremost in celebrating the brightest triumph of humanity since man began to oppress his brother. And so they would, if they were true worshippers at the shrine of freedom—if their hands were not red with innocent blood— if they were not actually preying upon their own species. Never were their inconsistency, their hypocrisy, their hard-heartedness, so apparent, as on this very day. In the West India islands, slavery has been totally and for ever abolished! Yet the people of the United States, (excepting a portion of them who are branded as fanatics and madmen,) not only feel no delight in view of this fact, but are absolutely offended at the experiment; nay, they hope it will prove an utter failure! And why? Simply because the victims, who have been released from thraldom, wear a skin ' not colored like their own ; ' and because they dread to be left without excuse for their oppressive conduct. O, if this day had been set apart for the restoration of the Poles to their civil and political rights, so cruelly wrested from them by the strong arm of Russia, this country would now be rocking ' from side to side ' with excitement! But the peaceful emancipation of five hundred thousand descendants of Africa, not merely from civil disabilities, but from the most horrible servitude ever borne by any people — from all that is beastly in rank and treatment, and all that is terrible in irresponsible power — this is an event in which free, republican, Christian Americans feel no joy, and evince no interest! In honor of it, they will not fire a single gun, nor hoist a single flag, nor ring a single bell. They leave it to the subjects of a monarchical government, to ' agitators,' ' incendiaries,' and ' madmen,' to ' free negroes,' to exult over it! O, I blush for my country, to think that an occurrence which is filling all heaven with gladness, excites not a throb in her obdurate heart. But how can she participate in the general festivity, while she is actively engaged in forging chains for the limbs of millions of her own children? The loudest in her boasts of liberty, she is the vilest of hypocrites and the worst of oppressors. Let her be clothed in sackcloth and ashes; let her brow and her lips be prostrate in the dust, for shame and confusion of face; and let her be the scorn of the earth, until she ceases to plunder the poor and defenceless, and to turn away the stranger from his right.

The event we are assembled to commemorate cannot be

overrated in importance, nor adequately described in any
human dialect. Its altitude exceeds the highest flight of
the imagination ; its circumference cannot be measured by
human calculation ; its ramifications extend through time
into eternity. It has terminated such an amount of human
suffering, effaced such frightful stains of blood, healed up so
many wounds, rolled back such a tide of licentiousness,
opened so many fountains of happiness, poured such a light
upon the darkness of ages, rescued so many victims from
destruction, brought such glory to God, and removed such
mountainous obstacles out of the path of the gospel of
Christ, that neither men nor angels can compute the aggregate of blessings bestowed, or of horrors dispersed, by the
extinction of West India slavery. It makes set phrases of
speech, and formal attempts at description, seem almost con-
temptible. Words are for the common transactions of life,
but not for an occasion like this. I tremble to proceed.
The subject should have been committed to some master-
mind, capable of doing something like justice to it. But
what am I, in my poverty of speech, and my tediousness of
manner, and my feebleness of mind, that I should adventure
to grapple with it, or ' soar to the height of this great argument ' ? I speak, because the loftiest intellects in the land
are dumb. A question of dollars and cents, respecting a
modification of the Tariff Bill, or the regulation of the cur-
rency, can induce a Webster loudly to declaim in Faneuil
Hall ; but the transformation of hundreds of thousands of
slaves into freemen is too trifling an affair to extort an
approving sentence from his lips ! And the same thing is
true of other giant minds. Politic men ! Not that they love
freedom less, but that they love popularity, ' that weed of
the dunghill,' more ! Verily, they shall have their reward.
Let them refuse to hail this glorious jubilee, if they will.
Their conduct demonstrates that they have shrivelled souls,

whatever may be the size of their intellect. Liberty, like her great author, GOD, is no respecter of persons; she chooses the foolish things of the world to confound the wise, and weak things of the world to confound the things which are mighty. If the rulers in Church and State are not prepared to celebrate the most important victory she has ever obtained over oppression, it is because they are recreant to her cause.

Before I proceed any further, let me call attention to a remarkable exemplification of the insincerity and effrontery of the anti-abolition party in this country, as manifested this day. What have they not done, for the last five years, to cast odium upon our principles and measures? Have they not ridiculed, without mercy, our demand for the immediate abolition of slavery as wild, chimerical, monstrous? Has not the idea of 'turning loose' so many unlettered, penniless, homeless creatures, seemingly filled them with horror? Have they not a thousand times declared, that a sudden emancipation would fill the land with blood, and be the signal for a war of extermination? Have they not attempted to show, that slavery is a divine institution, which has been approved by God, from patriarch Abraham to patriarch McDuffie, and is therefore perfectly consistent with Christianity? Have they not claimed to be the only true philanthropists, the best friends of the slaves, the most tenderhearted among mankind? Have they not represented the slaves as incapable of taking care of themselves, and vehemently insisted that their simultaneous liberation would bring forth another St. Domingo tragedy? Most certainly, all this they have said and done, and a great deal more, equally creditable to their common sense, benevolence and piety! Now, how do I prove them to be inconsistent, if not hypocritical; reckless of consequences, if not hard-hearted; lukewarm friends of humanity, if not her treacherous foes?

28 *

I will show you. It is known throughout the country, that an abolition experiment is to be made this day, in the British West Indies, on a scale such as the world has never witness-ed. All the slaves, belonging to the following islands, rose up this morning without a chain upon their limbs, free men, free women, free children; without an owner to oppress them, without a driver to order them into the field, without any other restraints upon them than those which bind all the subjects of Great Britain, whether at home or abroad! The cart-whip, the thumb-screw, the yoke, the fetter, all the infernal devices of slavery to extort unpaid labor and servile obedience, have disappeared as by enchantment!

Tortola emancipates 5,400; Montserrat, 6,200; Nevis, 6,600; Dominica, 15,400; St. Vincent, 23,500; Barba-does, 82,000; Jamaica, 323,000; making a grand total of 462,100.

Now, I ask, if the apprehensions expressed by our oppo-nents are not feigned; if they are sincere in their opinions; if they really credit their own assertions; if they are not actuated by selfishness; if they truly love their neighbors as themselves; if their humanity is not restricted by geographi-cal boundaries; if, in fine, they believe that to ' turn loose,' in the twinkling of an eye, large masses of imbruted slaves, will subject the planters to imminent peril, if not to certain destruction—why, in the names of consistency and humani-ty, are they so imperturbable, so entirely indifferent, so abso-lutely unconscious, as it were, in full view of what is now transpiring in the West Indies? How shall we account for their conduct, except at the expense of their understandings or their hearts? Why has not a national fast been ordered? Why do they not toll the bells, and sing funeral dirges? This they do, if but the President of the United States die a natural death! And, lovers of mankind as they are, can they do less when thousands of planters are given up to indis-

criminate butchery, with their wives and children, by 'turning loose' upon them a troop of infuriated slaves? At least,
can they not refrain from their usual merriment, or wear
upon their countenances a semblance of concern, or affect
to be horror-stricken? Do they not know that the abolitionists are looking them full in the face, and taking notes of
their behavior, for the very purpose of recording it in print?
Have they 'remembered to forget' that this is the first of
August? Verily, it would seem so, or else that they have
been playing the part of hypocrites, for a long time past, for
a very bad purpose, and with very bad success! How is it
with the newspaper press? Are there no editorial wailings,
no lachrymal forebodings, no ebullitions of grief and horror?
Why are not the Journal of Commerce, the Evening Star,
the New York Gazette, the Commercial Advertiser, the
Courier and Enquirer, the New York Observer, the Christian Advocate and Journal, dressed in deep mourning? Or
have they already imprinted upon their pages too many
black marks, in testimony of their regard and sympathy for
the robbers of God's poor, to render their multiplication
necessary? Black marks, indeed, which no chemical liquid
shall be able to efface, nor any element destroy. If these
shrewd, far-sighted, infallible editors shall tell us, as a reason for their present composure, that they mean to wait
until they learn how the experiment works in Jamaica,
before they commit themselves by shedding too many tears,
and uttering too many groans, why then let us acknowledge
that they have some method in their madness; but while we
commend their discretion, let us inquire after their consistency. Though they have been prophesying 'evil, and only
evil, and that continually,' of any and every scheme of
immediate emancipation; though they have advanced it as a
self-evident proposition, that bloodshed and ruin must be the
inevitable consequence of letting all the oppressed go free

at once, it seems, after all, that they knew nothing about the
matter.   What was beyond all doubt with them, a short
time since, is now full of uncertainty : they wait for intelligence !   It is possible that the thorns of emancipation will
produce some very fine grapes, that the thistles of liberty
will grow some very nice figs, that a bad tree will bring
forth some very choice fruits.   They wish to do nothing
rashly, for they are civilized and Christian men, and as
unlike the wild and headlong abolitionists as lynch-law is
worse than common law.   For once they are puzzled ; their
vision is dim ; they falter in their steps ; they really cannot
tell how many throats will be cut, or whether any mischief
will be done this day, in the emancipated colonies.   Every
thing with them is in suspense, problematical, betwixt daylight and dark.   They can hardly discern ' men as trees
walking.'   Yet these are the keen scrutators, the severe
admonishers, the discerning moralists, the profound logicians,
the wise philosophers, the infallible prophets, the quick-sight-
ed seers, who perceive the end from the beginning, ' looking
before and after '—these, I say, who are now stumbling,
doubting, waiting, in relation to a result they have all along
asserted to be inevitable, are the very men who have held
up the abolitionists to public scorn as fools or madmen, blind
as to ' consequences,' ignorant of the relation of cause and
effect, and incapable of understanding that bad principles
and bad measures, if successful, (or, in other words, the
sudden overthrow of the slave system,) must inevitably lead
to violence and bloodshed.   O, most surely, they are the
people, and wisdom will die with them !   But the sooner such
wisdom perishes from the earth, the better for mankind.   So
ends the serio-comico farce enacted three-hundred and sixty-
five times a year, (Sundays not excepted,) for the last five
years, by our unfortunate opponents.   In what a pitiable
plight do they stand !   For, in one hour, all their ingenious

sophistry, subtle jesuitism, metaphysical hair-splitting; their confident predictions, their false accusations, their legal postulates, and their biblical perversions; together with the blood-red scourges and galling fetters of that detestable system which they impiously labored to uphold; have been broken in pieces by the sledge-hammer of Freedom, and consumed in the fire of immediate emancipation.

Now, look at the abolitionists, and observe with what exultation they greet this most eventful era! Where are they, but where they should be — crowding the public halls and temples of worship, to return thanks to Almighty God for the wonderful salvation he has effected for a people 'peeled, meted out, and trodden under foot'? There is no fear in their hearts, no doubt in their eyes; for, in their reverence for the immutable principles of justice, they looked well to CONSEQUENCES. For a series of years, they have been proclaiming in the ears of oppressors, in season and out of season, the duty of instantly releasing all their slaves from bondage. They have marshalled together all the facts of history — the experience of the ages — the testimony of the wise and good of all nations — proofs without number, and 'strong as holy writ' — to demonstrate the impolicy, danger and wickedness of exercising oppression over the needy and defenceless. On the score of personal safety, of self-interest, they have strenuously urged the planters to give up their impious claim of property in human flesh. They have indignantly scouted the notion, as opposed to reason and revelation, as equally unphilosophical and unscriptural, that it is perilous to entrust men with their inalienable rights. They have challenged their opponents, in vain, to produce a single instance, in any quarter of the globe, from ancient or modern history, in which disastrous consequences have followed the removal of heavy burdens from the backs, and galling yokes from the necks of the oppressed, however feeble in intellect, or darkened in mind, or unprepared to enter upon ' liberty and the pursuit of happiness.' ' Give freedom to all whom you are unjustly retaining in bondage,' they have said to the masters, ' and, as true as the Lord liveth, there shall no evil befall you. Not a hair of your heads shall be injured, not a drop of your blood shall be shed, not a fragment of your property shall be destroyed. Instead of darkness, you shall have light ; instead of tribu- lation, joy ; instead of adversity, prosperity. For barren- ness, you shall have fertility ; for wasteful, indolent and revengeful serfs, provident, industrious and grateful labor- ers; for liability to servile insurrections, perfect exemption from danger. The execrations of your victims shall be turned into blessings; their wailings into shouts of joy ; the judgments of God into mercies. Your peace shall flow like a river, for there shall be none to molest or make afraid. " For the mouth of the Lord hath spoken it." '

Well, God be praised ! the planters of Jamaica have this day resolved, with perfect unanimity, to try the experiment. Are the abolitionists troubled, that they have been taken at their word ? Have they not some forebodings that all will not turn out so well as they have predicted ? None at all. They know whereof they affirm, and accurately perceive all the consequences of the emancipation act. They have taken a bond, not of fate, but of HIM who cannot lie, and thus have made ' assurance doubly sure.' Hence it is that, unlike those who have deprecated the measure as suicidal on the part of the planters, they do not feel constrained to wait until they can get intelligence from the West Indies, before they can pass judgment upon it. Hence it is, in various parts of the United States, throughout old Eng- land, among the highlands of Scotland, and in the Emerald Isle, they are now swelling the grand chorus of liberty —

> 'From every giant hill, companion of the cloud,
> The startled echo leaps, to give it back aloud!'

Now let 'the base of heaven's deep organ blow,' and all that is harmonious in heaven or on earth take up the thrilling strain, ' Glory to God in the highest!'

Our cautious opponents will perhaps admonish us not to be premature in our exultation. Perhaps they will sagely remind us, in the form of a homely adage, that it is not best to halloo until we get out of the woods. Sanguine as we are of good results, we may be wofully mistaken; and therefore we shall be on the safe side to follow their prudent example — WAIT FOR INTELLIGENCE ! Now, these admonitory suggestions prove the blindness, ignorance and skepticism of those who aspire to be our teachers and guides. If they would disburden their minds of prejudice, and calmly listen to the voice of reason, and believe what God has spoken, they would feel assured that tranquillity, order and happiness are reigning throughout the emancipated colonies. The difference between them and ourselves, in this matter, is, that we walk by faith, they by sight. We *believe* — therefore we rejoice ! They cannot yet *see* — hence their reluctance to change their position ! Now, was there ever a people so low and brutal as not to rejoice in being set free from bondage ? Is it not morally impossible, that the same act which fills them with gratitude and joy should inflame them with revenge ? If they will patiently suffer themselves to be

> 'Yoked to the beasts, and driven to their toil,' —

if they will not lift up a finger in self-defence, when they are horribly scourged, branded with hot irons, defrauded of

their earnings, sundered in traffic like cattle, and subjected
to the most dreadful torments,—is it to be supposed, for the
twentieth part of a moment, that, when they are released
from such a condition, and raised to the level of our
common humanity, (by the consent, too, of their masters,)
they will engage in butchery, ' cry havoc, and let slip the
dogs of war,' and make human blood flow like water?
Nay, can it be rationally apprehended, that they will resort
even to the slightest acts of violence ?   On the contrary, is
it not to be taken for granted, as a matter of course, that
they will manifest the liveliest gratitude, be docile as lambs,
perform their remunerated labor with alacrity, and make
each field and hill vocal with melody ?   ' Instinct is a great
matter ' — what says instinct, in reply to these interrogations ?   What says common sense ?   What says history ?
What says ' holy writ' ?   Are we, then, presumptuous in
observing this day as a joyful festival ?   Run we any hazard
of being premature in uttering our acclamations ?   Is it not
our opponents, who are forced into a painful and ridiculous
attitude ?   O, they are anxiously *waiting for intelligence !*
Why, what has been done in the West Indies, thus to fill
them with perplexity ; thus to shake their theory of right
and wrong ; thus to make it impossible for them to predict,
whether joy or sorrow, order or anarchy, gratitude or revenge, a reign of peace or a hurricane of fire and blood, is
to be the consequence ?

In the first place, all the laborers in the seven islands
which have been already specified,—comprising nine-tenths
of the whole effective population, — are henceforth to receive
wages for their work, instead of getting no compensation, as
heretofore.   They are no longer to be forced to their labor
under the lash of the driver.   No man may now strike or
oppress them with impunity.   Their labor is to be voluntary ; they may work as many or as few hours as they

please; they are free to make their own contracts, to choose their own employers, to acquire and possess as much as industry and economy will enable them. Slave mothers are no more to be compelled to toil from dawn of day to the approach of night, in the open field, beneath a burning sun, dragging their infants with them. They may now give heed to the cries of nature, and administer to the wants of their helpless offspring, without being lacerated for their motherly tenderness. In short, honesty is to take the place of robbery, voluntary action that of brute violence, recompense is to go hand in hand with toil, wages are to be substituted for the whip.

Under the slave-driving system in the Colonies, it appears, by returns made to the British Parliament, that not only was the natural increase of the slave population cut off, but, in the short space of eleven years, there had been a decrease, to the frightful amount of FIFTY-TWO THOUSAND, EIGHT HUNDRED AND EIGHTY-SEVEN, or about FIVE THOUSAND annually! Now, this wholesale butchery is to cease; the laborers cannot be worked to death with impunity. We turn to our opponents, and ask, whether this single item is not something gained to the cause of humanity—something that warrants, unattended by other favorable circumstances, a jubilee like the present? 'Well, they don't know; honesty *may* prove to be the best policy; fair dealing and humanity are very good things, if they only turn out well in the end!' They shake their heads doubtingly; they fear the experiment will prove ruinous to both the employers and the employed; at all events, they *wait for intelligence!* Let us try again.

In the second place, the claim of property, whether absolute or conditional, in the bodies and souls of half a million of our race, expired by limitation at twelve o'clock last night, and can never be renewed. There are to be no more slave auctions; no more sunderings of fathers and mothers,

29

husbands and wives, parents and children, lovers and friends, by the slave speculator. A legalized system of concubinage is ended, and upon its ruins is established the marriage institution, sacred to virtue and love! The broken links of parental, filial and conjugal ties are reünited in a golden chain. O, it is dreadful to contemplate the reeking licentiousness, the abounding impurity, the Sodom-like beastiality, generated by that foul system which abrogated marriage, removed all virtuous restraints, and offered premiums on pollution! Blessed be God, it is over the downfall of that system we are met to rejoice. Its lava tide of desolation is stayed, dried up, for ever! Now, we turn once more to our opponents, and demand, whether this is not a signal gain to the cause of morality — a triumph of purity over the filthiness of the flesh, in which all the virtuous in heaven and on earth may participate, never doubting as to the ' consequences,' either in time or in eternity ? 'Well, they are not prepared to answer! They hope for the best, but fear the worst!' 'All's well that ends well!' They *wait for intelligence!*

In the last place, (for it is needless, almost endless, to recapitulate the benefits of this great measure,) the most formidable obstacle to the progress of Christianity — greater than any which the Man of Sin, or the False Prophet, or Pagan Juggernaut, has been able to cast in her path — is taken out of the way, so far as relates to the West Indies ; and the gospel of Christ, not in isolated texts or perverted expositions, but in its completeness, can now be preached with all boldness, where but a short time since, the missionaries of the Cross were cast into prison, or compelled to flee for their lives, and their chapels burnt to the ground. The statutes are repealed, which made it a crime worthy of stripes, imprisonment, or death, to give light to the blind, knowledge to the ignorant, succor to the perishing ; which

prohibited instruction in letters, the establishment even of
primary schools, the circulation of the Scriptures, and all
measures for intellectual cultivation and moral improvement; which estimated the soul of a slave as the life of a
beast, denied the immortality of our race, claimed to be of
higher obligation than the commandments of God, and au-
thorised all manner of inflictions upon our common nature.
Ample protection is now given against violence and wrong;
all restrictions upon the liberty of the press, of speech, and
of locomotion, are taken off; those who, yesterday, had no
will or power of their own, may to-day go where they
please, give free utterance to their thoughts, consult their
own wishes; all the avenues to human elevation and infinite
progression are thrown wide open; the Bible may be read
and circulated without let or hindrance ; mind, intellect and
heart are all permitted to develop themselves in the sunlight
of liberty.   Again, therefore, we turn to our opponents, and
ask, whether here is not an incalculable gain to the cause of
justice, virtue and religion?   Can the ' consequences ' of
this change of administration be otherwise than good and
glorious?   May not the followers of Progress, the friends
of Philanthropy, the disciples of Christianity, rejoice over it
with all certainty as to its beneficent effects, even though not
a day has passed since the experiment was put into operation?   ' O, they are not inclined to answer; they are really
puzzled to know whether more harm than good will not
result from it; by the first of September, they hope to be
able to form an opinion.   They *wait for intelligence !* '
True, the slave system has been cast into the bottomless
pit; but then, they are persuaded a state of freedom is
pregnant with far greater evils !   True, the slaves can no
longer be bought, sold, mortgaged, branded, cropped, manacled, lacerated, murdered with impunity ; but then, for this
merciful exemption from suffering, it is to be apprehended

that they will cut their masters' throats! True, learning may now be encouraged, schools established, the gospel enforced, extraordinary privileges enjoyed; but then, as a consequence of this state of things, plantations may be ravaged, the dwellings of the planters fired, and the awful scenes of St. Domingo witnessed!! O, well may Bedlam laugh at such stolidity, and shudder at such insensibility! What shall we think of such men? or what shall we say of them? It cannot be that they are in their right minds; or, if they are, that they are sincere in what they affirm. Ignorant they cannot be, for they make high pretensions to wisdom and knowledge. Talents they certainly possess; but talents, ' though angel bright,' may be turned into foolishness by perversion. It is impossible to believe them to be honest, except at the expense of their understandings. They deny self-evident propositions. They proclaim that all men are created free and equal, and endowed with inalienable rights, and then mob us for enforcing their own doctrine! They contend for liberty of speech, and then subject us to lynch law for exercising that liberty! They expatiate upon the blessings of freedom, and then burn down our dwellings for proposing to extend those blessings to millions of our countrymen who are kept in the house of bondage! But, enigmatical as their conduct may at first appear, it finds an easy solution. They despise, loathe, repudiate, the colored man, as a MAN; though they value him, cling to him, extol him, run after him, from the borders of Texas to our north-eastern boundary, as a SLAVE! They hate the colored race, cordially, unceasingly, implacably — not all of them so much as to desire their perpetual enslavement, but hate them to an extent which requires their banishment from the soil. They wish them to be out of sight, out of the land, out of the world, — except they will go to Liberia, and then they will be pretty sure to be out of it in

a very short time. The fire of their prejudice is unquench-
able ; all the waters of the Atlantic cannot extinguish it.
They declare it to be an offence against good manners,
good morals, Christian decorum, and republican equality, to
treat men irrespective of their complexion — nay, subversive
of the American Union, and destructive of the peace of
Zion ! They maintain that it is ' an ordination of Heaven,'
as unalterable as the laws of Nature, that there should be
no intercourse between the white and colored races, except
as masters and slaves : hence, emancipation and expulsion
must be inseparable. The conformation of the black man
is to them a source of merriment. They sometimes affect
to doubt whether he belongs to the *genus homo ;* whether
he is, in fact, a member of the human family. If they have
enslaved him, the color of his skin is invaluable to identify
him, in case (as will most probably be the case) he shall
take to himself legs, and run away. If he is free in their
midst, his complexion is a nuisance. They send a man to
the hospital if he has the small pox or cholera, but if he has
a sable complexion, he must go to Liberia—and very poor
medical attendance will he receive when he gets there,
though he will need it greatly. The cholera may be cured,
but a sable skin admits of no remedy. Besides all this, a
very large portion of our opponents are slaveholders, and it
would be very strange if they were not found in array
against us. Whoever sides with them in this great controversy, takes part against their victims; that is, against justice
and humanity. They may, indeed —as we trust they
will — come over to us, in imitation of the cheering example which has been set them in the West Indies ; but we
can never go over to them. Subtract from the ranks of the
anti-abolition party all who own slaves, or have mortgages
upon slave property, or who are in any way interested in
the system; or their relations and connections, who sympa-
29 *

thize with them, or who cherish the brutal spirit of caste towards the victims of American brutality; all who love their denominational or political party more than mankind; all who are seeking the loaves and fishes of office in Church or State; and all who are licentious, profane, jacobinical in their spirit,—how many unprejudiced, tender-hearted, noble-spirited souls would be left ? Be they few or many, they are fast coming over to the side of bleeding humanity.   But, controlled by such influences, passions and interests, is it to be wondered at that our opponents, whenever they discourse upon the subject of slavery, and the rights of the colored race, talk like men in a state of lunacy; deny their own faith; insist that two and two make nine, and twice nine make forty-five; grow angry, spiteful, turbulent; conjure up raw-head and bloody-bones, dire chimeras, *black* ghosts; run away from the light of free discussion, as sheep-devouring wolves troop back to their murky dens at dawn of day; substitute rotten eggs for arguments, brickbats for syllogisms, and tar and feathers for victorious appeals; burn down buildings dedicated to ' VIRTUE, LIBERTY and INDEPENDENCE '; resort to bowie-knives and pistols as their weapons of defence, and imbrue their hands in the blood of innocency ? Why, these things should excite no marvel; they are the natural consequence of such principles.   The measures are adapted to the principles, and the principles to the measures.   Can a corrupt tree bring forth good fruit ?   Can that which is evil-disposed, which is proscriptive, oppressive, cruel, delight in peace, love, and good-will to all men ?

I have said that abolitionists believe, therefore they now rejoice; that their opponents walk by sight, and very short-sighted they are withal.   They wait for intelligence.   It will come by and by; come to their confusion, let me tell them ! Nay, deride the fact as they may, it has come already!

Though the sun of this time-consecrated day has not yet disappeared from the heavens, though it is not twenty-four hours since the event we are commemorating took place in distant islands; yet tidings of the result have been received in this city, from high authority, which I am permitted to announce in the ears of the people. They were brought by no human express, and are authenticated by no fictitious sign-manual. The messenger is the Spirit of Truth, sent down from heaven, his documents having the seal and signet of the Lord Almighty! What was done last night in Jamaica? At twelve o'clock, precisely, all the bands of wickedness were loosed, the heavy burdens undone, the oppressed set free, and every yoke broken, according to the command of God! What has followed in Jamaica? Its light broke forth as the morning, and its health shall spring forth speedily! Its darkness is as the noonday! It shall be satisfied in drought, and its bones made fat; yea, it shall be like a watered garden, and like a spring of water whose waters fail not. And they that shall be of it shall build the old waste places: it shall raise up the foundations of many generations; and it shall be called, The repairer of the breach, The restorer of paths to dwell in! 'For the mouth of the Lord hath spoken it.' Who discredits this intelligence? Who doubts whether the facts are just as they are represented? None who take God at his word; none who implicitly believe that he is faithful, and cannot lie; none but those who are practically infidels! If it be a dream, still, ' the dream is certain, and the interpretation thereof sure!'

But this will not satisfy our opponents; for, as they regard not the colored man, so neither in this matter do they fear God. They want better testimony; the reports of pro-slavery journals and colonization repositories, some four or six weeks hence, respecting the workings of the free-labor system; then, peradventure, they will believe, even if it con-firms what God foretold would certainly come to pass! They leave fanatics and madmen to cant about walking by faith; as for themselves, they will take nothing upon trust. They will believe their own eyes. They will see what the Journal of Commerce, or the Courier and Enquirer, or the Commercial Advertiser, or the New York Observer, or the Washington Globe, and other kindred prints, say of this affair, and make up their minds accordingly. 'A bird in the hand is worth two in the bush,' say they.

Very well; I will not stop to pick a feather from the wing of that full-fledged adage. Let them have their own way in the argument, for which ever path they choose, their escape is impossible. They will hear nothing, it seems, about faith, promises, light, darkness, repairs, ruins, or any such cabalistical nonsense. They are your practical, cautious, shrewd, calculating men. They know what they know, and believe what they believe; among other things, that to steal a sixpence out of their own pockets is a crime deserving the frown of heaven, and condign punishment by the magis-trate, but that to kidnap a whole plantation of negroes is no crime at all, but a patriarchal exploit, which Heaven smiling-ly approves! But I press to the point. Between them and us, for a long time past, there has been a warm controversy as to the consequences that would follow the immediate emancipation of large bodies of slaves, without education, ignorant even of its lowest rudiments. We have maintain-ed, that such an act, if voluntarily performed by the mas-ters, or effected in any peaceful manner, would be safe, bloodless, profitable, and mutually advantageous to all par-ties. They have asserted, that it would involve both mas-ters and slaves in one common ruin; that the soil would be left uncultivated, the plantations devastated, and butchery be the order of the day; that, in short, it would be ' chaos come again,' with thick-brooding darkness, and thronging horrors! Now for a practical trial of our conflicting theories. Our opponents very well know, that, four years ago, just such an experiment was made, on a large scale, under disadvantageous circumstances, where there were fifteen blacks to one white; a most unequal disproportion, surely! In one hour, no less than thirty thousand slaves were transformed into freemen! Now let them tell us, whether one of their frightful anticipations has been realized; whether all our happy predictions have not been fulfilled to the letter. One, two, three, four years have elapsed since that adventurous step was taken, though the planters might have retained their authority for the term of six years longer. Well, during all that time, has a single throat been cut, or a drop of blood spilt, or lynch law administered in a single case, or an embryo conspiracy detected, or the ghost of a rebellion seen? No. Has the property of the planters been injured to the amount of a farthing? No. Has any plantation been left uncultivated? No. Have the emancipated slaves refused to work? No. Have they shown the slightest disposition to be idle, turbulent, or intractable? No. On the contrary, has not the measure been attended with the happiest consequences, in detail and in the aggregate? Yes. Are not the employers (now masters no longer) enjoying unwonted security, an enviable peace of mind, and a splendid recompense of reward for well-doing? Yes. Are not the employed (now unpaid laborers no longer) industrious, economical, orderly, docile almost to a fault, filled with grateful emotions, aspiring after intellectual and moral cultivation, and rejoicing continually over the boon of liberty? Yes. These facts are notorious. How do our opponents get over them? They can neither get over, nor under, nor around them, nor escape their flaming omnipresence by flight. How is it that cause and effect have ceased relationship; that the best possible result has accompanied the worst possible act; that a firebrand, thrown into a powder magazine, creates no explosion; that water runs up hill, and a thousand other miracles are witnessed; that the planters are not torn limb from limb, and all their property annihilated; how is it, I repeat, that our opponents have witnessed the laws of nature reversed, (if we may believe them,) their own ingenious theories turned topsy-turvy, and every prediction of the 'fanatical abolitionists' literally fulfilled, and they have made no confession of error, uttered no exclamation of surprise, attempted no explanation of these remarkable phenomena? How is it, that they are so stoical, so phlegmatic, so dumb! I have conceded too much to their humanity. I have said that they are waiting for intelligence from Jamaica, in regard to the transactions of this day in that island, before they hail the emancipation act as a blessing. But they will not hail it, though it shall appear that the very windows of heaven have been opened, and such a blessing poured out that there was no room to receive it. They will be filled with chagrin, with ill-digested spleen, with undiminished hostility to the emancipation of their own downtrodden countrymen. They will behave precisely as they have done in the case of Antigua. They profess to be humane, patriotic, Christian men, anxious to see the cause of human freedom advancing in the earth; yet how have they welcomed the intelligence, that emancipation works well in Antigua, and is going on 'in the full tide of successful experiment'? Positively in a manner that would be disgraceful to barbarians! They have studiously attempted to garble and suppress facts, to wink out of sight what an adoring universe will ever contemplate with delight, to forget what shall be held in everlasting remembrance! I appeal to the world, steeped as it is in pollution and iniquity; I appeal to heaven, in its immaculate purity and resplendent glory, if they were virtuous men, would they not rejoice to know that a system of legalized concubinage and prostitution had come to an end? If they were patriotic, would they not exult at the peaceful overthrow of a worse than Turkish despotism? If they were philanthropic, would they not shout aloud in view of misery assuaged, broken hearts comforted, wounds and putrefying sores healed up, the lame leaping like the roe, the blind restored to sight, the deaf made to hear, and the dumb to speak? If they were lovers of justice, would they not delight in the fact, that the lynch code of slavery, as administered for ages to an immense multitude of their fellow-creatures, has been superseded by constitutional law, giving ample protection to the meanest of them all? If they were truly pious, would they not give glory to God, that where it was until recently fettered and gagged, the gospel may now have free course and be glorified? that a mighty obstacle to the progress of the Redeemer's kingdom has been removed out of the way? that where the Bible has been a prohibited book, it may now be freely circulated? that where mental and moral improvement has been forbidden under severe penalties, all restrictions are taken off, and light and knowledge are abounding? But they do not rejoice; they do not shout aloud, (no, not even whisper!) they do not give glory to God! How is their hypocrisy, their hard-heartedness, their contempt for the colored race, made manifest! How are they judged in the presence of angels and mankind!

They walk by sight, forsooth! Why not look, then, at Antigua? That is a sight worth looking at! But the light is too strong for their weak vision. If there had been blood and carnage in that island, they could have beheld it with 'philosophical composure;' it would have helped them to an argument, and arguments with them are very scarce; it would have served to make plausible their scare-crow theory

of emancipation, now, alack! proved, to the satisfaction of
the veriest cowards in Christendom, to be nothing but a
scare-crow, with an air-drawn dagger! They looked, but
hearing songs of praise instead of the agonies of the dying;
seeing every man's hand, instead of turning against another,
extended in fraternal kindness; beholding the whole face of
society renovated, and all things presenting an animated
aspect; why should they look more than once? Are disagreeable objects to be contemplated with satisfaction? Is
the mirror, that clearly reveals one's deformity, a source of
pleasure to the beholder? No, indeed! At least, so think
our opponents!

I proceed now, with all brevity, to show in what manner
the boon of freedom was received by the slaves of Antigua
and Bermuda; and the first witness I shall summon upon
the stand is LORD BROUGHAM, whose gigantic exertions in the
cause of emancipation entitle him to the gratitude of mankind. In an eloquent speech, delivered by him in the House
of Lords, February 20th, 1838, on this subject, he testifies
as follows : —

'The first of August arrived — that day so confidently and joy-
ously anticipated by the poor slaves, and so sorely dreaded by their
hard task-masters; and if ever there was a picture interesting to
look upon — if ever there was a passage in the history of a people,
redounding to their eternal honor — if ever there was a complete
refutation of all the scandalous calumnies which had been heaped
upon them for ages, as if in justification of the wrongs which we
had done them — that picture and that passage are to be found in
the uniform and unvarying history of that people throughout the
whole of the West India islands. Instead of the fires of rebellion
lit by a feeling of lawless revenge and resistance to oppression, the
whole of those islands were, like an Arabian scene, illuminated by
the light of contentment, joy, peace and good-will towards all men.
No civilized people, after gaining an unexpected victory, could have
shown more delicacy and forbearance than was exhibited by the
slaves at the great moral consummation which they had attained.

There was not a look or a gesture which could gall the eyes of their masters. Not a sound escaped from negro lips, which could wound the ears of the most feverish planter in the islands. All was joy, mutual congratulation and hope.'

So far the testimony of Lord Brougham. Thus much for the horrors of immediate emancipation! Thus much in proof that slaves are contented and happy, and would not be free if they could! O, if there were time, it would be a delightful task to give the details of events, as they transpired in Antigua, in 1834. But a single extract from Thome and Kimball's Journal must suffice : it contains an Alexandrian library of pathos and sublimity in a single paragraph : —

'The Wesleyans kept "watch-night" in all their chapels on the night of the 31st July [the evening preceding the day of emancipation.] The spacious chapel in St. John's was filled with the candidates for liberty. All was animation and eagerness. A mighty chorus of voices swelled the song of expectation and joy, and as they united in prayer, the voice of the leader was drowned in the universal acclamations of thanksgiving, and praise, and blessing, and honor, and glory to God, who had come down for their deliverance. In such exercises, the evening was spent until the hour of twelve approached. The missionary then proposed, that when the clock on the cathedral should begin to strike, the whole congregation should fall upon their knees, and receive the boon of freedom in silence! Accordingly, as the loud bell tolled its first note, the immense assembly fell prostrate on their knees. All was silence, save the quivering, half-stifled breath of the struggling spirit. The slow notes of the clock fell upon the ears of the multitude ; peal on peal, peal on peal, rolled over the prostrate throng, in tones of angels' voices, thrilling among the desolate chords and weary heart-strings ! Scarce had the clock sounded its last note, when the lightning flashed vividly around, and a loud peal of thunder roared along the sky.— God's pillar of fire, and trump of jubilee ! A moment of profoundest silence passed — then came the burst — they broke forth in prayer; they shouted, they sung, "glory," "alleluia;" they clapped their hands, leaped up, fell down, clasped

30

each other in their free arms, cried, laughed, and went to and fro, tossing upwards their unfettered hands; but, high above the whole, there was a mighty sound, which ever and anon swelled up — it was the utterings, in broken negro dialect, of gratitude to God. After this gush of excitement had spent itself, and the congregation became calm, the religious exercises were resumed, and the remainder of the night was occupied in singing and prayer, in reading the Bible, and in addresses from the missionaries, explaining the nature of the freedom just received, and exhorting the freed people to be industrious, steady, obedient to the laws, and to show themselves in all things worthy of the high boon which God had conferred upon them.'

Nothing can surpass the sublimity of the scene, or add to the power of its description : —

'Nought but itself can be its parallel' !

And yet, how natural the conduct, how reverent the spirit, how exquisite the sensibility, how overwhelming the gratitude of these contemned ones ! I say, how natural their conduct ! They had obtained all they wished for ; why should they think of butchering those who had set them free ? The idea is preposterous. Yet it is upon record, that several American vessels, which had lain for weeks in the harbor of St. John's, weighed anchor on the 31st July, and made their escape, through actual fear that the island would be destroyed on the following day ! There is a specimen of republican reverence for liberty ! That is the way we encourage tyranny to give up its victims ! What fit subjects for a slaveholding master the captains of those vessels must have been ! O, the cowardly, recreant unbelievers ; the liberty-hating, consistent members of a confederacy of oppressors !

No throats were cut in Antigua ! And an equally astonishing fact is, the slaves wanted to be free, and don't want to return to bondage ! And, perhaps, what will surprise our opponents most of all is, the Governor of Antigua being witness, ' the planters all concede that emancipation has been a great blessing to the island; he does not know of a single individual who wishes to return to the old system.' ' He is well acquainted with the country districts of England, and has also travelled extensively in Europe; yet he has never found such a peaceable, orderly, and law-abiding people as the emancipated slaves of Antigua.' On being interrogated as to the workings of the new system, one of the planters (Dr. Daniel) said—' The planters, by giving immediate freedom, had secured the attachment of their people; it had removed all danger of insurrection, conflagration and conspiracies.' Another planter (Mr. Hatley) said—' Formerly, it was whip, whip, whip, incessantly, but now we are relieved from this disagreeable task.' Another (Hon. Samuel O. Baijer) said—' I can cultivate my estate at least one third cheaper by free labor than by slave labor.' Another (Hon. N. Nugent) said—' there is not the slightest feeling of insecurity; quite the contrary. Property is more secure, for all idea of insurrection is abolished for ever. My family go to sleep every night with the doors unlocked, and we fear neither violence nor robbery.' Another said— ' Now, the security of property was so much greater in Antigua than it was in England, he thought it doubtful whether he should ever venture to take his family thither, as he had long contemplated doing.' Another (H. Armstrong, Esq.) said—' There is no possible danger of personal violence from the emancipated slaves. Should a foreign power invade our island, I have no doubt that the negroes would, to a man, fight for the planters.' Another (Dr. Ferguson) said—' The credit of the island has decidedly improved. Its internal prosperity is advancing in an increased ratio. More buildings have been erected since emancipation, than for twenty years before.' An estate which, previous to eman-

cipation, could not be sold for £600 current, lately brought
£2000. 'All persons, of all professions, testify to the fact,
that marriages are rapidly increasing. In truth, there was
scarcely such a thing as marriage before the abolition of
slavery. The whole number of marriages, during ten years
previous to emancipation, was but half as great as the number for a single year following emancipation.' The effect
wrought upon prejudice is very remarkable. Before emancipation, the spirit of caste was strong and rampant. How
is it now? 'All distinctions,' says the Governor of Antigua,
'founded in color, must be abolished every where. We
should learn to talk of men, not as colored men, but as men,
as fellow citizens and fellow subjects.' His secretary is a
colored gentleman. The language of one of the Wesleyan
missionaries to Messrs. Thome and Kimball was, 'Tell the
American brethren, that, much as we desire to visit the
United States, we cannot go, so long as we are prohibited
from speaking against slavery, or while that abominable
prejudice is encouraged in the churches. We could not
administer the sacrament to a church, in which the distinction of color was maintained.' The revolution of opinion
in the midst of the planters, respecting slavery and the abolitionists, is worthy of especial observation. Says the Hon.
N. Nugent, 'The anti-slavery party in England were detest-
ed here for their fanatical and reckless course. Such was
the state of feeling previous to emancipation, that it would
have been certain disgrace for any planter to have avowed
the least sympathy with anti-slavery sentiments. The humane might have their hopes and aspirations, and they might
secretly long to see slavery ultimately terminated; but they
did not dare to make such feelings public. They would
at once have been branded as the enemies of their country.'
Says another planter, (James Scotland, sen.) 'The opinions
of the clergymen and missionaries, with the exception of, I

believe, a few clergymen, were favorable to emancipation; but neither in their conduct, preaching or prayers, did they declare themselves openly, until the measure of abolition was determined on. Whoever was known, or suspected of being an advocate for freedom, became the object of vengeance, and was sure to suffer, if in no other way, by a loss of part of his business.' Now, how changed is the scene! 'Anti-Slavery is the popular doctrine among all classes. He is considered an enemy to his country, who opposes the principles of liberty. The planters look with astonishment at the continuance of slavery in the United States, and express their strong belief that it must soon terminate here, and throughout the world. They hailed the arrival of the French and American visitors on tours of inquiry as a bright omen. Distinguished abolitionists are spoken of in terms of respect and admiration. An agent of the English Anti-Slavery Society now resides in St. John's, and keeps a book-store, well stocked with anti-slavery books and pamphlets. The bust of GEORGE THOMPSON stands conspicuously upon the counter, looking forth upon the public street.' At a public meeting attended by the agents of the American Anti-Slavery Society, a resolution approving of their mission was adopted by rising. 'Not an individual in the crowded congregation kept his seat. The masters and the slaves of yesterday all rose together — a phalanx of freemen — to testify "their sincere sympathy" in the efforts and objects of American abolitionists!' At a dinner party in Barbadoes, the planters complimented Messrs. Thome and Kimball, by giving their health, and 'wishing success to their most laudable undertaking.' Though the contrary was pretended before the abolition of slavery, (as it is now in our country, in order to stop 'agitation,') the planters now ingenuously confess, that there was far less cruelty exercised by them during the anti-slavery excitement in England. 'They

30 *

were always on their guard to escape the notice of the abolitionists. They did not wish to have their names published abroad, and to be exposed as monsters of cruelty.'

There are many other equally instructive facts. ' *Before* emancipation, martial law invariably prevailed on the holidays; but the very first Christmas after emancipation, the Governor made a proclamation, stating that, in consequence of the abolition of slavery, it was no longer necessary to resort to such a precaution.' In fact, the main constabulary force is now composed of emancipated negroes, living on the estates. So, there can be no more slave insurrections in Antigua, though it is not impossible that there may now and then be a mob of ' gentlemen of property and standing.' No more is heard about Paul sending Onesimus back to his master — the passage ceases to be translated, ' *Slaves,* obey your masters ' — not an allusion is made to the example of the patriarchs — the Levitical code has suddenly become obsolete, in the light of the British Constitution, and the Gospel of Christ! As to the willingness of the emancipated slaves to work, there is abundant testimony. We have a proverb among ourselves, that one can tell whether a mechanic is at work by the day or by the job, by listening to the sound of his hammer. If by the day, the tune is ' *Largo*,' thus: — ' By —— the —— day ! by —— the —— day !' If by the job, it is ' *Prestissimo* ' — ' By the job, job, job ! by the job, job, job !' That is human nature ; that is the instinct of self-interest, which is indeed ' a great matter ' to white and black alike. It is just so in Antigua. The laborers work very industriously by —— the —— day, though they receive but eleven cents as compensation ; but they work still better *by the job.* One planter testifies — ' When they had jobs given them, they would sometimes go to work by three o'clock in the morning, and work by moonlight. When the moon was not shining, he has known them to

kindle fires among the trash, or dry cane leaves, to work
by. They would then continue all day, working until
four o'clock, stopping only for breakfast, and dispensing
with the usual intermission from twelve to two.' So much
for the laziness of the negroes, which nothing but a cart-
whip can stimulate! When we consider how small is the
pittance which they receive, it is amazing to learn 'how
that *the abundance of their joy and their deep poverty*
abounds unto the riches of their liberality.' For, besides
supporting their families, they are contributing to Sunday
schools, missionary objects, the support of religious worship,
the distribution of the Bible, and to a multitude of benevolent and moral associations, to the amount of thousands of
dollars annually! Injured, calumniated, wonderful people!
Lord Brougham, as a proof of their extraordinary industry, asserts that, ' during the year which followed the first
of August, 1834, twice as much sugar per hour, and of a
better quality, as compared with the preceding years, was
stored throughout the sugar districts; and that one man, a
large planter, has expressly avowed, that with twenty
freemen, he could do more work than with a hundred
slaves, or fifty indentured apprentices. Now, I maintain,'
continues Lord Brougham, ' that had we known what
we now know of the character of the negroes, neither
would the compensation (of £20,000,000 sterling) have
been given to the slave-owners, nor we have been guilty of
proposing to keep the negro in slavery five years, after
we were decided that he had a right to his freedom. The
money had, in fact, been paid to them by mistake; and,
were the transaction one between man and man, an action
for its recovery might lie.'

Such are some of the glorious ' consequences' which
have attended the immediate overthrow of slavery in Antigua; such they will be in Jamaica and the other islands,

and in the Southern States of America, whenever a similar event takes place. Think you there is one person in Great Britain, male or female, rich or poor, who has signed one memorial, or offered up one prayer, or made one effort, or contributed one mite, for the extinction of the West India slave system, that regrets the deed? O, no! They recur to it with pleasing satisfaction, lamenting only that they had not been more fervent in spirit, more liberal in giving, and more zealous in hastening so blissful a consummation!

Some people are quite astounded at the prosperous state of things in Antigua. They seem to regard it as almost miraculous. It is no miracle at all! It is no more surprising than the autumnal harvest obtained from sowing the seed in spring time. It is the natural result of well-doing, unattended by aught that is mysterious or incredible. Remembering what man is—in whose image he is created—what are the motives by which he is made to be controlled—under what government the Almighty has placed him, a free, moral, accountable agent—what promises that glorious Being holds forth to those who let the oppressed go free—I am surprised at nothing which has transpired in any of the West India islands. My surprise would have been unfeigned, my disappointment great, had there been a different result. As a believer in Divine Revelation—as a worshipper at the shrine of Christianity—is it for me to be astonished when God exactly fulfils his word? No. When he fails, in a single instance, to maintain his veracity, then may I well distrust him for ever!

What has GOD wrought! GOD, I say; not man—not any body of men—but GOD!

'Him first, him last, him midst, and without end!'

The means, the principles, the measures, the weapons, by which this mighty victory has been achieved, are all of Him. To Him, therefore, be ascribed all the honor, renown, praise and glory — exclusively, universally, eternally! Yea, 'let all the earth fear the Lord; let all the inhabitants of the earth stand in awe of him; for he spake, and it was done; he commanded, and it stood fast.' But, while 'no flesh shall glory' in this matter, we are permitted, and it is our duty, to remember with admiration and gratitude the instruments which God has used to effect his great design. This day, then — as philanthropists, lovers of our race, co-workers in the cause of human liberty — let us unite in proffering our heartfelt acknowledgments to the faithful and fearless, the indefatigable and uncompromising, the generous and victorious friends of negro emancipation across the Atlantic — the noble men and women of Great Britain — by whom, under God, the cause has been carried through to a triumphant termination. Animated by their example, and taking fresh encouragement from their success, let us redouble our exertions to deliver our own oppressed countrymen from the yoke of slavery. I have called them noble men and *noble women*; for let it never be forgotten, that the doctrine which has annihilated the slave system in the West Indies, and will yet subvert it in the United States, — the doctrine of IMMEDIATE EMANCIPATION, — was first promulgated in Great Britain by a WOMAN — the late ELIZABETH HEYRICK, an estimable member of the Society of Friends. Her memory shall be cherished by future generations, and diffuse

' Through the dark depths of Time its vivid flame.'

To recite the long catalogue of those who have been instrumental in achieving this unparalleled work of mercy would require a large amount of time. How impossible it is, then, to do justice to their merits on this occasion! But they need no panegyric, and most surely have their reward.

Friends of bleeding humanity, our work is before us!—
The slaveholders have impeached our motives, libelled our
characters, and threatened our lives. No indignity is too
great to be heaped upon us—no outrage too shocking to be
perpetrated upon our persons and property. And now,
we will have our revenge! God helping us, we will still
continue to use all lawful and Christian means for the overthrow of their suicidal slave system; so that when it
falls,—as fall it must,—we will repay them with all
the rich blessings that abound in Antigua. We will remove
from them all source of alarm, and the cause of all insurrection; increase the value of their estates tenfold; give an
Eden-like fertility to their perishing soil; build up the old
waste places, and repair all breaches; make their laborers
contented, grateful and happy; wake up the entombed
genius of invention, and the dormant spirit of enterprise;
open to them new sources of affluence; multiply their
branches of industry; erect manufactories, build railroads,
dig canals; establish schools, academies, colleges, and all
beneficent institutions; extend their commerce to the ends
of the earth, and to an unimagined amount; turn the tide
of Western adventure and of Northern capital into Southern channels; unite the North and the South by indissoluble ties; change the entire moral aspect of society; cause
pure and undefiled religion to flourish; avert impending
judgments and secure heavenly blessings; and fill the land
with peace, prosperity and happiness! Thus, AND THUS
ONLY, will we be revenged upon them for all the wrongs
and outrages they have heaped upon us, personally and
collectively,—for all the evil they are now doing, or may
hereafter do to us,—past, present, and to come!

West India Emancipation.

I.

Lo! the bondage of ages has ceased!
  The chains of the tyrant are riven!
No more, as a chattel or beast,
  Shall man to his labor be driven:
Where the groans and the shrieks of despair
  From heart-broken victims were heard,
Songs of rapturous joy fill the air,
  More sweet than the notes of a bird!

II.

Lo! the gloom and the blackness of night
  Have suddenly vanished away,
And all things rejoice in the light
  Of Freedom's meridian day!
Restored to their sight are the blind —
  No longer they grope for the wall;
All who seek may with certainty find,
  For clear is the vision of all!

III.

Hark! a voice from the Isles of the Sea!
  Its echoes are heard round the world;
O, joyful its message — 'WE ARE FREE!
  To the dust Oppression is hurled!
We are free as the waves of the deep,
  As the winds that sweep o'er the earth;
And therefore we Jubilee keep,
  And hallow the day of our birth!'

IV.

Praise, praise to the name of the Lord!
  What wonders his right hand hath done!
How mighty and sure is his word!
  How great is the victory won!

The Power that Jehovah defied,
　　In ruin and infamy lies :
O spread the intelligence wide —
　　For marvellous 'tis in all eyes !

V.

Columbia ! O shame on thee now !
　　Repent thee in ashes and dust !
There is blood on thy hands — on thy brow —
　　And thou art by Slavery cursed !
Thy millions of vassals set free,
　　Away with the scourge and the rod —
Then join with the Isles of the Sea,
　　In a shout of thanksgiving to God !

Independence Day.

PART I.

I.

THE bells are ringing merrily,
　　The cannon loudly roar,
And thunder-shouts for Liberty
　　Are heard from shore to shore ;
And countless banners to the breeze
　　Their ' stars and stripes ' display :
What call for sights and sounds like these ?
　　' T is Independence day !

II.

Our fathers spurned the British yoke,
　　Determined to be free ;
And, full of might, they rose and broke
　　The chains of tyranny !

O, long they toiled, with zeal unfeigned,
　And kept their foes at bay,
Till, by their valorous deeds, they gained
　Our Independence day !

III.

They fought not for themselves alone,
　But for the RIGHTS OF ALL,
Of every caste, complexion, zone,
　On this terrestrial ball :
To God they made their high appeal,
　In hope, not in dismay ;
For well they trusted He would seal
　Their Independence day !

IV.

Their creed how just — their creed how grand !
　'ALL MEN ARE EQUAL BORN !'
Let those who cannot understand
　This truth, be laughed to scorn !
Cheers for the land in which we live,
　The free, the fair, the gay !
And hearty thanks to Heaven we 'll give,
　For Independence day !

PART II.

I.

O God! what mockery is this !
　Our land how lost to shame!
Well may all Europe jeer and hiss,
　At mention of her name !
For, while she boasts of liberty,
　'Neath SLAVERY's iron sway
Three millions of her people lie,
　On Independence day !

31

II.

She may not, must not, thus rejoice,
    Nor of her triumphs tell:
Hushed be the cannon's thundering voice,
    And muffled every bell!
Dissolved in tears, prone in the dust,
    For mercy let her pray,
That judgments on her may not burst
    On Independence day!

III.

Lo! where her starry banner waves,*
    In many a graceful fold —
There toil, and bleed, and groan her slaves,
    And men, like brutes, are sold!
Her hands are red with crimson stains,
    And bloody is her way;
She wields the lash, she forges chains,
    On Independence day!

IV.

Friends of your country — of your race —
    Of Freedom, and of God!
Combine Oppression to efface,
    ⸏ And break the tyrant's rod;
All traces of injustice sweep,
    By moral power, away;
Then a glorious Jubilee we'll keep,
    On INDEPENDENCE day!

---

* 'United States, your banner wears
    Two emblems — one of fame;
  Alas! the other that it bears,
    Reminds us of your shame.
  The white man's liberty, in types,
    Stands blazoned by your stars;
  But what's the meaning of your stripes?
    They mean your Negroes' scars!' — CAMPBELL.

To Kossuth.

AMIDST the roar of public acclamation —
  The tempest-greetings of a mighty throng —
The cannon's thundering reverberation —
  The civic fête, with toast, and speech, and song —
The grand ' All hail ! ' of a rejoicing nation,
  A million times repeated, loud and long —

Can one lone voice, all tremulous with feeling,
  Be heard by thee, O glorified KOSSUTH,
To all thy noblest attributes appealing,
  As one who knows Oppression's bitter fruit;
And to thy listening ear the truth revealing,
  When sycophants and cowards all are mute?

My claims for audience thou wilt not discredit,
  For they are based on kindred love of Right;
And as for Liberty, world-wide to spread it,
  I, too, have suffered outrage, scorn and slight;
Known what the dungeon is, yet not to dread it,
  And still am zealous in the moral fight.

Thou dreaded foe of Austrian oppression,
  With earnest love of liberty imbued,
Since through America's strong intercession,
  Thy liberation has at last ensued,
'T is meet thou comest here to give expression
  To thy sincere and heartfelt gratitude.

But, while thy obligation thus admitting,
  O let it not thy generous soul ensnare !
Act thou, while here, a manly part, befitting
  Thy name and fame as one to do and dare,
Whate'er the peril of the hour, — acquitting
  Thyself right valiantly, a champion rare.

Is it for thee to deal in glowing fiction ?
  To call this land great, glorious and free ?
To take no note of its sad dereliction

From all that constitutes true liberty ?
To feel upon thy spirit no restriction
    By aught that thou canst learn, or hear, or see ?

While this republic thou art warmly thanking,
    For aiding thee once more to breathe free air,
Three million slaves their galling chains are clanking,
    Heart-broken, bleeding, crushed beyond compare,
At public sale with swine and cattle ranking,
    The wretched victims of complete despair !

The government that thou art now extolling,
    As well-deserving measureless applause,
By its strong arm these millions are enthralling,
    And persecuting those who plead their cause ! —
O, rank hypocrisy, and guilt appalling !
    Like Draco's code, in blood are writ its laws.

For 't is by law the father, son, and brother,
    Know nought of filial or parental ties ;
By law the sister, daughter, wife, and mother,
    Must claim no kindred here beneath the skies ;
All, at the fiendish bidding of another,
    Their God-given rights must basely sacrifice.

By law the fugitives from stripes and fetters,
    Who seek, like thee, a refuge safe and sure
From murderous tyrants and their vile abettors,
    Are hunted over mountain, plain and moor ;
Dragged back to slavery, as absconding debtors,
    To toil, like brutes, while life and strength endure.

By law 't is criminal the slave to pity,
    To give him food and shelter from his foes ;
For him no hiding-place in town or city ;
    He must be hunted wheresoe'er he goes ;
And they are branded as a vile banditti,
    Who for his freedom nobly interpose !

Behold what scenes are in our courts transpiring !
    Behold on trial placed the good and brave

For disobedience to the law requiring
    That he whom God made free should be a slave!
Arraigned as traitors with a zeal untiring,
    And, if convicted, hurried to the grave!

Thou hast proclaimed, in tones like ringing clarion,
    That freedom is the gift of God to all;
That as a man, not as a mere Hungarian,
    In its defence thou 'lt bravely stand or fall;
For Jew and Greek, for Scythian and Barbarian,
    Alike are summoned by its trumpet-call.

I take thee at thy word, out-spoken hero!
    Forget not those who are in bondage here;
For our humanity now stands at zero,
    And threatens utterly to disappear;
Rebuke each merciless plantation Nero;
    Reprove our land in accents loud and clear!

While praising us wherein we are deserving,
    Tell us our faults, — expose our crime of crimes;
Be as the needle to the pole unswerving,
    And true to Freedom's standard in all climes;
Thus many a timid heart with courage nerving
    To meet the mighty conflict of the times.

Say slavery is a stain upon our glory,
    Accursed of Heaven, and by the earth abhorred;
Show that our soil with negro blood is gory,
    And certain are the judgments of the Lord;
So shall thy name immortal be in story,
    And thy fidelity the world applaud.

Yet first, for this, thou shalt be execrated
    By those who now in crowds around thee press;
Thy visit shall be sternly reprobated;
    Thy friends and flatterers grow less and less;
Thy hopes for Hungary be dissipated;
    America shall curse thee, and not bless.

31 *

But if, alas! thy country's sad condition,
  And need of succor, a pretence be made,
Why from thy lips should fall no admonition,
  Lest she should lose our sympathy and aid;
No blessing can attend thy selfish mission —
  The cause of freedom thou wilt have betrayed.

O, shall the millions here in bondage sighing,
  Branded as beasts, and scourged with bloody whips,
The 'property' of tyrants God-defying,
  Hear not one word of pity from thy lips?
O be not dumb, to thy reproach undying —
  And thy great fame save from a dire eclipse!

Courage, KOSSUTH! Be true — fear not the trial!
  Pluck out thy right eye, and thy right hand lose!
Though on thy head be poured out every vial,
  To wear a padlock on thy lips refuse!
And·thou shalt gain, through lofty self-denial,
  A brighter crown than all the world can choose.*

---

* LEWIS KOSSUTH, the Hungarian leader, having fled to Turkey for protection, after the subjugation of Hungary by the allied forces of Austria and Russia, was finally extricated from his perilous situation through the intervention of the British and American governments, and arrived at New York, December 4th, 1851, where he was received with unparalleled popular demonstrations. The hope that he would prove true to the principles of impartial freedom, by at least an expression of his sorrow and surprise that there should be more than three millions of slaves in a land claiming to be Christian and republican, was soon dissipated by his public declaration, that it was his determination 'not to mix, and not to be mixed up with whatever domestic concerns of the United States' — meaning, that he was resolved to be deaf, dumb and blind, concerning American slavery, in order that he might subserve Hungarian liberty; acting on the jesuitical maxim, that 'the end sanctifies the means'!

Hope for the Enslaved.

I.

Ye who in bondage pine,
Shut out from light divine,
   Bereft of hope;
Whose limbs are worn with chains,
Whose tears bedew our plains,
Whose blood our glory stains,
   In gloom who grope : —

II.

Shout! for the hour draws nigh,
That gives you liberty!
   And from the dust,
So long your vile embrace,
Uprising, take your place
Among earth's noblest race —
   'Tis right and just!

III.

The night — the long, long night
Of infamy and slight,
   Shame and disgrace,
And slavery, worse than e'er
Rome's serfs were doomed to bear,
Bloody beyond compare,
   Recedes apace!

IV.

Lorn Africa, once more,
As proudly as of yore,
   Shall yet be seen
Foremost of all the earth
In learning, beauty, worth —
By dignity of birth,
   A peerless Queen!

V.

Speed, speed the hour, O Lord!
Speak! and, at thy dread word,
    Fetters shall fall
From every limb — the strong
No more the weak shall wrong,
But Liberty's sweet song
    Be sung by all!

To Isaac T. Hopper.

HOPPER! thou venerable friend of man,
  In heart and spirit young, though old in years;
  The tyrant trembles when thy name he hears,
And the slave joys thy countenance to scan.
A friend more true and brave, since time began,
  HUMANITY has never found: — her fears
  By thee have been dispelled, and wiped the tears
Adown her sorrow-stricken cheeks that ran.
If like Napoleon's appears thy face,*
  Thy soul to his bears no similitude;
He came to curse, but thou to bless our race —
  Thy hands are white — in blood were his imbrued:
His memory shall be covered with disgrace,
But thine embalmed among the truly great and good.

---

* The resemblance of this venerable Philanthropist, in person and features, to Napoleon, was said, by Joseph Bonaparte, to be most remarkable.

May Day.

I.

Up, ye slumberers, one and all!
Welcome in the smiling May!
Hear ye not her thrilling call?
Will ye waste in bed the day?
'Tis a morn for old and young,
Prodigal of joy and song.

II.

See! the watch-fires of the night,
One by one, are vanishing:
What a glorious tide of light
Issues from Morn's golden spring!
Flooding every land and clime,
Up the sun goes — slow — sublime.

III.

Birds of every kind and hue
Airily are glancing by,
And with notes expressive, true,
Fill the air with melody:
Who would lose their joyous strain?
Who, inert, abed remain?

IV.

Maiden, with the flashing eye,
Quench its brilliance not in sleep;
Let thy blushes, mounting high,
Shame Aurora's color deep;
Gather flowers to braid thy hair:
For a Queenly state prepare!

V.

Child, absorbed in sportive dream,
Be not Slumber's pretty dupe;

Up, and drive the mimic team,
    Fly the kite, or whirl the hoop;
Let the music of thy mirth
In a merry shout have birth!

VI.

Youth, in sweetest visions lying,
    Building worlds with busy thought;
Now exulting, smiling, sighing,
    O'er the labors thou hast wrought;
Fairest scenes, by Fancy drawn,
Cannot match so fair a morn.

VII.

Manhood, lift thy stately head —
    Stand erect, Creation's lord!
Leave the couch by dalliance spread —
    O'er thy empire walk abroad;
Earth and sky were made for thee,
Dressed in royal pageantry.

VIII.

All who pine in secret love,
    All whose hopes are high or low,
Ugly folks, who would improve,
    Handsome, who would prettier grow —
Rich and poor, gay, wise and witty,
Leave, at earliest dawn, the city.

IX.

Exercise will use his brushes
    With a Painter's matchless skill,
Covering palest cheeks with blushes,
    Giving eyes new power to kill:
O, then, slumber not, I pray —
Go, and welcome jocund May!

Dedicatory Lines to Liberty.

I.

ANOTHER year, devoted to thy cause,
   O LIBERTY! has swiftly fled away :
Not till the war is over would I pause,
   Nor for my spirit seek a holiday :
   It needs none, for its strength knows no decay.
This is no time for loitering, while thy foe,
   OPPRESSION, seeks thy precious life to slay :
His hand is raised to give the fatal blow,
That he may gorge himself afresh with human woe!

II.

Dispensing with all forms, I consecrate
   Anew, this day, my soul to God and thee,
Reckless of what may be my earthly fate:
   For this I know, that all shall yet be free,
   And God and thou shall gain the victory.
What though these eyes may ne'er behold the time?
   A coming age shall hail the jubilee,
When men of every caste, complexion, clime,
Shall burst their chains, and stand in dignity sublime.

III.

I care not, tyrants! for your strength or power,
   Your savage mien, your more than savage rage;
It is for you, not for myself, to cower ;
   Sustained by TRUTH and RIGHT, I dare engage
   Your fierce array, and single combat wage.
In FREEDOM's cause one shall a thousand chase,
   And two ten thousand drive from off the stage :
The brave are never found among the base —
Where Innocence is bold, Guilt hides his crimson face!

IV.

What is before me, Lord, is known to thee ;
   To me all is unknown, except thy will,

That I in all things should obedient be,
    Come weal or woe, come present good or ill —
    Nor fear those who the body only kill.
Thy will is mine, and let thy will be done !
    Thy light and love my spirit sweetly fill : —
Following with zeal the footsteps of thy Son,
With martyrs I rejoice the Christian race to run.

V.

E'en to this hour, to public gaze I stand,
    An object feared, rejected, and abhorred ;
And for my labors to redeem the land,
    Reproach and infamy are my reward :
    But time shall justice unto me accord.
To him, who, for Thy sake, takes up his cross,
    Thy promises are rich and sure, O Lord ! —
Fire from th' adulterate ore extracts but dross,
But the pure gold sustains, and can sustain, no loss.

VI.

Courage, O friends ! a thousand fields are won !
    Ten thousand foes lie prostrate in the dust !
Your task, though onerous, is nearly done ;
    Still in the LORD JEHOVAH be your trust,
    And victory crowns you, for your cause is just !
All yokes and manacles shall yet be riven ;
    The monster SLAVERY shall die accursed ;
Sweet freedom to the pining thrall be given,
And a grand jubilee be kept by Earth and Heaven !

APPENDIX.

[From the Boston Liberator of November 7, 1835.]

TRIUMPH OF MOBOCRACY IN BOSTON.

I SHALL give, as far as 1 am capable, an exact and faithful account of the ruthless disturbances which took place in Boston on Wednesday afternoon, Oct. 21st, and by which this city was suddenly transformed into an infuriated pandemonium. It is the most disgraceful event that has ever marred the character of Bostonians, whether reference be made to the time of its occurrence, or to the cause which was assailed, or to those who stood obnoxious to violent treatment. The recent pro-slavery meeting in Faneuil Hall supported the *theory* of despotism, and the tumultuous assembly of Wednesday carried it into *practice* — trampling all law and order, the Constitution and personal liberty, public decorum and private decency, common humanity and Christian courtesy, into the dust. The light of day did not cause a blush, nor the certainty of exposure restrain from indecent and barbarous behavior, nor profession or station deter ' respectable, wealthy and influential citizens' from enacting the part of ruffians and anarchists. All distinctions (excepting that of *color*, to the honor of the BLACK MAN be it recorded) were blended, for the purpose of gagging the advocates of freedom, and infusing new strength into the arm of the remorseless scourger of *Woman* at the South. The merchant and the aristocrat — the wealthy and the learned — the ' respectable' and the ' influential' — the professor and the profane — were all huddled together in

32

thick and formidable array, with every variety of feeling, but with one prevalent design, namely, to insult, annoy and disperse the Female Anti-Slavery meeting, (brave, gentlemanly, chivalric men!) and to tar-and-feather, or put to death, GEORGE THOMPSON or myself! Was it not a sublime spectacle to behold four or five thousand genteel ruffians courageously assembling together, to achieve so hazardous an exploit as the putting to flight one man and thirty defenceless females?

As the scenes of the last week are historically connected with those of the present, it is necessary to recapitulate them, in order that the beginning and the end of the late tumult may be seen at a glance by the reader; and that Boston, the boasted Cradle of Liberty, may obtain every particle of that infamous renown which she has so dearly earned, and of which she seems so insanely covetous.

The Boston Female Anti-Slavery Society has been in operation about three years, humbly aiding with its prayers and limited means the cause of bleeding humanity, and gradually increasing both in number and efficiency. Its members are industrious, estimable, intellectual and devout women, and exemplary mothers, wives and daughters. He who sneers at them, knowing their true character, must be destitute of honor, virtue and benevolence; and he who aims to suppress their association must first drag them to the stake, and consume them to ashes, before he can succeed. They are worthy to be ranked with the females of Great Britain, to whose untiring efforts EIGHT HUNDRED THOUSAND slaves in the British Colonies are mainly indebted for their emancipation — and what higher praise need be given? Hear what the great Irish champion of freedom — the fearless and eloquent O'Connell — said, in relation to the merits of the women, in his sublime and spirit-stirring speech, delivered in Exeter Hall, London, July 13, 1833:

'I have, however, moments of exquisite delight. I remember that 1,500,000 of the people of this country have joined in petitioning Parliament for the total and immediate abolition of slavery. (Cheers.) O, blessings upon them! Every age, every station, nay, *every sex*, has united in these petitions. THE WOMEN OF ENGLAND HAVE LED THE WAY; and *under the banners of the maids and matrons of England*, proud must that individual be, who shall have an opportunity of telling them, "*At your command we have done our duty, and* SLAVERY IS AT AN END !" (Cheers.) A ruffian in this country taunted the females who signed the petitions, by calling them the Dorothys, and Tabithas, and Priscillas. I stigmatized him as a ruffian, in my place in Parliament; and I stigmatize him as such here. (Loud cheers.)'

The constitutional period for holding the annual meeting of the Society occurred last week; and, accordingly, the Secretary gave public notice that the meeting would be held on Wednesday afternoon, Oct. 14, at Congress Hall, and that an address would be delivered on the occasion by GEORGE THOMPSON, at the request of the Society. It did not occur to the members, (but, surely, their forgetfulness is a pardonable offence,) that they were not competent to conduct their own business, or to choose a speaker to address them, without suitable instructions from the upholders of Southern slavery; and that they were solemnly bound to inquire of the editorial creatures who manage the Commercial Gazette, and Atlas, and Courier, and Centinel, — when, where, and how to assemble, and whom to invite to be present, and the proper manner of conducting their meeting. They felt perfectly able to transact all the business of the Society, independently of the assistance of profligate and impudent intermeddlers; nor could they readily believe that any thing in the shape of a man could be so lost to shame, or so great a dastard, as to assail their meeting in broad daylight, or threaten the personal safety of any of their number.

It was summarily stated in the Liberator of last week, that the reading of their notice from some of the pulpits on the preceding Sabbath excited the amiable fury and holy horror of many a hypocrite and pharisee — of those who take tithe of mint, anise and cummin, and neglect the weightier matters of the law, judgment, mercy and faith — in the various congregations; — that the Commercial Gazette, Courier, and Centinel, of Tuesday, put forth violent and seditious articles respecting the meeting, for the purpose of inflaming the worst passions of a slavery-loving community against it; — that, in consequence of the furious tone of those papers, and the alarming symptoms of a riot, the lessee of Congress Hall felt it to be his duty, as the

only chance of preserving his property from destruction,
publicly to forbid the Society occupying the hall; — that,
being thus unexpectedly deprived of a place in which to
assemble, the Society advertised in the morning papers of
Wednesday, that the meeting was necessarily postponed
until further notice; — that, notwithstanding their advertise-
ment, a crowd of 'respectable and well-dressed' disturbers
of the public peace gathered tumultuously around the hall,
vainly hoping to seize Mr. Thompson, that they might vent
their murderous spite upon his person; — that, being falsely
told that the Society was holding its meeting at Ritchie Hall,
thither they rushed with frantic joy, and finding a meeting
of the Ladies' Moral Reform Society convened together in
the hall, they behaved so infamously as to cause its disper-
sion; — that, in the sequel, the Mayor made his appearance,
and succeeded in causing the riotous 'gentlemen of respectability and influence' to withdraw, by assuring them
that the object of their hatred was not in the city — &c. &c.

  This unmanly, impertinent and anomalous procedure
failed to intimidate the members of the Female Anti-Slavery
Society, or to convince them that they ought not to hold
their annual meeting, agreeably to the precept of their Constitution. They were made of sterner stuff, and had too
clear an apprehension of the duty which they owed to God,
their country, and the perishing slaves, to be driven from a
lawful and holy purpose by an irruption of Goths and Van-
dals upon their assembly. To retreat, under such circumstances, would savor of apostacy from the cross of Christ;
and to be passive, would seem to argue an imbecility of
mind, a lack of Christian faith, or a sacrifice of principle.
They were not requested, by their shameless assailants, to
postpone or suspend their meeting for a limited time, on the
score of expediency; but they were virtually commanded
to desist, at once and for ever, on the ground of brutal
authority, from their Christ-like design to bind up the
broken-hearted, to open the prison-doors, and to set the captive free. They were threatened as slaves, not kindly
advised as equals. They had no other alternative, therefore,
than to move steadily onward to the regular discharge of
their duty, or to be branded as recreants to a cause which
they had pledged to support, under all circumstances, and

through all perils. Accordingly, they gave public information to the ladies of Boston, that their meeting would be
held in the Anti-Slavery Hall, 46, Washington street, on
Wednesday afternoon, Oct. 21, at 3 o'clock, and that several addresses might be expected on the occasion. It was
not advertised that Mr. Thompson would attend, nor was
his presence deemed to be essential or expedient, either by
himself or the Society. He therefore left the city on Tuesday, that there might be no pretext for causing an interrup-
tion of the meeting on the ensuing day. The aspect of
things looked tranquil until Wednesday morning, when
inflammatory articles appeared in some of the daily papers,
and it was stated that several store-keepers, in the immediate vicinity of the hall, had petitioned the Mayor and Aldermen to *suppress* the meeting, as it might endanger their
property *by* causing a riot! Yes, to accommodate their selfishness, they declared that the liberty of speech, and the
right to assemble in an associated capacity peaceably
together, should be unlawfully and forcibly taken away from
an estimable portion of the community, by the officers of
our city — the humble servants of the people! Benedict
Arnold's treachery to the cause of liberty and his bleeding
country was no worse than this. As properly might they
have petitioned for leave to slaughter every man who should
venture to maintain the exploded doctrine, that all men are
created equal. Such sordid men would sell their country
for less than thirty pieces of silver, under favorable circumstances. If they felt that the safety of their goods would
be endangered by the contemplated meeting, — or, rather,
by the ruffians who had conspired to break it up, — they
had an unquestionable right to warn the city authorities of
the fact, and to demand adequate protection, but not to ask
for the suppression of a benevolent and lawful meeting. Of
course, — however much inclined they might have been, in
spirit, to comply with so daring a request, — the Mayor and
Aldermen comprehended the limitation of their authority
too well, and had too much respect even for the equivocal
patriotism of the people, to interpose their authority. A
seditious and blood-thirsty placard, — printed, I presume, at
the office of the Commercial Gazette, — was circulated
through the city, stating that 'the infamous foreign scoun-

32*

drel, Thompson,' would hold forth in the Anti-Slavery Hall,
in the afternoon ; that ' the present was a fair opportunity
for the friends of the Union to snake him out'; and that ' a
purse of $100 had been raised by a number of *patriotic*
citzens to reward the individual who should first lay violent
hands upon him, so that he might be brought to the tar-
kettle before dark.' In consequence of the inflammatory
state of the public mind, the Mayor, THEODORE LYMAN, sent
a deputy to the Anti-Slavery Office, to ascertain whether
Mr. Thompson contemplated addressing the meeting ; for, if
he did not, the Mayor said he wished to be enabled to apprise
the multitude of the fact, and thus induce them to retire —
or, if he did, the Mayor was anxious seasonably to enrol an
efficient constabulary force to protect the meeting and preserve order. As this information was asked, not as a matter
of right, but seemingly with just intentions, I sent word to
the Mayor, that the Female Anti-Slavery Society could not
feel obligated, at any man's bidding, either to suppress or to
publish the names of those whom they had invited to speak at
their meeting ; but, as I trusted that his request was made in
the spirit of kindness, and not of impertinence or domination, I felt not only willing but desirous to inform him, that
Mr. Thompson was not in the city, nor would he be present
at the meeting, and that he might make proclamation to that
effect to all who should assemble for riotous purposes.

As the meeting was to commence at 3 o'clock, P. M., I
went to the hall about twenty minutes before that time.
Perhaps a hundred individuals had already gathered around
the street door and opposite to the building, and their number
was rapidly augmenting. On ascending into the hall, I
found about fifteen or twenty ladies assembled, sitting with
serene countenances, and a crowd of noisy intruders
(mostly young men) gazing upon them, through whom I
urged my way with considerable difficulty. ' That's Garrison,' was the exclamation of some of their number, as I
quietly took my seat. Perceiving they had no intention of
retiring, I went to them and calmly said — ' Gentlemen,
perhaps you are not aware that this is a meeting of the
Boston *Female* Anti-Slavery Society, called and intended
exclusively for *ladies*, and those only who have been invited
to address them. Understanding this fact, you will not be

so rude or indecorous as to thrust your presence upon this
meeting. If, *gentlemen*,' I pleasantly continued, ' any of you
are *ladies* — in disguise — why, only apprise me of the
fact, give me your names, and I will introduce you to the
rest of your sex, and you can take seats among them
accordingly.' I then sat down, and, for a few moments,
their conduct was more orderly. However, the stair-way
and upper door of the hall were soon densely filled with a
brazen-faced crew, whose behavior grew more and more
indecent and outrageous. Perceiving that it would be impracticable for me, or any other person, to address the
ladies; and believing, as I was the only male abolitionist in
the hall, that my presence would serve as a pretext for the
mob to annoy the meeting, I held a short colloquy with the
excellent President of the Society, telling her that I would
withdraw, unless she particularly desired me to stay. It
was her earnest wish that I would retire, as well for my
own safety as for the peace of the meeting. She assured
me that the Society would resolutely but calmly proceed to
the transaction of its business, and leave the issue with God.
I left the hall accordingly, and would have left the building,
if the stair-case had not been crowded to excess. This
being impracticable, I retired into the Anti-Slavery Office,
(which is separated from the hall by a board partition,)
accompanied by my friend, Mr. Charles C. Burleigh. It was
deemed prudent to lock the door, to prevent the mob from
rushing in and destroying our publications.

In the mean time, the crowd in the street had augmented
from a hundred to thousands. The cry was for ' Thompson! Thompson!' — but the Mayor had now arrived, and,
addressing the rioters, he assured them that Mr. Thompson
was not in the city, and besought them to disperse. As
well might he have attempted to propitiate a troop of ravenous wolves. None went away — but the tumult continued
momentarily to increase. It was apparent, therefore, that
the hostility of the throng was not concentrated upon Mr.
Thompson, but that it was as deadly against the Society and
the Anti-Slavery cause. This fact is worthy of special
note — for it incontestably proves that the object of these
' respectable and influential' rioters was to put down the

cause of emancipation, and that Mr. Thompson merely furnished a pretext for their lawless acts!

Let not any, therefore, who are disposed to be friendly to our cause, suppose that Mr. Thompson is the chief, or even the slightest obstacle in the way of its triumph, or that his departure would bring popularity and repose to the abolitionists. Is James G. Birney, or Theodore D. Weld, or William Jay, or Arthur Tappan, treated more tenderly than George Thompson by the enemies of liberty? No. Their grand design, then, is not simply to drive an English philanthropist from our shores, but to maltreat, gag and enslave AMERICAN, NATIVE-BORN CITIZENS! The struggle is between Right and Wrong — Liberty and Slavery — Christianity and Atheism — Northern Freemen and Southern Taskmasters. The great question to be settled is not merely whether 2,000,000 slaves in our land shall be immediately or gradually emancipated — or whether they shall be colonized abroad or retained in our midst; but whether freedom is with us — THE PEOPLE OF THE UNITED STATES — a reality or a mockery; — whether the liberty of speech and of the press, purchased with the toils and sufferings and precious blood of our fathers, is still to be enjoyed, unquestioned and complete — or whether padlocks are to be put upon our lips, gags into our mouths, and shackles upon that great palladium of human rights, the press; — whether the descendants of the Pilgrim Fathers, the sons of those who fell upon Bunker Hill, and the plains of Lexington and Concord, are to fashion their thoughts and opinions, and to speak or be dumb, and to walk freely or with a chain upon their spirit, and to stand upright or to crook the knee, and to obey Jehovah or worship Mammon, at the bidding of Southern slave-drivers and oppressors; — whether the truths of the Declaration of Independence are still to be acknowledged as 'self-evident,' and valuable beyond all price — or whether they are to be regarded as ingenious fictions and mere 'rhetorical flourishes'; — whether Equity, and Law, and Public Order, are to be enforced, irrespective of political or religious opinions — or whether Jacobinism, Anarchy and Confusion are to reign in our midst, to the prostration of all that makes life a blessing and society desirable; —

whether citizens, guiltless of crime, are to walk without molestation, and to repose without danger, and to assemble together without hindrance — or whether they are to be seized with impunity by lawless ruffians, dragged ignominiously through the streets, thrust into prison, and forced to fly from the endearments of home, for self-preservation. Nay, more. It is a question of life and death to this nation — of Christian freedom and abject bondage — that we have now to decide. I rejoice, and thank God, that it assumes such a shape, and is presented at such a crisis. The people — blinded and misled for a time — will in the end see and decide aright. Wo, then, to their deceivers! A tide of indignation shall sweep them from the high places of power, and sink them into the lowest depths of infamy. NEW ENGLAND will settle this question — for herself, the nation, and the world. Ere long, I have faith to believe,

> 'From her Green Mountains to the Sea,
> One voice shall thunder — *We are free!*'

But even if the sun of her own liberty has set for ever, still, the discussion of this great question can never be suppressed, so long as a single abolitionist is left alive upon her soil. Slaughter-houses must be erected in every town and village, and the scenes of the French revolution be re-enacted; and men and women, and children even, put to death by human butchers, until the earth be drunk with blood, and the slain cease to find a covering for their mutilated bodies. *The victims are ready to be sacrificed* — throughout the Commonwealth, and all over the land — a noble company of martyrs! *Is Boston prepared to commence the work of extermination?*

Notwithstanding the presence and frantic behavior of the rioters in the hall, the meeting of the Society was regularly called to order by the President.* She then read a select and an exceedingly appropriate portion of Scripture, and offered up a fervent prayer to God for direction and succor, and the forgiveness of enemies and revilers. It was an

---

* The late Miss MARY PARKER.

awful, sublime and soul-thrilling scene — enough, one would
suppose, to melt adamantine hearts, and make even fiends
of darkness stagger and retreat.   Indeed, the clear, untrem-
ulous tone of voice of that Christian heroine in prayer,
occasionally awed the ruffians into silence, and was heard
distinctly even in the midst of their hisses, yells and
curses — for they could not long silently endure the agony
of conviction, and their conduct became furious.   They
now attempted to break down the partition, and partially
succeeded ; but that little band of women still maintained
their ground unshrinkingly, and endeavored to transact their
business.

An assault was now made upon the door of the office,
the lower panel of which was instantly dashed to pieces.
Stooping down, and glaring upon me as I sat at the desk,
writing an account of the riot to a distant friend, the ruffians
cried out — ' There he is!   That's Garrison !   Out with
the scoundrel !' &c. &c.   Turning to Mr. Burleigh I said —
' You may as well open the door, and let them come in and
do their worst.'   But he, with great presence of mind, went
out, locked the door, put the key into his pocket, and by his
admirable firmness succeeded in keeping the office safe.

Two or three constables having cleared the hall and stair-
case of the mob, the Mayor came in and *ordered* the ladies
to desist, assuring them that he could not any longer guar-
antee protection, if they did not take immediate advantage
of the opportunity to retire from the building.   Accordingly,
they adjourned, to meet at the house of one of their number, for the completion of their business ; but as they passed
through the crowd, they were greeted with taunts, hisses,
and cheers of mobocratic triumph, from ' gentlemen of
property and standing from all parts of the city.'   Even their
absence did not diminish the throng.   Thompson was not
there — the ladies were not there — but ' *Garrison* is
there !' was the cry.   ' Garrison ! Garrison ! We must
have Garrison !   Out with him ! Lynch him !'   These
and numberless other exclamations arose from the multitude.
For a moment, their attention was diverted from me to
the Anti-Slavery sign, and they vociferously demanded its
possession.   It is painful to state, that the Mayor promptly
complied with their demand !   So agitated and alarmed had

he become, that, in very weakness of spirit, he ordered the
sign to be hurled to the ground, and it was instantly broken
into a thousand fragments by the infuriated populace. O,
lamentable departure from duty — O, shameful outrage upon
private property — by one who had sworn, not to destroy,
but to protect property — not to pander to the lawless
desires of a mob, however ' wealthy and respectable,' but
to preserve the public peace. The act was wholly unjustifiable. The Mayor might have as lawfully surrendered me
to the tender mercies of the mob, or ordered the building,
itself to be torn down, in order to propitiate them, as to
have removed that sign. Perhaps — nay, probably, he was
actuated by kind intentions ; probably he hoped that he
should thereby satisfy the ravenous appetites of these
human cormorants, and persuade them to retire ; probably
he trusted thus to extricate me from danger. But the
sequel proved that he only gave a fresh stimulus to popular
fury ; and if he could have saved my life, or the whole city
from destruction, by that single act, still he ought not to
have obeyed the mandate of the mob — no indeed! He
committed a public outrage in the presence of the lawless
and disobedient, and thus strangely expected to procure obedience to and a respect for the law ! He behaved disorderly
before rebels, that he might restore order among them !
Mr. HENRY WILLIAMS and Mr. JOHN L. DIMMOCK also
deserve severe reprehension for their forwardness in taking
down the sign. The offence, under such circumstances, was
very heinous. The value of the article destroyed was of
no consequence ; but the principle involved in its surrender
and sacrifice is one upon which civil government, private
property and individual liberty depend.

The sign being demolished, the cry for ' Garrison !' was
renewed, more loudly than ever. It was now apparent,
that the multitude would not disperse until I had left the
building ; and as egress out of the front door was impossible, the Mayor and his assistants, as well as some of my
friends, earnestly besought me to effect my escape in the
rear of the building. At this juncture, an abolition brother,
whose mind had not been previously settled on the peace
question, in his anguish and alarm for my safety, and in
view of the helplessness of the civil authority, said — ' I

must henceforth repudiate the principle of non-resistance. When the civil arm is powerless, my own rights are trodden in the dust, and the lives of my friends are put in imminent peril by ruffians, I will hereafter stand ready to defend myself and them at all hazards.' Putting my hand upon his shoulder, I said, 'Hold, my dear brother! You know not what spirit you are of. Of what value or utility are the principles of peace and forgiveness, if we may repudiate them in the hour of peril and suffering? Do you wish to become like one of those violent and blood-thirsty men who are seeking my life? Shall we give blow for blow, and array sword against sword? God forbid! I will perish sooner than raise my hand against any man, even in self-defence, and let none of my friends resort to violence for my protection. If my life be taken, the cause of emancipation will not suffer. God reigns — his throne is undisturbed by this storm — he will make the wrath of man to praise him, and the remainder he will restrain — his omnipotence will at length be victorious.'

Preceded by my faithful and beloved friend Mr. J——R——C——, I dropped from a back window on to a shed, and narrowly escaped falling headlong to the ground. We entered into a carpenter's shop, through which we attempted to get into Wilson's Lane, but found our retreat cut off by the mob. They raised a shout as soon as we came in sight, but the proprietor promptly closed the door of his shop, kept them at bay for a time, and thus kindly afforded me an opportunity to find some other passage. I told Mr. C. it would be futile to attempt to escape — I would go out to the mob, and let them deal with me as they might elect; but he thought it was my duty to avoid them, as long as possible. We then went up stairs, and finding a vacancy in one corner of the room, I got into it, and he and a young lad piled up some boards in front of me, to shield me from observation. In a few minutes, several ruffians broke into the chamber, who seized Mr. C. in a rough manner, and led him out to the view of the mob, saying, 'This is not Garrison, but Garrison's and Thompson's friend, and he says he knows where Garrison is, but won't tell.' Then a shout of exultation was raised by the mob, and what became of him I do not know; though, as I was immediately discovered, I presume he escaped without material injury. On seeing me, three or four of the rioters, uttering a yell, furiously dragged me to the window, with the intention of hurling me from that height to the ground; but one of them relented, and said —' Don't let us kill him outright.' So they drew me back, and coiled a rope about my body — probably to drag me through the streets. I bowed to the mob, and requesting them to wait patiently until I could descend, went down upon a ladder that was raised for that purpose. I fortunately extricated myself from the rope, and was seized by two or three of the leading rioters, powerful and athletic men, by whom I was dragged along bareheaded; (for my hat had been knocked off and cut in pieces on the spot,) a friendly voice in the crowd shouting, ' He shan't be hurt! He is an American!' This seemed to excite sympathy in the breasts of some others, and they reiterated the same cry. Blows, however, were aimed at my head by such as were of a cruel spirit, and at last they succeeded in tearing nearly all my clothes from my body. Thus was I dragged through Wilson's Lane into State street, in the rear of the City Hall, over the ground that was stained with the blood of the first martyrs in the cause of LIBERTY and INDEPEND-ENCE, in the memorable massacre of 1770; and upon which was proudly unfurled, only a few years since, with joyous acclamations, the beautiful banner presented to the gallant Poles by the young men of Boston! What a scandalous and revolting contrast! My offence was in pleading for LIBERTY — liberty for my enslaved countrymen, colored though they be — liberty of speech and of the press for ALL! And upon that 'consecrated spot,' I was made an object of derision and scorn, some portions of my person being in a state of entire nudity.

They proceeded with me in the direction of the City Hall, the cry being raised, ' To the Common!' whether to give me a coat of tar and feathers, or to throw me into the pond, was problematical. As we approached the south door, the Mayor attempted to protect me by his presence; but as he was unassisted by any show of authority or force, he was quickly thrust aside; and now came a tremendous rush on the part of the mob to prevent my entering the hall. For a time, the conflict was desperate; but at length a rescue

33

was effected by a posse that came to the help of the Mayor, by whom I was carried up into the Mayor's room.

In view of my denuded condition, one individual in the Post Office below stairs kindly lent me a pair of pantaloons; another, a coat; a third, a stock; a fourth, a cap — &c. After a brief consultation, (the mob densely surrounding the City Hall, and threatening the safety of the Post Office,) the Mayor and his advisers said my life depended upon committing me to jail, ostensibly as a disturber of the peace!! Accordingly, a hack was got in readiness at the door; and, supported by Sheriff Parkman and Ebenezer Bailey, Esq., (the Mayor leading the way,) I was put into it without much difficulty, as I was not at first identified in my new garb. But now a scene occurred that baffles the power of description. As the ocean, lashed into fury by the spirit of the storm, seeks to whelm the adventurous bark beneath its mountain waves, so did the mob, enraged by a series of disappointments, rush like a whirlwind upon the frail vehicle in which I sat, and endeavor to drag me out of it. Escape seemed a physical impossibility. They clung to the wheels — dashed open the doors — seized hold of the horses — and tried to upset the carriage. They were, however, vigorously repulsed by the police — a constable sprang in by my side — the doors were closed — and the driver, lustily using his whip upon the bodies of his horses and the heads of the rioters, happily made an opening through the crowd, and drove at a tremendous speed for Leverett street. But many of the rioters followed even with superior swiftness, and repeatedly attempted to arrest the progress of the horses. To reach the jail by a direct course was found impracticable; and after going in a circuitous direction, and encountering many ' hair-breadth 'scapes,' we drove up to this new and last refuge of liberty and life, when another desperate attempt was made to seize me by the mob, but in vain. In a few moments, I was locked up in a cell, safe from my persecutors, accompanied by two delightful associates, — a good conscience and a cheerful mind. In the course of the evening, several of my friends came to my grated window, to sympathize and confer with me, with whom I held a strengthening conversation until the hour of retirement, when I threw myself upon my prison-bed, and slept tranquilly. In the morning, I inscribed upon the walls of my cell, with a pencil, the following lines :

'Wm. Lloyd Garrison was put into this cell on Wednesday afternoon, Oct. 21, 1835, to save him from the violence of a " respectable and influential " mob, who sought to destroy him for preaching the abominable and dangerous doctrine, that " all men are created equal," and that all oppression is odious in the sight of God. " Hail, Columbia ! " Cheers for the Autocrat of Russia, and the Sultan of Turkey !
'Reader, let this inscription remain till the last slave in this despotic land be loosed from his fetters.'

> 'When peace within the bosom reigns,
>   And conscience gives th' approving voice ;
> Though bound the human form in chains,
>   Yet can the soul aloud rejoice.

> ''Tis true, my footsteps are confined —
> I cannot range beyond this cell ; —
> But what can circumscribe my mind?
> To chain the winds attempt as well ! '

> 'Confiné me as a prisoner — but bind me not as a slave.
> Punish me as a criminal — but hold me not as a chattel.
> Torture me as a man — but drive me not like a beast.
> Doubt my sanity — but acknowledge my immortality.'

In the course of the forenoon, after passing through the mockery of an examination, for form's sake, before Judge Whitman, I was released from prison ; but, at the *earnest solicitation of the city authorities*, in order to tranquillize the public mind, I deemed it proper to leave the city for a few days, accompanied by my wife, whose situation was such as to awaken the strongest solicitude for her life.

My thanks are due to Sheriff Parkman, for various acts of politeness and kindness; as also to Sheriff Sumner, Mr. Coolidge, Mr. Andrews, and several other gentlemen.

I have been thus minute in describing the rise, progress and termination of this disgraceful riot, in order to prevent (or rather to correct) false representations and exaggerated reports respecting it and myself. It is proper to subjoin a few reflections.

1. The outrage was perpetrated in Boston — the Cradle of Liberty — the city of Hancock and Adams — the head-quarters of refinement, literature, intelligence and religion! No comments can add to the infamy of this fact.

2. It was perpetrated in the open daylight of heaven, and was therefore most unblushing and daring in its features.

3. It was against the friends of human freedom — the liberty of speech — the right of association — and in support of the vilest slavery that ever cursed the world.

4. It was a dastardly assault of thousands upon a small body of helpless females.

5. It was planned and executed, not by the rabble, or the working-men, but by '*gentlemen* of property and standing from all parts of the city'; and now, that time has been afforded for reflection, it is still either openly justified or, coldly disapproved by the 'higher classes,' and exultation among them is general throughout the city.

6. It is virtually approved by all the daily presses, except the Daily Advocate and the Daily Reformer. These independent presses have spoken out in a tone worthy of the best days of the revolution.

7. It is evidently winked at by the city authorities. No efforts have been made to arrest any of the rioters. The Mayor has made no public appeal to the citizens to preserve order ; nor has he given any assurance that the right of free discussion shall be enjoyed without molestation ; nor did he array any military force against the mob, or attempt to disperse them, except by useless persuasion ; on the contrary, he complied with their wishes in tearing down the anti-slavery sign. He was chairman, too, of the pro-slavery meeting in Faneuil Hall, at which WASHINGTON was cheered for having been a SLAVEHOLDER!

What will be the effect of this riot ? Will it cause one abolitionist to swerve from the faith ? Will it prevent either men or women from assembling together, to devise ways and means for the destruction of the slave system ? Will it stop the freedom of discussion? Will it put down the Liberator ? Will it check the growth of the anti-slavery cause? Will it slacken my efforts? No! It will have a contrary effect. It will humble the pride of this city ; it will rouse up and concentrate all that is left of the free

spirit of our fathers; it will excite sympathy for the persecuted, and indignation against the persecutors; it will multiply sterling converts to our doctrines; it will increase the
circulation of anti-slavery writings; it will substitute a thousand agitators in the place of one, and make the discussion
of slavery paramount to all other topics; it will make the
triumph of truth over error, and of liberty over oppression,
and of law over jacobinism, and of republicanism over
aristocracy, more signal and glorious; it will enable the most
blind to see that the existence of Southern slavery is incompatible with the exercise of the rights and privileges of
Northern freemen; and it will nerve my arm to strike
heavier blows than ever upon the head of the monster
OPPRESSION. We give our enemies their choice of weapons, and conquer them easily. The TRUTH that we utter is
impalpable, yet real: it cannot be thrust down by brute
force, nor pierced with a dagger, nor bribed with gold, nor
overcome by the application of a coat of tar and feathers.
The CAUSE that we espouse is the cause of human liberty,
formidable to tyrants, and dear to the oppressed, throughout
the world — containing the elements of immortality, sublime
as heaven, and far-reaching as eternity — embracing every
interest that appertains to the welfare of the bodies and
souls of men, and sustained by the omnipotence of the Lord
Almighty. The PRINCIPLES that we inculcate are those of
equity, mercy and love, as set forth in the glorious gospel of
the blessed God — without partiality and without hypocrisy,
and full of good fruits. In the midst of tribulation, therefore, we rejoice, and count it all honor to suffer in the cause
of our dear Redeemer. 'God is our refuge and strength,
a very present help in trouble: Therefore will not we fear,
though the earth be removed, and though the mountains be
carried into the midst of the sea.' 'Gird thy sword upon
thy thigh, O Most Mighty, with thy glory and thy majesty;
and in thy majesty ride prosperously, because of truth, and
meekness, and righteousness; and thy right hand shall teach
thee terrible things.'

WM. LLOYD GARRISON.

33*

[From the Boston Liberator of November 7, 1835.]

LETTER FROM GEORGE THOMPSON.

THURSDAY EVENING, OCT. 22, 1835.

MY DEAR FRIEND AND FELLOW-LABORER IN THE CAUSE
OF FREEDOM FOR TWO MILLIONS TWO HUNDRED AND
FIFTY THOUSAND AMERICAN SLAVES:

Since despatching the few hasty lines which I wrote you
on receipt of the news of yesterday's proceedings in Boston,
I have yielded to a strong impulse to address you a longer
communication, more fully expressive of the views and feelings with which the signs of the times have inspired me.   I
despair, however, of finding words to express adequately the
deep sympathy I cherish with you in the midst of your trials
and persecutions, and the feelings of my soul, as I contemplate passing events, and follow out to its ultimate results
the headlong wickedness of this generation.   Surely, we can
enter somewhat into the experience of the lamenting prophet,
when he exclaimed, ' O that my head were waters, and mine
eyes a fountain of tears, that I might weep day and night for
the sins of this people ! '

How unutterably affecting is a view of the present aspect
of the country !   The enslavement of the colored population
seems to be but one of a hideous host of evils, threatening
in their combined influence the overthrow of the fairest
prospects of this wide republic.   Of the abolition of slavery
I feel certain.   Its doom is sealed.   I read it in the holy and
inflexible resolves of thousands who are coming up to the
contest with the spirit of martyrs, and in the strength and
under the leadership of Jehovah.   I read it in the blind fury
and unmitigated malignity of Southern tyrants and their
Northern participants in crime.   I read it in the gathering
frown and bursting indignation of Christendom.   The consummation of our hopes draws nigh.   The times are pregnant with great events.   America must witness another revolution, and the second will be far more illustrious in its
results than the first.   The second will be a moral revolution ;
a struggle for higher, holier, more catholic, more patriotic
principles : and the weapons of our warfare will not be car-

nal, but mighty through God to the pulling down of strong holds. During the progress of this latter revolution will be witnessed the advent of ' Liberty,' in the true sense of that now much abused and perverted name :

' O spring to light, auspicious babe, be born ! '

While, however, I have no fears respecting the ultimate effectuation of the object so dear to our hearts, I have many fears for the perpetuity of this nation as a Republic, for the continuance of these States as a Union, for the existence of that Constitution, which, properly respected and maintained, would bless the country and the world. These fears do not arise from any tendency to such results in the principles of abolition in themselves considered. Those principles are conservative of the peace, and happiness, and security of the nation ; and, if voluntarily acted upon, would heal many of the feuds and animosities which have endangered the integrity of the Union. My fears are founded upon the symptoms, every where exhibited, of an approach to mob-supremacy, and consequent anarchy. In every direction I see the minority prostrate before the majority ; who, despite of law, the Constitution, and natural equity, put their heel upon the neck of the weaker portion, and perpetrate every enormity in the name of ' public opinion.' ' Public opinion ' is at this hour the demon of oppression, harnessing to the ploughshare of ruin, the ignorant and interested opposers of the truth, in every section of this heaven-favored, but mob-cursed land. Already the Constitution lies prostrate — an insulted, wounded, impotent form. A thousand hands are daily uplifted to send assassin daggers to its heart. Look on the pages of the daily press, and say, if traitors to liberty and the Constitution are not sedulously schooling a hood-winked multitude to commit a suicidal act upon their own boasted freedom ! Count (if they can be counted) the disturbances occurring all over the land, and say, is not mob-supremacy the order of the day ? Where is the freedom of speech ? where the right of association ? where the security of national conveyances ? where the inviolability of personal liberty ? where the sanctity of the domestic circle ? where the protection of property ? where the prerogatives of the judge? where the trial by jury? Gone, or fast disappearing. The minority in every place speak, and write, and meet, and walk, at the peril of their lives. I speak not now exclusively of the Anti-Abolition mania, which has more recently displayed itself with all its froth and foam, and thirst for spoliation and blood. I have in mind the Anti-Mormonism of Missouri, and its accompanying heart-rending persecutions — the *Anti*-Anti-Masonic fury, with the abduction of Morgan, and its other grim features of destruction and death — the burning zeal of Anti-Temperance, with its bonfires and effigies, and its innumerable assaults upon persons and property — the Anti-Gambling and the Anti-Insurrection tragedies of Southern States, with their awful waste of human life, and the frequent sacrifice of the blood of innocent victims. But time would fail to tell of Anti-Whig, and Anti-Jackson, and Anti-Convent, and Anti-Bank, and Anti-Kean, and Anti-Anderson, and Anti-Graham, and Anti-Joel Parker, and Anti-Cheever, and Anti-Colored School, and Anti-House of Ill-fame riots, with all the other anti-men and anti-women, anti-black, and anti-red, and anti-meat, and anti-drink riots, and mobs, and persecutions, which have distinguished this age and land of revivals, and missions, and Bible Societies, and educational operations, and liberty, and independence, and equality! Suffice it to say, that, for some years past, all who have dared to act, or think aloud, in opposition to the will of the majority, have held their property and being dependent on the clemency of a mob. Were I a citizen of this country, and did there seem no escape from such a dreadful state of things — if I did not, on behalf of the righteous and consistent, (for, thank God, there are thousands of such, who cease not day nor night to weep and pray for their country,) hope and believe for brighter days and better deeds, I should choose to own the dominion of the darkest despot that ever sealed the lips of truth, or made the soul of a slave tremble at his glance. If I must be a slave, if my lips must wear a padlock, if I must crouch and crawl, let it be before an hereditary tyrant. Let me see around me the symbols of royalty, the bayonets of a standing army, the frowning battlements of a Bastile. Let me breathe the air of a country where the divine right of kings to govern wrong is acknowledged and respected. Let

me know what is the sovereign will and pleasure of the one
man I am taught to fear and serve. Let me not see my
rights, and property, and liberties, scattered to the same
breeze that floats the flag of freedom. Let me not be sacrificed to the demon of despotism, while laying hold upon
the horns of an altar dedicated to 'FREEDOM and EQUALI-
TY!' I hope, however, for the best; I trust to see the people saved from their infatuation and madness. I look very
much to the spread of anti-slavery principles for the salvation of the country, for they are the principles of righteous
government—they are a foundation for order, and peace,
and just laws, and equitable administration; and those who
embrace them will be likely to act wisely and righteously
upon other great questions.

A MOB IN BOSTON!! and such a mob!!! Thirty ladies
completely routed, and a board 6 feet by 2 utterly demolished by 3000 or 4000 respectable ruffians — in broad daylight and broad-cloth! Glorious achievement! and, as it
deserved to be—regularly Gazetted! Indeed, this noble
army of gentlemanly savages had all the customary adjuncts
of civilized warfare. There were 'Posts,' and 'Sentinels,'
and 'Couriers,' and 'Gazettes,' and a 'HOMER,' too, to
celebrate their praise!

A mob in Boston! The birth-place of the revolution—
the Cradle of Liberty! A mob in Washington (!) Street,
Boston, TO PUT DOWN FREE DISCUSSION!

'Hung be the heavens with black!'

Shrouded in midnight be the height of Bunker! Let the
bells of the Old South and Brattle Street be muffled, and let
the knell of the country's boasted honor and liberty be rung!
Ye hoary veterans of the revolution! clothe yourselves in
sackcloth! strew ashes on your heads, and mourn your
country's downfall!

'For what is left the patriot here?
For Greeks a blush — for Greece a tear!'

Would that you had died, ere the sad truth was demonstrated, that you fought and bled in vain!

A mob in Boston! O, tell it not in St. Petersburgh!
publish it not in the streets of Constantinople! But it will

be told; it will be published. The damning fact will ring
through all the haunts of despotism, and will be a cordial to
the heart of Metternich — sweet music in the ears of the
haughty Czar, and a prophetic note of triumph to the sovereign Pontiff. What American lip will henceforth dare to
breathe a sentence of condemnation against the bulls of the
Pope, or the edicts of the Autocrat? Should a tongue wag
in affected sympathy for the denationalized Pole, the out-
lawed Greek, the wretched Serf, or any of the priest-ridden
or king-ridden victims of Europe, will not a voice come
thundering over the billows : — .

'Base hypocrites! let your charity begin at home! Look
at your own Carolinas! Go, pour the balm of consolation
into the broken hearts of your two millions of enslaved children! Rebuke the murderers of Vicksburg! Reckon with
the felons of Charleston! Restore the contents of rifled
mail-bags! Heal the lacerations, still festering, on the
ploughed backs of your citizens! Dissolve the star-cham-
bers of Virginia! Tell the confederated assassins of Alabama and Mississippi to disband! Call to judgment the
barbarians of Baltimore, and Philadelphia, and New York,
and Concord, and Haverhill, and Lynn, and Montpelier;
and the well-dressed mobocrats of Utica, and Salem, and
Boston! Go, ye praters about the soul-destroying ignorance
of Romanism, gather again the scattered schools of Canter-
bury and Canaan! Get the clerical minions of Southern
taskmasters to rescind their " Resolutions " of withholding
knowledge from immortal Americans! Rend the veil of
legal enactments, by which the beams of light divine are
hidden from millions who are left to grope their way through
darkness here, to everlasting blackness beyond the grave!
Go, shed your "patriotic" tears over the infamy of your
country, amidst the ruins of yonder Convent! Go, proud
and sentimental Bostonians, preach clemency to the respectable horde who are dragging forth for immolation one of your
own citizens! Cease your anathemas against the Vatican,
and screw your courage up to resist the worse than papal
bulls of Georgia, demanding, at the peril of your ' bread
and butter,' the 'HEADS' of your citizens, and the passage
of GAG-LAWS! Before you rail at arbitrary power in foreign
regions, save your own citizens from the felonious intercep-
tion of their correspondence; and teach the sworn and paid

servants of the Republic the obligations of an oath, and the
guaranteed rights of a free people ! ''Send not your banners
to Poland, but tear them into shreds, to be distributed to the
mob, as halters for your sons !   When, next July, you rail
at mitres, and crosiers, and sceptres ; and denounce the bow-.
string, and the bayonet, and the faggot ; let your halls be
decorated with plaited scourges, wet with the blood of the
sons of the Pilgrims,— let the tar cauldron smoke — the gibbet rear aloft its head — and cats, and bloodhounds,* (the
brute auxiliaries of Southern Liberty men,) howl and bark
in unison with the demoniacal ravings of a 'gentlemanly
mob '— while above the Orator of the day, and beneath the
striped and starry banner, stand forth, in characters of blood,
the distinctive mottoes of the age :

Down with Discussion !
Lynch Law Triumphant !
Slavery For Ever !
Hail, Columbia !

---

* See the accounts in Southern newspapers of '*a curious mode of
punishment*' recently introduced, called 'CAT-HAULING.' The victim is stretched upon his face, and a cat, thrown upon his bare
shoulders, is dragged to the bottom of the back. This is continued
till the body is 'lacerated.'

'The Vicksburg (Miss.) Register says, that Mr. Earl, one of the
victims of mobocracy in Mississippi, was tortured a whole night to
elicit confession. The brutal and hellish tormentors laid Mr. Earl
upon his back, and drew a cat tail foremost across his body ! ! ! He
hung himself soon after in jail.'

See also the accounts of the Mississippi murders given by a correspondent in the Charleston Courier, dating his letter Tyger (how
appropriate !) Bayou, Madison County, Miss. The following is an
extract : — 'Andrew Boyd, a conspirator, was required by the Com-
mittee of Safety, and Mr. Dickerson, Hiram Reynolds and Hiram
Perkins (since killed) were ordered to arrest him. They discovered
he was flying, and immediately commenced the pursuit, with a
pack of TRAINED HOUNDS. He miraculously effected his deliverance
from his pursuers, after swimming Big Black River, and running
through cane-brakes and swamps until night-fall, when the party
called off THE DOGS. Early next morning they renewed the chase,
and started Boyd one mile from whence they had called off the
dogs. But he effected his escape on horse, (fortune throwing one in
his way,) *the hounds* not being accustomed to that training after he
quit the bush.'

Before you weep over the wrongs of Greece, go wash the
gore out of your national shambles—appease the frantic
mother robbed of her only child, the centre of her hopes,
and joys, and sympathies—restore to yon desolate husband
the wife of his bosom—abolish the slave marts of Alexan-
dria, the human flesh auctions of Richmond and New
Orleans—'undo the heavy burdens,' 'break every yoke,'
and stand forth to the gaze of the world, not steeped in
infamy and rank with blood, but in the posture of penitence
and prayer, a free and regenerated nation!

Such, truly, are the bitter reproaches with which every
breeze from a distant land might be justly freighted. How
long—in the name of outraged humanity I ask, how long
shall they be deserved? Are the people greedy of a
world's execration? or have they any sense of shame—
any blush of patriotism left? Each day the flagrant inconsistency and gross wickedness of the nation are becoming
more widely and correctly known. Already, on foreign
shores, the lovers of corruption and despotism are referring
with exultation to the recent bloody dramas in the South, and
the pro-slavery meetings and mobs of the country generally,
in proof of the ' dangerous tendency of Democratic principles.' How long shall the deeds of America clog the wheels
of the car of Universal Freedom? Vain is every boast—
acts speak louder than words. While

'Columbia's sons are bought and sold;'

while citizens of America are murdered without trial; while
persons and property are at the mercy of a mob; while city
authorities are obliged to make concessions to a bloody-mind-
ed multitude, and finally incarcerate unoffending citizens to
save them from a violent death; while ' gentlemen of standing and property' are in unholy league to effect the abduction and destruction of a ' foreigner,' the head and front of
whose offending is, that he is laboring to save the country
from its worst foe; while assemblages of highly respectable
citizens, comprising large numbers of the clergy, and some
of the judges of the land, are interrupted and broken up,
and the houses of God in which they met attacked in open
day by thousands of men, armed with all the implements of
demolition; while the entire South presents one great scene
of slavery and slaughter; and while the North deeply sym-

pathise with their ' Southern brethren,' sanction their deeds of felony and murder, and obsequiously do their bidding by hunting down their own fellow-citizens who dare to plead for equal rights ; and, finally, while hundreds of the ministers of Christ, of every denomination, are making common cause with the plunderer of his species ; yea, themselves reduce God's image to the level of the brute, and glory in their shame ; I say, while these things exist, professions and boasts are ' sounding brass ; ' men will learn to loathe the name of Republicanism, and deem it synonymous with mob despotism, and the foulest oppression on the face of the globe !

A word to the opposers of the cause of emancipation. You must stop in your career of persecution, or proceed to still darker deeds and wider desolations. At present, you have done nothing but help us. You have, it is true, made a sincere, though impotent attempt to please your masters at the South. The abolitionists have risen, after every attempt to crush them, with greater energy and in greater numbers. They are still speaking ; they are still writing ; still praying ; still weeping, (not over *their suffer- ings*, but *your sins*)—they are working in public and in private, by day and by night — they are sustained by prin- ciples you *do* not (because you *will* not) understand, prin- ciples drawn pure from the throne of God — they have meat to eat which you know not of, and live, and are nour- ished, and are strong, while you wonder that they do not wither under your frown, and fall into annihilation before the thunderbolts of your wrath. Some of you have con- versed with them. What think you of the abolitionists ? of their moral courage — their tact in argument — their knowl- edge of the Scriptures — their interpretation of the Constitu- tion ? Have you found them ignorant ? Have you found them weak ? Have you not often been driven to your wits' end by the probing questions or ready answers of these silly and deluded women and children ? How, then, do you ex- pect to conquer ? If finally by the sword, why delay ? Commence the work of butchery to-day. Every hour you procrastinate, witnesses an increase of your victims, a defection from your ranks, and an augmentation in numbers and influence of those you wish to destroy. You profess to

be republicans.   Have you ever asked yourselves what you
are doing for the principles you profess to revere ?   In the
name of sacred Liberty, I call upon you to pause. 'I conjure you,

> 'By every hallowed name,
> That ever led your sires to fame' — .

pause, and see whither your present deeds are tending.   Be
honest — be just — just to yourselves, just to us, before you
condemn us, still more, before you seek to destroy us.
'Search us, and know our hearts; try us, and know our
thoughts; and see if there be any wicked way in us.'   Condemn us not unheard.   'Strike, but hear.'   Remember, too,
that your violence will effect nothing while the liberty of the
press remains.   While the principles and opinions of abolitionists, as promulgated in their journals, are carried on the
wings of the wind over sea and land, you do but give a
wider circulation to those principles and opinions by your
acts of violence and blood.   You awaken the desire, the
determination, to know and understand what ' these babblers
say.'   Be prepared, therefore, to violate the Constitution by
annihilating the Liberty of the Press.

In this place, it may not be inappropriate to introduce a
passage from an able letter, recently addressed by the eloquent M. de Chateaubriand to the French Chamber of Dep-
uties, while that body were advocating the recent law for
imposing severe restrictions on the French press : —

'I could (says he) if I wished, crush you under the weight of
your origin, and show you to be faithless to yourselves, to your
past actions and language.   But I spare you the reproaches which
the whole world heaps upon you.   I call not upon you to give an
account of the oaths you have taken.   I will merely tell you that
you have not arrived at the end of your task, and that, in the perilous career you have entered upon — following the example of other
governments which have met with destruction — you must go on
till you arrive at the abyss.   You have done nothing till you establish the censorship; nothing but that can be efficacious against the
liberty of the press.   A violent law may kill the man, but the censorship alone kills the idea, and this latter it is which ruins your
system.   Be prepared, then, to establish the censorship, and be
assured that on the day on which you do establish it, you will perish.'

In concluding this lengthened communication, let me exhort you, my beloved brother, to ' be of good cheer,' and to exercise unwavering confidence in the God you serve — the God of Jacob, and of Elijah, and of Daniel, of all who, with singleness, prefer the faithful discharge of duty, and its consequences, to the suggestions of expediency, and the favor of the world. He is able to deliver you in the hour of peril, and give you the victory over all your enemies. To Him resort for refuge. He will be a hiding-place from the wind, and a covert from the tempest; as rivers of water in a dry place, as the shadow of a great rock in a weary land. To all, who, with you, are waging this holy war, I would say : — Let not passing events move you ! The turbulence and malignity of your opponents prove the potency and purity of your cause. But yesterday, the abolitionists were esteemed few, mean, silly, and contempti--b!e. Now, they are of sufficient importance to arouse and fix the attention of the entire country, and earth and hell are ransacked for weapons and recruits, with which to fight the ignorant, imbecile, superannuated and besotted believers in the doctrine of immediate emancipation. This is a good sign — an unequivocal compliment to the divinity of your principles. ' Ye are not of the world, therefore, the world hateth you. ' Blessed are ye when men shall revile you, and persecute you, and shall say all manner of evil against you falsely, for my sake. Rejoice, and be exceeding glad ; for great is your reward in heaven ; for so persecuted they the prophets which were before you.' Let your motto be, ' ONWARDS ! ' You have already accomplished much. You have awakened the country from its guilty slumber. You can reckon upon three hundred Auxiliary Associations, embracing a large portion of the effective moral energy of the land. The churches of the North are taking right ground upon the question. The principles of abolition are diffused through most of the seminaries of learning. The females of America are nobly devoting themselves to this work of mercy, regardless of the malignity of their heart-less and unmanly persecutors. Onwards, therefore ! A few years will witness an entire change in the sentiments of the American people ; and those who are now drawn up in opposition to your philanthropic movement, will blush to acknowledge the dishonorable part they have enacted. A voice, from the other side of the Atlantic, says, Onwards! You are supported by the prayers and sympathies of Great Britain. The abolitionists of the British empire are with you. They are the friends of the peace, happiness and glory of your country, and earnestly desire the arrival of the day, when, having achieved a victory over slavery on this continent, you will join them in efforts for its abolition throughout the world. While you pray fervently for strength in the day of conflict, pray also for grace to bear yourselves with meekness and charity towards those who oppose you. Pursue your holy object in the Spirit of Christ, 'giving no offence in any thing, that the (cause) be not (justly) blamed, but in all things approving yourselves as the servants of God, in much patience, in afflictions, in necessities, in distresses, in stripes, in imprisonments, in tumults, in labors, in watchings, in fastings; by pureness, by knowledge, by long suffering, by kindness, by the Holy Ghost, by love unfeigned, by the word of truth, by the power of God, by the armor of righteousness on the right hand and on the left, by honor and dishonor, by evil report and good report; as deceivers, and yet true; as unknown, and yet well known; as dying, and behold you live; as chastened, and not killed; as sorrowful, yet always rejoicing; as poor, yet making many rich; as having nothing, and yet possessing all things.'

> Your affectionate friend,
> and devoted fellow-laborer,
>
> GEORGE THOMPSON.

Wm. Lloyd Garrison.

TO WILLIAM LLOYD GARRISON.

Joy to thee, Son of Trial! — and so soon
  Hath it been given thee thy faith to prove?
Joy ! so that Heaven only grant this boon,
  That nought on earth thy steadfastness may move!
Yet when, but yesternight, I saw thee go,
  Surrounded by that fierce, insensate throng,
  Drunk with the wine of wrath, for evil strong,
I felt my soul with bitterest tears o'erflow.
O ! with what earnestness of passion went
  Forth from my heart, my whole soul after thee !
I knew that, though to bonds and prison sent,
  Thou from all stain of evil still wert free ;
Yet a strange feeling, half of joy arose,
That friend of mine should have such men his foes.

Boston, October 22, 1835.

THE AMERICAN COLONIZATION SOCIETY.

In proof that the American Colonization Society is not hostile to slavery ; is nourished by fear and selfishness ; is animated by a rabid and heathenish spirit of complexional caste ; is hostile to the emancipation of the slave population, except they are expelled from the country ; is the traducer and persecutor of the free people of color ; is in the hands and under the control of Southern slaveholders ; is a bulwark of strength and safety to the slave system, enhances the value of slave property, and thus directly tends to perpetuate what God and nature demand should be instantly abolished ; and is therefore a cruel, hypocritical, demonia-

34*

cal combination, — a conspiracy against justice and humanity on a colossal scale, — to be abhorred, denounced and
exposed by all who fear God and regard man ; the following quotations (which might be multiplied to the size of a
volume) from the Annual Reports of its Boards of Managers, and the ' African Repository,' the official organ of the
Society, indisputably demonstrate :—

   ' In every part of the United States, there is a broad and
impassable line of demarcation between every man who has
one drop of African blood in his veins, and every other
class in the community.   The habits, the feelings, all the
prejudices of society — prejudices which neither *refinement*,
nor *argument*, nor *education*, NOR RELIGION ITSELF, can subdue — mark the people of color, whether bond or free, as
the subjects of a degradation *inevitable* and *incurable*.   The
African in this country belongs by birth to the very lowest
station in society ; and from that station HE CAN NEVER RISE,
be his talents, his enterprise, his virtues what they may . . .
They constitute a class by themselves—a class out of
which *no individual can be elevated*, and below which none
can be depres ed.' — [African Repository, vol. iv. pp. 118,
119.]

   ' We have endeavored, but endeavored in vain, to restore
them either to self-respect, or to the respect of others (! ! !)
It is not our fault that we have failed ; (! ! !) it is not theirs.
*It has resulted from a cause over which neither we, nor they,
can ever have control* [that is to say, they have colored
skins ! ! !]   *Here,* therefore, they must be *for ever debased ;*
more than this, they must be FOR EVER USELESS ; more even
than this, they must be FOR EVER A NUISANCE, from which it
were a blessing for society to be rid.   *And yet they,* AND
THEY ONLY, *are* QUALIFIED *for colonizing Africa* ' (! ! !)
[Idem, vol. v. p. 276.]

   ' They constantly hear the accents, and behold the triumphs, of a liberty *which here they can never enjoy.*' . . . .
' It is against this increase of colored persons, who take but
a nominal freedom here, and *cannot rise from their degrad-*

ed condition, that this Society attempts to provide.' — [Idem, vol. vi. pp. 17, 82.]

' Is it not *wise*, then, for the free people of color and their friends to admit, *what cannot reasonably be doubted*, that the people of color must, *in this country*, REMAIN FOR AGES, PROBABLY FOR EVER, *a separate and inferior caste*, weighed down by causes, powerful, universal, inevitable ; which neither legislation nor CHRISTIANITY can remove ? ' — [Idem, vol. vii. p. 196.]

' *It* [the Society] *condemns no man because he is a slave-holder.*' * * * 'They [abolitionists] confound the *misfortunes* of one generation with the *crimes* of another, and would sacrifice both individual and public good to an *unsubstantial theory of the rights of man.*' — [Idem, vol. vii. pp. 200, 202.]

' The existence of slavery among us, though not at all to be objected to our Southern brethren as a *fault*, is yet a blot on our national character, and a mighty drawback from our national strength.' — [Second Annual Report of the N. Y. State Col. Society.]

' They do not perceive the propriety of confounding the crime of the kidnapper, with the *misfortune* of the owner of imported and inherited slaves.' — [North American Review, for July, 1832.]

' We hold their slaves, *as we hold their other property*, SACRED.' — [African Repository, vol. i. p. 283.]

' To the slaveholder, who had charged upon them the wicked design of interfering with the RIGHTS OF PROPERTY, under the specious pretext of removing a vicious and dangerous free population, they address themselves in a tone of conciliation and sympathy. We know your RIGHTS, say they, *and we respect them.*' — [Idem, vol. vii. p. 100.]

' It was proper again and again to repeat, that it was far from the intention of the Society to affect, in any manner, the tenure by which a certain *species of property is held.* He was himself a slaveholder ; *and he considered that kind of property as inviolable as any other in the country.*' [Speech of Henry Clay — First Annual Report.]

'The scope of the Society is large enough, but it is in no wise mingled or confounded with the broad sweeping views of *a few fanatics* in America, who would urge us on to the sudden and total abolition of slavery.'—[African Repository, vol. iii. p. 97.]

'What is to be done? Immediate and universal emancipation will find few if any advocates among judicious and reflecting men.' * * * 'Here, that race is in every form a curse, and if the system, so long contended for by the uncompromising abolitionist, could prevail, its effect would be to spread discord and devastation from one end of the Union to the other.'—[Idem, vol. iv. pp. 202, 363.]

'Were the very spirit of angelic charity to pervade and fill the hearts of all the slaveholders in our land, it would by no means require that all the slaves should be instantaneously liberated.'—[Idem, vol. v. p. 329.]

'No scheme of abolition will meet my support, that leaves the emancipated blacks among us.'—[Hon. Mr. Mason, of Virginia.—Idem, vol. ii. p. 188.]

'We would say, *liberate them only on condition of their going to Africa or to Hayti.*'—[Idem, vol. iii. p. 26.]

'I am not complaining of the owners of slaves; it would be as humane to throw them from the decks in the middle passage, as to set them free in our country.' * * * '*Any scheme of emancipation without colonization,* they know and see and feel to be productive of nothing but evil; evil to all whom it affects: to the white population, to the slaves, to the *manumitted themselves.*'—[Idem, vol. iv. pp. 226, 300.]

'If this question were submitted, whether there should be either immediate or gradual emancipation of all the slaves in the United States, *without their removal or colonization,* painful as it is to express the opinion, *I have no doubt that it would be unwise to emancipate them.*'—[Idem, vol. vi. p. 5.]

'All emancipation, to however small an extent, *which permits the persons emancipated to remain in this country,* is an evil, which must increase with the increase of the operation.' [First Annual Report.]

' They will annex the condition, that the emancipated *shall leave the country.*'—[Second Annual Report.]

' Colonization, to be correct, must be beyond seas—Emancipation, *with the liberty to remain on this side of the Atlantic, is but an act of dreamy madness !* '—[Thirteenth Annual Report.]

' The Society maintains, that no slave ought to receive his liberty, except on condition of being excluded, not merely from the State which sets him loose, *but from the whole country ;* that is, of being colonized.'—[North American Review, for July, 1832.]

' So far from being connected with the abolition of slavery, *the measure proposed would prove one of the greatest securities to enable the master to keep in possession his own property.*'—[Speech of John Randolph at the first meeting of the Colonization Society.]

' The slaves would be greatly benefitted by the removal of the free blacks, who now corrupt them, and render them discontented.'—[Second Annual Report.]

' We all know the effects produced on our slaves by the fascinating, but delusive appearance of happiness, exhibited in some persons of their own complexion, roaming in idleness and vice among them. By removing the most fruitful source of discontent from among our slaves, we should render them more industrious and attentive to our commands.' [Fourteenth Annual Report.]

' What is the free black to the slave ? A standing, perpetual incitement to discontent. *Though the condition of the slave be a thousand times the best*—supplied, protected, instead of destitute and desolate—yet, the folly of the condition, held to involuntary labor, finds, always, allurement, in the spectacle of exemption from it, without consideration of the adjuncts of destitution and misery. The slave would have, then, little excitement to discontent but for the free black.'—[Fifteenth Annual Report.]

' To remove these persons from among us will increase the *usefulness,* and improve the moral character of those who remain in servitude, and *with whose labors the country is unable to dispense.'* * * * '*Are they vipers, who are sucking our blood?* we will hurl them from us! It is not sympathy alone; not sickly sympathy, no, nor manly sympathy either, which is to act on us; but vital policy, self-interest, are also enlisting themselves on the humane side in our breasts.'—[Idem, vol. iii. pp. 67, 201.]

'Enough, under favorable circumstances, might be removed for a few successive years, if young *females* were encouraged to go, to keep the whole colored population in check.' [Idem, vol. vii. p. 246.]

'THE EXECUTION OF ITS SCHEME WOULD AUGMENT INSTEAD OF DIMINISHING THE VALUE OF THE PROPERTY LEFT BEHIND.'—[Idem, vol. ii. p. 344.]

'The removal of every single free black in America, would be productive of nothing but safety to the slaveholder.' [Idem, vol. iii. p. 202.]

'The tendency of the scheme, and one of its objects, is to SECURE SLAVEHOLDERS, AND THE WHOLE SOUTHERN COUNTRY, against certain evil consequences, growing out of the present threefold mixture of our population.'—[Address of the Rockbridge Col. Society.—Idem, vol. iv. p. 274.]

'There is but one way, [to avert ruin,] but that might be made effectual, fortunately!, It was to PROVIDE AND KEEP OPEN A DRAIN FOR THE EXCESS BEYOND THE OCCASIONS OF PROFITABLE EMPLOYMENT.'—[Speech of Mr. Archer.]

'What greater pledge can we give for the moderation and safety of our measures, than our own interests as *slaveholders*, and the ties that bind us to the slaveholding communities to which we belong?'—[Speech of Mr. Key.—Eleventh Annual Report.]

'THE SYSTEM ORIGINATED IN THE WISDOM OF THE ANCIENT DOMINION. It was generously countenanced by Georgia in its earliest stages. Maryland has done more for it than all the other States. Kentucky and Tennessee have declared themselves ready to support any legitimate interposition of the General Government in its favor. Louisiana and Mississippi are beginning to act vigorously.'—[North American Review, for July, 1832.]

' Your memorialists refer with confidence to the course they have pursued, in the prosecution of their objects for nine years past, to show that it is possible, without danger or alarm, to carry on such an operation, notwithstanding its supposed relation to the subject of slavery, and that they have not been regardless, in any of their measures, of what was due to the state of society in which they live. *They are, themselves, chiefly slaveholders*, and live with all the ties of life binding them to a slaveholding community.'—[Memorial of the Society to the several States.—African Rep., vol. ii. p. 60.]

' Let me repeat, the *friends* of the Colonization Society, three-fourths of them, are SLAVEHOLDERS; the legislatures of Maryland, Georgia, Kentucky and Tennessee, all slaveholding States, have approved it; *every member* of this auxiliary Society is, *either in himself, or his nearest relatives, interested in holding slaves.*'—['The Colonization Society Vindicated.'—Idem, vol. iii. p. 202.]

' About twelve years ago, some of the wisest men of the nation, *mostly slaveholders*, formed in the city of Washington the present American Colonization Society.'—[Address of the Rockbridge Colonization Society.—Idem, vol. iv. p. 274.]

' *Being, chiefly, slaveholders ourselves*, we well know how it becomes us to approach such a subject as this in a slaveholding State, and in every other. If there were room for a reasonable jealousy, we among the first should feel it; being as much interested in the welfare of the community, and having as much at heart, as any men can have,—the security of ourselves, our property, and our families.'—[Review of Mr. Tazwell's Report.—Idem. p. 341.]

' *It is no abolition Society;* it addresses as yet *arguments to no master*, and disavows with horror the idea of offering temptations to any slave. IT DENIES THE DESIGN OF ATTEMPTING EMANCIPATION, EITHER PARTIAL OR GENERAL.' ['The Colonization Society Vindicated.'—African Rep. vol. iii. p. 197.]

' They can impress upon the Southern slaveholder, by the strength of facts, and by the recorded declarations of hon-

est men, that the objects of the Colonization Society are
altogether pure and praiseworthy, and that *it has no intention to open the door to universal liberty*, but only to cut
out a channel, where the merciful providence of God may
cause those dark waters to flow off.' — [Idem, vol. iv. p.
145.]

'We do not ask that the provisions of our Constitution
and statute book should be so modified as to relieve and
exalt the condition of the colored people, *whilst they remain
with us*. LET THESE PROVISIONS STAND IN ALL THEIR RIGOR,
to work out the ultimate and unbounded good of this people.
Persuaded that their condition here is not susceptible of a
radical and permanent improvement, we would deprecate
any legislation that should encourage the vain and injurious
hope of it.' — [Memorial of the New York State Colonization Society.]

'There is a class, however, more numerous than all these,
introduced amongst us by violence, notoriously ignorant,
degraded and miserable, mentally diseased, broken-spirited,
acted upon by no motives to honorable exertions, SCARCELY
REACHED IN THEIR DEBASEMENT BY THE HEAVENLY LIGHT;
yet where is the sympathy and effort which a view of their
condition ought to excite? They wander unsettled and
unbefriended through our land, or sit indolent, abject and
sorrowful, by the "streams which witness their captivity."
Their freedom is *licentiousness*, and to many, RESTRAINT
[SLAVERY] WOULD PROVE A BLESSING.' — [African Rep. vol.
i. p. 68.]

'Free blacks are a greater nuisance than even slaves
themselves.' * * * 'They knew that where slavery had
been abolished, it had operated to the advantage of the masters, not of the slaves. They saw this fact most strikingly
illustrated in the case of the free negroes of Boston. If, on
the anniversary celebrated by the free people of color, of the
day on which slavery was abolished, they looked abroad,
what did they see? Not freemen, in the enjoyment of every
attribute of freedom, with the stamp of liberty upon their
brows! No, sir; they saw a ragged set, crying out liberty!
for whom liberty had nothing to bestow, and whose enjoyment of it was but in name. — [African Rep., vol. ii. p. 328.]

We, the undersigned, having observed with regret that the *American Colonization Society* appears to be gaining some adherents in this country, are desirous to express our opinions respecting it.

Our motive and excuse for thus coming forward are the claims which the Society has put forth to *Anti-Slavery* support. These claims are, in our opinion, wholly groundless; and we feel bound to affirm that our deliberate judgment and conviction are, that the professions made by the Colonization Society, of promoting the abolition of Slavery, are altogether delusive.

As far as the mere Colony of Liberia is concerned, it has no doubt the advantages of other trading establishments. In this sense, it is beneficial both to America and Africa, and we cordially wish it well. We cannot, however, refrain from expressing our strong opinion, that it is a settlement of which the United States ought to bear the whole cost. We never required of that country to assist us in Sierra Leone; we are enormously burdened by our own connection with Slavery; and we do maintain that we ought not to be called on to contribute to the expense of a Colony, which, though no doubt comprising some advantages, was formed chiefly to indulge the prejudices of American Slaveholders, and which is regarded with aversion by the colored population of the United States.

With regard to the extinction of the Slave Trade, we apprehend that Liberia, however good the intentions of its supporters, will be able to do little or nothing towards it, except on the limited extent of its own territories. The only effectual death-blow to that accursed traffic will be the destruction of slavery throughout the world. To the destruction of slavery throughout the world, we are compelled to say, that we believe the Colonization Society *to be an obstruction.*

Our objections to it are, therefore, briefly these:—While we believe its pretexts to be delusive, we are convinced that its *real* effects are of the most dangerous nature. It takes its root from a cruel prejudice and alienation in the whites of America against the colored people, slave or free. This being its source, the effects are what might be expected;

35

that it fosters and increases the spirit of caste, already so unhappily predominant; that it widens the breach between the two races, and exposes the colored people to great practical persecution, in order to *force* them to emigrate; and, finally, is calculated to swallow up and divert that feeling which America, as a Christian and a free country, cannot but entertain, that slavery is alike incompatible with the law of God, and with the well-being of man, whether the enslaver or the enslaved.

On these grounds, therefore, and while we acknowledge the Colony of Liberia, or any other colony on the coast of Africa, to be, *in itself*, a good thing, we must be understood utterly to repudiate the principles of the American Colonization Society. That Society is, in our estimation, not deserving of the countenance of the British public.

> WM. WILBERFORCE,
> WM. SMITH,
> ZACHARY MACAULAY,
> WM. EVANS, M. P.
> SAMUEL GURNEY,
> GEORGE STEPHEN,
> SUFFIELD, (Lord,)
> S. LUSHINGTON, M. P.
> THOS. FOWELL BUXTON, M. P.
> JAMES CROPPER,
> WM. ALLEN,
> DANIEL O'CONNELL, M. P.

London, July, 1833.

TESTIMONY OF THOMAS CLARKSON.

Extracts from a Letter addressed to WILLIAM LLOYD GARRISON, by THOMAS CLARKSON: —

DEAR SIR:

When you was in England on a former occasion, you did me the favor to call upon me, at Playford Hall, to take a part against the 'Colonization Society.' Long before this visit, my friend, Mr. Elliot Cresson, had engaged me in its favor, so that I fear that I did not show you the attention and respect (while you was at my house) due to so faithful an apostle of Liberty. You have lately been in England again, but your numerous engagements prevented you from seeing me, though it was your intention to have done so, and to have conversed with me on the same subject. I understand from your friends in London, who sent me a message to that effect, that you wished to know the particular reasons why I changed my mind with respect to that Society. I have no objection to give you a short account of the reasons which induced me to enter into it, and *finally to abandon it.* * * *

You will see in this narrative my reasons for patronizing, at first, the American Colonization Society, and my reasons, also, for having afterwards deserted it. I left it, first, because it was *entirely impracticable.* This is a *sufficient reason,* of itself; for no man in his senses would pursue a plan which he thought could never be accomplished. I left it, secondly, because I thought that *newly emancipated* slaves were not qualified to become colonists in Africa to any good purpose. How could persons be sent with any propriety to *civilize others,* who *wanted civilizing themselves* ? Besides, the advocates of the Colonization Society in America had no right to send the *scum of their population* to Africa, to breed a moral pestilence there. As far, however, as the *abolition of the slave trade concurred in the plan,* it must be allowed that Liberia has done a great deal of good. But then, this was *the first* colony planted, and the people sent there, as Mr. Cresson assured me, were more select. Many of these had been emancipated a considerable time before, and had got their own living, knowing something of the habits of civilized life. My argument relates only to *newly emancipated slaves,* who, according to the scheme, were to be hurried off from the plantation as soon as their liberty was given them. If the Society did not take these people, then the prospectus, offered to the public, had no meaning in it, and slavery could never, according to its promises, be *extinguished* in the United States. * * *

But I have not done with the subject yet. Mr. Cresson had scarcely left England the last time, when new information was given me on this same subject, by two American gentlemen, of the very highest moral reputation, by which I was led to suppose one of two things ; either that I had mistaken Mr. Cresson in his numerous conversations with me, or that he had allowed me to entertain erroneous impressions, without correcting them.   It was true, as my two friends informed me, that there had actually been a great stir or agitation in the United States on this subject, and quite as extensive and general as Mr. Cresson had represented it to be, but that the cause of it was not a *religious feeling*, as I had been led to imagine, by which the planters *had been convinced of the sin of slavery*, but a base feeling of fear, which seemed to pervade all of them, and which urged them *to get rid of the free people of color* by sending them to Africa.   These people were more knowing, intelligent and cultivated than the slaves, and, it was believed, were likely to join them, and be very useful to them, in the case of an insurrection ; so that if these were once fairly sent out of the country, they, the planters, might the more safely rule their then slaves with a rod of iron.   This information was accompanied by an account, by way of proof, taken from American newspapers, of different meetings held by the friends of the Colonization Society in different States of the Union, and of the speeches made there.   It appeared from these speeches, that the most violent supporters of this Society *were planters themselves*, and that the speakers did not hesitate to hold out the monstrous and hateful proposition, that the negroes were *not men and women*, but that they belonged to the *brute creation*.   It was impossible to read these speeches, which were so many public documents, and not perceive that the persons then assembled were no friends, but bitter enemies, to the whole African race, and that *nothing in the way of good intentions* towards the negro could be expected from them.   It is unnecessary for me to attempt to describe what my feelings were upon this occasion.   I will only say, that I saw the scheme — shall I say, *the diabolical scheme?* — with new eyes, and that the new light thus thrown upon it, added to the two arguments before mentioned, *determined me to wash my hands clean for ever of the undertaking.*   *   *   *

I am, dear Sir, with great esteem,

Very truly and cordially yours,

THOMAS CLARKSON.

SENTIMENTS OF THE FREE PEOPLE OF COLOR.

RESOLUTIONS PASSED BY THE COLORED INHABITANTS OF PHILADELPHIA.

Resolved, That we never will separate ourselves voluntarily from the slave population in this country; they are our brethren by the ties of consanguinity, of suffering, and of wrong; and we feel that there is more virtue in suffering privations with them, than fancied advantages for a season.

BY THE COLORED INHABITANTS OF NEW YORK.

Resolved, That we view the resolution calling on the worshippers of Christ to assist in the unholy crusade against the colored population of this country, as totally at variance with true Christian principles.

Resolved, That we claim this country, the place of our birth, and not Africa, as our mother country, and all attempts to send us to Africa, we consider as gratuitous and uncalled for.

BY THE COLORED INHABITANTS OF BOSTON.

Resolved, That this meeting look upon the American Colonization Society as a clamorous, abusive and peace-disturbing combination.

Resolved, That this meeting look upon the conduct of those clergymen, who have filled the ears of their respective congregations with the absurd idea of the necessity of removing the free colored people from the United States, as highly deserving the just reprehension directed to the false prophets and priests, by Jeremiah, the true prophet, as recorded in the 23d chapter of his prophecy.

BY THE COLORED INHABITANTS OF BALTIMORE.

Resolved, That it is the belief of this meeting, that the American Colonization Society is founded more in a selfish policy, than in the true principles of benevolence:—and, therefore, so far as it regards the life-giving spring of its operations, is not entitled to our confidence, but should be viewed by us with all that caution and distrust which our happiness demands.

BY THE COLORED INHABITANTS OF WASHINGTON, D. C.

Resolved, That this meeting view with distrust the efforts made by the Colonization Society to cause the free people of color of these United States to emigrate to Liberia, on the coast of Africa, or elsewhere.

Resolved, That it is the declared opinion of the members of this meeting, that the soil which gave them birth is their only true and veritable home, and that it would be impolitic, unwise and improper for them to leave their home without the benefits of education.

BY THE COLORED INHABITANTS OF HARTFORD, CT.

Resolved, That it is the opinion of this meeting, that the American Colonization Society is actuated by the same motives which influenced the mind of Pharaoh, when he ordered the male children of the Israelites to be destroyed.

Resolved, That it is the belief of this meeting, that the Society is the greatest foe to the free colored and slave population with whom liberty and equality have to contend.

Resolved, That, in our belief, we have committed no crime worthy of banishment, and that we will resist, even unto death, all the attempts of the Colonization Society to banish us from this, our native land.

BY THE COLORED INHABITANTS OF NEW HAVEN, CT.

Resolved, That we will resist all attempts made for our removal to the torrid shores of Africa, and will sooner suffer every drop of blood to be taken from our veins, than submit to such unrighteous treatment.

Resolved, That we consider the American Colonization Society founded on principles that no Afric-American, unless very weak in mind, will follow; and any man who will be persuaded to leave his own country and go to Africa, is an enemy to his country and a traitor to his brethren.

BY THE COLORED INHABITANTS OF COLUMBIA, PA.

Resolved, That it is our firm belief, that the Colonization Society is replete with infinite mischief, and that we view all the arguments of its advocates as mere sophistry, not worthy our notice as freemen.

HON. PELEG SPRAGUE.

Extracts from a Speech, delivered before an immense pro-slavery
gathering in Faneuil Hall, August 21st, 1835, by the Hon.
Peleg Sprague : —

The combinations and proceedings of the immediate abolitionists have produced and are producing, throughout the
South, feelings of bitterness and hatred toward the North. I
am aware that some of these gentlemen insist that all their
efforts are designed merely to produce a persuasive effect
on the masters. Sir, if such be really their object—if they
intend only persuasion—the course they adopt, the pouring
forth the most insulting and opprobrious language, even to
the pronouncing of all slaveholders indiscriminately to be
robbers and murderers, and thus arousing the most indignant
and embittered feelings, exhibits the most singular ideas of
the adaptation of means to ends that ever were presented in
the varieties of the human intellect. I have heard of persons who had a ' thousand winning ways to make folks hate
them,' and surely the abolitionists have employed them all
toward the South, and with wonderful success.

Sir, said Mr. S., the time has come when the great body
of the people, hitherto silent upon this delicate and momentous subject, should come forward and express their
sentiments. Our brethren of the South are *alarmed*, deeply, profoundly. Nor ought we to be surprised that they are
so. We know, indeed, that the agitators here are few, that
even the whole number of those who have permitted their
names to be enrolled in these societies is small, and I verily
believe that many of them disapprove the violence of their
leaders, and that more will do so when they contemplate the
consequences of their measures. But, seen from a distance,
they appear to occupy the whole field, and their incessant
activity produces an erroneous impression of their strength
and numbers.   *   *   *   *

If these abolitionists shall go on, if their associations shall
continue to increase, if their doctrines shall spread and their
measures be adopted, until they become the general sentiment and action of a majority of the people of the North,
and this shall be known, as known it will be, at the South,
the fate of our government is sealed—the day that sees that

consummation will look only upon the broken fragments of our Union. * * * * *

When the blood of our citizens, shed by a British soldiery, had stained our streets, had flowed upon the heights which surround us, and sunk into the earth upon the plains of Lexington and Concord, then, when HE — whose name can never be pronounced by American lips without the strongest emotions of gratitude and love in every American heart — when HE, *that slaveholder*, (pointing to the full length portrait of Washington,) who from this canvass smiles upon you, his children, with parental benignity, came with other slaveholders to drive the British myrmidons from this city and this hall, our fathers did not refuse to hold communion with him or with them. With slaveholders they formed the Confederation, neither asking nor receiving any right to interfere in their domestic relations. * * * *

Sir, these doctrines and that language to which I have felt it my duty to advert, tending as they do to the disruption of the Union, the prostration of Government, and to all the horrors of a civil and servile war, have attained their greatest prevalence and intensity within the past year, since a certain notorious foreign agent first landed upon our shores; who comes here, not to unite his fate with ours, not as other foreigners who would make this their home, and whom we cordially receive to the participation of all the immeasurable blessings of free institutions; but he comes here as an avowed *emissary*, sustained by foreign funds, a *professed agitator*, upon questions deeply, profoundly *political*, which lie at the very foundation of our Union, and in which the very existence of this nation is involved. He comes here from the dark and corrupt institutions of Europe, to enlighten us upon the rights of man and the moral duties of our own condition. Received by our hospitality, he stands here upon our soil, protected by our laws, and hurls ' fire-brands, arrows and death' into the habitations of our neighbors, and friends, and brothers — and when he shall have kindled a conflagration which is sweeping in desolation over the land, he has only to embark for his own country, and there look securely back with indifference or exultation upon the widespread ruin by which our cities are wrapt in flames and our garments rolled in blood. (! ! !)